The Navy of Henry VIII & Elizabeth I

Thomas Howard, Earl of Surrey
later third Duke of Norfolk. K. G. Lord High Admiral

The Navy of Henry VIII
& Elizabeth I

English Naval Warfare, Exploration & Vessels during
the 16th Century

W. Laird Clowes

LEONAUR

The Navy of Henry VIII & Elizabeth I
English Naval Warfare, Exploration & Vessels during the 16th Century
by W. Laird Clowes

FIRST EDITION

Leonaur is an imprint of Oakpast Ltd

ISBN: 978-1-78282-676-7 (hardcover)
ISBN: 978-1-78282-677-4 (softcover)

http://www.leonaur.com

Publisher's Notes

Contents

Civil History of the Navy, 1485-1603

Before the end of the fifteenth century, European seamen had ceased to be mere unscientific gropers in darkness. They knew how Eratosthenes had calculated the obliquity of the ecliptic by means of the *armilla*, or great copper circles, fixed in the square porch of the Alexandrian Museum, and how he had determined the circumference of the earth. He had heard that deep wells in Syene were enlightened to the bottom on the day of the summer solstice, and he therefore reasoned that Syene must be on the tropic. He had ascertained the latitude of Alexandria by observation, and he assumed that the two places were on the same meridian. The arc thus measured enabled him to calculate the proportion it bore to the whole circumference of the earth, and his result was a fair approximation to the truth.

Then again, the fifteenth-century seamen had the catalogue of the stars and constellations, the system of mapping by degrees of latitude and longitude, and the theory of the precession of the equinoxes—all bequeathed to them by Hipparchus, and preserved for them by Ptolemy. The system of Ptolemy was the navigator's text-book in the Middle Ages; and the Almagest, the Arabic translation of his work, was the foundation of astronomical knowledge. It was to learned men, well versed in the Almagest, that Alfonso X. of Castille, had entrusted the preparation of the astronomical tables which are called after him, and which, after they had remained in manuscript for about two hundred years, were first printed in 1483. Before the accession of Henry VII., Georg Peurbach and Johann Müller, better known as Regiomontanus, had lived and done their work, and the latter had not only constructed valuable instruments, but had also published his *Ephemerides*, with tables of the sun's declination calculated for the years from 1475 to 1566.

It was, however, in the lifetime of Henry VII. that greater progress was made than in any previous period of thrice the duration, and the chief authors of this remarkable progress were the two celebrated navigators, Martin Behaim, of Nuremberg, and Christopher Columbus.

Behaim, a merchant, was a pupil of Regiomontanus, and a student of the Almagest. While in Portugal, he adapted for Joäo I., as an instrument of navigation, the astrolabe, which had previously been used only in astronomy. A graduated metal ring, held so as to hang as a plummet, with a movable limb across it, fitted with two perforated sights, enabled the seaman to observe the angle between the horizon and the sun at noon; and with this, and the daily declination of the sun, as given by Regiomontanus, the discovery of the latitude involved only a simple calculation.

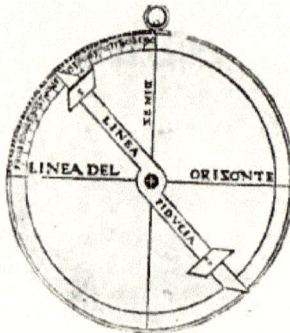

EARLY ASTROLABE.

This seems to have been about the year 1483. Not many years elapsed ere a more suitable instrument for observing the sun's altitude was devised. This was the cross-staff, the first known description of which dates from 1514, and is by Werner of Nürnberg. After accompanying Diogo Cão on his West African voyage in 1484-85, and then living for a time in the Azores, Behaim returned to Nürnberg, and constructed his great globe, concerning which Baron Nordenskiöld has written as follows to Sir Clements Markham:—

The globe of Behaim is, without comparison, the most important geographical document that appeared between A.D. 150, the date of the composition of Ptolemy's Atlas, and A.D. 1507, when Ruysch's map of the world was published. This globe is not only the oldest known to exist, but, from its size and its wealth of geographical detail, it far surpassed all analogous *monuments de géographie*, until the appearance of the globe of Mercator. It is the first geographical document which, with-

8

out any reserve, adopts the existence of antipodes. It is the first which plainly shows the possibility of a passage by sea to India and Cathay. It is the first on which the discoveries of Marco Polo are clearly indicated. It is true that the Behaim globe may be said to have been preceded, in some respects, by some other earlier maps of the fifteenth century—for instance, the map in a codex of Pomponius Mela of 1427, in the library of Rheims, and that of Fra Mauro.

But if these are impartially studied, it will be found that they are based on the idea of Homer, that the earth is a large circular island encompassed by the ocean, a conception totally incompatible with the new geographical discoveries of the Spaniards. These and analogous maps are, therefore, not in the slightest degree comparable with the globe of Behaim, which may be said to be an exact representation of the geographical knowledge of the period immediately preceding the first voyage of Columbus.

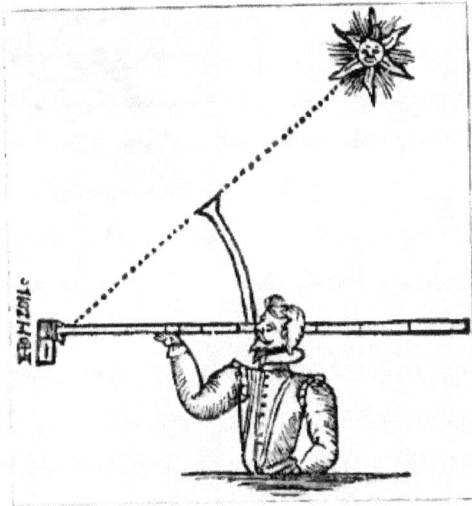

CROSS-STAFF.

The ascertaining of the longitude continued for many generations to be a difficulty, although Werner of Nürnberg; proposed the method of observing the distance of the moon from the sun with simultaneous altitudes—a method subsequently known as taking a "lunar"; and Gemma Frisius of Louvain had an idea, made public in 1530, that longitude might be found by comparison of times kept by small clocks, a foreshadowing of the modern use of the chronometer.

Columbus was the first to observe the variation of the needle. This was on September 14th, 1492. It afterwards attracted the attention of Sebastian Cabot. But the peculiarity was very generally believed at the time to be non-existent, the observations being inaccurate; and, as late as 1571, Sarmiento doubted it.

Globes, and not charts, were chiefly used by the early sixteenth century navigators who ventured into distant seas. The plane charts were fruitful sources of error and danger, owing to the degrees being shown in them as of equal length. Therefore, the discovery of a method of projection which obviated these disadvantages marked a very great advance in the progress of the art of navigation. The discoverer was Gerard Cremer, better known as Mercator. Gerard learnt astronomy at Louvain from Gemma Frisius, published his first map in 1537, and constructed his great globe, two feet in diameter, in 1541. But the chart of the world, on the new projection, did not appear until 1569.

The advantage of the system lies in the fact, as the author explains, that, although distances are distorted, the relative positions of places are correct. The actual chart is incorrectly drawn, and if Mercator really had a definite theory, he supplied others with no practical methods of working it out. The idea was not utilised in a scientific manner until Edward Wright of Garveston, in 1594, the year of Mercator's death, discovered the method of dividing the meridian. Five years later he published his treatise on *The Correction of Certain Errors in Navigation*, and only thereafter did charts, on what is still nevertheless called Mercator's projection, come into general use.

Other valuable aids to the advancement of the science of navigation were furnished, in the sixteenth century, by the work of Pedro Nunez, or Nonius, Martin Fernandez Enciso, Pedro de Medina, Martin Cortes, Bourne, William Borough, Blundeville, Hondius, Blagrave, Thomas Hood, Hues, Heriot, John Davis, and Gilbert of Colchester. Nonius gave the solution of several problems, including the determination of the latitude by the sun's double altitude, and was the first to introduce rhumb lines on charts. Enciso's *Suma de Geografia* was the first practical navigation book for the use of sailors. Medina, though a Spanish writer, was the mentor of the early Dutch navigators. Cortes's *Compendium* appeared in an English translation in 1561, and was used by John Davis, the navigator. Bourne's *Regiment of the Sea* (1573) was the earliest original English work on Navigation, and contains the first account of the modern method of measuring a ship's run by means of the log and line, an apparatus which Bourne elsewhere says was the invention of one Humphrey Cole, of the Mint in the Tower. Borough wrote on the Magnet and Loadstone in 1581. Blundeville published his very popular *Exercises* in 1594, with a table of meridional parts as furnished to him by his friend Edward Wright, and an explanation of the principle of Mercator's projection. Hondius, in 1595, published at Amsterdam a new chart of the world on Mercator's projection, in the preparation of which he utilised Wright's tables.

Blagrave and Hood improved the astrolabe and cross-staff. Hues expounded various problems in navigation, and included in his *Tractatus de Globis* (1594), a chapter by Heriot on the use of rhumbs. John Davis, the navigator, wrote *The Seaman's Secrets* in 1594, and invented the back-staff or, Davis's quadrant, which rapidly superseded the cross-staff, and which, improved by Flamsteed, remained in common use until Hadley's reflecting quadrant took its place in 1731. And Doctor Gilbert of Colchester, in the last year of the century, followed up the previous works by Borough, Norman, and others, on magnetism, by propounding the theory that the earth itself is a magnet. Nor must the invention of the telescope be forgotten. It is due to Zacharias Janssen, of Middelberg, about 1590, and the instrument, quickly improved, soon became part of the sea captain's equipment.

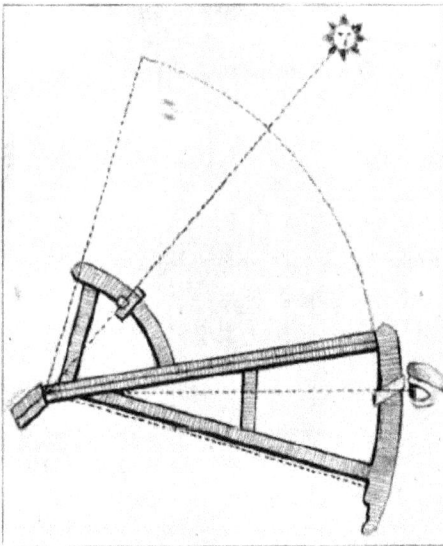

BACK-STAFF, OR DAVIS'S QUADRANT.

Henry VII., unlike some of his fifteenth-century predecessors, deemed it of importance to build some vessels specially for war, instead of relying entirely upon ships hired from the merchants, and more or less hastily and imperfectly adapted for it, and he strengthened the Navy Royal by adding to it at least two finer men-of-war than had been previously seen in England.

With the crown, he acquired the *Grace à Dieu*, (probably bought or built, 1473), the *Governor*, (bought, 1485), the *Martin Gareia*, (probably bought, 1470), the *Mary of the Tower*, (bought, 1478), the *Trinity*, the *Falcon*, and possibly the *Bonaventure*. He purchased the *Carvel of Ewe*, (*Caravel of Eu*, in Normandy); renamed *Mary and John*, and perhaps also a small craft called the *King's Bark*; he captured the *Margaret* in 1490; and he built the *Regent*, the *Sovereign*, the *Sweepstake*, and the *Mary Fortune*.

The tonnage and dimensions of the *Regent* and the *Sovereign* are unknown; but it is tolerably certain that both ships were larger and more powerful than any of their predecessors in the English navy. (It is known, however, that the *Regent* was copied from a French ship, the *Columbe*, of 600 tons.)

The *Regent* was constructed in Reding Creek, on the Rother, under the supervision of Sir Richard Guildford, and seems to have been launched in 1489 or 1490. (Richard, son of Sir John Guildford, of Hempsted. He was made Master of the Ordnance in 1486, then Controller of the Household, and, in 1500, a K.G.) She carried 225 serpentines, all apparently on the upper deck, forecastle, and poop. She had a foremast and foretop-mast, a main-mast, main top-mast, and main top-gallant-mast, a main mizen-mast, a bonaventure mizenmast, and a sprit-sail on the bowsprit. (The foretop-masts were separate spars, but fixed, and not strikable.) Each mast seems to have carried a yard. The *Regent* was burnt in 1512.

The *Sovereign* was constructed, partly out of the remains of the broken-up *Grace à Dieu*, under the superintendence of Sir Reginald Bray, and, in all likelihood, was launched in 1488. (Sir Reginald, later, a Privy Councillor and K.G. He was the architect of St. George's Chapel, Windsor, and of Henry VII's Chapel, Westminster.) She was smaller than the *Regent*, carrying only 141 serpentines. Her masts were like those of the *Regent*, except that she had no main topgallant-mast. (Nav. Accts. and Inventories of Henry VII.)

The *Sweepstake*, (renamed *Katherine Pomegranate* under Henry VIII.), and *Mary Fortune* were built in 1497, and were small craft, each

THE "HENRY GRACE À DIEU."
From a supposed contemporary panel, formerly in Canterbury Cathedral,
given by the dean and chapter to Admiral of the Fleet, Sir John Norris.

THE "HENRY GRACE À DIEU."

with three lower masts, a main top-mast, and a sprit-sail on the bowspit. (Nav. Accts. and Inventories of Henry VII.) One had eighty and the other sixty oars, for use as sweeps.

The *Regent*, the principal warship, bequeathed to Henry VIII. by his father, was, as will be seen later, burnt in the action off Brest, on August 10th, 1512, and it would appear that it was as a substitute for her that the famous *Henry Grace à Dieu* was laid down at Erith in the course of the autumn of the same year. On June 13th, 1514, the not extravagant sum of 6*s*. 8*d*. was offered at her "hallowing," (Letters and Papers, Hen. VIII.), from which fact it may be concluded that she was then launched; and in the course of the following year she seems to have been completed for sea. William Bond, the master-shipwright who built her under Brygandine's direction, is supposed to have been the first master-shipwright of the Royal Navy. A MS. Augmentation Office account, quoted by Charnock, indicates that in November, or December, 1514, she was moved from Erith to Barking Creek by a party which included twenty-one seamen who had been discharged from the *Lizard*, each of whom received 8*d*. for his share of the work.

Several alleged representations of this interesting ship exist, and some of them are reproduced here. One is found in a picture which was long hanging in Canterbury Cathedral, and which was presented to Sir John Norris, Admiral of the Fleet, by the dean and chapter. It is still in the possession of Sir John's descendants, and was exhibited at the Royal Naval Exhibition, 1891. Another occurs in the picture by Volpe of the embarkation of Henry VIII. at Dover on May 31st, 1520, to meet Francis I. on the Field of the Cloth of Gold. This picture, the property of the Crown, is at Hampton Court Palace. Another occurs in the well-known drawing preserved in the Pepysian collection at Cambridge. And there are two models in the museum at Greenwich.

The authenticity of these last was, however, so much doubted by the models committee of the Naval Exhibition, that they were merely described in the catalogue as probably representing large ships of the sixteenth century. Upon the whole, Volpe's picture, long ascribed to Holbein, seems to be the most trustworthy, although it does not represent the vessels which actually convoyed Henry, but rather those vessels which would have convoyed him, had the harbours where the king embarked and disembarked been deep enough to admit them.

The following account of Volpe's picture, which is of necessity here reproduced on a very diminished scale, and does not, therefore, show details with great clearness, will assist the student. Of it Pepys says:

EMBARKATION OF HENRY VIII, AT DOVER, MAY 31ST, 1520

I came a little too late (to receive the Communion at White-hall), so I walked up into the house, and spent my time in looking over pictures, particularly the ships in King Henry VIII.'s voyage to Bullaen, marking the great difference between those built then and now.

The *Henry Grace à Dieu* is the vessel which is sailing out of harbour, and which is immediately above the right tower. She has four pole masts, with two round tops on each, except the shorter mizzen, which bears only one. Her sails and pennants are of cloth of gold damasked. The royal standard of England flies on each of the four angles of the forecastle, and the staff of each standard is surrounded by a *fleur-de-lys Or*. Pennants fly from the mastheads, and at each angle of the poop is a banner of St. George. Her quarters and sides, as well as her tops, are hung with targets, charged differently with the Cross of St. George, Azure a *fleur-de-lys Or*, party per pale Argent and Vert a union rose, and party per pale Argent and Vert a portcullis Or, alternately and repeatedly.

In the waist stands the king, in a garment of cloth of gold, edged with ermine, the sleeves, jacket, and breeches, crimson. His round hat bears a white feather, lying on the brim. On his proper left stands a person in a dark violet coat, slashed with black, and with red stockings. On his right are three other persons, one in black, another in bluish-grey, and the third in red, guarded with black, and with a black slashed jacket. Behind are yeomen of the guard, with halberts. Two trumpeters, sounding their trumpets, sit on the break of the poop, and two more are on the break of the forecastle. On both forecastle and poop are many yeomen of the guard. Beneath the break of the forecastle are shown, party per pale Argent and Vert, within the garter, the arms of England and France, quarterly crowned; the supporters, a lion and a dragon, being those then used by the king. The same arms appear on the stern.

On each side of the rudder is a porthole, showing the muzzle of a

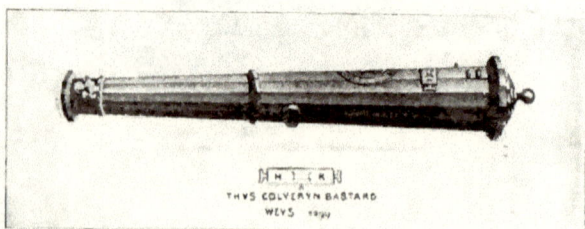

THVS COLVERYN BASTARD
WEYS 1899

CULVERIN BASTARD, XVITH CENTURY.

16

brass gun. The figure-head seems to represent a lion. Under the stern is a boat, having at her head two banners of St. George, and at her stern the same. Two yeomen of the guard, and other persons are in her. Both stern and forecastle are two decks higher than the waist, which itself appears to be two clear decks above the water.

Four other ships, all large, are shown in the picture. The king's squadron actually consisted of the *Great Bark*, the *Less Bark*, the *Katherine Pleasaunce*, the *Mary and John*, and two row barges, all comparatively small craft; but the painter obviously shows us some of the crack ships of the time. The visit to France was paid in Henry's twelfth year. In the thirteenth year of his reign, 1521-22, according to a MS. in Pepys' *Miscellanies*, the five largest ships in the English navy, with their tonnage, were as follows: *Henry Grace à Dieu*, 1500, (most authorities, however, agree that the tonnage was but 1000, see table further on); *Sovereign*, 800; *Gabriel Royal*, 650; *Mary Rose*, 600, (elsewhere generally described as of 500 tons); and *Katherine Forteleza*, 550; and it is very probable that these five vessels are the five depicted. On this assumption, the ship which men are boarding, and which is the innermost of the three lying alongside one another, would naturally be the *Sovereign*, since she alone, except the *Henry Grace à Dieu*, has four masts.

The heavy guns of the *Henry Grace à Dieu*, according to an account in *Archeeologia*, taken from a MS. in the Pepysian Collection at Magdalen College, Cambridge, were twenty-one in number, and were all of brass.

The following are the types and numbers of each, with the number and nature of the shot carried for them:—

Guns.	Number.	Shot.	Number.
Cannon	4	Iron	100
Demi-cannon . . .	3	,,	60
Culverin	4	,,	120
Demi-culverin . . .	2	,,	70
Saker	4	,,	120
Cannon Perer (Cannon Petro)	2	Stone or lead	67
Falcon	2	Iron	100

There were also the following light guns, *viz.*: port pieces, 14; slings, 4; demi-slings, 2; fowlers, 8; bassils, 60; top-pieces, 2; hail-shot pieces, 40; and hand-guns, 100. Her complement was made up of 301 mariners, 50 gunners, and 349 soldiers, making 700 in all.

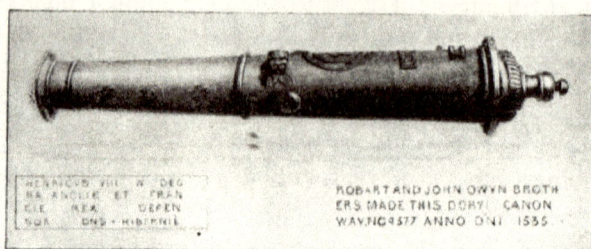

HENRICUS VIII N DEI / BA ANGLIE ET FRAN / CIE REX DEFEN / SOR DNS HIBERNIE

ROBART AND JOHN OWYN BROTH / ERS MADE THIS DOBY CANON / WAV.NG4577 ANNO D'NI 1535

BRASS GUN FROM THE "MARY ROSE."

It would be waste of time, in default of specific information on the subject, to endeavour to indicate how and where the different heavy guns were mounted; but some particulars as to the guns themselves can and should be attempted. In this we are assisted by the fact that several guns which went down in the abovementioned *Mary Rose* in 1545, off Portsmouth, have been recovered, and are still in existence, and by the further fact that little change in the size and nature of ships' heavy guns took place during the sixteenth century. A table of the principal guns of that period, compiled from extant specimens, and from what appear to be the most trustworthy ancient authorities, (see note following), is therefore appended:—

Name of Piece.	Calibre.	Length.[1]		Weight of Gun.	Weight of Shot.	Charge of Powder.
	Ins.	Ft.	Ins.	Lbs.	Lbs.	Lbs.
Cannon Royal . . .	8·54	8	6	8,000	74	30
Cannon	8·0	..		6,000	60	27
Cannon Serpentine .	7·0	..		5,500	42	25
Bastard Cannon . .	7·0	..		4,500	42	20
Demi-Cannon . . .	6·4	11	0	4,000	32	18
Cannon Pedro, or Petro[2]	6·0	..		3,800	26	14
Culverin[3]	5·2	10	11	4,840	18	12
Basilisk.	5·0	..		4,000	14	9
Demi-Culverin . .	4·0	..		3,400	8	6
Culverin Bastard . .	4·56	8	6	3,000	11	5·7
Saker[4]	3·65	6	11	1,400	6	4
Minion	3·5	6	6	1,050	5·2	3
Falcon	2·5	6	0	680	2	1·2
Falconet[5]	2·0	3	9	500	1	·4
Serpentine	1·5	..		400	·5	·3
Rabinet or Robinet .	1·0	..		300	·3	·18

18

[1] Monson puts the length of the guns mentioned by him at 8 ft. 6 in.; but specimens still extant, dating from about his time, indicate that this was not always correct.

[2] "Cannon Pedro" was the English form of "canon pierrier," and means a gun primarily intended for throwing stone shot.

[3] *I.e. couleuvrine*—serpent. Compare Basilisk.

[4] Named after the Saker hawk. Compare Falcon.

[5] In the grounds of the Seigneurie, Sark, is a well-preserved brass gun, apparently a falconet, 57 inches in length, and 1¾ inches in calibre, bearing the following inscription:—"Don de sa Majesté la Royne Elizabeth au Seigneur de Sarcq, A.D. 1572."

★★★★★★

The paper Dom. Eliz. Cclii, 64 is printed at length as an appendix to the *State Papers relating to the Defeat of the Spanish Armada* (Nav. Rec Soc.), and contains a table from which the following is extracted:—

——	Height (calibre) of the Piece.	Weight of the Piece.	Weight of the Shot.	Weight of the Powder.	Point blank (range) by the Quadrant.	Random (range with elevation).
	Inches.	Lbs.	Lbs.	Lbs.	Score Paces.	Paces.
Cannon Royal	8½	7000	66	30	..	1930
Cannon	8	6000	60	27	17	2000
Cannon Serpentine	7½	5500	53½	25	20	2000
Bastard Cannon	7	4500	41¼	20	18	1800
Demi-Cannon	6½	4000	30¼	18	17	1700
Cannon Pedro	6	3000	24¼	14	16	1600
Culverin	5½	4500	17⅓	12	20	2500
Basilisco	5	4000	15¼	10	..	..
Demi-Culverin	4½	3400	9⅓	8	20	2500
Bastard Culverin	4	3000	7	6¼	18	1800
Saker	3½	1400	5⅓	5⅓	17	1700
Minion	3¼	1000	4	4	16	1600
Falcon of 2⅓ inches	2⅓	800	3	3	15	1500
Falconet	2	500	1¼	1¼	14	1400
Serpentine	1½	400	⅓	⅓	13	1300
Robinet	1	300	½	½	12	1000
Falcon	2½	660	2¼	2¼	15	1500

The charges are for "cannon corn powder" (serpentine meal powder). When "fine corn powder" (small arm powder) was used, 25 per cent. less of it was to be employed. The table and directions are signed "Jo. Sheriffe."

★★★★★★

The weights of guns of the same denomination, and of the shot for them, nay, even the calibres, seem to have varied considerably, and the windage was greater than was ever allowed in the seventeenth or eighteenth century. In the cannon royal, it must have amounted to a full half-inch at least, and if, as some authorities say, the cannon royal threw only a sixty-six-pound shot, the windage must have been in some cases as much as three-quarters of an inch. In his preface to the *Defeat of the Spanish Armada*, Professor Laughton speaks loosely of the shot being "a good inch and a half less in diameter than the bore of the gun." This is surely an exaggeration. Had the proportions been so, the iron shot for an 8-in. gun would have weighed less than 40 lbs.; that for a 7-in. gun less than 24 lbs.; that for a 6-in. gun about 13 lbs.; and that for a 5-in. gun only about 6 lbs.

The relatively large charges of powder may be explained by this great windage, and the excessive badness and weakness of the explosive. In the eighteenth century, twenty-five pounds was a proof charge for a 42-pounder, and the heaviest sea-service charge for it was only seventeen pounds, while the proof charge for an 18-pounder was fifteen pounds, and the sea-service charge was but nine pounds. (Montaine's *Practical Sea Gunner's Companion*, 1747.)

The ships of Henry VII. appear to have been the first English ones to be fitted with regular port-holes. The *Regent* and *Sovereign* certainly had them in their poops and forecastles. The invention of the device has been ascribed to Descharges, a shipbuilder of Brest, about the year 1500, but there is no doubt that it was of a rather earlier date. The numerous small guns of the *Henry Grace à Dieu*, and of the other large ships of her time, were mounted on the upper deck, in the tops, in the poop and forecastle, and under the break of the poop and forecastle, so as to command the waist and sweep it, should boarding be attempted there.

ELIZABETHAN FALCONET, AT THE
SEIGNEURIE, SARK.

Among these small guns were:—Fowlers, short, light weapons, with or without a separate breech which could be unshipped and reloaded while another was being discharged; port-pieces, small fowlers with the same peculiarities; curtalds, short heavy guns, apparently employed for high-angle fire; slings, demi-slings, bassils or small basilisks, and top-pieces, all of diminutive calibre and relatively large powder-charge, working on swivels or pivots; hail-shot pieces, carrying a charge of cubical dice; and hand-guns or calivers, which, though fired from the shoulder, required to be supported on a pivot or staff.

Among the stores of the *Henry Grace à Dieu* at her commissioning were two lasts, or 4800 pounds of "serpentyn" powder in barrels, and six lasts, or 14,400 pounds of "corn" powder, also in barrels. (From a MS. in the Pepysian Library). This, and the provision of shot, must have been more than ample, for the larger guns could be fired only very seldom, there being no mechanical contrivances for working them; and it is recorded as a marvellous thing by Du Bellay that in the action of 1545, when about two hundred ships were hotly engaged at close quarters for two hours, there were not less than three hundred cannon-shot fired on both sides. Du Bellay, as a military contemporary, no doubt wrote what was quite true, (though another contemporary says that not less than 300 guns were engaged); but he probably included only the shots thrown from the heavier guns engaged, and paid no attention to the fire of light pieces.

A GENOESE CARRACK.

Still, the expenditure was remarkably small, and it cannot have permitted the heaviest guns to be discharged more than twice or thrice apiece. The seamen of the period had not, however, begun to depend exclusively, nor even chiefly, upon firearms as their weapons of offence, and this abundantly appears from the fact that, among the stores of the *Henry Grace à Dieu* were 500 bows of yew, ten gross of bowstrings, 200 morris pikes, 200 bills, ten dozen lime pots, and great quantities of arrows and darts. As late as 1578, (from a MS. of Dr. Samuel Knight), there were, among the stores of Queen Elizabeth's ships, 300 bows, 380 sheaves of arrows, 460 morris pikes, and 460 bills; nor had the gun fully asserted its supremacy until several years after the time of the Armada. It should be added that in the case of the largest guns of the Tudors, the powder was made up on board into cartridges in canvas cases, paper cases being used for the charges of the medium and lighter guns. Hence the comparatively early origin of the term cartridge-paper.

No picture, print, or model of the *Henry Grace à Dieu* suggests to the modern technical critic that the vessel was in the least suited for sea work; yet the ship was undoubtedly a good sailer, for, writing to the king on June 4th, 1522, from the Downs, Vice-Admiral Sir William Fitzwilliam reported that she sailed as well as, and rather better than, any ship in the fleet, weathering all save the *Mary Rose*.

An inventory of her gear, made in 1521, shows that she possessed a 22-inch cable, a 20-inch cable, and an 8-inch hawser. Her mainstay was sixteen inches in diameter. When she was still building, the authorities paid for a streamer or pennant, fifty-one yards long, for her mainmast, a sum of £3, and for two flags; with crosses of St. George, 10*d.* each. These last may have been boat-flags; for, of course, she carried boats, though it is not clear how she hoisted them out and in, and where she stowed them. They must have lain, possibly on chocks, on deck in the waist. The boat davit was a much later invention.

Some notes as to the prices of certain gear for other ships, from records of the year 1513, may be added here: For the *Trinity of Bristol*, otherwise the *Nicholas of Hampton*, a spirit-sail yard cost 9*s.* (she was a craft of 200 tons); 100 feet of oak plank, 6*s.*; a hundredweight of small ropes, 11*s.* 4*d.*; a boathook, 4*d.*; a compass, 2*s.*; a foreyard, 14*s.*; and two gallons of vinegar, "to make fine powder for hand-guns," 8*d.* A mizzenmast for the *Katherine Pomegranate*, otherwise the *Sweepstake*, of 65 (or 80) tons, cost 10*s.*, and an anchor for the same craft, 20*s.*

Contemporary literary references to naval matters of the sixteenth

VESSELS, 14TH CENTURY

century are so rare, and so very few of them are attributable to writers who seem to have been at all familiar with the technical aspects of naval life, that no excuse is necessary for printing here an extract from a volume which was published at Edinburgh in 1801, and which is entitled *The Complaynt of Scotland*. The work was written by an unknown author in 1548; and it takes the form of a satire directed against those responsible, or supposed to be responsible, for the misfortunes of the northern kingdom. In the first part, the author laments his country's woes, and considers the causes of them; in the second, as if endeavouring to escape from the sadness of his reflections, he gives a vivid description of a number of characteristic scenes. Among these is the following naval picture, (translation follows at the end):—

Than I sat doune to see the flonying of the fame; quhar that I leukyt fart furth on the salt flude. There I beheld ane galiasse gayly grathit for the veyr, lyand fast at ane ankir, and her salis in hou. I herd many vordis amang the marynalis, bot I vist nocht quhat tai menit. Zit I sal reherse and report ther crying and ther cal. In the fyrst, the maister of the galiasse gart the botis man pas vp to the top, to leuk fart furth gyf he cnld see ony schips. Than the botis man leukyt sa lang quhit that he sae ane quhyt sail. Than he cryit vitht ane skyrl, quod he, 'I see ane grit schip.' Than the maister quhislit, and bald the marynalis lay the cabil to the cabilstok, to veynde and veye. Than the marynalis began to veynde the cabil vitht mony loud cry. And as ane cryit, al the laif cryit in that samyn tune, as it hed bene ecco in ane hon heuch. And, as it aperit to me, thai cryit thir vordis as eftir follouis: 'Veyra, veyra, veyra, veyra, gentil gallandis, gentil gallandis! Veynde; I see hym: veynde; I see him. Pourbossa; pourbossa! Hail al and ane! Hail al and ane! Hail hym vp til vs! Hail hym vp til vs!'

Than, quhen the ankyr vas halit vp abufe the vattir, ane marynal cryit, and al the laif follouit in that sam tune; 'Caupon caupona; caupon caupona; caupun hola; caupun hola; caupun holt; caupun holt; sarrabossa; sarrabossa.' Than thai maid fast the sthank of the ankyr.

And the maister quhislit and cryit: 'Tua men abufe to the foir ra! Cut the raibandis, and lat the foir sail fal! Hail doune to steir burde! Lufe harde aburde! Hail eftir the foir sail scheit! Hail out the bollene!'

Than the maister quhislit and cryit; 'Tua men abufe to the mane ra! Cut the raibandis, and lat the mane sail and top sail fal! Hail doune the lufe close aburde! Hail eftir the mane sail scheit! Hail out the mane sail bollene!' Than ane of the marynalis began to hail and to cry, and al the marynalis ansuert of that samyn sound: 'Hou! Hou! Pulpela! Pulpela! Boulena! Boulena! Darta! Darta! Hard out strif! Hard out strif! Afoir the vynd! Afoir the vynd! God send! God send! Fayr vedthir! Fayr vedthir! Mony pricis! Mony pricis! God foir lend! God foir lend! Stou! Stou! Mak fast and belay!'

Than the maister cryit and bald: 'Eenze ane bonet! Vire the trossis! Nou heise!' Than the marynalis began to heis vp the sail, cryand: 'Heisau! Heisau! Vorsa! Vorsa! Vou! Vou! Ane lang draucht! Ane lang draucht! Mair maucht! Mair maucht! Zong blude! Zong blude! Mair mude! Mair mude! False flasche! False flasche! Ly a bak! Ly a bak! Lang suak! Lang suak! That! That! That! That! Thair! Thair! Thair! Thair! Zallou hayr! Zallou hayr! Hips bayr! Hips bayr! Til hym al! Til hym al! Viddefullis al! Viddefullis al! Grit and smal! Grit and smal! Ane and al! Ane and al!

Heisau! Heisau! Nou mak fast the theyrs!'

Than the maister cryit: 'Top zour topinellis! Hail on zour top sail scheitis! Vire zour listaris and zour top sail trossis, and heise the top sail hiear! Hail out the top sail boulene! Heise the myszen, and change it ouer to leuart! Hail the loriche and the seheitis! Hail the trosse to the ra!'

Than the maister cryit on the rudirman: 'Mait, keip ful and by! A luf! Cunna hiear! Holabar! Arryva! Steir clene vp the helme! This and so!'

Than, quhen the schip vas taiklit, the maister cryit: "Boy to the top! Schaik out the flag on the top mast! Tak in zour top salis and thirl them! Pul doune the nok of the ra in daggar vyise! Marynalis, stand be zour geyr in taiklene of zour salis! Euery quartar maister til his aen quarter! Botis man, bayr stanis and lyme pottis ful of lyme in the craklene pokis to the top, and paucis veil the top vitht pauesis and mantillis! Gunnaris, cum heir, and stand by zour astailzee, euyrie gunnar til hir aen quartar! Mak reddy zour cannons, culuerene moyens, culuerene bastardis, falcons, saikyrs, half saikyrs, and half falcons, slangis, and half slangis, quartar slangis, hede stikkis, murdresaris, pasau-olans, bersis, doggis, doubil bersis, hagbutis of croche, half hag-gis, culuernis, and hail schot! And ze soldaris and coupangzons of veyr, mak reddy zour corsbollis, hand bollis, fyir speyris, hail schot, lancis, pikkis, halbardis, rondellis, tua handit sourdis and tairgis!'

Than this gaye galiasse, beand in gude ordour, sche follouit fast the samyn schip that the botis man hed sene; and for mair speid the galiasse pat furht hir stoytene salis, and ane hundretht aris on euerye syde.

The maister gart al his marynalis and men of veyr hald them quiet at rest, be rason that the mouying of the pepil vitht in ane schip stopes hyr of hyr fair. Of this sort, the said galiasse in schort tyme cam on vynduart of the tothir schip. Than eftir that thai hed hailsit vthirs, thai maid them reddy for battel.

Than quhar I sat I hard the cannons and gunnis mak mony hiddeus crak—*duf, duf, duf, duf, duf, duf.* The bersis and falcons cryit *tirduf, tirduf, tirduf, tirduf, tirduf.* Than the smal artailze cryit *tik, tak, tik, tak, tik, take.* The reik, smeuik, and the stink of the gunpuddir fylit al the ayr, maist lyik as Pluto is paleis hed been birnand in ane bald fyer. Quhilk generit sik mirknes and myst that I culd nocht see my lynth about me.

******

The following is a fairly close translation, so far as the above extract appears to be translatable. In the original, some inconsistencies of spelling and obvious inaccuracies are corrected. In the translation, obscure passages are left in italics:—

Then I sat down to see the flowing of the foam; where I looked far forth on the salt flood. There I beheld a *galliass* gaily caparisoned for the war, lying fast at an anchor, with her sails furled. I heard many words among the mariners, but I knew not what they meant. Yet I shall rehearse and report their crying and their call. In the first (place) the master of the *galliass* bid the boatsman, (*i.e.* the first officer), pass up to the top, to look far forth if he could see any ships. Then the boatsman looked so long out that he saw one white sail. Then he cried with an oath, quoth he: 'I see a great ship.'

Then the master whistled, and bade the mariners lay the cable to the cable-stock, (windlass), to wind and weigh. Then the mariners began to wind the cable with many (a) loud cry. And as one cried, all the rest cried in that same tune, as it had been (an) echo in a cave. And, as it appeared to me, they cried their words as after follows: 'Veer, veer, veer, veer, gentle gallants, gentle gallants! Wind; I see him. Wind; I see him. *Pourbossa; pourbossa!* Haul all and one! Haul all and one! Haul him up to us! Haul him up to us!'

Then, when the anchor was hauled up above the water, one mariner cried, and all the rest followed in that same tune: '*Caupon caupona; caupon caupona; caupun hola; caupun hola; caupun holt; caupun holt; sarrabossa; sarrabossa!*' (Apparently corrupted Mediterranean terms. *Capone* in Italian means "cable.") Then they made fast the shank of the anchor.

Then the master whistled, and cried: 'Two men above to the foreyard! Cut the lashings, and let the foresail fall! Haul down to starboard! Luff hard aboard! Haul aft the foresail sheet! Haul out the bowline!'

Then the master whistled, and cried: 'Two men above to the mainyard! Cut the lashings, and let the mainsail and topsail fall! Haul down the luff close aboard! Haul aft the mainsail sheet! Haul out the mainsail bowline!' Then one of the mariners began to hail and to cry, and all the mariners answered that same sound: '*Hou! Soul Pulpela! Pulpela! Boulena! Boulena! Darta! Darta!* (Probably more Mediterranean corruptions). Hard out strif! Hard out strif!" (Unintelligible.) Before the wind! Before the wind! God send! God send! Fair weather! Fair weather! Many prizes! Many prizes! Good fair land! Good fair land! Stow! Stow! Make fast and belay!'

Then the master cried, and bade: 'Out with a bonnet! (Extra cloth laced to a sail or course for line-weather sailing.) Veer the trusses! Now hoist!' Then the mariners began to hoist up the sail, crying: '*Heisau! Heisau! Vorsa! Vorsa! Vou! Vou!* One long pull! One long pull! More power! More power! Young blood! Young blood! More mud! More mud! False flesh! False flesh! Lie aback! Lie aback! Long *suak*! Long *suak*! That! That! That! That! There! There! There! There! Yellow hair! Yellow hair! Hips bare! Hips bare! To him all! To him all! *Viddefullis al! Viddefullis al!* Great and small! Great and small! One and all! One and all! *Heisau! Heisau!* Now each make fast his!'

Then the master cried: 'Top your *topinellis*! Haul on your topsail sheets! Veer your leeches, and your topsail trusses, and hoist the topsail higher! Haul out the topsail bowline! Hoist the mizen, and change it over to leeward! Haul the leeche and the sheets! Haul the truss to the yard!'

Then the master cried to the steersman: 'Mate, keep full and by! Luff! Con her! Steady! Keep close! Steer straight ahead! That will do!'

Then, when the ship was under sail, the master cried: 'Boy to the top! Shake out the flag on the topmast! Take in your topsails and *thirl* them! Pull down the *nok* of the yard in dagger-wise! Mariners, stand to your gear for handling of your sails! Every quartermaster to his own quarter! Boatsman, bear stones and lime-pots full of lime in the *craklene pokis* to the top, and *paucis* veil the top with pavises and mantlets! Gunners, come here, and stand by your artillery; every gunner to his own quarter! Make ready your cannons, medium culverins, culverins bastard, falcons, sakers, half sakers, and half falcons, slings and half slings, quarter slings, head sticks, murdering pieces, passevolants, bassils, dogs, double bassils, arquebusses with crooks, half arquebusses, calivers, and hail shot! And ye soldiers and companions of war, make ready your crossbows, hand-bows, fire spars, hail shot, lances, pikes, halberds, rondels, two-handed swords, and targes!'

Then this gay *galliass*, being in good order, she followed fast the same ship that the boatsman had seen; and for more speed the *galliass* put forth her studding sails and a hundred oars on every side. (If "stoytene" be really "studding," the vessel employed studding sails as well as bonnets. The translation is doubtful.)

The master bid all his mariners and men of war hold themselves quietly at rest, by reason that the moving of the people within a ship stops her on her course. In this manner, the said *galliass* in short time came to windward of the other ship. Then, after that they had hailed one another, they made them ready for battle.

Then where I sat I heard the cannons and guns make many hideous cracks—*duf, duf, duf, duf, duf, duf.* The bassils and falcons cried *tirduf, tirduf, tirduf, tirduf, tirdut.* Then the small artillery cried *tik, tak, tik, tak, tik, take.* The reek, smoke, and the stink of the gunpowder rilled all the air, most like as Pluto's palace had been burning in one bad fire: which generated such murkiness and mist that I could not see my length about me.

★★★★★★

As the period now under consideration was that of the infancy and early growth, if not of the actual birth of that magnificent creation, the British Navy, some lists of the royal fleet, as it stood at different dates, will here be appropriate:—

LIST[1] OF WARSHIPS BUILT, PURCHASED, OR OTHERWISE ACQUIRED, BY
HENRY VIII. (1509–1547), AND APPARENTLY LOST OR DISPOSED OF BEFORE
THE ACCESSION OF EDWARD VI.

SHIP.	*Built. †Bought. ‡Taken.	Tons.	SHIP.	*Built. †Bought. ‡Taken.	Tons.
1. *Anne Gallant*	†1512	140	13. *Great Elizabeth*	†1514	900
2. *Artigo*	†1544	100	14. *Great Nicholas*	†1512	400
3. *Bark of Boullen*	‡1522	80	15. *Great Zabra*	*1522	50
4. *Bark of Morlaix*	‡1522	60	16. *Henry Galley*	*1512	?
5. *Black Bark*	†1513	?	17. *Henry of Hampton*	†1513	120
6. *Christ*	†1512	300	18. *Jennet Perwyn*	‡1511	70
7. *Dragon*	*1512	100	19. *John Baptist*	†1512	400
8. *Fortune*	*1522	160	20. *John of Greenwich*	‡1523	50
9. *Gabriel Royal*	†1509	700	21. *Katherine* Galley	*1512	80
10. *Galley Blancherd*	‡1546	?	22. *Katherine Forteleza*	†1512	700
11. *Great Bark*	*1512	400	23. *Katherine Pleasaunce*	*1518	100
12. *Great Barbara*	†1513	400			

[1] Compiled mainly from information in Oppenheim's 'Admin. of Royal Navy.'

SHIP.	*Built. †Bought. ‡Taken.	Tons.	SHIP.	*Built. †Bought. ‡Taken.	Tons.
24. *Less Bark* . . .	*1512	160	37. *Mary James (II.)*.	‡1545	120
25. *Less Pinnace* . .	*1545	60	38. *Mary Odierne* .	‡1545	70
26. *Lesser Barbara* .	†1512	160	39. *Mary Rose*. . .	*1509	500
27. *Lesser Zabra* . .	*1522	40	40. *Mary Thomas* . .	‡1545	100
28. *Lion*	‡1511	120	41. *Mawdlyn of Dept- ford* . . . . }	*1522	120
29. *Lizard*	*1512	120			
30. *Mary George* . .	†1510	300	42. *Minion* . . .	*1523	180
31. *Mary Gloria* . .	†1517	300	43. *Primrose* . . .	*1523	160
32. *Mary Grace* . .	‡1522	?	44. *Rose* Galley . .	*1512	?
33. *Mary and John* .	†1521	?	45. *Roo*.	*1545	80
34. *Mary Guildford* .	*1524	160	46. *Sovereign* (rebuilt)	*1509	600
35. *Mary Imperial* .	*1515	120	47. *Swallow* . . .	*1512	80
36. *Mary James (I.)* .	†1509	300	48. *Sweepstake*. . .	*1523	65

2. Called also *L'Artique.* Sold 1547.
3. "Bullen," *i.e.* Boulogne.
5. Also called *Black Bark, Christopher,* and *Mark Florentine.*
6. Also called *Christ of Lynn.* She was captured in 1515.
9. Perhaps called also *Mary Lorette.*
10. Taken from the French.
12. Formerly *Maudlin.*

13. Formerly *Salvator,* of Lübeck. Wrecked in 1514.
15. *Zabra* means pinnace.
18. Taken from Barton.
19. Formerly *John Hopton.*
22. Genoese built.
27. See 15.
28. Taken from Barton.

30. Probably ex *Mary Howard.*
35. Rebuilt 1523.
36. Possibly ex *James,* of Hull.
39. Rebuilt 1536. Overset 1545.
42. Rebuilt of 300 tons, about 1536. Given to Sir T. Seymour.
45. Taken by the French, 1547.
47. Rebuilt 1524.

LIST OF THE ROYAL NAVY ON JANUARY 5TH, 1548 (1 EDW. VI.) IN ARCHÆOLOGIA V., 218 (WITH DATES SUPPLIED FOR THE MOST PART FROM OPPENHEIM, 'ADMIN. OF ROY. NAVY').

SHIP.	* Built. † Bought. ‡ Taken.	TONS.	MEN.	GUNS.[1] Brass.	Iron.
[2] *Henry Grace à Dieu* (rebuilt) .	* 1540	1000	700	19	103
[3] *Peter* (rebuilt)	* 1536	600	400	12	78
[3] *Matthew*	† 1539	600	300	10	121
[3] *Jesus*	† 1544	700	300	8	66
[3] *Pauncy (Pansy)*	* 1544	450	300	13	69
[3] *Great Bark*	† 1539	500	300	12	85
[3] *Less Bark*[a].	† 1539	400	250	11	98
[3] *Murryan*[b]	† 1545	500	300	10	53
[3] *Struce of Dawske*[c].	† 1544	450	250	0	39
[3] *Christopher*[d]	† 1546	400	246	2	51
[3] *Trinity Henry*.	* 1519	250	220	1	63
[3] *Sweepstake*.	* 1539	300	230	6	78
[3] *Mary Willoughby*[e]	* 1536	140	160	0	23
[4] *Anne Gallant*	* 1545	450	250	16	46
[4] *Salamander*	‡ 1544	300	220	9	40
[4] *Hart*	* 1546	300	200	4	52
[4] *Antelope*	* 1546	300	200	4	40
[4] *Swallow*	* 1544	240	100	8	45
[4] *Unicorn*[f]	‡ 1544	240	140	6	30

[1] The armament certainly varied at different times.
[2] At Woolwich.
[3] At Portsmouth.
[4] Galleys at Portsmouth.

[a] Ordered to be rebuilt, 1551.
[b] Sold, 1551.
[c] Dawske—Danzig. Sold, 1551.
[d] Ordered for sale, 1551, but not sold till 1556.
[e] Taken by the Scots; retaken, 1547; rebuilt, 1551.
[f] Ordered for sale, 1551 ; sold, 1555.

SHIP.	* Built. † Bought. ‡ Taken.	TONS.	MEN.	GUNS.[1]	
				Brass.	Iron.
[4] *Jennet*	* 1539	180	120	6	35
[4] *New Bark*	* 1523	200	140	5	48
[4] *Greyhound*[g]	* 1545	200	140	8	37
[4] *Tiger*	* 1546	200	120	4	39
[4] *Bull*	* 1546	200	120	5	42
[4] *Lion*[h]	* 1536	140	140	2	48
[4] *George*	† 1546	60	40	2	26
[4] *Dragon*[i]	* 1544	140	120	3	42
[5] *Falcon*	* 1544	83	55	4	22
[5] *Black Pinnace*	?	80	44	2	15
[5] *Hind*[j]	* 1545	80	55	2	26
[5] *Spanish Shallop*	?	20	26	0	
[5] *Hare*	* 1545	15	30	0	10
[6] *Sun*	* 1546	20	40	2	6
[6] *Cloud in the Sun*	* 1546	20	40	2	7
[6] *Harp*	* 1546	20	40	1	6
[6] *Maidenhead*	* 1546	20	37	2	6
[6] *Gillyflower*[k]	* 1546	20	38	0	0
[6] *Ostrich Feather*	* 1546	20	37	1	6
[6] *Rose Slip*	* 1546	20	37	2	6
[6] *Flower de Luce*	* 1546	20	43	2	7
[6] *Rose in the Sun*	* 1546	20	40	3	7
[6] *Portcullis*	* 1546	20	38	1	6
[6] *Falcon in the Fetterlock*	* 1546	20	45	3	8
[7] *Grandmistress*[k]	* 1545	450	250	1	22
[7] *Marlion*	‡ 1545	40	50	4	8
[7] *Galley Subtle, or Row Galley*	* 1544	200	250	3	28
[7] *Brygandine*	* 1545	40	44	3	19
[7] *Hoy Bark*	?	80	60	0	5
[7] *Hawthorn*	* 1546	20	37	0	0
[8] *Mary Hamborow*[l]	† 1544	400	246	5	67
[8] *Phœnix*	† 1546	40	50	4	33
[8] *Saker*	* 1545	40	50	2	18
[8] *Double Rose*	* 1546	20	43	3	6
53 ships		11,268	7,780	237	1,850

[1] The armament certainly varied at different times.　[5] Pinnaces at Portsmouth.
[d] Row Barges at Portsmouth. Most of these were sold in 1548–49.
[7] At Deptford Stronde.　[8] In Scotland.

[g] Wrecked off Rye, 1552.　[j] Sold in 1555.
[h] Ordered to be rebuilt, 1551.　[k] Condemned, 1551 ; sold in 1551.
[i] Ordered to be rebuilt, 1551.　[l] Sold in 1555.

Of the 7780 men in the fleet, 1885 were soldiers, 5136 mariners, and 759 gunners. The importance of Portsmouth, where no fewer than forty-one of the fifty-three vessels were stationed, will not fail to be noticed.

By August, 1552, as a list in Pepys's *Miscellanies*, viii. shows, there had been added to the above the *Primrose* (launched in 1551), *Gyrfalcon* (120 tons), *Swift* (30 tons), *Moon*, *Seven Stars* (35 tons), and *Bark of Bullen* (60 tons), and the *Henry Grace à Dieu* had apparently been renamed the *Edward*. (But she was again known as the *Henry Grace à Dieu* when

she was accidentally burnt on August 25th, 1553.—Machyn's *Diary*.)
There had also been added a French prize, the *Black Galley*, taken in
1549, and the *Lion*, taken from the Scots by the *Pauncy*, but presently
lost off Harwich.

In 1558, the year of the death of Queen Mary, the Royal Navy
had been reduced to twenty-six vessels of 7110 tons in all. In 1565,
the eighth year of Elizabeth, there were but twenty-nine ships, of an
unknown total tonnage. In 1575, the eighteenth year of Elizabeth, the
number of ships had further fallen to twenty-four, and the tonnage
was but about 10,470.

THE GALLEY "SUBTILE."

At that time, there were in England one hundred and thirty-five
other ships of 100 tons and upwards, six hundred and fifty-six of from
40 to 100 tons, about a hundred hoys, and a large but unstated number
of small barks and smacks. Practically the whole of the Royal Navy
was engaged against the Spanish Armada in 1588; and an account of
the fleet then employed will be found later in the appendix to the history of Philip's attempted invasion.

I insert, for reference purposes, an alphabetical key list of all the
vessels (except a few small prizes taken in 1562, and apparently returned in 1564), which, I have been able to satisfy myself, were acquired for the Royal Navy during the reign of Elizabeth. The tonnag-
es given are only approximate. Almost every contemporary document
that pretends to show them differs more or less from every other:—

SHIP.	*Built. †Bought. ‡Taken.	Tons.	SHIP.	*Built. †Bought. ‡Taken.	Tons.
Achates [1]	*1573	100	Mary Rose (rebuilt) [13] .	1589	600
Advantage	*1590	200	Mercury	*1592	?
Advantagia . . .	*1601	?	Mer Honour . . .	*1590	?
Adventure	*1594	250	Merlin	*1579	50
Advice	*1586	50	Minion [14]	†1560	?
Aid [2]	*1562	250	Minnikin	*1595	?
Answer	*1590	200	Moon	*1586	60
Antelope (rebuilt) . .	1581	400	Nonpareil (rebuilt) [15] .	1584	500
Ark Royal . . .	*1587	800	N. S. del Rosario . .	‡1588	?
Black Dog . . .	‡1590	?	Popinjay	*1587	?
Bonovolia, galley [3] .	1584	?	Post	*1563	?
Brygandine . . .	*1583	90	Primrose [16] . . .	†1560	800
Bull (rebuilt) [4] . .	1570	200	Primrose, hoy . .	*1590	80
Charles	*1586	70	Quittance . . .	*1590	200
Crane	*1590	200	Rainbow [17] . . .	*1586	500
Cygnet	*1585	30	Revenge [18] . . .	*1577	500
Defiance . . .	*1590	500	St. Andrew [19] . . .	‡1596	900
Dreadnought [5] . .	*1573	400	St. Mathew [20] . . .	†1596	1000
[Due] Repulse . . .	*1596	700	Scout [21]	*1577	120
Eagle [6]	†1592	?	Search	*1563	?
Eleanor, galley [7] . .	‡1563	?	Seven Stars . . .	*1586	?
[Elizabeth] Bonaventure [8]	†1567	600	Speedwell, galley [22] .	*1559	?
Elizabeth Jonas [9] . .	*1559	900	Spy	*1586	50
Foresight . . .	*1570	300	Sun	*1586	40
Flight	*1592	?	Superlativa . . .	*1601	?
French Frigate . .	‡1591	?	Swallow [23] . . .	?1573	360
Gallerita	*1602	?	Swiftsure [24] . . .	*1573	400
Garland	*1590	700	Talbot	*1585	?
George, hoy (rebuilt) .	1601	100	Tiger (rebuilt) [25] . .	1570	200
[Golden] Lion (rebuilt)	1582	500	Tremontana . . .	*1586	150
Greyhound . . .	*1585	?	Triumph [26] . . .	*1561	1100
Guide	*1563	?	Trust	*1586	?
Handmaid . . .	*1573	80	Tryright, galley [27] .	*1559	?
Hope [10]	*1559	600	Vanguard [28] . . .	*1586	500
Lion's Whelp (I.) [11] .	*1590	?	Victory [29] . . .	†1560	800
Lion's Whelp (II.) [12] .	†1601	?	Volatilla	*1602	?
Makeshift (I.) . .	*1563	?	Warspite . . .	*1596	600
Makeshift (II.) . .	*1586	?	[White] Bear [30] . .	*1563	1000

[1] Converted to a lighter.
[2] Condemned, 1599.
[3] Ex Eleanor, rebuilt. Sold 1599.
[4] Broken up, 1594.
[5] Rebuilt, 1592.
[6] A Lübecker, used as a bulk.
[7] Probably taken from Havre.
[8] Rebuilt, 1581.
[9] Rebuilt, 1598.
[10] Rebuilt, 1584 and 1602.

[11] Lost, May 17th, 1591.
[12] Bought from E. of Nottingham.
[13] Built, 1556.
[14] Condemned, 1570.
[15] Ex Philip and Mary, rebuilt.
[16] Sold, 1575.
[17] Rebuilt, 1602.
[18] Taken by Spain, 1591.
[19] Taken at Cadiz.
[20] Taken at Cadiz.

[21] Converted to a lighter.
[22] Disposed of ca. 1580.
[23] Condemned, 1603.
[24] Rebuilt, 1582.
[25] Converted to a lighter.
[26] Rebuilt, 1596.
[27] Disposed of ca. 1580.
[28] Rebuilt, 1599.
[29] (?) Ex Great Christopher. Re-built, 1586.
[30] Rebuilt, 1599.

At the death of the great queen in 1603, the effective Royal Navy, according to a list preserved by Monson in his *Tracts*, corrected and here supplemented, as to certain details from other contemporary sources, (MS. list of 1599, printed in *Archaeologia*), was as follows:

SHIPS	Tons.	Mariners	Gunners	Soldiers	Total, all Men	Cannon	Demi Cannon	Culverin	Demi Culverin	Saker	Minion	Falcon	Falconet	Total Heavier	Portpieces	Portpiece Chambers	Fowlers	Fowler Chambers	Curtalls	Total Lighter	Total, all Guns
Elizabeth Jonas	900	340	40	120	500	3	6	8	9	9	1	2	..	38	1	2	5	10	..	18	56
Triumph	1,000	340	40	120	500	4	3	17	8	6	..	..	..	38	1	4	5	20	..	30	68
White Bear	900	340	40	120	500	3	11	7	10	..	..	..	..	31	2	..	7	..	..	9	40
Victory	800	268	32	100	400	..	..	12	18	9	..	..	..	39	..	..	7	13	..	20	59
Mere Honour	800	268	32	100	400	..	4	15	16	4	..	..	..	39	..	..	2	..	..	2	41
Ark Royal	800	268	32	100	400	4	4	12	12	6	..	..	..	38	4	7	2	4	..	17	55
St. Matthew	1,000	340	40	120	500	4	4	16	14	4	4	2	..	48	..	..	..	..	..	0	48
St. Andrew	900	268	32	100	400	..	..	8	21	7	2	..	..	38	..	..	3	7	2	12	50
Due Repulse	700	230	30	90	350	2	3	13	14	6	..	..	..	38	2	4	2	4	..	12	50
Guardland	700	190	30	80	300	..	..	16	14	4	..	..	..	34	2	4	2	3	..	11	45
Warspite	600	190	30	80	300	2	2	13	10	2	..	..	..	29	..	..	..	..	..	0	29
Mary Rose	600	150	30	70	250	..	4	11	10	4	..	..	..	29	3	7	..	..	..	10	39
Hope	600	150	30	70	250	2	4	9	11	4	..	..	..	30	4	8	2	4	..	18	48
Bonaventure	600	150	30	70	250	2	2	11	14	4	2	..	..	35	2	4	2	4	..	12	47
Lion	500	150	30	70	250	..	4	8	14	9	..	1	..	36	..	..	8	16	..	24	60
Nonpareil	500	150	30	70	250	2	3	7	8	12	..	..	..	32	4	8	4	8	..	24	56
Defiance	500	150	30	70	250	..	..	14	14	6	..	..	..	34	2	4	2	4	..	12	46
Rainbow	500	150	30	70	250	..	6	12	7	1	..	..	..	26	..	..	..	..	..	0	26
Dreadnought	400	130	20	50	200	2	..	4	11	10	..	2	..	29	..	..	4	8	..	12	41
Antelope	350	114	16	30	160	..	..	4	13	8	..	1	..	26	2	4	2	4	..	12	38
Swiftsure	400	130	20	50	200	2	..	5	12	8	..	2	..	29	..	..	4	8	..	12	41
Swallow	330	114	16	30	160	..	..	..	..	..	2	1	..	3	..	2	..	3	..	5	8
Foresight	300	114	16	30	160	..	..	..	14	8	3	3	..	28	..	..	3	6	..	9	37
Tide	250	88	12	20	120	?	?	?	?	?	?	?	?	?	?	?	?	?	?	?	?
Crane	200	76	12	20	108	..	..	..	6	7	6	..	..	19	..	..	2	3	..	5	24
Adventure	250	88	12	20	120	..	..	4	11	5	..	..	..	20	..	..	2	4	..	6	26
Quittance	200	76	12	20	108	..	..	2	6	7	4	..	..	19	..	..	2	4	..	6	25
Answer	200	76	12	20	108	..	..	..	5	8	2	..	..	15	..	..	2	4	..	6	21
Advantage	200	76	12	20	102	..	..	4	11	5	..	..	..	20	..	..	2	4	..	6	26
Tiger	200	70	12	20	102	..	..	..	6	14	..	2	..	22	..	..	..	..	..	0	22
Tremontana	140	52	8	10	70	..	..	..	..	12	7	2	..	21	..	..	..	..	..	0	21
Scout	120	48	8	10	66	..	..	..	..	4	..	6	..	10	..	..	..	..	..	0	10
Achates	100	42	8	10	60	..	..	..	6	..	2	5	..	13	..	..	..	..	..	0	13
Charles	70	32	6	7	45	..	..	..	..	8	..	2	..	10	..	..	2	4	..	6	16
Moon	60	30	5	5	40	..	..	..	..	4	4	1	..	9	..	..	..	..	..	0	9
Advice	50	30	5	5	40	..	..	..	..	4	2	3	..	9	..	..	..	..	..	0	9
Spy	50	30	5	5	40	..	..	..	..	4	2	3	..	9	..	..	..	..	..	0	9
Merlin	45	26	5	4	35	..	..	..	..	..	..	7	..	7	..	..	..	..	..	0	7
Sun	40	24	4	2	30	..	..	..	1	..	..	4	..	5	..	..	..	..	..	0	5
Cygnet	20	?	?	?	20	..	..	..	..	..	1	2	..	3	..	..	..	..	..	..	3
George, hoy	100	?	?	?	10	?	?	?	?	?	?	?	?	?	?	?	?	?	?	?	?
Primrose hoy	80	?	?	?	2	?	?	?	?	?	?	?	?	?	?	?	?	?	?	?	?
42 ships	17,055	5,534	804	2,008	8,346	32	60	232	326	213	43	50	2	958	29	58	78	149	2	316	1,274

1 The original and meaning of this name are obscure. The ship sometimes is called *Mere Honour*, sometimes *Mer Honour*; sometimes *Honour de la Mer*; and sometimes *Mary Honora*.   2 Or *Dieu Repulse*.   3 Later corrupted into "Garland."   4 Also called *Golden Lion*.   5 *I.e.* "Swift Pursuer" probably. Later corrupted into "Swiftsure."   6 Doubtful whether this belonged to the Royal Navy; perhaps hired.   7 These, converted to lighters, were in use to support the chain at Upnor.

During the reign of Henry VII. the position of officers and men, as regards their pay and "rewards," seems to have remained much as before. The men were given 1*s*. a week in harbour, and 1*s*. 3*d*. at sea. Their victuals, early in the reign, cost 1*s*. 0½*d*., and later 1*s*. 2*d*. a week. Masters received 3*s*. 4*d*.; pursers and boatswains, 1*s*. 8*d*.; quartermas-

AN ELIZABETHAN SHIP OF WAR.

ters, 1*s*. 6*d*; and stewards and cooks, 1*s*. 3*d*. a week in harbour, (1 and higher pay at sea. But early in the reign of Henry VIII. an alteration was effected. The nature of this is shown in an agreement, (2 made in 1512 between the king and Sir Edward Howard, captain-general of the armed force at sea (or Lord High Admiral). Part of this agreement had better be given at length. It runs thus:—

> The said admiral shall have under him in the said service three thousand men, harnessed and arrayed for the warfare, himself accounted in the same number, over and above seven hundred soldiers, mariners and gunners that shall be in the King's ship, the *Regent*. A thousand seven hundred and fifty shall be soldiers; twelve hundred and thirty-three shall be mariners and gunners.

...And the said admiral shall have for maintaining himself, and his diets and rewards, daily during the voyage, ten shillings. And for every of the said captains, for their diets, wages, and rewards, daily during the said cruise, eighteen-pence. . . . And for every soldier, mariner, and gunner, he shall have, every month, during the said voyage, accounting twenty-eight days for the month, five shillings for his wages, and five shillings for his victuals, without anything else demanded for wages or victuals, saving that they shall have certain dead shares, as hereafter doth ensue; all which wages, rewards and victual money the said admiral shall be paid in manner and form following:—

He shall, before he and his retinue enter into the ship, make their musters before such commissioners as it shall please our said sovereign Lord to depute and appoint; and immediately after such musters shall have been made, he shall receive of our sovereign Lord, by the hands of such as his Grace shall appoint, for himself, the said captains, soldiers, mariners, and gunners, wages, rewards, and victual money, after the rate before rehearsed, for three months then next ensuing, accounting the month as above. And, at the same time, he shall receive for the cost of every captain and soldier four shillings, and for the cost of every mariner and gunner twenty pence; and at the end of the said three months, when the said admiral shall with his navy and retinue resort to the port of Southampton and then and there victual himself and the said navy and army and retinue. He shall make his musters before such commissioners as it shall please his Grace, the King, therefore to appoint within board; and after the said musters so made, he shall, for himself, the said captains, soldiers, mariners, and gunners, receive of our said sovereign Lord, by the hands of such as his Grace shall appoint, new wages and victual money, after the rate before rehearsed, for the three months next ensuing; and so, from three months to three months continually during the said time. . . . The said admiral shall have for his dead shares of the ships as hereafter ensueth, that is to say, for the *Regent*, being of the portage of 1000 tons, 50 dead shares and four pilots; and for the—

Mary Rose	of 500 tons, 30½ dead shares.		
Peter Pomegranate	„ 400	„ 23½	„ „
Nicholas Reede	„ 400	„ 23½	„ „

Mary and John	of 260 tons	24½ dead shares		
Ann, of Greenwich	„ 160	„ 24½	„	„
Mary George	„ 300	„ 20½	„	„
Dragon	„ 100	„ 22½	„	„
Barbara	„ 140	„ 20½	„	„
George, of Falmouth	„ 140	„ 20½	„	„
Nicholas of Hampton	„ 200	„ 22	„	„
Murtenet	„ 140	„ 22½	„	„
Jennet	„ 70	„ 22½	„	„
Christopher Davy	„ 160	„ 22½	„	„
Sabyan [1]	„ 120	„ 20	„	„

[1] There are accidentally omitted from this copy of the agreement:—

" John Hopton's Ship "	400 tons.
Lion	120 „
Peter, of Fowey	120 „

These bring the strength of the fleet up to eighteen sail (as mentioned elsewhere in the indenture), or, with the crayers, to twenty sail.

And for the victualling and refreshing the said ships with water and other necessaries, the said admiral shall . . . have two crayers, the one being of three score and fifty tons, wherein there shall be the master, twelve mariners, and one boy; and every of the said masters and mariners shall have for his wages five shillings, and for his victual money five shillings, for every month, accounting the month as above; and every of the said two buys shall have for his month's wages two shillings and sixpence, and for his victuals live shillings; and either of the said masters shall have three dead shares; and the other crayer shall have a master, ten mariners, and one boy, being of the burden of 55 tons, with the same allowances.

Also, the said soldiers, mariners, and gunners shall have of our sovereign Lord conduct money, that is to say, every of them, for every day's journey from his house to the place where they shall be shipped, accounting twelve miles for the day's journey, sixpence; of which days they shall give evidence, by their oaths, before him or them that our said sovereign Lord shall appoint and assign to pay them the said wages and conduct money.

And forasmuch as our said sovereign Lord, at his costs and charges, victuals the said army and navy, the said admiral shall therefore answer our said Lord the one-half of all manner of gains and winnings of the war, that the same admiral, or his retinue, or any of them, shall fortune to have in the said voyage, by land or water: all prisoners, being chieftains, or having our said sovereign Lord's adversary's power; and one ship royal, being of the portage of 200 tons or above, with the ordnance and apparel of every such prize that shall fortune to be taken by them in the said war, reserving to our said sovereign Lord all artillery contained within any other ship or ships by them to be taken.

SIX ANGEL PIECE OF
EDWARD VI.

The document, to put it briefly, shows that at the time of the armament of 1512 the daily pay of an admiral was 10s.; the daily pay of a captain, 1s. 6d.; the lunar monthly wage of master, soldier, mariner, or gunner, 5s., together with 5s. for victuals, and the lunar monthly wage of a boy, 2s. 6d., together with 5s. for victuals.

★★★★★★

Lunar months, of thirteen to the year, were there, and long afterwards, the ordinary official divisions of the year. A MS. list of the services of captains from 1688 to 1717 (in the Author's Coll.) contains such entries as one to the effect that Captain John Norris entered on the command of the *Content*, prize, on March 24th, 1695, and was discharged from it on February 25th, 1696 (O, S.), having, served in the ship for 0 years, 12 months, 0 weeks, and 3 days. For many purposes, the naval month remained twenty-eight days until after the beginning of the nineteenth century. At present, in the Navy, 1 month equals 30 days; 2 months equal 61 days; 3 months equal 91 days; 4 months equal 121 days; 5 months equal 152 days; 6 months equal 182 days; 7 months equal 212 days; 8 months equal 243 days; 9 months equal 273 days; 10 months equal 303 days; 11 months equal 334 days; and 12 months (1 year) equal 365 days, unless otherwise provided.

★★★★★★

It also shows that the men were allowed conduct money to the port of embarkation at the rate of 6*d*. per twelve miles; that the profits of prizes were to be divided, one–half, together with one vessel of 200 tons or more, and all ordnance and "apparel" (? movable fittings) going to the king, and the rest to the captors in stipulated proportions; and it appears to show that, as head money, a sum of 4s. for each captain and soldier, and of 20*d*. for each mariner and gunner, was payable to the admiral, although this is not quite clear.

The "dead shares" were non–existent men, something like the widows' men of a later date. Pay on their behalf was allowed, and the pay so granted was divided among the really existent ship's company. This extra pay took the place of the "rewards" of an earlier period. But it does not appear certain that, after the reign of Henry VIII., the seamen participated in the dead shares.

In the earlier years of Elizabeth, the seaman's lunar monthly pay was 6*s*. 8*d*. In 1586, on the representation of Hawkyns, (*Dom. Eliz.* clxxxv.), this was raised to 10*s*., and other pay was raised in proportion, so that a captain's pay, which had been 1*s*. 8*d*., became 2*s*. 6*d*. a day, besides certain allowances which varied according to ship and circumstances.

The practice of allowing dead shares continued; but little, if any, of the proceeds can have gone to the men, seeing that masters and master-gunners each received a whole dead share, boatswains probably the same; quartermasters half a dead share; some of the gunners one-third of a dead share, and so on. But the subject is still in much obscurity.

AN ELIZABETHAN
SEAMAN.

In 1588, the superior officers who served against the Armada had daily pay as follows, (from a paper, printed in *Defeat of Spanish Armada* by Prof. J. K. Laughton):—

	£	s.	d.
The Lord High Admiral	3	6	8
Lord Henry Seymour, as his Vice-Admiral	2	0	0
Sir John Hawkyns, as his Rear-Admiral	0	15	0
Sir Henry Palmer ⎫			
Sir William Wynter ⎬ commanding under Lord Henry Seymour	1	0	0
Sir Martin Frobiser ⎭			
Thomas Gray, "Vice-Admiral" under Lord H. Seymour (while in command of a detached force)	0	6	8
Sir Francis Drake, "Captain and Admiral"	1	10	0
Thomas Fenner, his "Vice-Admiral"	0	15	0
Nicholas Gorges, "Admiral" of the merchant coasters, for him and his lieutenant	0	13	8

It would appear from the above that both rule and consistency were lacking in the apportionment of the pay of these officers; and the fact is that the rate depended quite as much upon the social rank and title of the recipient as upon his position in the fleet. In all these cases there were allowances, though of unknown amount in addition. In the Armada period, it may be added, the master in a flagship was virtually her captain in all senses; and the Thomas Gray, who is mentioned above as having commanded an independent or detached squadron with the temporary rank of vice-admiral, had previously held, and may have reverted to, the position of master of the *Ark*.

The instructions of Howard of Effingham and Essex to the officers under their command for the Cadiz Expedition of 1596 are so interesting, and throw so much light upon the naval customs of a very important period in English history, that they are here printed at length, so far as they can be deciphered from the damaged manuscript in which they are contained. They are among the earliest instructions extant, and seem to have served as a basis for many subsequent regulations of the same sort.

Instructions and Articles set down by us, Robert, Earl of Essex, and Charles, Lord Howard, Lord High Admiral of England, Generals of Her Majesty's forces employed in this action, both by sea and land, to be observed by every captain and chief officer of the Navy: And that every ship's company may not be ignorant hereof, we do hereby straitly charge and command all captains to give order that, at Service time, they may be openly read, twice every week.

1. *Imprimis*, that you take special care to serve God, by using of Common Prayers twice every day, except urgent cause enforce the contrary, and that no man, soldier or other mariner do dis-

pute of matters of religion, unless it be to be resolved of some doubts; and, in such case, that he confer with the ministers of the army: for it is not fit that unlearned men should openly argue of so high and mystical matters. And if any person shall forget himself and his duty herein, he shall, upon knowledge thereof, receive open punishment to his shame, and after be banished the army. And if any shall hear it, and not reveal it to us, generals, or to his captain, or some other especial officers, whereby the knowledge thereof may come to us, the generals, he shall likewise receive punishment, and be banished the army.

2. Item. You shall forbid swearing, brawling, diceing, and such like disorders as may breed contention and disorders in your ships; wherein you shall also avoid God's displeasure and win His favour.

3. Picking and stealing you shall severely punish; and, if the fault be great, you shall acquaint us, generals, therewith, that martial law may be inflicted upon the offenders.

4. You shall take great care to preserve your victuals, and to observe such orders therein as you shall receive by particular directions from your generals. And that every captain of each ship receive an account once a week how his victuals are spent, and what remains, that their provision may be lengthened by adding more men to a mess in time.

5. All persons whatsoever, within your ship, shall come to the ordinary services of the ship without contradiction.

6. You shall give special charge for avoiding the danger of fire, and that no candle be carried in your ship without a lantern; which, if any person shall disobey, you shall severely punish. And if any chance of fire or other dangers (which God forbid) should happen to any ship near unto you, then you shall, by your boats and all other your best means, seek to help and relieve her.

7. Your powder you shall carefully preserve from spoil and waste; without which we cannot undertake any great service.

8. You shall give order that your ship may be kept clean daily, and sometimes washed; which (with God's favour) shall preserve from sickness and avoid many other inconveniences.

9. You shall give order and especial charge that your top-masts

be favoured, and the heads of your masts, and that you have care not to bear too high sail when your ships go by the wind, and especially in a head-sea; for the spoil of our masts may greatly lander us, and endanger the enterprises which otherwise (with God's help) we should perform with safety.

10. All such as are in ships under the government (of the admiral in char—there is a hiatus, these words are conjecturally supplied) ge of a squadron, shall, as near as in them lieth, keep with it, and not for chase of other ships, or any other cause, go from that squadron, but by the command of the admiral of that squadron; unless any of the two chief generals shall send for them, or, by message, appoint them to any service, or that, by weather, they be separated. And then, as they may, they shall endeavour to repair to the place appointed by such instructions as shall be set down.

And if there be any sail perceived by any of the ships of any squadron, it shall be lawful for the next ship, having the wind, to give chase, the ship descried being to the windward; and the like of any that shall be nearest to bear up, if the sail be descried to the leeward. (This permission is difficult to reconcile with the first clause of the instruction. Apart from that, it is wrongly expressed. But the meaning is clear.) But because, upon every chase, all will be apt to follow the same, and so be led away upon every occasion from the Fleet, it shall not be lawful for any second ship to follow any chase (one having undertaken the same), unless the admiral of the squadron hang out two flags, one over another.

If it be necessary that three do follow, then shall the general, or admiral of the squadron hang out three flags, one over another, which shall be for warrant to the next and fittest to follow as aforesaid. But if the admiral bear up, and come upon a wind himself, then may all the squadron give chase, and follow. Which, if it should seem convenient to any of the Lords Generals of the army, if it please any of them to hang out the flag of council, the same may be a warning that the chase is misliked, and that then all give over and keep their course.

11. Every ship shall, towards the evening, seek to come, as near as she conveniently may, to speak with the admiral of the squadron, to know his pleasure and what course he will keep; and

that the admiral of a squadron do bear up, or stand upon a wind, to speak with us, their generals, if he conveniently may. The rest of the squadrons may, notwithstanding, keep their course and distance. And if the admiral of the squadron cannot recover the head of his fleet before night, the rest shall then follow the light of the vice-admiral of the said squadron.

12. That every squadron keep a good breadth one from another, and that the squadrons do, in themselves, keep a reasonable breadth one from another, that they fall not foul one of another, whereby danger may grow; and that the great ships have especial regard not to calm the smaller ships. And if any of these smaller ships shall negligently bring themselves in danger of the greater ships, the Captains and Masters especially shall be severely punished. Ami further, that either the admiral, or rear-admiral of the squadron be always in the rearward of his fleet.

13. When there is a flag of council of the red cross (the St. George's flag), out in either one of the two generals' ships, half-mast high against the main mizzen, (apparently the third mast of a four-masted ship), then the captains and masters of every ship shall repair on board that ship where the flag is so hung out. And when the flag of arms (*i.e.,* with the queen's arms), shall be displayed, then shall the selected Council only come on board. (The Council of Five Officers, and the extra members, if any, appointed by the generals.)

14. If your ship happen to spring a mast, to fall into a leak, or such mischance (which God forbid), you shall shoot off a piece and spring a loose. (Seventeenth-century instructions bade the disabled ship haul up her courses. "Spring a loose" seems to mean, "let fly.") If it be in the night, you shall shoot off two pieces and bear two great lights, one a man's height and a half above another.

15. Every captain and master of the Fleet shall have a social regard that no contention be found betwixt the mariners and the soldiers. And in time of sickness (if any do happen amongst you), you shall, of such good things as are to be had and are needful for them, distribute unto them in such convenient sort as you may.

16. (The MS. is too much damaged to admit of this instruction being intelligible.) If you happen to lose company, your token

shall be (. . . .) main-topsail twice, if it be foul weather, th (. . . .) strike your main mizzen twice, or as often as you list (. . . .) nder (. . . .) re your white pennant on your mizzen yard. And if you shall be of the company of us, your generals, you shall find us at such place as we will give you instructions for, at sea.

17. If in chasing of any ship you happen to fetch her up, if she be a ship in amity with Her Majesty, you shall treat her well, and bring her to us. But if you find her to be an enemy, you shall make no spoil of the goods in her, but shall take the captain and master of her aboard you, and put into her some sufficient persons to bring her forthwith unto us, your generals, or to such as we shall assign, that order may be taken what shall be done with her.

18. When you shall he appointed to give chase, and that you shall surprise any enemy's ship that shall have treasure or merchandise of value in her, you shall take great care that those commodities in her he preserved; in respect whereof, and for your loyal and faithful service to be done in this voyage, Her Majesty's favour, bounty, and pleasure is that a third part of that which shall be taken from the enemy, so it be not the king's treasure, jewels, or a carrack, shall be employed to the commodity and benefit of the whole company, over and above his ordinary wages, according to his desert.

19. No captain or master shall suffer any spoil to be made aboard any ship or bark that shall be taken by them or any of their companies, upon pain to be displaced of their offices, or some great punishment, according to the offence given; because the rest of the company have interest in everything that shall be taken. Therefore, the value of every such thing, be it of great or small importance, must especially be regarded and considered of. And whatsoever soldier or mariner that obeyeth not accordingly shall be despoiled of that which he hath gotten, and his person extremely punished.

20. Whosoever shall enter aboard any ship, he shall give account of those things which shall be wanting and taken out of her; for that no other company shall board her, unless there shall be need of their help.

21. If we happen to meet with any great fleet, supposed to be the army of the King of Spain, you shall endeavour yourself to

come as near us, generals, or to the admiral of your squadron, or, in our absence, to the vice-admiral, or rear-admiral of the Fleet (as possible), to know what you shall be directed unto, as you will answer it upon the peril of your lives.

22. The watch shall be set every night by eight of the clock, either by trumpet or drum, and singing the Lord's Prayer, some of the Psalms of David, or clearing the glass. And after the watch is set, no trumpet or drum shall be heard, or any piece whatsoever shall be shot off, without such great cause offered as is before signified, or such like.

23. You are to take especial care of your watch by night, and that the soldiers do watch, as well in harbour as at the seas, one-third part of them every night, and that there be a captain of the watch appointed, who shall take care that no fire or light be suffered, but only such candles in lanterns as are allowed to the quartermasters, or otherwise upon necessity: and that in harbour a certain number be appointed to keep diligent watch in the forecastle or beak-head of your ships, for fear of cutting of cables, which is a practice much used in hot countries.

24. If at any time the generals have occasion to order a chase, and that order be given to any other ships (. . . possibly insert, "to take them on board, and to carry") their flags until their return unto the Fleet, all the (. . . . probably insert, "other ships") shall follow the flag, in what ship soever it be placed: and that whatsoever ship shall be next, the same shall take up our, your general's, boats, (*i.e.*, the boats in which the generals had proceeded on board the temporary flag-ships), when we give chase, or the boats of any of the admirals of squadrons or others whatsoever.

25. No man, upon pain of death, shall presume to land in any country until his return into England, without order from us, your generals, or such as we shall appoint to command.

26. No person shall depart out of the ship wherein he is placed into another, without special leave of his captain: and no captain or master shall receive such person without the knowledge of us, your generals, or such as we shall appoint.

27. In fogs (if any happen), when your ships are becalmed, you shall cause some noise to be made, by drum, by trumpet, by shooting off a musket or calliver now and then, or by some

other like means, that, hearing you to be near, every one may take heed lest he fall foul of another.

28. No person whatsoever shall dare to strike any captain, lieutenant, master, or other officer, upon pain of death. And, furthermore, whatsoever he be that shall strike any inferior person, he shall receive punishment, according to the offence given, be it by death or otherwise.

29. There shall be no report or talk raised in the Fleet, wherein any officer or gentleman in the same may be touched in reputation; or matter of importance spoken, without his author shall be severely punished as an evil member amongst us.

GOLD RIAL OF ELIZABETH.

Up to the twenty-third year of Queen Elizabeth there was no regular provision for the maintenance of seamen disabled in the service of their country. In that year an Act was passed to assess every parish at a certain weekly sum for the support of the disabled sailors and soldiers belonging to the county. In 1590, thanks to the interest displayed in the matter by Nottingham, Hawkyns and Drake, the Chest at Chatham was established. The origin of the mutual benevolent fund known by this name arose out of the consideration "that by frequent employment by sea for the defence of this kingdom" . . . divers and sundry, "masters, mariners, shipwrights, and seafaring men, by reason of hurts and maims received in the service, are driven into great poverty, extremity and want, to their great discouragement."

It was therefore determined that perpetual relief should be afforded in such cases, and, in order to be able to afford it, it was voluntarily agreed that every man and boy in the navy should regularly forfeit to the fund a small proportion of his monthly wages, such contributions to be from time to time placed "in a strong chest with five locks, to that purpose especially provided." The chest, which is of iron, still exists in Greenwich Hospital, where it was placed by the Admiralty in

1846. The fund, which, before the utilisation of banks, and the value of investments became properly appreciated, the chest contained, continued, under varying regulations, to exist, until in 1803 it was transferred to the supervisors and directors of the chest at Greenwich, and practically became part of the relief funds at Greenwich Hospital. Not until 1829 did the stoppage on behalf of it of sixpence a month from the wages of every seaman of the Royal Navy cease.

Henry VIII. contributed greatly to the creation and development of the bases and arsenals of the navy, and built numerous important works of defence along the coast. He founded Woolwich Dockyard, and much improved the yards at Portsmouth and Deptford, erecting at the latter large magazines and storehouses.

★★★★★★

The land here, on the east side of Portsmouth Haven, runneth further by a great way straight into the sea, by south-east from the haven mouth, than it doth at the west point. There is, at this point of the haven, Portsmouth town, and a great round tower, almost double in quantity and strength to that which is on the west side of the haven, right against it; and here is a mighty chain of iron to draw from tower to tower. About a quarter of a mile above this tower is a great dock for ships, and in this dock lieth part of the ribs of the *Henri Grace à Dieu*, one of the biggest ships that have been made *in hominum memoria*. There be above this dock creeks in this part of the haven.

The town of Portsmouth is fended from the east tower ... with a mud wall armed with timber, whereon are great pieces both of iron and brass ordnance; and this piece of the wall, having a ditch without it, runneth so far flat south-south-east, and is the most apt to defend the town there open on the haven. There runneth a ditch almost flat east for a space, and within it is a wall of mud like to the other, and so thence (it) goeth round about the town to the circuit of a mile. There is a gate of timber at the north-east end of the town; and by it is cast up a hill of earth ditched, wherein are guns to defend entry into the town by land. There is much vacant ground within the town wall. There is one fair street in the town, from west to northeast. I learnt in the town that the towers in the haven mouth were begun in King Edward the Fourth's time, and set forward in building by Richard the Third. King Henry the Seventh ended them at the procuration of Fox, Bishop of Winchester. King

Henry the Eighth, at his first wars into France, erected in the south part of the town three great brewing-houses, with the implements, to serve his ships at such time as they should go to the sea in time of war.

One Carpenter, a rich man, made of late time, in the middle of the High Street of the town, a Town House. The town is bare, and little occupied in time of peace.—Leland, *Itinerary*, iii. Leland was on his journey between 1536 and 1542; so that this description of Portsmouth applies to the town as it then was. The allusion to the ribs of the *Henri Grace à Dieu* is obscure, seeing that the ship was in existence until a later date.

★★★★★★

The fortification of Gravesend and Tilbury was his work, as was also the building of the castles at Walmer, Deal, Sandgate, Sandown, Portland, Hurst, Cowes, Camber, Southsea, Queenborough, Pendennis, and St. Mawes. At several of these places there were earlier castles or towers, but Henry's strongholds were, for the most part, much finer coast defences than had previously been seen in England. The sums thus spent may be regarded as having been to a large extent wasted; for, even in those days, they might have been to better advantage assigned to the increase of the fleet; but in an age when ships were much more at the mercy of the winds and waves than they were when the art of navigation had somewhat further progressed, it would perhaps have been injudicious of the government to neglect these works altogether.

At one crisis during his reign, Henry was threatened with a combination between France and the Empire; and, had such an alliance attacked him with all its resources, and seized the most favourable occasion for doing so, it is possible that the coast castles might have proved very useful. Upnor Castle on the Medway, and works at Portland, Hurst, Southsea, Calshot, and elsewhere were built under Elizabeth, who also founded Chatham Dockyard, on the site of the modern Gunwharf. The yard was transferred to its present situation about 1622. Elizabeth, too, improved the defences of Plymouth.

★★★★★★

Camden describes Chatham Dockyard as "stored for the finest fleet the sun ever beheld, and ready at a minute's warning, built lately by our most gracious sovereign Elizabeth, at great expense, for the security of her subjects and the terror of her enemies, with a fort on the shore for its defence." The original

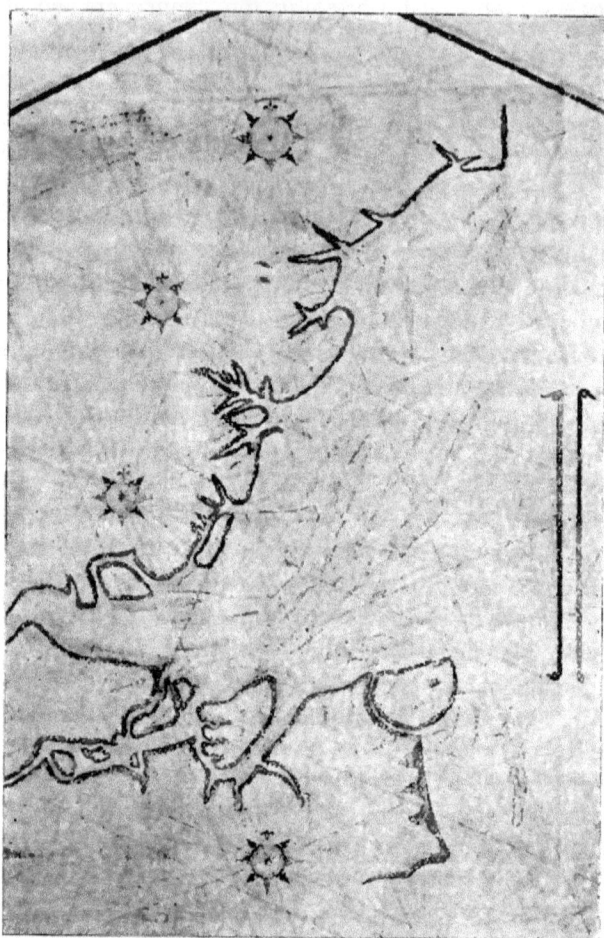

CHART OF THAMES MOUTH, 1580.

dockyard became the gun wharf in the reign of James I., who began the existing yard on a site farther to the north. This was enlarged and much improved under Charles I.

The most ancient fort for the defence of Plymouth was built in the reign of Edward III. by Edmund Stafford, Bishop of Exeter, and is described by Leland as "a strong castle quadrate, having at each corner a great round tower." This fortress stood on the south of the town, near the Barbican. In the reign of Elizabeth, numerous blockhouses and platforms were erected on different points of the shore of the harbour; and several of them were, about the year 1592, combined into a fort, called the Fort on the Hoe Cliffs. This was demolished upon the building of the citadel in 1670-71.

★★★★★★

Scilly was first garrisoned, and St. Mary's Guernsey, and Jersey were fortified in 1593, when the Treaty of Melun was concluded with France against Spain.

The first real dry dock in England was built at Portsmouth under Henry VII., the superintendent of the work being Robert Brygandine, Clerk of the Ships, and the business being completed in 1496. This dock was of wood and stone, but was not closed by a caisson, or a dock gate on hinges. What were called the "dock gates" were two walls of wood or stone, one within the other, which overlapped and partially blocked the entrance. When a ship, after passing between these walls, had been berthed, the space between the two walls was filled with earth, etc., and the dock then pumped out. Such, at least, are the only conclusions to be plausibly drawn from contemporary accounts of the manner in which this dock was utilised. (Chapter House, bk. vii., *Nav. Accts. and Inventories of Hen. VII.*)

Although, as has been said, dockyards were established or improved, the number of dry docks in the country remained very small until after the end of the sixteenth century. From a letter addressed to the Lord High Admiral in 1583, and preserved among Pepys' *Miscellanies* (viii.), it appears that there were then only two queen's dry docks in the Thames, one at Woolwich, and the other probably at Deptford. The writers, Sir John Hawkyns, William Wynter, and William Folstoke, proposed "to enlarge that at Woolwich to that length and bigness that two royal ships at one time might be brought in to be repaired and built within the same."

Before the time of Henry VIII., the general executive government of the navy and some of the various other functions now discharged by the Admiralty were for a long period in the hands of the admirals-in-chief, no matter whether they happened to be called at the moment Admirals of the North and of the West, and held divided but co-equal authority, or whether the single head was Lord High Admiral. The civil work was done by the Clerk of the Ships, and occasionally by the King's Chancery. But the increasing business of the service necessitated the erection of more elaborate machinery. A Lord High Admiral continued to be appointed as before. To relieve him, however, of various branches of his duty, especially in his administrative work, civil officers, known as commissioners, were appointed in April, 1546, to attend to victualling, construction and repair of ships, procuring of suitable ordnance, etc. These civil officers constituted the Navy Board.

★★★★★★

The Navy Board was established by patent of April 24th, 1546. The officers then appointed were a Lieutenant of the Admiralty (whose post was never refilled after the death of the second occupant); a Treasurer; a Comptroller; a Surveyor; a Master of the Ordnance of the Navy (whose post was not refilled when it fell vacant for the third time, in 1598); and, at first, a couple of extra officers. In 1550, a Surveyor of Victuals was also appointed. The sequence of officers in these posts, up to the end of the reign of Elizabeth, was as follows:—

Lieutenant of the Admiralty:

April 24, 1546, Sir Thomas Clere.
Dec. 16, 1552, Sir William Woodhouse.

Treasurer of Marine Causes:

April 24, 1546, Robert Legge.
July 8, 1549, Benjamin Gonson, senr.
Jan. 1, 1578, John Hawkyns.
(*In abeyance from Nov.* 12, 1595.)
Dec. 22, 1598, Fulke Greville, Lord Brooke

Comptroller of Ships:

April 24, 1546, William Broke.
Dec. 12, 1561, William Holstock.
1589, William Borough.
Dec. 20, 1598, Sir Henry Palmer.

Surveyor of Ships:

April 24, 1546, Benjamin Gonson, senr.
July 8, 1549, William Wynter.
July 11, 1589, Sir Henry Palmer.
Dec. 20, 1598, John Trevor.

(A continuation of these lists will be found in the last chapter.)

★★★★★★

To assist in the executive business of the Lord High Admiral, the Admiralty Office or Admiralty Board was formed. Full regulations for the conduct of all these officials do not seem to have existed until the time of Edward VI.; and, indeed, it may be assumed that no department of such great importance could, at the mere *fiat* of an individual, leap at once into full activity and usefulness. The commissioners of the Navy Office met, apparently from the time of their first appointment, on Tower Hill, in a building which, under Elizabeth, was known as the Queen's Consultation Room. The Board of Admiralty, in the earlier days of its existence, had no fixed home, and met sometimes at the Lord High Admiral's residence and sometimes even afloat. (It may still meet wherever convenience dictates.)

At the instance of Sir Thomas Spert, Henry VIII. also, in 1513, established what is usually known as Trinity House, but is properly entitled "The Guild of the Holy and Undividable Trinity and St. Clement, at Deptford Strond." (Sir Thomas died in 1541. On his monument in St. Dunstan's, Stepney, he is called "Comptroller of the Navy," but there was no such office in 1541. The error arises from the monument being of a much later period. He was Clerk of the Ships in 1538.) It was at first associated to some extent with the navy, part of its duty being to examine into the professional qualifications of officers and petty officers, and to supply seamen as they were needed. In 1566, the master, wardens, and assistants of the Guild were empowered to set up beacons and seamarks; and, gradually, lighting, buoying, and pilotage fell more and more under their control, until their original connection with the navy became obscured.

Naval punishments, "according to the custom of the sea," which was extremely barbarous, were'much the same in the sixteenth century as they had been in previous ages; but in the account of Drake's dealings with Thomas Doughty, in 1578, and with Captain William Borough, and the other mutinous people in the *Golden Lion* in 1587, we have indications of the gradual evolution of the court-martial, and of a more just, if scarcely less severe, administration of marine law. Doughty, charged with a plot against Drake's life, was brought before a body of officers, who, hearing him confess himself guilty, as is alleged, unanimously signed the sentence by which he was condemned to death. Borough, convicted before "a general court holden for the service of Her Majesty aboard the *Elizabeth Bonaventure*" was, with his abettors, sentenced *in contumaciam*, "to abide the pains of death" in case of their being caught. "If not, they shall remain as dead men in law." (This quarrel between Drake and Borough was afterwards peaceably patched up.)

The regular seafaring population of England, as distinct from the numerous other people who went to sea upon occasion, was small at the beginning of the sixteenth century, and not large even in the early days of Elizabeth. In 1583, a census of the maritime inhabitants of the country, Wales being excluded, showed that there were 1484 masters, 11,515 mariners, 2299 fishermen, and 957 Thames wherrymen, or in all, 16,255 persons who were in some sort accustomed to the water.

The number does not seem to be proportionate to the very considerable sea-borne trade of the country at that time. Henry VII. had furthered commerce, and at the same time benefited himself, by hiring out to the merchants his own men-of-war, when they were not needed for the service of the State. He also enacted navigation Acts in his first and fourth years, for the encouragement of English shipping. Henry VIII. had hired out many of his ships of war; but the practice had fallen into disuse about 1534. The discoveries of Columbus, Cabot, and the Portuguese had opened fresh markets. The trade with Iceland had received great impetus, owing to the convention of 1488, whereby Denmark undertook not to interfere with it.

An advantageous commercial treaty had been concluded with Castillo. Henry VIII. had freed the principal rivers of England from weirs and obstructions; suppressed illegal tolls; improved many of the harbours, including Dover, where he built a new pier; encouraged commerce, especially with the Levant, where he appears to have appointed the first consul; and employed his diplomatic agents to advance the interests of the merchants. Under Edward, and under Mary, the Newfoundland trade had been increased and freed from restrictions: English merchants on the continent had been signally protected and encouraged; the African trade had largely grown; the judicial privileges of the merchants of the Steelyard had been withdrawn, and their other privileges curtailed; the Russia Company had been established; and there had been enlarged commercial intercourse with Spain.

But it is true that in 1583, the date of this census, the stimulating atmosphere of the Elizabethan era had not yet produced its full effect upon the energies of the country. The letters patent to the Company of Traders to Barbary were not granted until 1585; and the origins of the East India Company date only from 1600.

Elizabeth seldom neglected an opportunity of asserting the dignity of her country, and vindicating the interests of her subjects, especially where trade was concerned. Her conduct in 1597, in the matter of the dispute with the Hanse Towns, may be taken as typical of her general attitude in such cases. Commercial jealousy had induced the Hanse Towns to persuade the emperor to prohibit the traffic of English merchants with Germany. Elizabeth made remonstrances to the emperor and the electoral princes, and, obtaining no satisfaction, adopted prompt retaliatory measures. By proclamation she ordained that upon the day fixed for the English traders to leave Germany, all merchants of the Hanse Towns should quit England, and the Lord Mayor should seize that locality in London known as the Steel Yard, which the merchants of the Hanse Towns had been privileged to occupy. This was the deathblow to the influence of the Hanseatic League in England. The ultimate effect of it was to throw into English hands great part of that Northern European trade which had previously, for a long period, been the almost exclusive appanage of foreigners.

Military History of the Navy, 1485-1603

Henry VII. loved commerce, and was himself a great trader; he was a miser, and disliked any expenditure which did not appear to him to be absolutely necessary; his title to the throne was bad, and his seat upon it was consequently precarious; and he was a wise man, possessed of marked diplomatic ability. His qualities moulded his policy. His reign was, upon the whole, pacific; and, although he invaded France, he had no insatiate thirst for military glory, and no tyrannous lust of conquest; and he gladly seized the first opportunity for concluding a fairly honourable peace. His only other important foreign expedition, that for the repression of Ravenstein, in 1492, was undertaken in the interests of commerce.

Upon his accession, he appointed John de Vere, 13th Earl of Oxford, to be Lord High Admiral from September 21st, 1485, and this officer held the post until after the king's death.

It was Henry's misfortune that the fallen House of York remained for many years popular with the common people of the country, and especially of Ireland, and that the lost cause still had a most powerful and unscrupulous supporter in the person of Margaret, Duchess of Burgundy, a sister of Edward IV. Her court became the natural headquarters of all conspirators who sought the overthrow of the House of Tudor.

The best possible claimant among the Yorkist princes to the crown was Edward Plantagenet, Earl of Warwick, son of George, Duke of Clarence and nephew of Edward IV.; but Warwick was a prisoner in the hands of Henry. As, therefore, Warwick was not available as a tool for the malcontents, a false Warwick was invented in the person of Lambert Simnel, a baker's son, who appears to have been carefully trained for his part by Richard Simon, a priest in the confidence of the Yorkist leaders. Lambert was recognised by the Earl of Kildare, Lord Deputy of Ireland, by John de la Pole, Earl of Lincoln, a nephew of Edward IV., and, of course, by the unscrupulous Margaret of Burgundy; and at Dublin the pretender was proclaimed King of England, as Edward VI., in May, 1487.

Henry replied by parading the real Warwick through the streets of London; but this measure seems to have had little or no effect upon the infatuated people, and the movement continued. It may have been owing to Henry's parsimony that the Narrow Seas were so inefficiently policed as to allow the pretender and his friends, accompanied by two thousand Germans, under Martin Schwartz, to land in Lancashire; but it is more probable that the king, realising the importance of capturing his impudent rival, deliberately preferred to permit him to invade England. Here Simnel gathered few fresh adherents, except a small body of men under Sir Thomas Broughton.

He determined to attack Newark; but Henry judiciously placed himself between the rebels and that town, and so, on June 16th, 1487, provoked the battle of Stoke, where, after a well-fought action, Simnel was defeated and taken. His patron Simon was imprisoned for life. Hardly one of the remaining supporters of his claims who happened to be present escaped with his life. As for Simnel himself, he was contemptuously made a scullion in the royal kitchen, and subsequently promoted to be a falconer.

Edward, Lord Woodville, was the indirect cause of the hostilities with France. This nobleman, an uncle of the queen, was Governor of the Isle of Wight; and, happening to be in sympathy with the Duchess of Brittany, who was then in conflict with Charles VIII. of France, he took advantage of his position, and, in spite of Henry's positive orders to do nothing of the kind, raised four hundred men early in 1488, and crossed to the assistance of the princess. (This expedition is mentioned by Holinshed.) He and his followers were cut to pieces at St. Aubin, on July 28th, and the disaster, though perhaps richly merited, gave rise to so much public feeling in England, that Henry felt himself obliged to send to Brittany eight thousand men under Lord Brooke. But he still had some kind of secret arrangement with Charles, and possibly no further forces would have been dispatched, had not Anne of Brittany, in 1491, betrayed her English friends and astonished Europe by marrying her whilom enemy Charles VIII.

In 1490, Scotland, which, owing to the unworthy machinations of Henry VII. with the object of seizing the person of the young king, James IV., had no cause to spare England, dealt her two small but stinging blows at sea, and at the same time discovered that she possessed at least one exceptionally able naval officer. This was Sir Andrew Wood, of Largs. Upon the murder of James III. he had declared, against the Council, for that monarch's son, James IV., and he served the new king bravely; for not only did he, with two ships, capture five English vessels, (apparently hired craft), but also, when three more were sent against him under the command of Stephen Bull, he took them likewise. The only capture from the Scots during these operations seems to have been the *Margaret*, which was added to the navy. James IV. established the first efficient navy ever possessed by Scotland.

Towards the end of his reign he had thirteen men-of-war, the largest of which, the *Michael*, was, in her day, a marvel of size. And in Sir Andrew Wood, and the equally famous Andrew Barton, he had commanders who, in a very short period, gave the young Scots navy all the prestige it needed. Both Wood, and Barton whose exploits will be noted later, were somewhat piratical in their methods, although they acted under letters of marque; but piracy—especially on land, and where cattle was concerned—was a recognised and characteristic Scots institution until a much later day. It must also be remembered that the Scots of the fifteenth and sixteenth centuries were, in most respects, less civilised than their southern neighbours.

The marriage of Anne with Charles VIII. gave Brittany to France, and was undoubtedly a great blow at English prestige, the more so seeing that she had been previously supposed to be about to marry the Archduke Maximilian, the ally of Henry. These and other considerations determined Henry to appear to fall in with the obvious desires of his people for a war with France; and in 1491 and 1492 great preparations were made in consequence. But, privately, the king had no wish for hostilities. The acts of Woodville had forced his hand in 1488; the excitement of his people might force his hand again.

The king, however, made up his mind that he would not be driven so long as he could stand still; and that if he should be driven, he would do his utmost to bring the war to a speedy conclusion. In the meantime, the patriotism of Parliament and the enthusiasm of his subjects supplied him with large sums of money, some of which were expended in preparations, but still more of which remained in the coffers of the tenacious monarch, much to his personal advantage.

An occasion soon arose for pleasing the people by dealing a bye-blow at France, while, at the same time benefiting commerce, and obliging the Archduke Maximilian. A subject of the latter, Philip von Kleve-Ravenstein, was in rebellion against his sovereign, and, aided by citizens of Ghent and Bruges, had seized the town of Sluis, and had formed a piratical stronghold there. It is supposed that he was in receipt of some countenance from France, for his master, Maximilian, was, like Henry, on unfriendly terms with Charles, and Philip himself subsequently entered the French service.

Be this as it may, it is certain that the pirate chief had done much harm to English trade and shipping in the North Sea, and that for this reason, if for no other, Henry was glad to tender his help to Maximilian against the rebel. A squadron of twelve ships was in consequence fitted out, and the command of it was entrusted to Sir Edward Poynings. (Second son of Robert, 5th and last Lord Poynings under writ of 11 Edw. III. He was a lifelong friend of Henry VII. He died in 14 Hen. VIII. a K.G. One of his natural sons, Thomas, was created Baron Poynings in 1545.)

Sir Edward cruised at sea for a few days, and then approached Sluis, where he learnt that the place was besieged on the land side by the Elector of Saxony. He therefore blockaded it by water, and attacked it on that side. Its main defences consisted of two towers or castles, which were connected by a bridge of boats, Poynings made attempts on one or other of these castles every day for twenty days in succession; but failed to produce any impression, and suffered considerable losses, until he succeeded, during a night assault, in burning the bridge of boats. This brought about the surrender of the town to the elector, and of the castles to the English. In the course of the siege, a brother of the Lord High Admiral, the Earl of Oxford, lost his life.

In the same year (1492), on October 2nd, Henry reached Dover with an army of twenty-five thousand men and sixteen hundred horses, and was transported to Calais, by the aid of a large fleet which had been assembled for the purpose. About October 19th, he laid siege to Boulogne; but he had not been many days before the town ere peace with France was in principle agreed on. Peace was, in fact, signed at Etaples on November 3rd, (*Foedera*, xii.); and on December 17th, the king returned to London. The chief article in the stipulations was the payment to Henry of the sum of £149,000. Another was that the person calling himself Richard, Duke of York, should receive no more shelter and assistance in France.

This person was in reality one Perkin Warbeck, or Osbeck, supposed to be the son of a Jew of Tournay, but by a few believed to be a natural son of Edward IV. He claimed to be the Prince Richard whom Richard III. is generally charged with having caused to be murdered in the Tower; and in 1492 he appeared as such in Cork, and was so well received there that Charles VIII. of France invited him to Paris. He had previously been recognised by the unscrupulous Margaret of Burgundy. But, as has been seen, the Treaty of Etaples drove him out of France; and he went to his patroness Margaret.

His presence in Flanders encouraged a dangerous conspiracy in England; but Henry was ruthless in searching it out and stifling it; and when, on July 7th, 1495, the pretender, furnished by the duchess with a few ships and troops, landed some men near Sandwich, the intruders were at once captured by the country people. This miserable attempt led to the hanging of one hundred and sixty persons.

Warbeck returned to his patroness in Flanders; but the conclusion in February, 1496, of the treaty known as "The Great Intercourse," between England and Burgundy, proved that commercial advantages were stronger and weightier than dynastic considerations. The treaty stipulated for his expulsion; and the pretender went, first to Ireland, and then to Scotland. James IV. welcomed him as the lawful King of England, and gave him in marriage Lady Katherine Gordon, a member of the Scots royal house. Twice Warbeck attempted an invasion from the north. By July, 1497, James had grown tired, if not suspicious, of him; and Warbeck, escorted from Scots waters by the celebrated Andrew Barton, again became a fugitive.

******

At about that time there was in Scots waters a considerable English force under Robert, Lord Willoughby de Broke, including, besides the king's ships *Regent, Mary Fortune*, and *Sweepstake*, the hired vessels, *Anthony*, of Saltash, *Henry*, of Bristol, *Mary Bird*, of Bristol, *Mary Tower*, of Bristol, *Andrew*, of Plymouth, *Michael*, of Dartmouth, and a bark of Penzance (Augm. Off. bk. 316), as well as, possibly, the *Margaret Bull, Hermitage, Ellen*, of Calais, *Christopher*, of Calais, *Mary Hastings, Peter, Anne*, of Maiden, *John*, of Hampton, *Gregory Ismay, John Castelyn*, and numerous transports. *Nav. Accts. and Invts.*, 1485-88 and 1495-97.

******

He was leading a precarious existence in Ireland, when he was invited by some malcontents of Cornwall and Devonshire to join them. On September 27th, 1497, he accordingly arrived in Whitsand

Bay, near Penzance, with four small vessels, and landed with a few followers. He took St. Michael's Mount, gathered as many as three thousand men, and laid siege to Exeter; but on the approach of Giles, Lord Daubeny, (Sixth Baron Daubeney, died a K.G. in 1507), with the royal forces, he fled to Taunton, and subsequently to Beaulieu Abbey in Hampshire, where, on October 5th, he surrendered himself. His life was spared, and he was generously treated, until repeated attempts to escape, and participation in a plot with the Earl of Warwick, led to his execution in 1499.

During the earlier years of the reign of Henry VII. there were fewer examples than might have been expected of piracy and unofficial warfare in the Narrow Seas; and in 1497, the year of Warbeck's surrender, England and France came to an agreement which had the effect of rendering such proceedings less common than ever, especially in time of nominal peace between the two countries. A treaty was signed, in pursuance of which shipowners were required, ere sending their vessels to sea, to famish good and efficient bail that they would observe the peace.

In the year 1500, the plague then raging in London, the king and his family went to Calais, arriving there on May 8th, and returning about the end of June. Thereafter, until the death of Henry, there were few events which, by any stretch of the imagination, can be associated with naval affairs. The voyages and explorations undertaken during the reign are separately dealt with elsewhere; and it only remains to note that when, in 1506, Philip of Austria, who had succeeded to the kingdom of Castille, and who was on the way, with his queen, from the Netherlands to Spain, was driven by bad weather into Weymouth, and, contrary to the advice of his suite, ventured ashore, he was speciously detained by Henry, under various polite pretexts, until he had consented to a renewal, very advantageous for England, of the treaty of commerce between the two countries, (*Foedera*, xiii.), and had engaged to deliver up Edmund de la Pole, Duke of Suffolk, who had fled the kingdom, and who, being a nephew of Edward IV., was a possible thorn in Henry's side. The duke, on his surrender, was sent to the Tower. The king died at Richmond on April 22nd, 1509.

Henry VIII. came to the throne, a handsome and accomplished young man, in his eighteenth year. He was as able as his father, but in every other respect utterly unlike him. Generous, genial, and fond of amusement and display, he was also intensely ambitious; and, as his treasury was full, and the state of Europe was troubled, he was able to indulge his inclinations.

In the second year of his reign he joined Ferdinand of Spain and Maximilian of Germany in the Holy League against Louis XII. of France; and, about the middle of May, dispatched a body of a thousand archers under Thomas, Lord d'Arcy, to co-operate with Ferdinand against the Moors. The expedition left Plymouth, escorted by four men-of-war, and landed at Cadiz on June 1st. Its mere appearance was sufficient to secure the objects for which it had been demanded. The Moors made terms with the king, and the English, dismissed with presents, returned, without fighting, about August.

In July of the same year, another force of fifteen hundred men, under Sir Edward Poynings, was sent into Flanders to assist the Duke of Burgundy against the Duke of Gelderland. After effecting the desired ends, it returned with small loss and much honour.

But by far the most important naval event of 1511 was the action off the Goodwin with the famous Scotsman, Andrew Barton. Barton had obtained from his sovereign letters of marque and reprisals against the Portuguese, who were alleged to have killed his father, and seized his father's ship, and who had afforded no satisfaction for the outrage. Barton had thereupon equipped two vessels, the *Lion*, carrying thirty-six, and the *Jennet Perwyn*, a "pinnace" or tender, carrying thirty guns, if we may trust the popular Elizabethan ballad on the subject. (Their gun strength, unless the guns were extremely small, must be greatly exaggerated in the ballad, for the tonnage of the vessels was but 120 and 70 respectively.) The one seems to have had upwards of three hundred, and the other, one hundred and eighty men on board.

But, under pretext of cruising against the Portuguese, Barton seized and plundered many neutral vessels, including English ones, under the pretence that they had Portuguese goods on board; and complaints on the subject were made to Henry VIII. (Surrey, on hearing the complaints, remarked that "The Narrow Sims should not be so infested while he had estate enough to furnish a ship, or a son capable of commanding it." Lloyd's *State Worthies*.)

To Lords Thomas and Edward Howard, the two sons of Thomas, Earl of Surrey, and subsequently second Duke of Norfolk, was apparently entrusted the duty of dealing with this piratical adventurer. According to the generally received account, they were assigned by the king two ships for the purpose; but Colliber, (*Columna Hostrata*), though he does not say on what authority, states that these young noblemen fitted out two vessels at their own charges. (Surrey's words quoted in the note above seem to indicate that he fitted out the vessels.) Lord Edward Howard, the younger of the two brothers, had been knighted for his bravery in the expedition against Kleve-Ravenstein, and, perhaps on account of the experience thus gained, was appointed senior officer.

The brothers fell in with Barton off the Goodwin, brought him to action, and, after a determined struggle, killed him, and captured his vessels. (Stowe, says that the *Lion* struck to Lord Thomas. Herbert's *Life of Henry VIII.*, says that both ships were brought into the Thames on August 2nd, 1511.) The ballad has it that they sunk the pinnace with all on board, and took only the *Lion*; but the fact is that both vessels were added to the English navy.

The ballad mentions Barton's use of a whistle, probably to direct his men; and adds that Lord Edward Howard, or Sir Edward, as he is commonly called, received as part of his reward Sir Andrew's jewel and chain. Soon afterwards, on August 15th, 1512, Lord Edward was made Lord High Admiral.

★★★★★★

Lord Edward Howard, second son of the Duke of Norfolk. He had served with Sir Edward Poynings in the expedition against Sluis in 1492. Henry VIII. made him his standard-bearer (Pat. 1 Hen.VIII. p. 1, m. 24). He fell in action, as will be seen. He had married Alice, daughter of William Lovel, Lord Morley.

★★★★★★

The account of his death, presently to be given, shows that as badge of his rank he wore a. gold whistle, besides a chain of gold nobles about his neck; and it may well be that this whistle was the one which had been taken from Barton, and that the practice, long continued by Lord High Admirals, of wearing a whistle as their ensign of office, commemorated the defeat and death of the noted Scots seaman.

The Barton affair caused much ill blood between Scotland and England, and ultimately served as one of the pretexts for the invasion which ended at Flodden Field on September 9th, 1513. Henry's attitude, when James IV. remonstrated, was "that punishing pirates was never held a breach of peace among princes." (Drummond, *Hist, of Five Jameses.*)

In 1512, in furtherance of the objects of the Holy League, Henry VIII. fitted out a fleet of twenty vessels, and entrusted it to the command of Lord Edward Howard, whom he had made Lord High Admiral for the purpose. The immediate mission of this force was to convoy an English Army, under the Marquis of Dorset, to co-operate with King Ferdinand in the south of France. The troops were carried in Spanish ships; and the expedition sailed on May 16th, and reached the coast of Guipuscoa on June 8th.

As soon as the army had been landed, the Lord High Admiral proceeded on a cruise off the coasts of Brittany, where he attacked several places in the neighbourhood of Le Conquêt and Brest, and burnt some shipping.

France had afloat in the same waters a force under Jean de Thénouënel, Admiral of Brittany; another of her admirals, Prégent de Bidoux, was on his way from the Mediterranean with a reinforcement of four large galleys; and a French ship of great force, the *Marie la Cordeliere*, (said to have carried 1200 men), which Anne, Queen of France, had some years before caused to be built at her own cost, had lately been commissioned by a noted Breton seaman, Captain Hervé de Portzmoguer, (amusingly Anglicised as "Sir Piers Morgan"); and King Henry, conscious that Howard's command was scarcely equal to contending with such a combination, collected twenty-five other vessels at Portsmouth, and, after having himself reviewed them, dispatched them to the assistance of the commander-in-chief.

Among these ships were the *Regent* and the *Sovereign*, the two finest in the service. The former was commanded by Sir Thomas Knyvett, Master of the Horse, with Sir John Carew as his second; and the latter by Sir Charles Brandon, with Sir Henry Guildford.

★★★★★★

Sir Thomas Knyvett, of Buckenham, had been made a K.G. in 1509, on the occasion of Henry's coronation. He married Muriel, daughter of Thomas, Duke of Norfolk, and widow of John Grey, Lord Lisle.
Sir Charles Brandon, created Viscount Lisle in 1513, and Duke of Suffolk in 1514. He was also a K.G., He died in 1545.
Sir Henry Guildford, son of Sir Richard Guildford, of Hemsted, who had been Master of the Ordnance under Henry VII. Sir Henry died a K.G., 23 Henry VIII.

★★★★★★

In each case both officers were called captain; so that in the arrangement we may distinguish a foreshadowing of the modern practice of appointing a commander as well as a captain to a large man-of-war. Other captains in the fleet were Sir Anthony Oughtred, Sir Edward Echyngham, and William Sydney. (Sydney, who was knighted at about this time, became chamberlain and steward to Henry VIII., and died at the end of the reign of Edward VI.)

A GALLEY

Howard, with his reinforced fleet, made the mouth of Camaret Bay on August 10th, just as the French fleet of thirty-nine sail was coming out. Grafton, his spelling modernised, shall continue the story, he says:

When the Englishmen perceived the French Navy to be out of Brest Haven, then the Lord Admiral was very joyous; then every man prepared according to his duty, the archers to shoot, the gunners to loose, the men of arms to fight. The pages went to the topcastle with darts. Thus, all things being provided and set in order, the Englishmen approached towards the Frenchmen, which came fiercely forward, some leaving his anchor, some with his foresail only, to take the most advantage; and when they were in sight, they shot ordnance so terribly together that all the sea coast sounded of it.

The Lord Admiral made with the great ship of Dieppe, and chased her still. Sir Henry Guildford and Sir Charles Brandon, being in the *Sovereign*, made with the great *carrack* of Brest (*Marie la Cordelière*) and lay stem to stem with the *carrack*; but by negligence of the master, or else by smoke of the ordnance, or otherwise, the *Sovereign* was cast at the stern of the *carrack*, with which advantage the Frenchmen shouted for joy; but when Sir

Thomas Knyvett, which was ready to have boarded the great ship of Dieppe, saw that the *Sovereign* had missed the *carrack* which Sir Henry Oughtred chased hard at the stern and bowged (rammed) her in divers places, and set afire her powder as some say, suddenly the *Regent* grappled with her along board; and when they of the *carrack* perceived that they could not depart, they let slip an anchor, and so with the stream the ships turned, and the *carrack* was on the weather side, and the *Regent* on the lee side.

The fight was very cruel, for the archers of the English part, and the crossbows of the French part, did their uttermost; but, for all that, the Englishmen entered the *carrack*, which seeing, a varlet gunner, being desperate, put fire in the gunpowder, as others say, and set the whole ship of fire, the flame whereof set fire in the *Regent*; and so, these two noble ships, which were so grappled together that they could not part, were consumed by fire. The French Navy, perceiving this, fled in all haste, some to Brest, and some to the isles adjoining.

The English, in manner dismayed, sent out boats to help them in the *Regent*; but the fire was so great that no man doted approach: saving that, by the *James*, of Hull, were certain Frenchmen that could swim saved. This burning of the *carrack* was happy for the French Navy, or else they had been better assailed of the Englishmen, which were so amazed with this chance that they followed them not. The captain of this *carrack* was Sir Piers Morgan, and with him nine hundred men slain and dead. And with Sir Thomas Knyvett and Sir John Carew, seven hundred men drowned and burnt; and that night all the Englishmen lay in Bartram (Bertheaume) Bay, for the French fleet was dispersed as you have heard.

Such was the English account. As might be expected, the French accounts bore a somewhat different complexion; and it is perhaps but fair to append Monsieur Guérin's summary of them, although it must be premised that he attributes the battle to a wrong year, (1513, as Daniel and other French historians also do), that in some other particulars, his story is demonstrably incorrect, and that the entire description is obviously rather picturesque than historical in its mode of expression, he says:

The English fleet appeared on August 10th off Saint Mahé or

Saint Mathieu, at the extremity of the peninsula of Brittany. The French fleet, which was chiefly composed of Norman and Breton vessels, was inferior in number by one-half, and, moreover, believing the enemy to be well occupied in Picardy, was taken unawares. The presence of mind of the leaders compensated for the awkwardness of the moment; their courage and that of their men took the place of numbers.

The French fleet, which Prégent de Bidoux had hurried to join with his galleys, (it is extremely doubtful, however, whether Prégent did join at all that year), was careful to retain the advantage of the wind, and it paid its attention solely to boarding, smashing or sinking about half the enemy's vessels. In the midst of this general French attack, there was to be noted above all others a large and beautiful *carrack*, decorated superbly, and as daintily as a queen.

She, of herself, had already sunk almost as many hostile vessels as all the rest of the fleet; and now she found herself surrounded by twelve of the principal English ships, which had combined all their efforts against her. She was the *Marie la Cordelière,* which Anne of Brittany, Queen of France, had caused to be built at great cost at Morlaix, and the command of which she had entrusted to the gallant Portzmoguer, the worthiest Breton captain of his day. The *Cordelière*, alone among so many foes, struggled with a courage which was almost miraculous.

Of the twelve vessels surrounding her, she put several out of action and drove off some more. A large English ship, commanded by Sir Charles Brandon, had been completely dismasted by the gun-fire of the *Cordelière*, whose triumph was on the point of being assured, when, from the top of a hostile vessel, there was flung into her a mass of fireworks, the flame from which instantly took hold of her. Some of the soldiers and seamen were able to save themselves in boats, but Captain Portzmoguer, after having given every one the option of relinquishing a fight which now seemed hopeless, declined, in spite of the entreaties of his people, to avail himself of the chance, open to him also, of saving his life.

His life was entirely bound up with the existence of the vessel which had been so specially entrusted to him by the queen; the one was to end with the other. Suddenly the *Cordelière* sighted the *Regent*, of 1000 tons, in which Thomas Knyvett, squire to

Henry VIII., fulfilled the functions of Vice-Admiral of England; and, like a floating volcano, bore down, a huge incendiary torch, upon her, pitilessly grappled her, and wound her in her own flaming-robe.

The powder magazine of the *Regent* blew up, and with it the hostile ship, her commander, and thousands of burnt and mangled limbs went into the air; while the *Cordelière*, satisfied, and still proud amid the disaster, blew up also, and, a whirl of fire and smoke, vanished beneath the waves, like her immortal Captain Portzmoguer, who from a top had thrown himself, fully armed, into the sea. The ships of Dieppe were in great danger, when they were very opportunely succoured by three or four Breton ships belonging to Croisic, which made chase after the enemy. The English fleet took to flight, and was followed up as far as the coast of England.

Portzmoguer appears in many French histories as "Primoguet"; and Hubert Veille, the continuator of Robert Gaguin, Latinises him as Primangaius. The fight of the *Cordelière*, like that of the *Vengeur* in 1794, and of our own *Revenge* in 1591, has, thanks to patriotism, poetry, and vulgar tradition, been clouded over with the rosy mists of myth, and has become a naval legend. So much so is this the case that, although the French fleet in modern days has always included a vessel supposed to be named after the gallant captain of the *Cordelière*, he is commemorated, not as Portzmoguer, but as Primauguet.

Little or nothing was done during the winter, it being then and long afterwards the opinion of naval officers that it was almost madness to attempt to keep fleets of heavy ships at sea between the end of autumn and the beginning of spring. (This was the view even of Sir Clowdisley Shovell at the beginning of the eighteenth century.) But in March, 1513, the Lord High Admiral sailed again for the coasts of Brittany, with forty-two men-of-war, besides small craft. Among his captains were Sir John Wallop, Sir Thomas Cheyne, Lord Ferrers, Sir Henry Sherburn, Sir William Sydney, Sir William Fitz-William, Sir Edward Echyngham, Sir Richard Cromwell, Stephen Bull, Compton, and others.

★★★★★★

Sir John Wallop was made a K.G. in 1544. He died in the fifth year of Edward VI.

Lord Ferrers, Sir Walter Devereux, K.G. He was the third Baron

Ferrers, and in 1550 was created Viscount Hereford.

Sir William Fitz-William, Son of Sir Thomas Fitz-William, Kt., was knighted after the siege of Tournay, and was wounded off Brest in the action of 1513. In 1536, he was made Lord High Admiral and Earl of Southampton. He died a K.G. in 1543.

★★★★★★

The immediate object of the expedition seems to have been to clear the seas in order to permit Henry himself to pass over to France and personally conduct the campaign there.

Upon arriving off Brest, Lord Edward learnt that the French fleet lay within ready to sail, and awaiting only the appearance from the Mediterranean of the galleys, (as noted above, they do not appear to have arrived in 1512), under Prégent de Bidoux. He blockaded the enemy, who, to protect himself, threw up batteries on each side of the harbour, and drew across it four-and-twenty hulks chained together. (Holinshed, ii.) The English fleet entered Le Goulet, the narrow mouth of the harbour, and, manning its boats, made a feint as if to attempt a landing.

This brought down the French in great numbers to the shore; and while the admiral held them there, he advanced farther into the harbour, and landed a force on the peninsula of Plougastel, opposite the town. Bodies of men ravaged the country between the rivers Landerneau and Aven; but, owing to the lack of stores and provisions in the fleet, the operations could not then be followed up. Howard, however, continued to hold Le Goulet, and to blockade the port. These events took place in the first and second weeks of April.

The expected stores were meanwhile on their way, under the convoy of Sir Edward Echyngham, who, in a letter preserved in the Cottonian Library, has left an account of his proceedings. He left England on Wednesday, April 13th, and almost immediately sighted a vessel which he. recognised as French, and which he chased until she made for the coast of Friesland. On Thursday, the following day, he sighted fifteen sail, which proved to be Spanish, and which appear to have joined company with him. On the morning of the 15th he fell in with three French ships and prepared for action, making arrangements to protect his people with cables and mattresses, encouraging his men, and getting ready his morris pikes and other weapons.

Observing his good countenance, the French fled, making for Fécamp, under the walls of which Echyngham chased them. When beyond pursuit they fired at him. On the 16th the wind was S.S.W.

Nothing particular happened on the two following days; but on the 19th, at 10 a.m., while chasing a Breton ship and some transports, Echyngham discovered several French galleys among the rocks. The chased transports were two miles from the galleys. The Spaniards are reported to have been extremely terrified on this occasion. Presently Echyngham sighted the masts of other ships, and, approaching them, found, when he had made about ten miles, that they were those of the English fleet in Brest Harbour. He went on board the admiral, who received him very cordially; for the stores which he brought were sadly needed, the English, for the previous ten days, having been reduced to a single meal a day.

The French galleys which Echyngham had observed must have been those of Prégent de Bidoux from the Mediterranean. Four had originally started, but there were now six; and with them were four "foists" or tenders. Echyngham, of course, reported to Howard what he had seen, but no steps seem to have been then taken to deal with Prégent; and the omission had serious consequences; for on Friday, the 22nd, Prégent, with his galleys and tenders, made a dash at part of the English fleet, probably with the idea of joining his friends at Brest, or of forcing the raising of the blockade. He sank the vessel commanded by Compton, and so severely damaged another ship commanded by Stephen Pull, that she narrowly escaped foundering.

One of the tenders was taken by the English boats; and Prégent, apparently baffled for the time, went into Blanc-sablon Bay, where he remained throughout Saturday, the 23rd, placing his squadron between the two islets; it the mouth of the bay, and fortifying both.

On the night of Saturday, he intended to disembark six thousand men on the little peninsula between the bays of Blanc-sablon and Le Conquêt, so as to take the galleys in the rear, but the movements of the enemy caused him to abandon his design and to take, his fleet back to Le Goulet, it appearing to him that an effort was to be made to throw supplies into the town of Brest.

On St. Mark's Day, Monday the 25th, Howard determined to essay an attack upon the galleys, which were so situated that they could not be approached at all by large vessels, and that the batteries on the rocks commanded the approach of even boats. Captains Sir Thomas Cheyne, Sir John Wallop, Sir Henry Sherburn, and Sir William Sydney, with Lord Ferrers, were associated with him in the hazardous venture; and two small galleys, two large barges and two boats formed the cutting-out force, which advanced to the attack at about 4 p.m.

Howard, in the galley which he personally commanded, got alongside the galley of Prégent. He had told off fifteen men to fling into the French vessel his own anchor, so as to hold her, and to make fast the cable of it to his own capstan, with directions that if the French ships caught fire, the cable was to be cut; but either the cable was at once cut by the enemy, or the Englishmen failed to carry out their orders; for, as Howard, followed by a Spaniard named Charrau and sixteen others, clambered into the forecastle of Prégent's ship, his own craft swung clear and drifted away, leaving the admiral and his gallant companions fighting for their lives.

At the instant of boarding, Charrau, who had forgotten his pistol, sent a servant back for it. When the man had found it, he was unable to rejoin his master owing to the distance between the vessels. The admiral and his followers were quickly driven overboard by the pikes of the Frenchmen, and nearly all were drowned. Charrau's servant saw the admiral swimming, and hailing his galley to come to him. When he saw that he could not be saved, he took off his chain of gold nobles and his gold whistle of office, and threw them from him, so that the insignia of an English admiral, even after his death, might not fall into the hands of the enemy. After that he disappeared.

A second English craft came up, but her commander being killed, she retired. Cheyne, Wallop, Sydney and Sherburn all arrived not long afterwards; and the two latter boarded Prégent and did him some damage; but, seeing that the other vessels had withdrawn, and not knowing that the Lord High Admiral had ever quitted his galley, they also withdrew and rejoined the fleet.

For a short time Howard's fate was in doubt. To ascertain it, Cheyne, Cromwell, and Wallop presently went ashore in a boat under a flag of truce; and, upon hearing of their arrival, Prégent rode down on horseback to meet them. He assured them that his only prisoner was a seaman, but added that an officer with a gilt shield on his arm had boarded him, and had been thrust into the sea by the pikes; and that the prisoner declared this officer to have been the English admiral.

Lord Ferrers, in the second English galley, had engaged the other French vessels, but, after expending all his powder and shot and two hundred sheafs of arrows, saw that the admiral's galley had relinquished the combat, and followed it out of action.

On Saturday, April 30th, the fleet, in mourning, reached Plymouth; and on the following day it disembarked its sick, two of whom, according to Echyngham, (upon whose letter the above account is chiefly based), fell dead as they landed.

Echyngham makes some suggestive comments on this lamentable disaster. He says that after Howard's death it was the unanimous wish of the fleet that the king would send it a commander who, in addition to noble birth, should possess wisdom and firmness, and who should make himself equally loved and feared, no fleet having ever been more in need of a man who would keep it in good order. To do better in the future against the French, there must be brave captains and better seamen; the rowers must be chained to their benches; there must be plenty of archers; and those who should distinguish themselves must be rewarded, and those who should fail in their duty, punished.

These expressions seem to imply that Howard, brave and able though he certainly was, had suffered the discipline of the fleet to deteriorate; that some, at least, of the captains had disappointed expectations; that the seamen were inefficient; that the rowers had abandoned their posts; and that these and other shortcomings had not been duly punished. It may well be that such were the facts. Yet Howard's devotion and gallant death deserve to be remembered.

Lord Thomas Howard, (later, Earl of Surrey, was eldest son of the Duke of Norfolk, whom he succeeded, died 1554, aged 66), who had but recently returned from the expedition to Picardy, was at once (May 4th, 1513), appointed Lord High Admiral, in succession to his younger brother, and took the sea within a very few weeks; but, in the meantime, Prégent de Bidoux had followed up his success, landing some men in Sussex and ravaging the country. During the course of this raid he lost an eye.

Lord Thomas Howard chased him back to Brest, then returned to convoy the king and a large army in four hundred vessels to Calais, and on July 1st, 1513, landed at Blanc-sablon Bay and pillaged the adjacent country in revenge for Prégent's raid upon Sussex. Thence he hurriedly returned to co-operate against the Scots, who were endeavouring by an invasion of England to get satisfaction for the death of Andrew Barton. Howard, who had been so intimately concerned in that affair, commanded the van of the English Army when it crushed the invaders at Flodden Field on September the 9th. In the following year, the Lord High Admiral, for his various services, was created Earl of Surrey.

In 1514, Prégent again made a descent upon Sussex, and burnt Brighton, or, as it was then and long afterwards called, Brighthelmstone. Sir John Wallop was entrusted with the duty of carrying out the retaliatory measures, and he did it thoroughly, landing in Normandy and burning twenty-one towns and villages ere he withdrew. This was one of the last operations of the war of the Holy League, and for about seven years following there was peace with France.

The naval events of the peace were neither numerous nor important, the most striking of them being, perhaps, the transport by Vice-Admiral Sir William Fitz-William of Henry VIII. to Calais in 1520 to meet Francis I. of France on the Field of the Cloth of Gold. Some notice of the ships engaged on that occasion will be found in the previous chapter.

The war recommenced in 1522, England again allying herself with the emperor. Vice-Admiral Sir William Fitz-William was at once sent to sea with a fleet of twenty-eight sail to protect English commerce and annoy French trade, which he effectually did. Another squadron of seven ships went to the Firth of Forth, and, as a precautionary measure, burnt such Scots vessels as lay there. A little later, on June 8th, a great compliment was paid to England and to her Lord High Admiral, by Surrey's appointment as commander-in-chief of the combined fleets of England and the Empire.

The emperor's patent to Surrey, signed in London, after reciting that Henry had fitted out a fleet "under the command of the most illustrious Thomas, Earl of Surrey, our most dear cousin, Knight of the most noble Order of the Garter, Lord High Admiral of England, Wales, Ireland, Normandy, Gascony, and Aquitaine," and that it had been determined that the English and Imperial fleets were to act together, and that one captain-general was better than many, gave the command of the whole to the said Admiral of England, he to exercise exactly the same power and authority over the Imperial as over his own fleet.

Sailing immediately after the receipt of this patent, Surrey, with the combined fleet, appeared off Cherbourg, and, landing on June 13th, executed a rapid raid on the neighbouring country. After having returned to Portland, he recrossed the Channel, and on July 1st, landed near Morlaix, and took and sacked that town. He also burnt seventeen sail of French ships, and then carried a great amount of booty to Southampton, leaving Sir William Fitz-William to cruise in the Channel. (This booty included, apparently, the ships later taken into the navy, as the *Bark of Morlaix, Mary Grace*, and *Bark of Boulogne.* Roy. MSS. 14, Bk. xxii. A.) At Southampton, Surrey found the emperor waiting for a passage to Spain. His majesty and suite embarked on board the fleet on July 6th and were conveyed without mishap to Santander.

In this and the following year, the Lord High Admiral served on land as well as afloat, and was continuously and very arduously employed. It was probably owing to his many preoccupations, and to the fact that he had to provide for the transport to France of an army of thirteen thousand men in August, 1523, that he did not cruise during that summer. Sir William Fitz-William commanded the main fleet of thirty-six vessels; and Anthony Poyntz was entrusted with an inferior, yet still considerable, squadron which cruised to the westward. (Anthony Poyntz, afterwards knighted. Seems to have been High Sheriff of Gloucestershire in 1522 and 1527, and to have died 26 Hen.VIII.)

Fitz-William's orders were, if possible, to intercept John, Duke of Albany, who, after having been Admiral of France, had become Regent of Scotland, and who had collected in France a large force with which he intended to enter Scotland, or to invade England. The vice-admiral was so fortunate as to meet a Scoto-French division of twelve vessels which had on board, among other dignitaries, the Archbishop of Glasgow.

He took two of these ships, (possibly including the one which was added to the navy as the *John of Greenwich*), and chased the rest into Boulogne and Dieppe, off which places he left small blockading squadrons. With the rest of his fleet he ravaged the French coast, took and burnt Tréport, destroyed many vessels, and captured much booty; but he returned prematurely to England; and Albany, who had recognised the futility of attempting to cross the sea while Fitz-William was active there, and who had laid up his ships and quartered his troops ashore, no sooner learnt of the withdrawal of the vice-admiral than he quickly re-manned his vessels, sent his troops on board, and sailing with great promptitude, landed in Scotland on September 24th.

In the same year, one Duncan Campbell, described as a Scots pirate, was, according to Holinshed, taken after a long fight by John Arundel of Cornwall.

Peace was made with France in 1525; and thenceforward for many years, few naval events of sufficient importance to demand notice occurred. On July 16th, 1525, Henry Fitzroy, Duke of Richmond, a natural son of the king by Elizabeth Blount, later, wife of Sir Gilbert Baron Tailbois, was, though only about nine years of age, (he was already a K.G.), appointed Lord High Admiral in supersession of Surrey, who had succeeded to the dukedom of Norfolk in 1524;

but when Richmond died in 1536, the office was more deservedly conferred upon Sir William Fitz-William, K.G., (he assumed office on August 16th, 1536), who, in the following year was made Earl of Southampton and Lord Privy Seal, being already Treasurer of the Household and Chancellor of the Duchy of Lancaster.

At the end of 1539, Southampton, with a fleet of sixty sail, escorted Anne of Cleves to England. This was almost his last naval service. In 1540, he was succeeded as Lord High Admiral by John, Lord Russell, afterwards Earl of Bedford, (he assumed office on July 18th, 1540); and he in turn was succeeded on January 27th, 1543, by John Dudley, Lord Lisle, who subsequently became Earl of Warwick and then Duke of Northumberland, and who was the father-in-law of Lady Jane Grey.

The year 1544 found Henry VIII. again, in alliance with the emperor, and again at war with France and Scotland. Lisle, with a considerable fleet, (Sir William Wynter was in this fleet), picked up at the mouth of the Tyne a convoy of two hundred transports laden with troops under the Earl of Hereford, and escorted them to the Forth, where the army was landed near Leith on May 5th. (At Leith were taken the *Unicorn* and *Salamander*, which were added to the navy.) Edinburgh was taken and sacked, but the castle held out so stoutly that the English withdrew, and the fleet returned to the south ravaging and plundering the Scots coasts on its way.

Later in the year the Earl of Lennox, father of Lord Darnley, who had temporarily joined the English party, manifested his zeal by heading a squadron of twelve or fourteen ships, with which he harassed Arran, Bute and Argyll. He brought back much spoil to Bristol, and then made a second raid with a smaller force.

More important operations were undertaken in France. Henry in person landed at Calais on July 14th, and took the field with an army of thirty thousand men. He laid siege to Boulogne, Lord Lisle at the same time blockading it by sea; and on September 14th the place surrendered.

Sir Thomas Seymour, afterwards Lord Seymour of Sudeley, was appointed vice-admiral, and directed on October 29th, 1544, to take command of a fleet for the conveyance of a quantity of stores to the newly captured fortress, and, after having accomplished that service, to lie in mid-Channel, and, "if opportunity may serve thereunto, appoint a convenient number of the small shallops and other small vessels to pass in the River Estaples (the Canche) and there burn and bring away such vessels of the enemy as may be there found, or do other such annoyance to the enemy as the time will serve." If the ships in the Canche could not be attacked, other annoyance might be caused on the coasts of Normandy. Finally, after leaving a certain number of ships to cruise in the Channel, Seymour was to return to Portsmouth for more supplies for Boulogne.

Seymour proceeded at once, and on November 6th, wrote from off Dover to the Privy Council that he had quitted the mouth of the Orwell in a fog; that he had learnt of seventeen men-of-war being at Etaples; that the place was difficult to approach, and more difficult to get out of; and that he begged to be allowed to operate instead upon the coasts of Brittany.

Permission to attack Brittany was given, provided Boulogne was first attended to, and fourteen ships were left to guard the Narrow Seas; but, in the meanwhile, Seymour was driven from Dover by a gale. He tried to make Boulogne, but was carried too far to the westward; and then, hearing that seventeen sail of the enemy lay in Dieppe, and seventeen more in the Seine, determined to attack them. But the gale veered to E.S.E., and he was obliged to abandon his design. With much difficulty, and with the loss of all his boats, he reached the shelter of the Isle of Wight.

Henry wrote angrily to Seymour on November 13th; but the sailor returned a straightforward explanation, and the king was satisfied.

★★★★★★

A transport, with 259 out of 300 souls on board, was lost. Another transport, under Sir Henry Seymour, went ashore at Dartmouth, but her people were all saved except three.
Pat. Rolls, 36 Hen. VIII. 23, where Seymour is given a grant of land on January 16th, 1545.

★★★★★★

The supplies, however, did not go to Boulogne that winter.

This loss of the valuable fortress spurred France to great exertions. Francis I. concentrated his whole available western fleet on the coasts of Normandy under Claude d'Annebaut, Huron de Retz and Admiral of France, and reinforced it in 1545 with twenty-five galleys from the Mediterranean under, Baron de la Garde, and Strozzi, Prior of Capua.

★★★★★★

This distinguished seaman, Polain's real name was Antoine Escalin. For some unknown reason, he was nicknamed Polain (young horse) or Le Poulin. He was born about 1498 of poor and humble parents at La Garde, in Dauphiné. He gained his rank of captain in an infantry regiment, and always was known as Captain Polain, even when he had attained the highest commands. (Life by Richer, and by Turpin.)

******

Second in command under D'Annebaut was Vice-Admiral de Moüy de la Meilleraye. Polain's own galley was the largest and strongest built up to that time, and was remarkable as having five slaves to each oar. Previous galleys had never had more than four. This combined fleet was directed to take station so as to prevent English supplies from being thrown into Boulogne, which Francis purposed to besiege by land.

In the meantime, English cruisers and privateers captured many richly laden vessels; and wine and fish became drugs in the markets of London. Holinshed, quoting Stowe, also mentions that the English fleet under Lord Lisle looked into the mouth of the Seine where the French fleet lay, and exchanged some shot with it, so inducing the galleys to come out; but that, it beginning to blow, both parties drew off, the galleys because they made very bad weather of it, and Lord Lisle because he had not sufficient sea room among the shoals. The latter returned to Portsmouth.

D'Annebaut, while waiting for Polain, had collected from between Montreuil and Bayonne all the merchantmen and privateers which he could lay hands upon, and had got together an enormous fleet, which, when Lord Lisle saw it in June, numbered two hundred sail without the galleys. Du Bellay says that when it sailed it consisted of one hundred and fifty large ships, fifty vessels of smaller burden, and twenty-five galleys; and although some modern French writers admit only forty-eight ships, fifty smaller craft, and twenty-five galleys, they do not appear to be able to give any good authority for their figures. Francis, not being yet ready to begin the siege of Boulogne, ordered this large force to attack Portsmouth. The English fleet at anchor at or off Portsmouth included only sixty sail, apart from small craft.

The various divisions of the French fleet sailed simultaneously from Le Hâvre, Honfleur, Harfleur, and other ports in the estuary of the Seine, on July 6th. Francis I. had gone to Le Hâvre to watch them put to sea, and had intended to give a grand banquet on board the flagship *Caraquon*, 800 tons, while some of the other ships were moving out. Owing to the negligence of the cooks, the ship caught fire, and the flames could not be extinguished. The galleys managed to approach and take off the treasure which had been placed on board for

A GALLEY

the payment of the seamen and troops. The king, his suite, and some of the ship's company were also saved. But in consequence of the heating of the guns, which were loaded, the galleys were soon obliged to pull clear to avoid the shot, and numbers of people perished miserably. (Guérin, ii.)

Arrived off the Isle of Wight on July 18th, D'Annebaut sent Polain with four galleys to reconnoitre the situation of the English fleet which still lay within, and which had for the time completely surrendered the command of the sea. Fourteen English vessels weighed with a very light land wind, and stood out of harbour as if to cut off the galleys, which fell back upon the advancing body of the French. Thereupon, the rest of the English ships weighed and went slowly out; and an interchange of shot at long range ensued, no particular damage however being done on either side. The English manoeuvred to draw the enemy among the shallows on the Spit Sand and under the guns of the defences of the town; but D'Annebaut was too wary to be thus caught, and, as night came on, retired to St. Helen's Road, where he found that his largest ship, the *Maîtresse*, was making so much water that he had to send her back to Le Hâvre to be docked.

During the night D'Annebaut rearranged his order of battle, dividing his larger ships into three squadrons, with himself in command of thirty vessels in the centre; Do Boutières with thirty-six vessels on the right, and Baron de Curton with thirty-six vessels on the left.

The galleys under Polain were ordered to approach the English in the morning, and attempt to induce them, by firing at them, to follow the French to sea. But it would seem that these orders were not carried out very early.

On the 19th, King Henry was with Lord Lisle in the *Henry Grace à Dieu* when the first movement of the enemy was noticed, and he at once ordered an attack and went ashore. In moving out the *Mary Rose*, of 500 tons, being very low in the water, heeled so much when her helm was put hard over, that the sills of her open lower ports, only 16 inches out of the water ere she heeled at all, were submerged.

★★★★★★

Oppenheim, *Admin, of Royal Navy*, says, referring to this statement, which comes from Ralegh, "There is the great improbability that, after at least fifty years' experience of gunports, they should have been cut so low, since she (the *Mary Rose*) had been rebuilt in or before 1536. Moreover, Anthony's drawings show them to have been pierced very much higher in other vessels." The *Life of Sir Peter Carew*, in fact, attributes the disaster to the insubordination and disorder which reigned on board. Yet still, the port-sills may have been low, and even lower than normal, and so may have conduced to the accident. When the *Duke of Wellington* left Spithead during the Russian war, her lower port-sills, owing to the extra men and stores on board, were little more above water than those of the *Mary Rose* are alleged to have been.

★★★★★★

She rapidly filled and sank, carrying down with her her captain, Sir George Carew, and all hands, except about thirty-five persons. This awful catastrophe was witnessed from the shore, not only by the king, but also by Lady Carew, the wife of the gallant and unhappy commander. (*Life of Sir Peter Carew*.)

French historians are almost unanimous in asserting that the *Mary Rose* was sunk in action, some, as Du Bellay, attributing the result to gun-shot, and others, as Guérin and other modern writers, claiming the ship as the victim of the galleys of Polain. There is not a shadow of doubt that she perished as has been related, before she had an opportunity of getting into action.

The wind was too light to enable the English ships to manoeuvre properly; and, as the French galleys did not depend upon wind, they were able to inflict a certain amount of annoyance, especially upon the

Henry Grace à Dieu. But the armed boats of the fleet and the row-barges made a good fight with the enemy until, late in the day, the wind freshened. The galleys were then driven off, and, had not D'Annebaut moved to their assistance, would have suffered heavily. No serious effort, however, was made to engage the main force of the French; and once more the English spent a night among the shoals.

On July 20th, the French landed men at three separate places in the Isle of Wight and plundered some villages, but were easily driven off. Soon afterwards the whole fleet withdrew, coasting as far as Dover, landing at Brighton and Newhaven, but being repulsed there; and then crossing to Boulogne, near which place D'Annebaut put ashore four thousand soldiers and three thousand workmen to assist in the long-deferred siege.

An easterly wind presently drove D'Annebaut from off Boulogne, and obliged him to anchor near the English coast, probably somewhere off the Sussex shore. By that time Lord Lisle, his fleet reinforced to one hundred sail, was cruising in the Channel, and, on August 15th, sighted the enemy to leeward. D'Annebaut had already weighed, and most of the day was spent in manoeuvring for the weather gauge, which the English eventually lost; whereupon the galleys under Polain attacked, hut were not properly supported by their consorts; and, the wind increasing considerably towards night, the galleys knocked about so much and shipped so many seas that they were in danger not less of foundering than of being taken.

The skill of Polain, the best galley commander of his age, saved them; and although firing continued until dark, little damage was done on either side. This does not prevent Du Bellay from declaring that in the morning the French saw a number of dead bodies and much wreckage floating on the water. Night separated the combatants. The English returned to Portsmouth, and the French, who had undoubtedly gained the honours of the affray, went to Le Hâvre.

The indignities thus put upon England were in part revenged by Lisle, who, crossing to the coast of Normandy, landed 6000 men near Tréport on September 2nd, defeated the French forces opposed to him, burnt the town, the abbey, and thirty ships in harbour, losing only fourteen men, and went back unmolested to Spithead.

All this time the plague was raging to a terrible extent in Lisle's fleet. The number of men who returned from Tréport was 12,000. This was about the 4th or 5th of September. Some were subsequently discharged, but it is clear from the tone of a letter written on Sep-

Gilkicker.

Henry Grace à Dieu.

Mary Rose, sunk.

Southsea Castle.

's Galleys attacking.

French Fleet.

THE ENCAMPMENT OF THE ENGLISH FORCES NEAR PORTSMOUTH, JULY 19th, 1545.

Showing the Commencement of the Action with the French Fleet.

tember 11th by Lisle, Seymour, and Lord St. John (who reported that thirteen out of thirty-four ships were then infected) that the disease was very virulent; and musters taken on the 12th showed that only 8488 men remained fit for duty. (Sir William Paulet had been created Lord St. John in 1539. In 1515, he was made Lord Steward; in 1550 Earl of Wiltshire, and in 1551 Marquis of Winchester. He died a K.G., in 1572.) This number was on that day further reduced by discharges to 6445, a number far too small for the exigencies of the service, even on the brink of winter, for as Lisle and St. John lamented, "the men fall daylie sick." (S.P. Dom. i.)

The discharges, however, were very necessary. Russell, writing to the Council from Exeter on August 22nd, when the fleet was still fully manned, said, alluding to the Devon and Dorset fishermen:

Many of them, or the most part, are taken from hence as mariners to serve the king, and all the coast here (is) so barren of them that there is no fish almost to be gotten here for money; but that such as we have, the women of the fisher towns, eight or nine of them, with but one boy or one man with them, bring it in, adventuring to sail sixteen or twenty miles into the sea afishing; and have been sometimes chased home by the Frenchmen. And I myself, being upon occasion on the coast, have seen the fisher boats brought in with women which I think hath not been seen (before).—S. P. Dom., i.

In 1546, the French renewed their attempts on Boulogne, and, in order to sever the communications by land with Calais, tried to seize Ambleteuse. But they were disappointed by the vigilance of Lord Lisle and the Earl of Hertford; and a force of nine thousand troops encamped near it for its protection. In the spring, there were several naval skirmishes off the place; and in one of these, which occurred on May 18th, eight English men-of-war engaged an equal number of French vessels, and took a galley, (taken into the navy as the *Galley Blancherd*), with one hundred and eighty soldiers and one hundred and forty rowers; but the operations were of no great importance, and they were put an end to by the conclusion of peace on June 7th. In the following year D'Annebaut, Baron de Betz, came over with a large suite and with twelve galleys, to pay a state visit to England. He landed under a salute at Tower Wharf, and, proceeding to the king at Hampton Court on August 24th, solemnly swore in the name of his sovereign to perform the articles of peace.

This was the last naval event of the reign. On January 28th, 1547, Henry VIII. died, leaving the crown to his son Edward VI., who was then little more than nine years of age. On February 17th, Sir Thomas Seymour, who was brother of Edward, Duke of Somerset and Lord Protector, and who seems to have been already on excellent terms with the Queen Dowager, Katherine Parr, whom he married a few weeks later, was created Lord Seymour of Sudeley and Lord High Admiral.

Henry VIII. in his last years had cherished a project for the marriage of his son Prince Edward with the Princess Mary, daughter of James V. of Scotland; and he had succeeded in inducing the Scots Government to enter into an agreement that the marriage should take place. After Edward's accession, the plan was as warmly taken up by the Lord Protector; but the idea of the union was unpopular in Scotland, and was especially offensive to France, which, as a Catholic power, strongly objected to see a Catholic princess of a house long friendly with France allied to a Protestant prince of a house which was France's traditional enemy. The Lord Protector determined to endeavour to force Scotland to observe its undertaking.

On the other hand, France determined to endeavour to secure the princess for the *dauphin*, and dispatched Leo Strozzi, general of the galleys of France, with a force which on July 3rd, 1547, seized St. Andrews, in Fifeshire, and there captured the leading Scots Protestants who were partisans of the English match.

Before England could strike any forcible blow, there were several border skirmishes and small encounters at sea. In one of the latter, if Hayward may be credited, an English man-of-war called the *Pensée*, (or *Pauncy*, or *Pansy*, of 450 tons, but her force is unknown), was attacked by a Scots ship called the *Lion*, which, although of superior force, she took. But the prize, with most of her men, was lost off Harwich as she was being brought south.

There was no unnecessary delay in England. A fleet of sixty-five sail, including thirty-four large ships and one galley, was placed under the command of Admiral Edward, Lord Clinton, and Vice-Admiral Sir William Woodhouse, and a large army under Somerset in person marched northward. On September 10th, the Scots were defeated with enormous slaughter at Pinkie Cleuch, near Musselburgh, (often called the Battle of Musselburgh), the fleet co-operating with great effect on the Scots flank; and Leith (here the *Mary Willoughby*, previously been taken by the Scots, was re-taken), was taken immediately afterwards and Edinburgh plundered.

But in spite of this decisive English triumph, and of the damage done along the coast by the fleet, which burnt many towns, and practically annihilated the little Scots fleet, the Scots were more than ever determined to oppose the English marriage, and more than ever inclined to further a French one. France reciprocated in 1548 by sending to Scotland six thousand men under André de Montalembert, Baron d'Essé, and by carrying into practice a cleverly laid scheme for the transport of Mary Stuart, the subject of the dispute, from Scotland to Brittany.

Villegagnon, Vice-Admiral of Brittany, commanded the squadron which conveyed the expeditionary corps to Scotland. (This officer, who served with distinction in South America, gave his name to the island and fort of Villegagnon in Rio de Janeiro Harbour.) He landed the troops at Dunbar on June 18th, and they proceeded to lay siege to Haddington, while he, announcing his intention of returning to France, put to sea. But as soon as he was out of sight of the shore, he steered north instead of south, and passing between the Orkneys and the Shetlands, rounded Scotland, and so reached Dumbarton, where, by arrangement, Mary Stuart awaited him. Sailing again without unnecessary delay, he entered the Channel by way of the Irish Sea, and safely landed his charge in Brittany on July 13th, 1548. (Guérin, ii.)

A month afterwards, a squadron under the Lord High Admiral, Lord Seymour of Sudeley, was sent to the eastern coast of Scotland to cause a diversion. (Burnet, ii.) Seymour landed a force at St. Ninian's, in Fifeshire; but it was met by James Stuart, (4 later known as the Regent Murray, and driven back to its ships with a loss of six hundred killed and about one hundred taken. (James Stuart, natural son of James V., by Lady Margaret Erskine; born 1530; Earl of Murray 1562; Regent 1567; murdered 1570.) Seymour made an attempt upon Montrose, but he fell into an ambush organised by Erskine of Dun, and losing six hundred men was obliged to retreat. Although in the course of his cruise he destroyed a few vessels, he returned to England with little gain and no glory.

Peace nominally continued with France; but in July, 1548, the French off Boulogne fired on people who were engaged in building a mole there, and subsequently they captured three or four English victuallers, and made incursions within the English pale. (S. P. MSS. Dom.) Remonstrance was in vain, and at length the Council decided to permit the people of the western ports secretly to proceed to sea to intercept the homecoming French fishery fleet from Newfoundland, and to entrust the conduct of this strange privateering expedition to Seymour, Sir Peter Carew, and other officers of rank. But the political events preceding the fall and execution of the Lord High Admiral hindered the carrying out of the design. Seymour was deprived of his office in January, 1549, and was beheaded on March 20th.

Open war with France was resumed in 1549. Henry II. attacked Boulogne; and Leo Strozzi, with twelve galleys convoying transports with two thousand troops, blockaded Jersey and Guernsey. It was then that Captain William Wynter, who, under Elizabeth, showed himself to be a commander of unusual ability, first began to build up his reputation, although he had served as early as 1544 during the operations in the Firth of Forth. Entrusted with a small squadron and eight hundred soldiers, he, in spite of his inferior force, so boldly attacked Strozzi that he took or burnt all his galleys, killed a thousand of his men, and drove the rest of the expedition ignominiously back to France.

It is but just to add that the French histories contain no mention of this affair. They do, however, assert that on August 1st, 1549, Strozzi off Boulogne gained a brilliant victory over an English fleet, and drove the shattered remnant of it to Guernsey; and this action is not mentioned by English writers. The evidence as to Wynter's victory is, nevertheless, too strong to be neglected; while the evidence as to the French success is exceedingly and even suspiciously weak. There is less doubt as to the successes of the French on land. They pressed Boulogne severely, cutting off all communication with it save by sea; and by the treaty of March 14th, 1550, they were given possession of it and its dependencies upon payment of 400, 000 crowns.

Dudley, Earl of Warwick, who, since October 28th, 1549, had held the office of Lord High Admiral for the second time, relinquished it on May 4th, 1550, to Edward, Lord Clinton, who had been governor of the beleaguered fortress, and who had negotiated the treaty.

The peace between England and France was very displeasing to the emperor, who, in consequence, allowed and probably encouraged his Flamand subjects to cruise against the French in the English seas in a manner destructive to all security of commerce and intercommunication. The French naturally retaliated, the result being that the Narrow Seas became the scene of all sorts of piratical irregularities. The English Government did its best to stop these proceedings, and to protect the merchants, whose interests were seriously prejudiced.

A squadron of six ships with four pinnaces and a brigantine was sent on a preventive cruise in July, 1551; and the brigantine in question, or another craft of the same type, was dispatched to Dieppe to warn the French against the Flamands in the Channel. It is noteworthy as showing the respect with which the English naval power was then treated, that when this brigantine in her course encountered some Flamand vessels, they lowered their topsails to her. Yet the Flamands were not invariably so subservient. In February, 1552, a Flamand ship had the temerity to attempt to search the *Falcon*—probably the English pinnace of that name—for Frenchmen, whereupon the *Falcon* boarded and took her.

In 1551 there occurred the earliest recorded English voyage to Guinea. It was made by Thomas Windham, who, in the following year, repeated it, and opened a remunerative trade. In 1553, he made a third voyage, with three ships, but perished on the coast.

On March 1st, of 1552, four *barks* and two pinnaces were sent to reinforce the cruisers policing the Channels, and on March 26th Sir Henry Dudley, with four ships and two *barks*, was sent to sea with directions to protect the trade. He captured two pirates and carried them into Dover; but he appears upon the whole to have performed his task but indifferently, (Edward's *Journal*, Mar. 26, 1552), for the lawless proceedings continued, and those of the French, which in a space of twenty months cost English merchants a loss of £50,000, became so insufferable that very sharp remonstrances were addressed to the court of France. These led to strained relations, and a rupture appeared to be imminent when, on July 6th, 1553, Edward VI. died.

Mary, who in spite of the opposition of the partisans of the unfortunate Lady Jane Grey, succeeded her brother, owed her elevation, in a large measure, to the attitude of the navy. The Duke of Northumberland, on behalf of Lady Jane, sent a squadron of six ships, immediately after the king's death, to blockade Yarmouth with a view to preventing Mary, who was in the eastern counties, from leaving the country. But it happened that forces for Mary's support were at that moment being levied in the town, where the princess's interest was strong. Sir Henry Jernegan, one of the officers engaged in this levy, had the courage to put off to the squadron in an open boat, and the ability to persuade the whole command to declare for Queen Mary.

At about the same time the Warden of the Cinque Ports took the same course, and the result of these and other pronouncements was that opposition ceased before blood had been shed, and that Mary mounted the throne peaceably. (*Journal of P. C. Haynes*). In the following year, on March 26th, she appointed William, first Lord Howard of Effingham, to be Lord High Admiral.

In the meantime, Captain William Wynter had been sent with a squadron to Ostend to bring to England the ambassadors of the Emperor Charles V., who were charged to negotiate the preliminaries of a marriage between his son, Philip of Spain, and the new queen. The emperor on this occasion sent Wynter a chain of gold, which upon his return to England the honest seaman showed to Sir Nicholas Throgmorton, who exclaimed: "For this gold chain you have sold your country." (Both Wynter and Throgmorton nearly suffered for this. The trial is in Holinshed.) Such indeed was the unpopularity of the proposed match that Sir Thomas Wyatt's abortive rebellion was the instant outcome of the arrival of the ambassadors. But nothing sufficed to stay the execution of the project, and in the summer of 1551, Philip with an imposing fleet of one hundred and sixty sail set out for England.

Effingham, with twenty-eight ships, had ere this begun to cruise in the Channel, nominally to guard the trade, but really to welcome the arrival of the future King Consort, he welcomed it in strange fashion. Philip came up Channel with the Spanish flag at his main, and when he sighted Effingham's squadron, proudly kept the flag flying in expectation that Effingham would salute it. The Lord High Admiral did salute, but it was with a shotted gun. It did not seem fitting to him that any foreigner, no matter his rank and pretentions, should enter the seas of the Queen of England without paying the accustomed deference to her rights there.

The shot caused Philip to strike his colours and lower his topsails, the marriage being too important a part of his plans to permit of his then disputing the English claims; and the gallant Effingham at once returned the salute in the usual friendly way. Hervey calls this "a noble instance of spirit which well deserves to be commemorated." Campbell considers it "a circumstance worthy of immortal remembrance, and one would think too of imitation."

Philip landed at Southampton on July 19th, and the marriage took place at Winchester on the 25th of the same month. On August 12th, the royal pair made their public entry into London, amid the barely repressed disgust of the greater part of the nation.

Philip remained in England only until September, 1555, and did not revisit the country, save for a short period in 1557; yet he was not without influence upon its policy; and his accession to the throne of Spain, upon the abdication of his father in January, 1556, enabled him to involve England in disastrous wars with France and Scotland. Nor, in all probability, was he entirely irresponsible for the supersession, on February 10th, 1557, as Lord High Admiral, of Howard of Effingham by Edward, Lord Clinton; although, no doubt, Howard's devotion to the Princess Elizabeth was the ostensible reason why the change was made.

The French campaign opened well. William Herbert, Earl of Pembroke, with seven or eight thousand men, and in co-operation with Spanish troops, contributed to the victory of St. Quentin, in Picardy, on July 7th, 1557; but there was soon a great misfortune to be set off against this somewhat useless success. On January 1st, 1558, Francis, Duke of Guise, suddenly appeared at the Bridge of Nieullay, close to Calais, and surprised the defences there. Next day, D'Andelot de Coligny, (brother of Gaspard, the Admiral of France), seized Fort Risban on the sea front; and on the 5th, the citadel was carried by assault.

On the 7th, Lord Wentworth, the governor, who had but five hundred men at his disposal, capitulated; and so, after upwards of two hundred years of English occupation, this important strong place was lost, owing to the culpable indifference of the English Government, which, although it was war time, had failed to provide it with necessary men and supplies. On January 20th, Earl Grey de Wilton had to surrender Guines; and presently there remained to England not a single foot of her once splendid dominions in France.

Thirty years later, had England still held Calais, the Spanish Armada might, in all probability, have been completely destroyed there.

The naval campaigns of 1557 and 1558 were hardly more satisfactory. In the former year a squadron of twelve sail, under Sir John Clere of Ormesby, Vice-Admiral of England, was sent to sea to annoy the Scots, and to protect the home-coming Iceland fleet of fishing vessels. A descent was made by it on the mainland of Orkney on August 12th; but on the day following, an overwhelming force of Scots fell upon the landing party, killed three captains belonging to the squadron, took all Clere's artillery, and drove the survivors to their ships. Clere's boat, as he was being pulled off, was upset, and he was drowned.

In the summer of 1558, Lord Clinton put to sea with a fleet of one hundred and forty sail, reinforced by thirty ships belonging to Philip's Netherlands possessions, with orders to attempt the reduction of Brest. Part of the command seems, however, to have been detached to the northward; for, on July 13th, twelve English ships, chancing to find themselves off Gravelines, where a battle was being fought between

Count Egmont and the Marshal de Thermes, were able so to gall the French with their gun-fire as to decide the fight, which resulted in a decisive victory for Egmont.

But the main fleet, under the Lord High Admiral, effected no good. It landed seven thousand men in Brittany, and on July 31st, 1558, took and burnt Le Conquêt. Against Brest, however, it did nothing; and a party of Flamands, who had wandered into the country out of gun-shot of their ships, was cut off by the French.

Queen Mary died on November 17th, 1558.

Queen Elizabeth, who succeeded her sister, was a little more than twenty-five years of age. As Campbell remarks:

> There never was, perhaps, a kingdom in a more distressed condition than England at the accession of this princess. It was engaged in a war abroad for the interest of a foreign prince; at home, the people were divided and distracted about their religious and civil concerns. Those of the reformed religion had been lately exposed to the flames, and those of the Roman communion found themselves now in a declining state. On the continent, we had no allies; in this very island, the Scots were enemies, and their queen claimed the English crown. The exchequer was exhausted, most of the forts and castles throughout the kingdom were mouldering into ruins; at sea, we had lost much of our ancient reputation, and a too sharp sense of their misfortunes had dejected the whole nation to the last degree.

Happily, Elizabeth was a woman of ability, good education, lofty patriotism, high spirit, devotion to her exalted duties, and something more. Her youth had been stormy, and she had often been the unwilling centre of intrigues, which had taught her much concerning both men and women. She never forgot her early lessons, nor did she fail to apply them. They made her independent and self-reliant; and although she was fortunate in having as able advisers and servants as had ever lent aid to an English sovereign, she trusted, throughout her long reign, first of all to herself; and she deserves, in consequence, the first credit for the many glories and triumphs of the Elizabethan age.

The naval affairs of the time are intermixed, more than those of any other period, with affairs not purely naval. During much of the reign, unofficial warfare, not now very easily distinguishable from piracy, was waged by the queen's subjects against foreign powers; and many of the chief leaders in these operations had been, or were to become, officers in the Royal Navy. Again, queen's ships were, on more than one occasion, employed for purposes of private gain, adventure, or discovery, and were wholly or partially fitted out and maintained at private charges. And still, as previously, vessels and seamen of the merchant marine were frequently used for national purposes.

Unusual difficulty is, therefore, experienced in drawing a satisfactory line between the naval operations proper of the reign and those operations which were more particularly adventurous, commercial, exploratory, or piratical. It is hoped, however, that assisted by the references in the notes below, the reader will easily find in a further chapter an account of such expeditions as are not here treated of; since it has been deemed most convenient to confine the present chapter mainly to the consideration of the warlike undertakings of the State, and of those naval events which directly affected, or proceeded from, the national policy.

One of Elizabeth's first cares was for the safety of the Narrow Seas. On November 21st, ere she had been queen a week, she ordered Malyn, the vice-admiral, to collect as large a fleet as possible for the protection of the trade, and for the prevention of unauthorised persons from entering or leaving the kingdom. So strictly was the service performed that it was presently found necessary to relax the orders, and to explain that the queen had no intention of unduly restraining her subjects in the prosecution of their lawful concerns. Lord Clinton, although he had not been conspicuously successful in his operations during the previous reigns, was confirmed in his office as Lord High Admiral.

On April 2nd, 1559, peace was concluded with France at Cateau Cambrésis. Among the stipulations was one for the restitution of Calais to England at the expiration of eight years, or for the payment then of fifty thousand crowns by way of penalty. Another stipulation was to the effect that the fortresses built and manned by the French upon the Scots border should be evacuated and razed; and it was further agreed that the *dauphin*, later Francis II., and the *dauphiness*, Mary of Scots, should confirm the treaty and recognise the right of Elizabeth to the crown of England.

But nothing came of these arrangements. Religious considerations had induced Elizabeth, as early as February 27th, 1559, to take the Protestant party in Scotland under her protection; and similar considerations induced France to strain every nerve to assist the Roman Catholic party there. Nor would the *dauphin* and *dauphiness* confirm the treaty. And when the *dauphin*, in July, 1559, by the death of his father, was elevated to the throne of France, and, in the character of King of Scotland also, sent large forces thither, open war naturally recommenced.

Early in 1560, Elizabeth concluded the Treaty of Berwick with the Scots Lords of the Congregation, promising to assist them in the expulsion of the French; and, immediately afterwards, she dispatched to the north an army under Earl Grey de Wilton, a fleet under Wynter having already sailed for the Firth of Forth. Wynter attacked the French ships in the roadstead, and took or destroyed them. He then rigidly blockaded Leith; and, had the army of Grey and the Confederates been as active as the navy was, the place would probably have fallen. Wynter had not only to co-operate with the besiegers, but also to guard against the daily expected arrival from France of a relieving fleet under the Marquis d'Elbeuf. This fleet, however, was dispersed by a storm, and obliged to return to France; and Francis II., realising the difficulty of conducting operations at so great a distance from his bases, and the probability that, in spite of all his efforts, Leith would fall sooner or later, came to terms.

The Treaty of Edinburgh, signed on July 6th, 1560, (*Foedera*, xv.), procured the evacuation of Scotland by French troops, the razing of the fortifications of Leith and Dunbar, and the payment of a fine for Mary's blazoning of the arms of England with those of Scotland and France.

Mary declined to be a party to this arrangement; but as her husband, Francis II., died on December 5th, 1560, and as France was thenceforward less intimately concerned with the affairs of Scotland, Mary's refusal gained her nothing. Indeed, a full and frank concession of the English demands in 1560 might have spared her the long tragedy which ended at Fotheringay in 1587. Mary returned to Scotland from France in August, 1561. An English squadron, then at sea, is generally supposed to have received orders to intercept her, in order that she might be detained in England until she should ratify the Treaty of Edinburgh; but she was not sighted by it, and she landed without any interference.

It was ever part of Elizabeth's policy to encourage and support the Protestant party on the continent. After the accession of Charles IX. to the throne of France, the long growing tension between the Protestants and Catholics in France reached breaking point; and in 1562, (the year John Hawkyns made his first voyage to the West Indies), as a consequence of the massacre of Vassy, religious war broke out there. As the chief strength of the Protestants lay along the north-west coasts of the country, the civil war extended to the Channel, whither each party dispatched numerous privateers. Most of these vessels confused piracy with their privateering, and the trade of neutrals suffered so intolerably that Elizabeth found no difficulty in discovering a pretext for lending material support to the Huguenots. (The queen's manifesto is given by Stowe.) They had long begged for her assistance, and had offered to put the port of Le Hâvre into her hands. In 1562, therefore, she accepted the offer, and in October sent over Ambrose Dudley, Earl of Warwick, with a squadron conveying a considerable body of troops, to occupy the place. (Eleven small French vessels were taken in the port.)

France at once declared all English ships good prize, so long as Elizabeth held Le Hâvre. The queen replied by declaring all French ships good prize also. In this informal war, the English privateers made immense gains at sea. One Francis Clarke, for example, by means of three vessels which he had fitted out, captured no fewer than eighteen ships, valued at £50,000, within three weeks.

But the English privateers, like the French ones, soon developed piratical tendencies; it became necessary to restrain their operations by proclamation, and an embassy was sent to France to excuse their practices. Sir William Woodhouse, with a small squadron, composed of the *Lion, Hope, Hart, Swallow,* and *Hare,* was sent to sea to repress piracy, and at the same time to render such aid as might be possible to the Huguenots; and he seems to have cruised with success, lying at intervals at Portsmouth, during the winter.

But Elizabeth was soon deserted by her *protégés.* On March 12th, 1563, the French Protestant and Catholic leaders concluded peace at Amboise; and, as the English continued to hold Le Hâvre, formal war between France and England was declared on July 7th. and the reunited parties combined to press with equal energy the siege of the town, under the direction of the Constable Anne de Montmorenci. Warwick held out until the 28th, a fleet of sixty sail, sent to succour him, arriving only in time to carry off his forces. The campaign was put an end to on April 11th, 1564, (the year John Hawkyns made his second voyage to the West Indies), by the Treaty of Troyes. (*Foedera,* xv.) In virtue of this, the French queen-mother agreed to pay 120,000 crowns to England; free trade between the two countries was conceded; and French hostages in English hands were released.

Late in 1500, a little trading expedition, under George Fenner, consisting of three ships and a pinnace, left Plymouth for Guinea and Cape Verde. In May following, off Terceira, one of the English vessels was treacherously attacked by seven Portuguese craft, nearly all of which were of superior force. She gallantly resisted them for two entire days, and finally beat them all off. (Hakluyt, ii.)

A new religious war broke out in France in 1667, (the year John Hawkyns made his third voyage to the West Indies); and once more, in spite of the treatment which she had previously received from them, Elizabeth rendered assistance to the Protestants, sending them 100,000 crowns in gold and a park of artillery. She also showed favour to the persecuted Protestants of the Spanish Netherlands. Her attitude was even more resented by Spain than by France; and soon other difficulties arose to intensify the ill-feeling which had been sown early in the reign by Elizabeth's refusal to listen to the matrimonial advances of her brother-in-law, Philip.

Early in 1568, (the year the Russia Company sent agents to Persia), some Genoese merchants, purposing to establish a bank in the Netherlands, obtained from King Philip a licence to transport thither in Spanish bottoms a large sum in specie. As the vessels entered the Channel, they were chased by some French privateers into Plymouth, Falmouth, and Southampton, where they were well received. At the request of the Spanish ambassador, the specie was carried ashore. But in the meantime, the queen was informed that the Duke of Alva, who was Governor of the Netherlands, intended to seize the money on its arrival, and to use it to the prejudice of the Protestants. She therefore impounded it, promising, however, to return it with interest to the Genoese, should it prove to be indeed intended for their legitimate business, or to hand it over to the King of Spain, should he make good a claim to it.

The real object of the somewhat high-handed proceedings appears to have been to prevent Alva from getting improper possession of the treasure. Both Alva and Philip strongly resented the act. Philip attempted to tamper with certain English statesmen, and to stir up a rebellion in Ireland; and Alva laid hands on all English property in Flanders and granted letters of marque and reprisals. (*Burleigh's Diary*). Elizabeth thereupon permitted reprisals also; but, as before, the privateers soon developed piratical tendencies, and had to be repressed by proclamation. The matter was presently compromised, but it did not fail to leave much bad blood on both sides. Nevertheless, when in

1570 Philip was about to marry his niece, the Archduchess Anne of Austria, Elizabeth very politely sent a squadron under Charles Howard, afterwards Lord Howard of Effingham, to honourably escort the princess from Zeeland to Spain.

In 1572 (the year Drake made his first great expedition), there was a new treaty with France; yet Elizabeth was unable to regard the proceedings of her nearest continental neighbour without the gravest anxiety and suspicion. The massacre of St. Bartholomew's Day served to increase her misgivings; and, as a fourth religious war, which centred about La Rochelle, had broken out, the sympathies of most Englishmen were in an excited condition, which, even taken alone, was a source of difficulty and of danger to peace. Nor was the Protestant struggle going on only in France. The Prince of Orange had entered the Netherlands at the head of an army recruited in Germany.

Elizabeth was as desirous of avoiding formal war as she was of befriending the Protestant cause. She dispatched help to the Prince of Orange, under Thomas Morgan and Sir Humphrey Gilbert; and, at first less openly, she assisted the Protestants of La Rochelle. The celebrated Captain Polain blockaded that port; but he had only five galleys and three ships, besides small craft; and the success of one of the Protestant commanders named Miran, in running the blockade and throwing provisions into the town, seems to have encouraged Gabriel de Montgomeri, a Protestant leader who was at the time a refugee in England, to attempt an enterprise of a similar kind on a larger scale.

He fitted out a fleet of fifty-three vessels, not, of course, without the more or less active co-operation of the English Government; and he had as his second in command Jacques Sore, the best naval commander that Protestant France had then produced. Yet, in spite of these advantages, when, in April, 1573, he appeared off the beleaguered town, he effected nothing; nor, although he persisted in his efforts, did he succeed in breaking down Polain's guard before the conclusion of the arrangement in virtue of which the siege was raised on June 25th.

When the French ambassador in London complained of this expedition having been suffered to leave the shores of England, and of English merchants having supplied the besieged with provisions, the queen was able to disown personal knowledge of Montgomeri's design. Concerning the other allegation, she very aptly said that merchants were men who followed their gain, wheresoever they hoped to find it; and that since they, being Protestants, were in danger of being butchered in every other port of France, it was no wonder that they carried their goods where they might hope to vend them in safety.

A fifth war of religions raged in France from 1574 to 1576. As usual, Elizabeth, while countenancing the Huguenots, endeavoured to keep on terms of peace with France; and, at the height of the struggle, she sent the Earl of Worcester on a complimentary mission to the French Court. The Protestants of La Rochelle had, as on previous occasions of the kind, taken advantage of the civil strife to fit out privateers, which eventually began to commit piratical acts against vessels of all nations. Some of these cruisers were so rash as to seize a vessel containing part of the earl's baggage, and in the affray, they killed three or four people.

This was more than the queen could suffer, even from her *protégés*. The Lord High Admiral, who, in 1572 had been created Earl of Lincoln, was instructed to clear the Narrow Seas of all freebooters, Protestant or Catholic. He appointed the Controller of the Navy, William Holstock, as his vice-admiral, and entrusted him with the command of three fast vessels, having three hundred and sixty men on board. With these, in about six weeks, Mr. Holstock took twenty privateers, with nine hundred men, and retook fifteen merchantmen. The prizes were sent into Sandwich, Dover, and Portsmouth; and in one of them were found three of the persons who had been concerned in the plundering of the Earl of Worcester's baggage. These, after trial, were hanged as pirates.

In 1575, (the year John Oxenham made a voyage to the "South Seas"), the Prince of Orange and the States General of the Netherlands offered Elizabeth the possession, or, if not, the protectorate of Holland and Zeeland. The queen graciously declined the offer, but promised, if possible, to use her influence with Spain to procure peace for the United Provinces. Had she accepted the responsibility, she would probably have experienced great trouble in controlling her new subjects; for in the following year, 1576, the privateers of Holland and Zeeland, under the pretence that English merchants had been assisting Dunquerque, Spain and Antwerp, did so much damage to English shipping that the repressive services of Mr. Holstock had to be again called for.

He proceeded to sea with a small squadron and captured a number of Dutch seamen, two hundred of whom he sent to English prisons. The queen, moreover, sent Sir William Wynter and Mr. Robert Beal, Clerk of the Council, to Zeeland to endeavour to obtain restitution of wrongfully captured goods; but in this they were not successful.

(In 1576 John Barker made a voyage to the West Indies, and Martin Frobiser started on the search for a N.W. passage.)

Elizabeth, nevertheless, did not cease to show numerous kindnesses to the continental Protestants, and especially to those of them who took refuge in England. This policy of hers had the incidental effect of drawing into her realm many excellent artificers and workpeople, whose advent greatly benefited the trade and manufactures of the country and correspondingly weakened those of the places whence they came. Spain deeply resented the injury thus done to her Netherlands dominions; and signs are not wanting that, as early as 1580 or before, the more far-seeing of English statesmen realised that Spain's enmity was of a kind which would not exhaust itself in vapourings, nor indeed in hostile action of the ordinary kind.

It was perceived that sooner or later there must come a moment when the great champions of Catholicism and of Protestantism, antagonised not only by differences of religion and by trade rivalry, but also by the savage piratical warfare that had long unofficially subsisted between them in the New World, would stake their all, the one for dominion, and the other for liberty and existence. (Drake began his famous voyage round the world in 1577.)

Yet probably it was not then understood, and assuredly it has not always been since comprehended, how much depended upon the result of the struggle. It was not merely that Spain and England were pitting themselves one against the other; it was not merely that Catholicism challenged Protestantism; it was not merely that the Latin race threatened the Anglo-Saxon one. Viewed from the present, the long growing and carefully nourished hatreds, which settled their disputes in the English Channel in 1588, were mainly important to the world at large because, indirectly, they involved the fate of America.

Had Spain, and not England, been victorious, the American continent might still have developed into a congeries of republican states; but we may be sure that the prevailing republicanism of those states would have been rather of the central than of the northern American type, and we may well doubt whether a republican union, such as was founded under Washington, and kept together under Lincoln, would have been ever possible in the New World. (In 1578 Martin Frobiser again attempted a N.W. passage.)

Before publicly putting forth her whole strength against England, Spain more than once tried to injure her enemy by surreptitious blows. In 1580, (the year Charles Jackman and Arthur Pett sought a

N.W. passage), for example, Munster was in the throes of civil war, and the opportunity seemed a good one for dispatching from Corunna a little expedition to foment the rebellion against the English power. Italians as well as Spaniards took part in it.

They landed at Smerwick, in Dingle Bay, in September: but Arthur, Earl Grey de Wilton, who, as Lord-Lieutenant, had gone to Ireland earlier in the same year with a large body of picked troops, speedily made himself master of a fort which had been built on the coast in the previous year by James Fitzmaurice and a feeble Papal force, and which was occupied by the new invaders, hardly one of whom escaped to tell the story. In his preface to Vol. XII. of the new series of Acts of the Privy Council of England, Mr. J. B. Dasent notes a curious coincidence in connection with this abortive invasion, he says:

> On some unknown day (generally said to have been September 26th), in 1580, the *Pelican*, soon to be re-named the *Golden Hind,* (she had, in fact, been so re-named in August, 1578), which had sailed with her consorts from Plymouth in November, 1577, returned alone to England, laden with the plunder of the Spanish settlements in the Pacific, and cast anchor in Plymouth Sound after circumnavigating the globe, thus narrowly escaping, as she crossed the mouth of the Bay, the Spanish squadron which bore the invaders from Corunna to Dingle. As these luckless invaders, who could show no commission from Philip, were treated by Grey, so, no doubt, would the Spaniards have treated Drake, who had no commission from Elizabeth. . . . The Smerwick invasion following so soon after that of James Fitzmaurice no doubt rendered it difficult for the Spanish ambassador to press his complaints against Drake. (In 1582 Edward Fenton set out on his voyage to South America, and in 1583 Sir Humphrey Gilbert set out on his expedition to Newfoundland.)

On the death of Edward, Earl of Lincoln, in 1585, the office of Lord High Admiral was conferred, on July 8th, upon Charles, Lord Howard of Effingham, K.G. (He was then forty-nine. He had succeeded his father, the first Lord, in 1573.)

After Elizabeth's refusal to become either sovereign or protector of Holland and Zeeland, the United Provinces had made a similar offer to, and had received a similar refusal from, Henry III. of France. In 1585, (the year Sir Richard Greynvile made a voyage to Virginia), being hard pressed by Spain, they renewed the offer of the sovereignty to Elizabeth. The queen declined once more; but this time she agreed to furnish them with five thousand infantry and a thousand cavalry, upon condition that after the conclusion of an advantageous peace, the States should pay the cost, and that, in the meantime, as security for the payment, Flushing and Rammekins in Zeeland, and Brielle in Holland should be delivered to her. She also agreed to take the United Provinces under her protection, and she stipulated that if she should see fit to send a fleet to sea, the States should contribute an equal number of ships, to be placed under the command of an English admiral. (*Foedera*, xv.)

These measures and the increasing boldness of the English in the West Indies might well have provoked Spain to an immediate plunge into active war, but that slow-moving power was not yet ready to deal the great blow which she had in contemplation. She only redoubled her enormous preparations and the strength of her determination. Indeed, England risked much by the Netherlands alliance. And she risked scarcely less by the attitude which she adopted in the same year towards the Huguenots of France. Henri de Condé came as a suppliant to Elizabeth's court.

She received him well, gave him 50,000 crowns in money, and lent him ten ships, with which he was able to contribute to the relief of La Rochelle, where Henry of Navarre was besieged. Happily, for England, the Spanish cause in the Netherlands was already a lost one, and the star of Henry of Navarre in France was in the ascendant; so that Elizabeth, in both instances, ranged herself with the winning side. But Spain was still strong at sea—the strongest Power in the world. It had already been determined to launch the whole sea power of Spain, of Spain's Italian dependencies, and of Portugal, all under Philip's direction, against the island kingdom. It was now determined to launch it with as little delay as possible.

The nature of Spanish feeling and policy was shown in the case of the *Primrose*, 150 tons, of London, Foster, master. On May 26th, 1585, (the year Drake led an expedition to the West Indies), the ship, a trader, lay off Bilbao, and was visited by seven Spaniards, including the *corregidor*, or chief magistrate, of the province. After these people had been hospitably entertained, four of them, including the *corregidor*, returned to the shore. Presently a boat containing seventy people, with another containing four-and-twenty, was observed approaching the vessel. The people looked like merchants. They betrayed a desire to go on board;

but Foster, being suspicious, and having only twenty-seven men with him, refused to admit more than the *corregidor*, who was of the party, and three or four others; and he made the rest promise to remain in their boats. But, instead of doing so, they all, in a short time produced hidden arms and boarded, the *corregidor* summoning Foster to yield and causing him to be seized.

The men, however, determined to rescue their captain, and, attacking gallantly, killed many of the enemy and drove the rest overboard. Four of them, who were wounded and drowning, were taken up again, one being the *corregidor*; and they were carried prisoners to England. Asked for explanations of his treacherous conduct, the official produced a commission from the King of Spain for a general embargo upon all English, Netherlands, and German shipping along the coast. (Hakluyt, ii. Doubtless by error, the affair is attributed to May 26th, and Philip's commission of embargo, to May 29th, 1585. The latter was, of course, anterior to the former.) Thenceforward, the two countries were in a state of war, although, for a time, Spain still postponed her grand stroke.

Another case was that of the engagement in the Mediterranean, on July 13th, 1586, between some vessels of the Turkey Company and thirteen Spanish craft. Not content with the produce of the embargo which he had laid on ships in his ports, Philip had ordered his galleys in the Levant to take all English ships which they could meet with, the intention being to utilise for the service of the Armada, then preparing, all craft that might be deemed suitable for the purpose. The Turkey Company, in consequence, took care to send only well-built ships to sea; to arm and man them thoroughly; and to oblige several of them to sail in company. Five left England together in November, 1585, the *Merchant Royal*, the *Toby*, the *Edward Bonaventure*, the *William and John*, and the *Susan*.

Off Sicily they separated, each proceeding to her port of destination, and all agreeing to a rendezvous off Zante for the return voyage. When they met again, having learnt that the Spaniards were in search of them, they appointed Edward Williamson, master of the *Merchant Royal,* as their "admiral" or leader, and undertook to obey him. Off Pantelaria, they sighted eleven galleys and two "frigates" (fast sailing vessels), flying the colours of Sicily and Malta, places then in the pay and service of Spain. The "frigates" were sent forward to order the English captains and pursers to repair on board the Spanish admiral, Don Pedro de Leyva. The captains and pursers, as a body, refused; but sent a supercargo, Mr. Rowet, who was very haughtily received, and informed that the English ships must surrender at discretion. Rowet, in the name of all, declined, and had no sooner returned to his ship than the Spanish admiral fired a shot; whereupon a general engagement began. After five hours' hot fight, the enemy's vessels, some of which appeared to have suffered badly, made off; nor were they pursued; for the English, who had lost only two men, had no wish to hazard their ships. (Hakluyt, ii.) Reprisals were, long ere this, of course allowed by the English Government. Sir William Monson says:

I was then a youth of sixteen years of age, (1585-86, also, the year of John Davis's departure to search for a N.W, passage), and so inclined to see the world abroad that, without the knowledge of father or mother, I put myself into an action by sea, where there was in company of us two small ships fitted for men-of-war, that authorised us, by commission, to seize upon the subjects of the King of Spain. We departed from the Isle of Wight, to which place we returned with our dear-bought prize. She was a Biscayner, of three hundred tons, well manned, sufficiently furnished, and bravely defended. (This vessel, which afterwards belonged to Sir Geo. Carew, was re-named *Commander*.)

She came from Grand Bay, in Newfoundland, which, at our first arrival upon the coast of Spain we met with, and (she) refusing to yield to us, we suddenly boarded, and by consent of all our men entered her. But, the waves of the sea growing high, we were forced to ungrapple, and to leave our men fighting on board her from eight of the clock in the evening till eight in the morning. The Spaniards betook themselves to their close-fight, and gave two attempts, by trains of powder, to blow up her decks on which we were. But we happily prevented it by fire-pikes.

Thus, continued the fight till seven in the morning, when the Spaniards found they had so many men killed and disabled that they were forced to yield. When we came to take a view of our people, we found few left alive but could show a wound or shot through their clothes in that fight. We were a woeful spectacle, as well as the Spaniards; and I dare say that in the whole time of the war there was not so rare a manner of fight, or so great a slaughter of men on both sides.

It was in 1580 that George Clifford, Earl of Cumberland, one of the most distinguished adventurers of an adventurous age, fitted out the first of his numerous privateering expeditions. It consisted of three small ships, the *Red Dragon, Bark Clifford*, and *Roe*, and a pinnace, the *Dorothy*, belonging to Ralegh, the whole being under the command of Robert Widrington. In the Channel, the adventurers rifled some Hamburg ships which were alleged to have Spanish goods on board; on the west coast of Africa they came into what appears to have been unnecessary hostile collision with the negroes; off the Rio de la Plata they captured two Portuguese craft, from one of which they learnt of the taking of John Drake of the *Francis*, of Fenton's expedition; at Bahia they seized more Portuguese ships; and, after making other prizes, they returned to England, having abandoned their original design of cruising in the Pacific.

In the same year, Ralegh fitted out two little pinnaces, the *Serpent* and the *Mary Sparke,* for a cruise to the coast of Spain and the Azores. After having taken several prizes and started on their return to England, they fell in with four-and-twenty Spanish merchantmen, with which they maintained a running fight for thirty-two hours. Ralegh did not himself accompany this expedition.

In pursuance of her promise to the Netherlander, Elizabeth, at the beginning of 1586, sent the Earl of Leicester to Flushing with a fleet of fifty sail, and, in addition to troops, a body of five hundred gentlemen. Leicester, to the great displeasure of his royal mistress, accepted from the States the title of Governor and Captain-General of Holland, Zeeland, and the United Provinces, and was informed by the queen that although she was ready to relieve her distressed neighbours, she never meant to assume any power over them. The earl, in spite of his considerable force and large powers, did no good, and returned at the end of the year in something very like disgrace.

A more important event of 1586, as bearing upon the prospects of England, around which the thickest clouds were gathering, was the conclusion of a treaty of alliance and "stricter amity" with Scotland. The execution in the following year (1587, also the year Cavendish departed on his voyage round the world), of James's mother, Mary of Scots, did not disturb this alliance nor prevent King James from cooperating in the preparations against the Spanish Armada.

Philip's preparations were not ignored in England, nor was there any misapprehension concerning their aims and objects. Walsyngham, always well-informed, had private intelligence from Madrid to the ef-

ARRIVAL AT FLUSHING OF ROBERT DUDLEY, EARL OF LEICESTER. 1586

fect that the King of Spain had written to the Pope, advising him of the projected invasion of Elizabeth's dominions, and asking for the Papal blessing upon the undertaking. And not only the intentions of the Spaniards, but also the whereabouts and extent of their ever-growing armaments were matters of common knowledge among English naval officers, who, although there was then not even an embryo Naval Intelligence Department, made up in individual zeal, keenness, observation, and intelligence for what they lacked in corporate organisation.

It was therefore determined, early in 1587, to attempt a blow at the Spaniards while they were still in their ports and busy with their uncompleted preparations; and Sir Francis Drake was chosen to lead a naval expedition for the purpose.

The squadron entrusted to him was not a powerful one. Strype says that it included forty sail: Hakluyt and Monson put the number at only thirty. But nearly all these were hired merchantmen, not to be compared, either force for force, or in general efficiency, with regular war ships. Only four large vessels and two small pinnaces seem to have belonged to the Navy Royal. Drake hoisted his flag in the *Elizabeth Bonaventure*, of 600 tons, 250 men. and 47 guns. William Borough, a distinguished navigator and hydrographer, but no warrior, either by inclination or experience, was second in command, and sailed in the *Lion*, or, as she was commonly called, the *Golden Lion*, of 500 tons, 250 men, and 38 guns. Captain Henry Bellingham commanded the *Rainbow*, of 500 tons, 250 men, and 54 guns; and Captain Thomas Fenner, a most excellent officer, had command of the *Dreadnought*, of 400 tons, 190 men, and 32 guns.

These ships, and the majority of their officers and men, undoubtedly formed the backbone of the expeditionary force. Borough, however, contributed little to the end in view. The temerity of Drake's projects frightened him and, having been put under arrest, he fled home with his vessel, professing to go in fear of his life. In a rambling letter to Burghley, (S. P. Dom. ccviii.), dated from the *White Bear*, off Queenborough, on February 21st following, he pleaded that he had received "great discontent" "through Sir Francis Drake's injurious, ungodly, and extreme dealings, which are unsupportable," and complained that he had been "openly defamed and causelessly condemned;" but as Drake had sentenced him in *contumaciam*, and as the formal document which Borough styled "mine answer touching an objection against me for the coming away of the *Lion*," though enclosed with the letter to Burghley, has not been preserved, it is now impossible to sift all the merits of the case. We know, however, that, thanks to Burghley's good offices, the affair was smoothed over, and that in 1588 Borough commanded the galley *Bonavolia* against the Armada.

Early in April the squadron sailed from Plymouth. On the 16th, when off the mouth of the Mondego, it fell in with two Middelburg traders, and from them learnt that at Cadiz there were enormous supplies of provisions and ammunition, ready to be sent to Lisbon, where the Armada was collecting. Passing Lisbon, therefore, Drake steered for Cadiz, and arrived off the town on April 19th.

He at once drove in, under shelter of the castle, six galleys which made a show of opposing him, and then, boldly entering the bay, sank or took about a hundred vessels, chiefly laden with stores and ammunition. Most serious among the Spanish losses were a galleon of 1200 tons, belonging to the Marquis of Santa Cruz, and a richly freighted Ragusan merchantman of 1000 tons, mounting 40 brass guns. The whole brilliant operation was performed with insignificant loss in the space of a day and two nights, and the comparative ease with which it was carried to a conclusion cannot have failed to give Drake and his companions an encouraging assurance for the future.

From Cadiz, which he quitted on the 21st, Drake ravaged the coast westward as far as Cape St. Vincent, where he surprised the castle and three neighbouring works. His methods were stern and perhaps a little barbarous. He regarded not only the military forces of Spain, but also Spanish fishermen and their nets, as legitimate objects on which to wreak his vengeance; but he effectually attained the end which he had in view, and most thoroughly intimidated the enemy. So much, indeed, was this the case that when, on arriving off Cascais, at the mouth of the Tagus, he formally invited the Marquis of Santa Cruz to come out and engage him, the distinguished vanquisher of Strozzi neither accepted the challenge nor adopted any measures for stopping his opponent's further depredations. Drake therefore took and plundered or burnt about a hundred more ships, besides again harrying the coasts.

Huge quantities of military stores were thus destroyed or taken. But there was small gain of rich stuffs, of spices, and of treasure, and the numerous merchant adventurers who had associated themselves with the fortunes of the expedition naturally looked for some other reward than the spectacle of exploding powder-magazines and burnt accumulations of provisions. It was to satisfy them that, after quitting Cascais, Drake, although his ships were falling short of food and water, headed westward for the Azores.

On a day in June, off the island of St. Michael, the English squadron fell in with the great *carrack*, *San Felipe*, homeward bound with a rich cargo from the East Indies. Her foes were too many for her, and she was speedily taken. The booty found in her more than delighted the merchants, yet it was perhaps the least valuable part of her lading; for in her cabin were discovered papers which so convincingly drew attention to the enormous profits of the East India trade, and so clearly described the methods by which that trade had been prosecuted by the Spaniards, that the English adventurers, upon returning home, were able to establish a similar trade upon their own account, and, a very few years later, founded the East India Company—probably, upon the whole, the most successful as well as the most gigantic commercial association of which history provides any record.

It has been said that Drake's descent upon Cadiz had the effect of postponing the sailing of the Spanish Armada from 1587 to 1588. This scarcely appears to be true. But, undoubtedly, Drake's operations greatly confused and complicated the difficulties in Philip's way, and rendered the attempt of 1588 not only much more costly, but also far less formidable than it would otherwise have been. The whole expedition was well planned and well carried out; and at that juncture England could hardly have been better served, the enemy more seriously injured, or the adventuring merchants more signally benefited. (Letter of Drake to Burghley, April 27th, 1587, in Strype iii.)

The history of the Armada of 1588 is of so much importance, and has to be told in such detail and at so much length, that it has been made the subject of a separate chapter.

The objects of the Armada were effectually frustrated; but when the immediate danger was overpast, thinking minds began to ask themselves whether, after all, the general policy of national defence would not be furthered rather by attacking the enemy in his own waters, than by merely checking his attacks upon England. The victory over the Armada had been won in English waters, and within sight of the English shores. Should the struggle have been fought out there? Ought it not to have been fought out in Spanish waters, seeing that Queen Elizabeth claimed to be sovereign of the Narrow Seas, and that, granting her claim, her realm had been actually invaded, and that the invasion had been repelled only after it had insulted her territory?

These and similar considerations led to the adoption of a more active policy. The moral value attaching to a vigorously offensive defence obtained recognition; and, while Cumberland, to whom the queen lent the *Golden Lion* for the purpose, was commissioned to undertake a privateering venture to the South Seas, (in this expedition, the earl accomplished very little), it was determined to vigorously attack Spain at home, ere she should have time to organise a new offensive expedition.

Philip, as has been seen, had added Portugal to his dominions. The popular candidate for the throne of that country, Dom Antonio, was a refugee in England, and believed that, with a little naval assistance, he could gain a crown. Moreover, Portugal had been the scene of the fitting out of one Armada, and might be the scene of the fitting out of a second, Lisbon being the most convenient Atlantic port in Spanish hands. For more than one reason, therefore, Portugal seemed to be the best point at which to strike.

An expedition was accordingly fitted out in 1589, partly at the queen's expense, but chiefly at the charges of private individuals, among whom Sir Francis Drake and Sir John Norreys, with their immediate friends, were the most conspicuous. The States of Holland also co-operated. Some pieces of artillery for land service, a number of horses, several Dutch ships, and a considerable body of men either failed to join the fleet ere it sailed, or failed to get across the Bay of Biscay; so that the expedition was in many respects ill-found, and inadequate for the work in hand. It put to sea, however, in April from Plymouth, with eighty, or, as some say, one hundred and forty-six ships, of which six belonged to the Royal Navy, (*Revenge*, Sir Francis Drake; *Dreadnought*, Capt. Thomas Fenner; *Aid*, Capt. William Fenner; *Nonpareil*, Capt. Sackvile; *Foresight*, Capt. William Wynter, jun.; *Swiftsure*, Capt. Goring), and with eleven thousand soldiers under Sir John Norreys. Dom Antonio was with the fleet, and the Earl of Essex, in some vessels privately fitted out at his own expense for other objects, joined it off the coast of Portugal.

The first attempt was made upon Corunna, where troops were landed, and the defenders driven into the town. On the following day, the lower town, after an assault by land and by water, was carried, and the governor, Don Juan de Luna, was taken, a great quantity of ammunition and stores being destroyed. The English discipline was, unfortunately, lax, and the men got drunk with the captured wine in the cellars, while the Spaniards annoyed them by burning such of their own ships as lay in harbour, after having first overloaded their guns, which as they burst or went off caused some damage to the invaders. An attack upon the upper town was unsuccessful.

FERROL AND CORUNNA (THE GROYNE).

Hearing of the approach of a Spanish relieving force, Norreys, on May 6th, advanced with about two-thirds of his troops to meet it, and defeated it with great slaughter, and with very little loss to himself. But when, having burnt the enemy's camp and the neighbouring villages, he returned, the chiefs decided to abandon the siege. On May 8th, therefore, the lower town was set on fire, and the expedition re-embarked.

From Corunna, the fleet proceeded to the coast of Portugal, and on May 16, arrived off Peniche, in Estremadura. The troops were landed, and, after the place had surrendered to Dom Antonio, were marched overland towards Lisbon, (Monson's *Nav. Tracts*), taking Torres Vedras on their way. As for the fleet, it coasted southwards as far as Cascais, at the mouth of the Tagus.

The army arrived before Lisbon on May 25th, and seized the suburb of Santa Caterina; but the inhabitants betrayed no enthusiasm for Dom Antonio, guns and ammunition for a siege were wanting, and there was a great amount of sickness. A council of war decided upon a retreat, and, after lying unmolested for two days, the force marched to Cascais, which in the meantime had been taken by the fleet.

This expedition did no good to the cause of Dom Antonio, and was in many ways a failure; yet it greatly injured Spain. On its way south, it had captured many vessels, including fifteen bound for Lisbon

LISBON.

with men and provisions destined for the preparation of a new Armada; and at Cascais it took sixty sail, belonging to the Hanse Towns, laden with provisions and stores for the same object

The army was re-embarked, and the fleet weighed to return home. No sooner was it at sea than it was set upon by about twenty Spanish galleys, which, however, were easily driven off. On the way north, Vigo was attacked and burnt; but nothing further occurred until England was reached. Camden and others aver that a hundred and fifty cannon, and a large booty rewarded the adventurers, but this is doubtful; and there is evidence that the expedition cost a great number of lives, (Captain Thomas Fenner, of the *Dreadnought*, was mortally wounded in the attempt on Lisbon), the amount of sickness in the fleet being most terrible.

The captured ships belonging to the Hanse Towns would have been released, after the confiscation of the goods found in them, had not the queen been piqued by the action of an assembly which was convened at Lubeck to consider the matter, and which talked somewhat wildly about measures of revenge. Her majesty, upon this, made prize of all but two, which she returned that they might inform the authorities of the Hanse Towns of the fate of the rest.

Sir William Monson, commenting on the affair, points out that the landing at Corunna imperilled the main object of the expedition, not only by permitting the men to drink new wine, which seriously affected their health, but also by exposing them to a check which acted as a discouragement. But the real cause of failure was the ill-provided state of the fleet, some of the ships not having four days' victuals when they left Plymouth. Drake was blamed for having lain at Cascais instead of pushing up the Tagus to Lisbon; but it must be remembered that his ships were not in a position to supply the army, and that, had he mounted the river, he would have had to run the gauntlet of three castles, one of which Monson held to be the most impregnable, from seaward, in Europe. Moreover, if he had gone up, he might have been unable to get down again, the place being subject to contrary winds, and a strong current running in the estuary. And finally, there was a squadron of galleys at Lisbon.

Luring the absence of Drake and Norreys, Cumberland, having returned from his abortive second expedition, fitted out a new one of seven sail, including H.M.S. *Victory*, lent him by the queen, and commanded, under the earl, by Christopher Lister, and the armed vessels *Megg*, Captain William Monson, *Margaret*, and a *caravel*. Quitting Plymouth on June 18th, 1589, they took several prizes in the chops of the Channel, and were able to relieve some of the home-coming ships of Drake. Off the coast of Spain, they removed a quantity of Portuguese goods from some Hansa merchantmen. Off St. Michael's, in the Azores, they cut out some valuable vessels.

At Fayal they did likewise, and, moreover, took the town. Numerous other successes were won, but not without considerable loss. Lister, on the way home in charge of one of the prizes, was drowned, and the rest of the expedition, including two or three English vessels which had joined it at sea, suffered great privations ere it again reached England.

Another privateering voyage was made in 1589 by the *Dog*, 70 tons, William Michelson, master. She took several prizes in the Gulf of Mexico; but a number of her people were treacherously killed by the Spanish under a flag of truce, and she had to come home owing to being short-handed. (Hakluyt, iii.)

The disappointments of Drake's voyage did not discourage either queen or country. In 1590, Elizabeth patriotically set apart £8970 yearly out of her revenue for the repair of the navy; and ten ships, in two squadrons, under Sir John Hawkyns and Sir Martin Frobiser respectively, were commissioned to cruise off the coast of Spain to intercept the trade from the Indies. Philip heard of these preparations, and fitted out a squadron of twenty ships under Don Alonso de Bazan to cover the home-coming of his rich *carracks*. But, presently thinking better of the matter, he recalled Don Alonso, and sent a dispatch to the Indies, ordering the treasure ships to postpone their departure. Spain had learnt to depend for much of her prosperity upon the annual arrival of the *carracks*; and the delay caused much distress and many bankruptcies. But on the other hand, the English squadrons spent seven months in fruitless cruising, without taking so much as a single prize. As they returned, they made an ineffectual attempt upon Fayal, which since its capture by the Earl of Cumberland in 1589 had been re-fortified.

In the same year, 1590, a very gallant action was fought near Gibraltar between ten English merchantmen, homeward bound from the Levant, and twelve Spanish galleys. It occurred on April 24th. In the course of it, two Flamand vessels joined the English; but, seeing the great odds against them, one of them presently struck. For six hours the fight continued, and then the galleys, much disabled, withdrew, the English having lost neither ship nor man. (Hakluyt, iii.)

Cumberland fitted out a fourth expedition in 1591, consisting of H.M.S. *Garland* and seven armed vessels. He took some prizes; but two of them were subsequently recovered by the Spaniards, Captain William Monson being taken with them and carried prisoner to Peniche. Learning of the Spanish preparations at Corunna, the earl inquired as to them, and sent word to Lord Thomas Howard, and then, his ship being in an unsatisfactory state, returned to England.

In 1591, also, an effort, somewhat similar to that of 1590, to capture the treasure ships was made by a squadron of seven vessels of the Royal Navy, (*Defiance*, Lord Thomas Howard; *Revenge*, Sir Richard Greynvile—as vice-admiral); *Nonpareil*, Sir Edward Denny; *Bonaventure*, Captain Robert Crosse; *Lion*, Captain Thomas Former; *Foresight*, Captain Thomas Vavasour; *Crane*, Captain Duffield), with six victuallers and some pinnaces, under Lord Thomas Howard, (second son of the Duke of Norfolk), who sailed to Flores, in the Azores, and remained in the neighbourhood for six months. He narrowly escaped being surprised there by Don Alonso de Bazan, who had been sent out with a fleet of fifty-three ships to meet and convoy home the expected carracks.

The Earl of Cumberland, as has been mentioned above, had happened to learn of the fitting out of this fleet at Corunna, and had, with much foresight, ordered Mr. Middleton, master of the *Moonshine* pinnace, to discover its force and object, and then, if necessary, to proceed with all speed and warn Lord Thomas. Middleton kept the Spaniards in sight until there was no longer any doubt of their intentions; and thereupon set all sail for Flores, arriving very little ahead of the enemy. This was on August 31st.

Howard at once weighed. His second in command, Sir Richard Greynvile, of the *Revenge*, had a number of men ashore, and, according to some accounts, waited for them. Camden, and others, have it that he refused to turn his back upon the enemy, and so allowed himself to be hemmed in between the Spaniards and the island. Some also suppose that he mistook the squadron of Don Alonso for the expected treasure ships, and therefore disobeyed the orders of his commander-in-chief. But, be this as it may, he was presently surrounded and attacked by practically the whole of the best part of the Spanish fleet. Howard, with the remaining six men-of-war, seems to have been engaged for a considerable time with the enemy, but not in such a position as to afford any support to Greynvile. The *Foresight* made a serious effort to assist the *Revenge*, but, owing to the wind, could not get very near her.

The *Revenge* fought against these overwhelming odds for fifteen hours; and Greynvile, no matter whether he was, as has often been asserted, or was not, blameworthy as being rash, stubborn, and disobedient, immortalised himself by a defence such as has never, either before or since, been witnessed upon the sea.

At one time, his ship was simultaneously laid aboard by five large vessels, including the *San Felipe*, of 1500 tons and seventy-eight guns. At no time had she less than two vessels alongside, and in hot and close action. As one Spaniard withdrew disabled, another, with fresh men, cool guns, and new supplies of ammunition, took her place. Fifteen ships engaged her. Of these she sank at least two, including the *Asuncion*. Early in the fight, one of the victuallers, the *George Noble*, of London, at great peril to herself, drew near, and, falling under the lee of the *Revenge*, asked Sir Richard if he had any commands. Greynvile bid her shift for herself, and leave him to his fortune.

The fight had begun at about three o'clock in the afternoon. Soon afterwards Greynvile had been wounded, but he refused, until 11 p.m., to quit the deck, and then, receiving a wound in the body from a musket bullet, went unwillingly below to get it dressed. The surgeon who attended to him was killed at his side, and, for a third time, Greynvile was wounded, on this occasion in the head.

In the small hours, the situation of the devoted ship was deplorable.

All her best men lay killed or wounded; she was perfectly unmanageable, and her last barrel of powder had been expended. Greynvile, seeing the futility of further fighting, ordered the *Revenge* to be sunk; but to this the surviving officers would not agree, and terms were at length made with the Spaniards upon the understanding that the lives and liberties of the gallant ship's company should be spared.

When the *Revenge* surrendered, she had six feet of water in her hold, not a mast standing, and but about sixty men, nearly all of whom were wounded, alive, out of a crew which, at the outset, may have numbered two hundred and fifty, if all were on board. But sickness had been rife in the fleet, and no matter what may have been the number of men victualled in the *Revenge* on the day of the action, only about a hundred of them went into the fight fit for duty.

Greynvile, with every mark of admiration and respect, was carried on board the Spanish admiral. Two days later he died. His ship, overtaken five days after the battle by a storm, foundered off St. Michael's with two hundred Spaniards in her, and in the same storm there perished fifteen or sixteen Spanish men-of-war.

Within twenty-four hours of the fight, the home-coming carracks fell in with the fleet of Don Alonso de Bazan, and by it were safely convoyed to Spain.

Lord Thomas Howard's squadron, after maintaining a distant fight until nightfall, got away. On its homeward passage, it made several valuable prizes. A little force of victuallers, fitted out in London to carry supplies to it, had sailed on August 17th, but had been dispersed by bad weather, and obliged to put back. Some of the vessels, however, before they reached port, picked up three rich prizes in the Bay, and took one of them into Plymouth.

That year, 1591, saw some other very gallant actions, which, although not strictly naval, must be here recorded. Three English ships and a *barque*, belonging to Sir George Carey, who was afterwards second Lord Hunsdon, were in the West Indies, engaged apparently in trade, when, off Cape Corrientes, they fell in with six Spanish vessels, four of which were large. The English promptly attacked the three ships, two of which were named *Hopewell* and *Swallow*, engaging one, and the *barque*, named the *Content*, engaging the other of the two biggest Spaniards. After some fighting, the three English ships, for some reasons not fully explained, drew off, leaving the little *Content* to her fate. For three hours, after she had got away from her original opponent, she fought the two smallest Spanish vessels. She then maintained a running fight with two of the large and one of the small ships, endeavouring meanwhile to get into shallow water by using her sweeps.

The Spaniards, when they could no longer follow her with their deeper craft, double-manned the small vessel, and towed and rowed her after the *Content*. The Englishman was being slowly forced between the big ships and the shore, and was in a most precarious position, when a lucky shot from her temporarily disabled one of the larger Spaniards. This accident freed her, and enabled her to make an offing; but no sooner had she done so than she fell in with two fresh Spanish galleys, one of which presently tried to board. But the *Content* drove off her enemies on two occasions, and at last, after a contest which lasted, with intermissions, from 7 a.m. until 11 p.m., made her escape with a loss, strange to say, of but two men wounded, though her hull and rigging were cut to pieces. She had no more than twenty-three officers and men on board, and of these only thirteen took part in the action, the rest being below. (Hakluyt, pt. iii. The *Content's* master was Nicholas Liste.)

Another gallant affair was the action fought by the *Centurion*, Turkey merchant, Robert Bradshaw, master, with five Spanish galleys, near the Gut of Gibraltar. Three vessels simultaneously tried to board her, but she drove them all off, and, after more than five hours, induced them to leave her. Bradshaw, whose crew consisted of forty-eight men and boys, lost four killed and ten wounded. (Hakluyt, ii.)

Attempts against Spanish treasure and Spanish treasure ships remained for many years among the most attractive ventures for English seamen. One of these attempts was organised in 1592 by Sir Walter Ralegh and his friends, with assistance from the queen's government. Ralegh's original plan seems to have been either to await the homecoming Spanish fleet in the Atlantic or to cross to the Isthmus of Darien and seize the town of Panama, where the Spaniards were accustomed to assemble treasure, prior to shipping it home by way of the East Indies. Sir Walter was at the time in a restless and dissatisfied condition, owing to the queen's favour for him having diminished, and he may have thought it necessary to achieve some new exploit in order to reinstate himself.

Two only of her majesty's ships, the *Garland*, of 700 tons, 300 men, and 45 guns, and the *Foresight*, of 300 tons, 120 men, and 37 guns, participated in this expedition. With them were associated thirteen armed merchant vessels. Sir Walter Ralegh, in the first instance, took chief command, but, as will be seen, returned ere the adventure had fairly begun, and was superseded by Frobiser. Captain Robert Crosse commanded the *Foresight*, and the land forces on board the squadron were under Sir John Burgh, although he also exercised some kind of naval direction. (Sir John Burgh, a descendant of the famous Hubert de Burgh, was third son of William, fifth Baron de Burgh. He was killed in action on March 7th, 1595, being then in his fifty-third year, and lies buried in Westminster Abbey.)

After two or three months' detention by contrary winds, the expedition sailed on May 1st; but on the day following, Sir Martin Frobiser, in the Lord Admiral's pinnace *Disdain*, overtook it, bringing from Elizabeth letters revoking Ralegh's command in favour of Frobiser, and commanding Ralegh to return. Sir Walter seems to have been hurt and disappointed, and to have determined to proceed in defiance of orders; but when, upon reaching the latitude of Cape Finisterre, he learnt that the Spaniards had received intelligence of his preparations, and had, in consequence, decided that none of their ships should leave America that year, (judging from the result, this intelligence was false), he quitted the squadron and went home.

SIR MARTIN FROBISER, KT.

His departure caused much confusion, many of the merchant captains never having undertaken, and being unwilling, to serve under Frobiser. Several, therefore, quitted the squadron, and cruised on their own account; but before they separated they took, off the coast of Spain, a Biscayan ship of 600 tons, laden with ironwork, and sent her to England. After the parting, Sir John Burgh captured a fly-boat, which, however, cost him a long chase to the southward, and drew him within sight of a considerable Spanish fleet, which was to seaward of him, and which threatened to hem him in with the shore. He nevertheless escaped by the exercise of superior seamanship, and rejoined the *Foresight* and one other vessel which had been placed by Frobiser under his command, with orders to cruise to the Azores. Frobiser himself, with three or four ships, remained off the Spanish coast, and his craft being all indifferent sailers, did but little.

Taking several *caravels* on their passage, Sir John Burgh and Captain Crosse reached Flores, and there fell in with three ships belonging to the Earl of Cumberland's expedition, (this was the fifth of the earl's expeditions), which were in chase of a *carrack*. The Portuguese crew, despairing of escape, ran this *carrack* ashore, took out some of her cargo, and set her on fire; but the English, landing a hundred men, extinguished the flames, and saved part of the lading. They also captured the *carrack's* purser, who was by threats induced to admit that another carrack had been ordered to make the island, and was probably in the neighbourhood.

Sir John Burgh joined his friends in the search for this vessel, and the ships of the two commanders were so disposed northward and southward, on a line about seven leagues westward of Flores, as to cover and observe one hundred and twenty or one hundred and thirty miles of sea.

Thus, the united squadrons lay, from June 29th to August 3rd, when some *carracks* being sighted, a sharp engagement presently ensued with them. The English were still scattered, and the enemy appears to have concentrated on the ships of Sir John Burgh and of those captains nearest to him. Sir John himself was reduced to an almost sinking condition, and might have been taken had not Captain Robert Crosse, in H.M.S. *Foresight*, (some accounts say *Providence*; but Crosse's ship was the *Foresight*), placed himself athwart the threatened vessel's stern, and gallantly borne the brunt of the attack for three hours. This gave time for other English ships to come up. How many *carracks* were originally engaged does not appear, but it would seem that ere the bulk of the

English forces arrived on the scene, all save one of the enemy had withdrawn from the fight. Crosse then carried that remaining one by boarding. She proved to be the *Madre de Dios*, a seven-decked ship, (among these seven decks were, of course, included the numerous superimposed short decks, forming the lofty stern-castle or poop), measuring one hundred and sixty-five feet from stem to stern, and carrying six hundred men, and a miscellaneous cargo valued, upon its arrival in England, and after the vessel had been partially looted, at £150,000. The *Madre de Dios*, which was of 1600 tons' burthen, was brought to England. Most of the profits of the venture were confiscated by the queen, in spite of the fact that only two of her ships had been concerned, and that of these the smaller alone had had a hand in the taking of the *carrack*. The adventuring merchants were, in consequence, greatly discontented.

Don Alonso de Bazan, who had been directed by his sovereign to proceed direct to Flores to await the coming of the carracks, had disobeyed his instructions, and had sailed instead, with twenty-three galleons, to St. Michael's, for which he had a consignment of guns, intending to go on to Flores later. When he heard of what had occurred, he pursued the English resolutely enough for a hundred leagues, but failing to catch them, he was, upon his return to Spain, and in spite of his great previous services, broken for his disobedience and negligence.

Cumberland's fifth expedition, which had thus united with Burgh, consisted of five vessels, none of which belonged to the navy. The earl did not accompany it, but gave the command to Captain Norton.

Other expeditions of 1502, were Christopher Newport's privateering voyage, in the course of which Ocoa, and two other towns in what is now Haiti, were sacked, Puerto Carballo's, in the Bay of Honduras, was plundered, and several ships were taken or destroyed; and William King's voyage to the Gulf of Mexico. This was not less successful than Newport's venture, though King's operations were confined to the sea. The *Amity*, of London, Thomas White master, on her way home from a voyage to Barbary, fell in with two Spanish vessels, both of which, after a very stubborn fight, he took. They proved to be laden with quicksilver, wine, missals, and indulgences, and wen; extremely valuable prizes.

The year 1593 witnessed the setting out of Richard Hawkyns's expedition to the South Sea. The following year saw the inception of Lancaster and Vernier's expedition to Brazil, and of Dudley's voyage to Trinidad.

Few purely naval events occurred in 1593, the year of the Treaty of Melun; but, in the course of it, the Earl of Cumberland went to sea in command of his sixth privateering expedition, with H.M. ships *Golden Lion* and *Bonaventure*, and seven armed vessels, and with Sir William Monson and Sir Edward Yorke as his seconds. Monson records that his ship, the *Lion*, during this cruise, obliged twelve foreign "hulks" to strike to her, in spite of their refusal to do so until they were forced. The earl, on account of illness, had to return prematurely; but three of his smaller vessels went on to the West Indies, and there did a good deal of damage to the Spaniards.

Even prior to the conclusion of the Treaty of Melun, friendship between England and France, to the prejudice of Spain, had become very close and cordial, and Elizabeth had sent Sir John Norreys with three thousand men to co-operate with Henry IV. against the League, and against the Spaniards who were actively supporting the League in the neighbourhood of Brest. Henry, fearing lest Spain might dispatch naval as well as military assistance to his domestic enemies, persuaded Elizabeth, in 1594, to send a fleet to blockade Brest by sea. The League had by that time collapsed, owing to Henry's abjuration of Protestantism in 1593, and Norreys, with his troops, had been withdrawn. But the Due de Mercosur, who had pretensions to the independent sovereignty of Brittany, and whose only hope lay in Spanish help, was still hostile to Henry, and rather than submit, delivered to his Spanish friends Blavet, now Port Louis, in Morbihan, and winked at, if he did not actually facilitate, their seizure of the peninsula of Camaret, between the Bay of Douarnenez and the roadstead of Brest.

The Spaniards began to strongly fortify themselves there; and as their position threatened Brest and Le Conquêt, and bade fair presently to enable them to obtain the mastery of the chief naval station on the Atlantic seaboard of France, Norreys was ordered back to assist Marshal d'Aumont on the land side, and Sir Martin Frobiser, with a squadron, was directed to co-operate from the sea for the expulsion of interlopers who, had they ever securely established themselves in Brest, must have become highly dangerous neighbours for England.

Frobiser's force, according to Monson, included only four of her majesty's ships, (*Vanguard*, 500 tons, Sir Martin Frobiser; *Rainbow*, 500 tons, Captain Thomas Fenner; *Dreadnought*, 400 tons, Captain Alexander Clifford; and *Quittance*, 200 tons, Captain Savile), but to these there seem to have been added six, or possibly more, armed merchantmen. The main Spanish work was at Crozon, and to the Bay of Crozon Frobiser proceeded in October. Norreys and D'Aumont, in the meantime, reduced Morlaix and Quimper, and on November 1st, arrived before Crozon and opened communications with the squadron.

The attack on the fort was at once begun, and prosecuted with great energy; but the defence was not less sturdy, and the loss of life on both sides was great. The final and successful assault was made with the help of Frobiser and the officers and seamen of his squadron. In the course of it, Sir Martin received a ball in the side. The wound was not in itself very serious, but it was rendered so by the inexperience of the surgeons; and although Frobiser brought his squadron back to Plymouth, he survived but a few weeks after he had landed. (Dying in January, 1595.)

He was one of the most able seamen of an age which produced an unusual number of distinguished sailors; his courage and resource were remarkable, and he seems to have been in private life an admirable character; but he was blunt in manner, and so exceedingly strict a disciplinarian that he was never popular with his commands. It is probable, from the fact that no holograph letters of his appear to be extant, that he had been ill-educated, and that he could write little if any more than his name.

The Earl of Cumberland's seventh expedition left Plymouth on April 6th, 1594. The squadron consisted of the armed ships, *Royal Exchange*, 250 tons, George Cave, master; *Mayflower*, 250 tons, William Anthony, master; *Samson*, Nicholas Downton, master; a caravel and a pinnace. It made for the Azores, and, about ten days after having sighted them, fell in with a large and very richly laden Spanish carrack. The *Royal Exchange, Mayflower*, and *Samson* engaged her simultaneously at close quarters, but had to cast off from her, as she presently caught fire, and the flames threatened to involve them also, and actually did them some damage.

The *carrack* finally blew up, very few out of about 1100 souls on board being saved. In the struggle, William Anthony was killed, and George Cave was so badly wounded that he died in consequence after his return to England. The expedition refreshed at Flores, and, on June 20th, met with and engaged another large carrack. She beat them off, yet not without difficulty, and, having suffered severely, the English vessels made their way back to England.

In the meantime, there were apprehensions of renewed Spanish attempts upon a large scale against England. There was some small foundation for the rumours which prevailed, but the report received unmerited attention, especially in Ireland, where local disaffection was always in haste to credit foreign enemies with more than Irish hatred for Elizabeth and her representatives.

These apprehensions led to the fitting out, in the summer of 1594, of a small English squadron, which, designed to cruise in home waters, effected nothing, and met with no extraordinary adventures; for, although an insignificant Spanish force of four galleys did, in fact, make a descent in July upon Mount's Bay, and burnt Mousehole, Newlyn, and Penzance, the English squadron was not then in the neighbourhood, and the enemy escaped without interruption. The affair was relatively of small importance, and did not cost a single Englishman either his life or his liberty. It was, indeed, a mere momentary raid.

Another squadron, designed to act against the Spanish possessions in the West Indies and Central America, was placed in 1595 under the command of Sir Francis Drake and Sir John Hawkyns, and consisted of six-and-twenty vessels, of which the following, and possibly others, were ships of her majesty:—

Ships.			Tons.	Men.	Guns.	Commanders.
Defiance	.	.	500	250	46	Sir Francis Drake.
Garland	.	.	700	300	45	Sir John Hawkyns.
Hope	.	.	600	250	48	Captain Gilbert Yorke.
Bonaventure	.	.	600	250	47	Captain Troughton.
Foresight	.	.	300	160	37	Captain Wynter.
Adventure	.	.	250	120	26	Captain Thomas Drake.

The land forces embarked were commanded by Sir Thomas Baskerville.

This squadron was fitted out upon the express recommendation of Drake and Hawkyns. Both were, no doubt, animated by a sincere and patriotic desire to injure Spain, as well as by the personal desire of gain and glory; but Hawkyns was probably influenced by yet another motive. His son Richard, in the *Dainty* had been captured by the Spaniards on June 21st, 1594, and was still detained by them; and the father may have hoped to take some distinguished Spaniard who would form a suitable exchange. (Sir H. Hawkyns's *Observations on Voyage to the South Seas.*)

The original intention was to proceed to Nombre de Dios, land there, and march across the isthmus to Panama, in order to seize a

116

Spanish treasure reported to have been brought thither from Peru. But five days before the squadron sailed, the commanders were advised by the queen that, according to news received from Spain, a treasure ship dismasted had put in for shelter at Puerto Rico; and they were ordered to call at that island on their way, and, if possible, to possess themselves of the disabled vessel and her contents, Puerto Rico being but weakly defended.

The squadron left Plymouth on August 28th, 1595, (also the year of the departure of Sir Walter Ralegh for Guiana), and arrived off Grand Canary on September 27th. Drake and Baskerville were of opinion that the place should be attempted in order that the ships might be victualled. Hawkyns desired to proceed at once; but as the people were importunate, provisions short, and Baskerville confident that he could gain his object in four days, Hawkyns reluctantly consented to an attack being made.

It was, as he had anticipated, unsuccessful; and the squadron, no doubt somewhat discouraged by the initial failure, steered for Dominica, where it arrived on October 29th. Time was wasted there and at Guadaloupe in trafficking with the natives, and in building pinnaces; and opportunity was given to the Spaniards, not only to learn all that was intended against them, but also to concert measures of defence. The enemy captured a small English vessel, the *Francis*, (on October 30th), which had straggled from the main body, and by torture forced her master and seamen to disclose the English plans. They then forwarded the intelligence with all haste to Puerto Rico, where the treasure was promptly buried; and they warned both the islands and the main of the impending blow.

Thus, when, on November 12th, Drake and Hawkyns found themselves before San Juan de Puerto Rico, the place was prepared to receive them. As the squadron anchored, it was fired at by the forts, and Sir Nicholas Clifford, second in command of the troops, was mortally wounded. A still heavier blow to the expedition was the death of Sir John Hawkyns, which occurred on the same day. According to Hakluyt, this great commander had been dispirited by the knowledge that the capture of the *Francis* could not but result in the disclosure of all his plans to the enemy, and had from that moment sickened. (Monson attributes Sir John's death to causes which could not have influenced it.)

The Spaniards had blocked the mouth of the port by sinking a skip across the centre of the channel, and by fixing booms thence to the forts on shore; and within they had five well-armed and well-manned vessels; but on the evening of November 13th, Baskerville, manning and arming the pinnaces and boats of the squadron to the number of five-and-twenty, forced a way in under a heavy fire from the Spanish guns, and set fire to the five ships. A most obstinate fight was carried on for some time in the harbour. The English, however, were finally repulsed, and, concluding that any further attempt would be equally futile, they re-embarked, and sailed across to the mainland.

On December 1st, they burnt La Hacha, in the modern United States of Columbia, in spite of the willingness of the inhabitants to ransom the place for thirty-four thousand *ducats*. Other places in the neighbourhood were treated with similar barbarity, and some prisoners and pillage were secured. Santa Marta was taken and burnt on December 19th, but no loot was found there. The Spaniards at Nombre de Dios made some resistance; but that place also fell on December 28th, and with it were captured several vessels, and some silver, gold, jewels, and money.

From Nombre de Dios, a landing party of seven hundred and fifty soldiers, under Sir Thomas Baskerville, started across the isthmus for Panama, but, finding the march very arduous, being galled by fire from unseen foes, and learning that forts obstructed their passage, the troops returned, and, harassed and half-starved, rejoined the squadron on January 2nd, 1596.

The misfortune affected the health of Drake, who fell ill with dysentery. He was, nevertheless, contemplating an attack upon Puerto Bello when, on January 28th, death overtook him. (Monson says that Drake "grew melancholy upon this disappointment, and suddenly, and, I hope, naturally, died." He seems to have suspected a violent death, but upon what grounds is unknown.) His body, enclosed in a leaden coffin, found a fitting resting-place in the sea; and the expedition, deprived of both its admirals, set sail for England.

Thus, within a space of less than three months, did a single and only very moderately successful expedition cost England the lives of two of her most notable sea captains.

Hawkyns was a man of unusual and cultivated ability, and of exceptional skill as a seaman. Although his early life had been stormy, and his whole career had been adventurous in the highest degree, he remained to a large extent unspoilt to the end, in that he was merciful in action, ready to forgive, and ever a strict observer of his word. Unlike some of his distinguished naval contemporaries, he was cautious, reserved, and slow in making up his mind. The navy, of which he was treasurer for seventeen years, owed, and still owes, much to him; and although he had faults, chief among which may be ranked extreme bluntness of manner, jealousy, and an excessive love of money, he was withal a man of great and remarkable character.

Drake possessed at least equal ability, but had little acquired knowledge of many arts save those connected with navigation and war, in which he stood unrivalled. Less cautious and provident than Hawkyns, he was also less greedy of gain, and, indeed, appears to have generally set the welfare of his queen and country far above his own private advantage. He had many fine qualities, most of which were expressed in his person, which was that of a healthy, strong, and genial adventurer; and among his defects there seem to have been none much more serious than love of display, occasional quickness of temper, lack of reserve when among his equals, and a habit of boasting.

This fatal expedition was brought home by Sir Thomas Baskerville and Captain Troughton. A Spanish fleet had been sent from Europe to intercept the squadron, and lay waiting for it near the Isla de Pinos, off Cuba. There were twenty sail of Spaniards in company when the English wen; sighted; and, the forces on each side being nearly equal, a hot action resulted. After about two hours' firing, the enemy sheered off, having lost one vessel by fire, and having had several badly mauled; and the English, proceeding, reached England without further adventure in May, 1596. (The year of Keymis's Voyage to Guiana, of Shirley's expedition to the West Indies, and of Parker's cruise to the West Indies.)

The year 1595 witnessed two other expeditions of some importance. One was the voyage of a little squadron under Amyas Preston and George Somers to the West Indies. It was a privateering venture, and, in the course of it, the island of Porto Santo, near Madeira, was taken and pillaged, and considerable damage was done to the Spaniards on the coast of what is now Venezuela. The other was the eighth of the Earl of Cumberland's voyages. For the occasion, the earl had built the *Scourge of Malice*, 900 tons, at Deptford. His intention was to personally lead the expedition, and, indeed, he actually started with it, but was recalled by the queen.

The other ships were the *Alcedo*, Captain William Monson; the *Anthony*, David Jarret, master; and an old "frigate." Cumberland's appointment of Captain Langton to take his place as "admiral" disgusted Monson, who left the other ships, and cruised, but to no effect, on his own account. The remaining vessels made several prizes, but narrowly escaped falling into the hands of a large Spanish fleet.

119

It is interesting to note here that the *Scourge of Malice*, a famous ship in her day, was sold, after Cumberland had done with her, to the East India Company, and, re-named the *Dragon*, distinguished herself against the Portuguese in the Eastern seas in the time of James I.

Rumours of a renewed intention on the part of Spain to invade England still persisted. Indeed, Spain had apparently forgotten the catastrophe of the Armada, and, there is little doubt, harboured some fresh designs against Elizabeth, and particularly against her dominions in Ireland. Yet it is more than possible that the great English expedition of 1596 would not have sailed when, and struck as, it did, but for the fact that, owing to French mismanagement and folly in declining proffered English help, the Spaniards succeeded in making themselves masters of Calais. This stirred England, just in the same way as the probability of a Spanish occupation of Brest had stirred it in 1594. Preparations for an expedition against Cadiz were in progress before Calais fell. After the fall of Calais, they were hastened to such good effect that the fleet sailed about six weeks later.

The ships of Her Majesty engaged in this important adventure were—

Ships.	Tons.	Men.	Guns.	Commanders.
Ark Royal . .	800	400	55	The Lord High Admiral, Joint-Adml. Captain Amyas Preston.
Repulse . . .	700	350	50	Robert, Earl of Essex, Joint-Admiral. Captain William Monson.
Mere Honour . .	800	400	41	Lord Thomas Howard, Vice-Admiral.
Warspite . .	600	300	29	Sir Walter Ralegh, Rear-Admiral.
Lion . . .	500	250	60	Sir Robert Southwell.
Rainbow . .	500	250	26	Sir Francis Vere.[2]
Nonpareil . .	500	250	56	Sir Robert Dudley.[3]
Vanguard . .	500	250	31	Sir John Wingfeild.
Mary Rose . .	600	250	39	Sir George Carew.[4]
Dreadnought . .	400	200	41	Alexander Clifford.[5]
Swiftsure . .	400	200	41	Robert Crosse.[5]
Quittance . .	200	108	25	Sir George Gifford.
Tremontana . .	140	70	21	— King.
Crane . . .	200	108	24	

[2] Son of Geoffrey de Vere, and grandson of the fifteenth Earl of Oxford. He wrote 'The Commentaries of Sir F. Vere' (published in 1657). Dying in 1608, he was buried at Westminster.

[3] Son of Robert, Earl of Leicester, by Douglas Howard, sister of the Lord High Admiral. He married as his third wife a daughter of Sir Robert Southwell. His great nautical work, 'L'Arcano del Mare,' was written while he was serving the Grand Duke of Tuscany, with whom he took refuge upon failing to establish his legitimacy, his father having denied the marriage.

[4] Created Baron Carew, of Clopton, 1605, and later Earl of Totness; author of 'Hibernia Pacata.' He died Master of the Ordnance, March 27th, 1629.

[5] Knighted for this service.

—with probably three more, making seventeen in all. (There were originally to be only twelve ships of her majesty, twelve ships of the City, and twenty ships of the Netherlands; but the force was considerably increased. Cal. of Hatfield MSS.). With these, according to Speed, there were associated three vessels belonging to the Lord High Admiral, twenty-four belonging to the States-General, and armed merchantmen and victuallers sufficient to bring up the total number of sail to 150. De Jonge, (*Nederlandsche Zeewesen),* says that eighteen of the twenty-four Dutch vessels were of from 200 to 400 tons burden, and carried from sixteen to twenty-four guns apiece, with from 100 to 130 men. The contingent was under the orders of Jonkheer Jan van Duijvenvoorde, Lord of Warmond and Admiral of Holland; but the English Lord High Admiral was naval commander-in-chief, and for the first time a Dutch fleet obeyed an English flag-officer.

******

For the first time, also, the Dutch fleet seems to have carried a regular national flag to sea. A Resolution of the States-General of April 5th, 1596, directed that the arms of the States, a lion and arrows, should be worn on the colours, which were a tricolour of orange, white and blue. The flag was afterwards changed, red being substituted for orange on account of its superior visibility, and the arms being omitted. In Tromp's time, the orange (or red), white and blue flag was known as the prince's flag, since it represented the colours of the Prince of Orange.

******

On board the fleet there were, in addition to the Dutch, 7360 landsmen and 6772 seamen. The troops were under the Lord High Admiral and Essex, as joint generals. (This arrangement foreshadows the appointment under the Commonwealth of 'Admirals and Generals at Sea,' and, to some extent, the later practice of giving naval officers concurrent commissions in the Marines.)

Queen Elizabeth's instructions to Howard of Effingham and Essex (Cotton MSS.), may be briefly summarised. The generals were advised that the armament had been originally collected because of the prevalence of reports that Spain was preparing a greater Armada than that of 1588 to invade England, and to aid the Irish rebels. The reports had turned out to be exaggerated. Moreover, the Spanish fleet had been scattered, partly for the pursuit of Drake and partly for the reinforcement of the Indies. But there was still danger that the Irish rebels might be assisted, and that might best be prevented by the cap-

JAN VAN DUIJVENVOORDE, ADMIRAL OF HOLLAND.

ture or destruction of "some good number" of the King of Spain's ships in his ports.

The duties of the generals would, therefore, be to discover the strength, whereabouts, and designs of the Spanish Navy, and the nature and quantity of stores collected in Spain for purposes of aggression over sea; to destroy any vessels intended for Ireland, the Narrow Seas, or Calais, to generally injure the naval power of Spain, to avoid the unnecessary hazarding of ships and men, to take undefended towns, especially if they should be understood to contain treasure; not to injure non–combatants, and to preserve all booty for her majesty's disposal.

The two generals were to be assisted by a council of five, composed of Lord Thomas Howard, Sir Walter Ralegh, Sir Francis Vere, Sir Conyers Clifford, and Sir George Carew, (the generals had power to add to this Council); and the proceedings of the generals and council were to be from time to time recorded for the queen's information by Anthony Ashley, one of the clerks of her Privy Council, who would accompany the fleet for the purpose. (Anthony Ashley grandfather of the first Earl of Shaftesury, became Secretary to the Privy Council under James I., was made a baronet in 1622, and died in 1628.) If, after the attainment of the main objects of the expedition, the generals should learn of the home-coming of any rich Spanish carracks from the Indies, they might exercise; their discretion as to effecting their capture; but the fleet was not to be kept abroad longer than needful.

Before the sailing of the expedition, the queen's attitude towards it, and especially towards Essex, changed; and, almost at the last moment, the two leaders received letters of recall. These were withdrawn only upon the urgent remonstrances of Lord Thomas Howard, Sir Francis Vere, and other subordinate officers. (*Sir Francis Vere: Elizabeth I's Greatest Soldier and the Eighty Years War* by Clements R. Markham is also published in book and kindle format by Leonaur.)

The instructions issued by Howard of Effingham and Essex to the captains of the fleet will be found at length in the previous chapter.

★★★★★★

It is noteworthy that in all the documents relating to this expedition, Essex is given precedence over Howard, although the latter was Lord High Admiral, and the former was new to naval command. The navy was not yet recognised as the senior service.

★★★★★★

Before sailing, the joint generals also published in Spanish, French, Italian, and Dutch a manifesto "to all Christian people," setting forth the causes and objects of the expedition, proclaiming friendship to neutrals, and hostility to Spain and her allies, and requiring all who might have aided Philip in the past to withdraw from him upon pain of being made to suffer for their continued adherence to Elizabeth's enemies.

The fleet sailed from Plymouth on June 1st, 1596. With a north-easterly breeze, it quickly made Cape Ortegal; and there, being off the enemy's coast, was organised for instant action. We do not know what was its formation; but Monson says that the *True Love*, the *Lion's Whelp*, and the *Witness,* the three best sailers in the command, were dispatched ahead to look out for Spanish scouts or advice-boats, and to prevent any such from returning with news of the approaching danger. (It is probable that these were the three vessels belonging to the Lord High Admiral. A *Lion's Whelp* was bought from him for the navy in 1601. Pipe Off. Accts. 2239.)

By way of additional precaution, a course was taken well out of sight of land. Every captain had been already provided with sealed instructions, to be opened only in case of separation from the fleet, or after rounding Cape St. Vincent, directing him to make rendezvous off Cadiz; and he had been ordered, in the event of his capture by the enemy appearing imminent, to sink these instructions.

On June 10th, the three advanced ships, two of which were commanded by Richard Leveson and Charles, Lord Mountjoy, respectively, fell in with and took three Hamburg fly-boats, fourteen days out from Cadiz. From them they learnt that the garrison had no suspicions of the intentions of the English.

★★★★★★

Richard Leveson, of Lilleshall, born 1570, served as volunteer in the *Ark* against the Armada, and was knighted for his service in the Cadiz expedition. He died in 1605, Admiral of the Narrow Seas and Vice-Admiral of England. He had married in 1587 Margaret, a daughter of Lord Howard of Effingham. He lies buried at Wolverhampton.

Charles, Lord Mountjoy, second son of the sixth Lord Mountjoy, born 1563. He had been knighted in 1587, and had succeeded his elder brother in 1594. In 1603, he was made Lord Lieutenant of Ireland, and created Earl of Devonshire. He died in 1606. But in some accounts, it is said that not Lord Mountjoy, but Sir Christopher Blount was with the advanced squadron.

★★★★★★

ROBERT DEVEREUX, EARL OF ESSEX

On June 12th, the *Swan*, a London ship, commanded by Sir Richard Weston, was added to the advanced squadron. She presently came up with and fought a Flamand fly-boat, homeward bound from the Straits; but the stranger got away, and was next day making for Lisbon with the intention of alarming the Spaniards, when, within a league of the shore, she was fortunately taken by the *John and Francis*, another London ship, commanded by Sir Marmaduke Darell. Thus, everything contributed to keep the Spaniards in ignorance of the English design; and on June 18th, when an Irish craft returning from Cadiz was spoken, the generals had the satisfaction of learning from her that the people of the town were tranquil in their fancied security, that the garrison was small, and that the port was full of vessels richly laden for the Indies.

Owing to some miscalculation on the part of the masters, the fleet arrived off Cadiz a few hours sooner than had been anticipated, early in the morning of June 20th. At a council held previously, it had been determined to land on the peninsula of San Sebastian, the westernmost point of the Isle of Leon, on which Cadiz stands; and the fleet therefore dropped anchor off the peninsula; but, the wind being brisk and the sea high, and four galleys lying in such a position under the land as to be able to intercept incoming boats, nothing was that day attempted.

After some hours had been spent in communications between the generals, a scheme, which Monson says that he had himself recommended, was resolved upon. The project of first landing was given up, and it was decided to begin operations by boldly entering the harbour and seizing the shipping.

Essex demanded to have the honour of leading the way in; but the Lord High Admiral had been strictly charged by the queen not to suffer the earl to expose himself unnecessarily, and Essex had to appear to submit. That night the order of attack was arranged, the posts of honour being assigned to Lord Thomas Howard, (who, as the *Mere Honour* drew too much water, went on board the *Nonpareil*), Sir Walter Ralegh, Sir Robert Southwell, Sir Francis Vere, Sir George Carew, Captain Crosse, and others of less note.

At dawn on June 21st, these officers, having rounded the north end of the island, passed Fort San Felipe and the galleys moored near it, and, in the face of a heavy fire, made for the mass of Spanish ships within the port.

★★★★★★

Monson says that Ralegh, having entered, anchored out of gunshot of the Spaniards, and urged lack of water as an excuse for not going farther in; and that not until the *Rainbow* had passed him did Ralegh weigh and proceed.

★★★★★★

These fell slowly back, but the galleys, which were so stationed as to present their heavy bow armament to the advancing English, and which were covered by the town batteries behind them, very severely galled the advance, and especially inconvenienced Sir Francis Vere in the *Rainbow*. Essex, who witnessed this from the northern side of the entrance to the port, could no longer be restrained, and gallantly threw himself into the fight.

CADIZ HARBOUR.

Howard of Effingham, at about the same time, entered in a pinnace, being unwilling to risk the *Ark Royal* in such narrow waters. The English pressed forward steadily, driving the Spanish galleons and merchantmen up the harbour past more galleys, which were moored in Puntal Road, and which fought furiously. The Isle of Leon was joined to the mainland by a bridge at Suaco. Upon reaching the neighbourhood of the bridge, the fugitive Spanish vessels fell into great confusion. There was, however, a narrow canal whereby they could reach the open sea on the south side of the island. Entrance to this canal seems to have been obtainable by means of a swing opening near the island end of the bridge. (Monson says that the fleeing ships broke through the bridge itself.) Into the canal the fleeing ships crowded pell-mell, only to discover that at the seaward end of it was stationed Sir John Wingfield in the *Vanguard*. A good many, however, succeeded in thus escaping, though Sir John was exceedingly vigilant and arrested several.

In the meantime, very hot fighting between the English and Spanish men-of-war continued in Puntal Road, where Howard himself was engaged. But towards noon the action slackened, (it did not wholly cease until 4 p.m.), many of the Spanish vessels having by that hour been destroyed by the English fire, or sunk or set fire to by their own people to save them from capture. The Spanish flagship *San Felipe*, a ship of 1500 tons' burden, blew up and, by her explosion, destroyed two or three craft that lay near her. So rapidly did the flames make progress that the Spaniards, having fired their vessels, often had no time to take to their boats, and, throwing themselves into the water, would have perished, had they not been taken up by the English. Numbers, however, were drowned.

Two ships only of any importance were taken, the *San Mateo* and the *San Andres*, galleons of 1200 tons. These were saved by the exertions of the Lord High Admiral and Sir Thomas Gerard, and for several years afterwards they figured in the English navy as the *St. Matthew* and the *St. Andrew*. (Sir Thomas Gerard was created Baron Gerard in 1603. He was at the time a colonel of the land forces. He died in 1618. It may be of interest to add that he returned home in the *St. Mathew*.) All the rest, except those which escaped by way of the canal, were sunk, burnt, or driven ashore.

While these events were in progress, the Dutch contingent gallantly attacked and carried Puntal, and Essex soon afterwards landed eight hundred men a league from the city, with a view to storming it on the land side. (The landing-place, according to Monson, was commanded by Puntal Fort, but the garrison promptly abandoned that work. Monson also declares that Essex landed without Howard's privity.) But first Sir Conyers Clifford, Sir Christopher Blount, and Sir Thomas Gerard were dispatched with a party to Suaco to destroy the entrance to the canal by which the fugitive ships had escaped, and to cut the bridge in order to prevent the arrival of succours from the mainland.

When these measures of precaution had been carried out, Essex advanced upon Cadiz. The town was fortified on the south by means of a wall running across the island, and from this wall the enemy kept up a troublesome fire upon the English. But it is probable that the wall was enfiladed by the guns of the; English ships in the port, and that it could not have been held easily. A body of about five hundred Spaniards outside the wall retired precipitately, and was so closely followed up that the attackers almost succeeded in entering with it.

Sir Francis Vere, at the head of a small body, was one of the first to reach the gate; and while he was forcing it, another party, led by some young military officers, scaled the wall. In a few moments, the English were in the narrow streets. From the flat roofs of the houses the inhabitants aided those of their friends who still struggled below, by flinging down stones, and by firing occasional shots; but the defenders were gradually driven into the market-place, where, at length, the fight ceased. Such of the garrison as retreated to the castle and the townhouse surrendered the next day, promising 520,000 *ducats* for their lives, (Stow says 620,000), and giving forty hostages for the payment of that sum.

The loss of life on the English side was exceedingly small; but Sir John Wingfield was killed while serving ashore, and Sir Walter Ralegh was wounded.

Immediately after the place had fallen, the generals, by proclamation, ordered that no violence should be offered to unoffending citizens; and that the women, priests, and children should be conveyed across the harbour to Puerto Santa Maria in English vessels. Essex in person superintended the embarkation of the ladies, suffering them to carry off their richest apparel and jewels, and preserving them from all insult.

Ralegh's wound was not serious, and he was at once detached by the Lord High Admiral to proceed with a light squadron to Puerto Reale, to burn such merchantmen as had taken refuge there. The Spaniards offered Howard 2,000,000 *ducats*, (Hakluyt and Harris say 2,500,000), if he would stay his hand; but the Lord High Admiral answered that he had come to burn and not to ransom. The short time spent in negotiation, however, enabled the Duke of Medina Sidonia to remove a certain amount of goods from some of the ships ere they were fired.

The loss to Spain was estimated at 20,000,000 *ducats*. Besides the merchantmen which were destroyed and the two large galleons which were taken, thirteen men-of-war, eleven ships freighted for the Indies, and thirteen miscellaneous vessels were sunk, burnt, or bilged. About twelve hundred pieces of ordnance were also taken or sunk. Nearly sixty naval and military officers, whose names are given at length by Camden, were knighted in consequence of their behaviour upon the occasion; and Howard of Effingham, for the service, was subsequently created Earl of Nottingham.

Having gained the town, the leaders discussed what they should do with it. Essex desired to retain it, and offered to hold it with four hundred men and three months' provisions. Sir Francis Vere and Admiral Duijvenvoorde were also of opinion that it should be garrisoned and kept; but Howard and all the other senior officers were opposed to the project, and anxious to return to England. The place, therefore, was given over to pillage, its fortifications were razed, and many of its principal buildings, the churches excepted, were burnt.

On July 5th, the fleet weighed again and proceeded to Faro in Algarve, a hundred miles to the westward. The town had been deserted, the inhabitants carrying off nearly all their goods, and little spoil beyond the bishop's library was taken. (This booty fell to Essex, who succeeded in retaining it in spite of Elizabeth's efforts to secure it. He afterwards gave part of it to Sir Thomas Bodley, and so it became the nucleus of the Bodleian Library.)

Essex was not wholly satisfied with what had been done, and suggested sailing to the Azores, and there lying in wait for the homecoming East India *carracks*. Lord Thomas Howard and Admiral Duijvenvoorde concurred; but all the other officers seem to have been beset by a fear of losing what they had gained, and by a desire to hasten home to enjoy it. Essex thereupon asked that those ships which were short of stores or had many sick on board might be sent to England, together with the land forces, and that he, with two of her majesty's ships and ten other vessels, might be suffered to go to the Azores and look for the *carracks*. The council would not, however, consent even to this; whereupon Essex insisted upon each member delivering his views in writing, in order that his own attitude might be vindicated.

The sole concession that he succeeded in obtaining was that on the homeward voyage a visit should be paid to Corunna; but neither in Corunna, nor in the neighbouring port of Ferrol, was a single Spanish ship found. Essex, still anxious to effect something more, would have taken Corunna, and attacked such Spanish vessels as were in Santander and San Sebastian. Once more the gallant Duijvenvoorde supported him, and once more the two were overruled. And so, the fleet returned to England, with the two galleons, a hundred brass guns, and an immense amount of very valuable miscellaneous booty. (The fleet reached Plymouth on August 8th, 1696. Essex, who convoyed the *St. Andrew*, and a fly-boat laden with ordnance, arrived two days later.)

Then followed an amusing and undignified struggle for the plunder, most of the officers protesting that little or none had fallen to them, and the queen's commissioners doing their best to secure as much as possible. The queen's anxiety on the subject was probably well reflected in a letter addressed on August 10th from the Council at Greenwich to the joint generals.

In spite of all his efforts to vindicate his conduct, Essex fell into some disfavour at court. Lediard suggests that the uneasiness thus occasioned him may have led him into the extravagant projects which in the end cost him his life. Probably he proved himself at times a difficult colleague of the Lord High Admiral: possibly he often allowed zeal to outrun discretion. But it is abundantly clear that in all he did during the Cadiz expedition he was animated by the best motives, and not by that personal greed which remains a blot upon the record of some of his most noted contemporaries: and the fact that all his proposals for the more complete humiliation of Spain seem to have been supported by Duijvenvoorde, a seaman of experience, is one which speaks very strongly in favour of his general conduct. (Duijvenvoorde was knighted for his services on the occasion. Camden, iii.)

In 1596, Cumberland sent his ninth expedition to sea. He first fitted out the *Scourge of Malice*, obtained the *Dreadnought* from her majesty, and chartered some small craft. With these he sailed, but the *Scourge of Malice* was presently disabled in a storm, and the expedition had to put back. He then fitted out a vessel called the *Ascension*, of 300 tons and thirty-four guns, and dispatched her to cruise under Francis Slingsby. She also was damaged and forced home by a gale, but, sailing again, fought some gallant, though indecisive, actions off Lisbon ere she returned. (Thirty-six sail were reported to have been lost in this storm.)

The immediate effect of the Cadiz expedition was to stimulate Spain to a fresh effort. Philip lost no time in assembling at Lisbon as many ships as he could collect from all parts of his extensive dominions and in taking up such suitable foreign vessels as lay in his ports. The fleet thus formed proceeded in the spring of 1597 to Ferrol, and there received on board a considerable body of troops and a great number of fugitives from Ireland. The intention seems to have been to land all these forces in Ireland; but soon after the fleet had quitted Ferrol it fell in with such terrible weather, and suffered so severely, that it put back, incapable of prosecuting its mission. The attempt is said, by contemporary writers, to have been so secretly and so quickly prepared that the news of its disablement and dispersion actually reached England before the news of its sailing.

The failure, costly though it was, did not deter Philip from at once organising a fresh attempt. He was upon the point of liberating some of his resources by concluding a separate peace with France, which had been the ally of Elizabeth since 1593; there still remained a considerable part of his shattered fleet; there were yet other vessels in his Galician ports; and the state of affairs in Ireland appeared, as before, to invite him thither. This time, however, early news of Philip's intentions reached England, and steps were promptly taken for providing employment for the enemy ere he should be in a condition to sail.

A fleet was fitted out with a view, first, to surprise the Spaniards in Corunna and Ferrol, and then to seize Terceira or some other island of the Azores, so as to secure a base from which to watch for the homecoming Spanish treasure ships from the Indies. The expedition, known as the Voyage to the Islands, was entrusted to the supreme command of the Earl of Essex, who had as his vice-admiral Lord Thomas Howard, as his rear-admiral, Sir Walter Ralegh, and, as general of his land forces, Charles Blount, Lord Mountjoy. Sir Francis Vere went as camp-marshal or, as would now be said, general of a brigade; Sir George Carew as lieutenant of the ordnance, and Sir Christopher Blount as first colonel. Among the volunteers were the Earls of Rutland and Southampton, and Lords Cromwell, Grey de Wilton, and Rich.

★★★★★★

Edward Cromwell, third Baron, he joined in Essex's rebellion, but was pardoned, and lived till 1607.

Thomas Grey, fifteenth Baron Grey de Wilton. Involved in Ralegh's conspiracy, he died in the Tower in 1614.

Robert Rich, third Baron. In 1618 he was created Earl of Warwick, and in the same year died.

★★★★★★

Accounts of the expedition have been left by various participants, including Sir Arthur Gorges, Essex, Lord Thomas Howard, Lord Mountjoy, Sir Walter Ralegh, and others whose relations will be found in Purchas's *Pilgrims*, Sir William Monson, and several more; yet there is some little doubt as to the exact number of her majesty's ships taking part in it, and as to the names of their commanders at different periods. Careful comparison of the lists and statements seems to indicate that the naval portion of the fleet was composed and officered as follows:—

Ships.	Tons.	Guns.	Men.	Commanders.	Military Officers.
Mere Honour [1]	800	400	41	Earl of Essex. Sir Robt. Mansell, Capt.	
Due Repulse [2]	700	350	50	Lord Thos. Howard, V.-A. — Middleton, Capt.	
Warspite . .	600	300	29	Sir Walter Ralegh, R.-A. Sir Arthur Gorges, Capt.	
Garland . .	700	300	45	(?)	Henry, Earl of Southampton.[3]
Defiance . .	500	250	46	Sir Amyas Preston, Capt.	Lord Mountjoy.
Mary Rose .	600	250	39	John Wynter, Capt.	Sir Fras. Vere.
St. Matthew .	1000	500	48	(?)	Sir Geo. Carew.[4]
St. Andrew .	900	400	50	— Throckmorton, Capt.	
Rainbow . .	500	250	26	Sir Wm. Monson, Capt.	
Bonaventure .	600	250	47	Sir Wm. Harvey, Capt.	
Dreadnought .	400	200	41	Sir Wm. Brooke, Capt.	
Swiftsure .	400	200	41	Sir Gelly Meyrick,[5] Capt.	
Antelope [6]	350	160	38	Sir Thos. Vavasour, Capt.	
Nonpareil [7]	500	250	56	Sir Rich. Leveson, Capt.	
Foresight . .	300	160	37	Carew Reynell,[8] Capt.	
Tremontana .	140	70	21	— Fenner, Capt.	
Moon . . .	60	40	9	Edwd. Mitchelburne, Capt.	
Lion . . .	500	250	60	(?)	
Hope [9] . .	600	250	48	(?)	

[1] Essex afterwards shifted his flag to the *Due Repulse.*

[2] Howard afterwards shifted his flag to the *Lion,* which went out with stores after the main fleet had sailed.

[3] Henry Wriothesley, third Earl of Southampton, seems to have gone as a military volunteer, although in Monson's and Gorges's lists he appears as commanding the *Garland.* He was attacked and imprisoned for complicity with Essex, but re-created Earl in 1603, and made a K.G. He died in 1624.

[4] In Gorges's and Monson's lists, Carew figures as commanding the *St. Matthew.* He may have held naval as well as military command.

[5] Son of Rowland Meyrick, Bp. of Bangor, 1559–63; had been knighted for services at Cadiz. He was executed in 1600 for complicity with Essex.

[6] Sir John Gilbert, who did not sail, seems to have been originally appointed to the *Antelope.*

[7] Sir Thos. Vavasour seems to have been originally appointed to the *Nonpareil.*

[8] Fifth son of Rich. Reynell, of East Ogwell, was knighted in 1599 for services in Ireland, and died in 1624.

[9] Sir Rich. Leveson seems to have been originally appointed to the *Hope.*

"Some of her Majesty's small pinnaces" also "attended the fleet." (Account of Gorges).

To the whole force was added a Dutch squadron of ten men-of-war under the command of Admiral van Duijvenvoorde.

The fleet sailed on July 9th, 1597, from Plymouth, but it met with bad weather, was obliged to put back and repair damages, and did not sail again until August 17th. Monson says that, before the second departure, five thousand troops were disembarked, and only one thousand veterans remained on board. This step was taken with a view to making the provisions and stores last longer than had been originally intended.

In the Bay, more bad weather overtook the expedition. The *Mere Honour* sprang a dangerous leak; the *St. Matthew* carried away her mainmast and some yards, and narrowly escaped driving ashore; and the *St. Andrew* for a time lost sight of the fleet. After the gale had moderated, the course was ill-advisedly steered parallel with the coasts of Asturias and Galicia, so that the ships were sighted from the shore, and warning of their approach was conveyed to the enemy in Corunna.

The English and Dutch stood on and off for some time between Cape Ortegal and Cape de San Adrian in hopes of enticing the Spaniards to come out. When it appeared that they would not do so, Essex was desirous of entering Ferrol and Corunna; but the risk to the ships and to the larger objects of the expedition, and the smallness of the available landing party, seem to have led to the abandonment of the project; and, after a council of war had been held, it was decided to proceed to the Azores, Ralegh, in the *Warspite*, which had lost her mainyard, was not present when this decision was arrived at, but rightly conjecturing what would be the result of the council, he steered for the Azores as soon as he had made good his damages, and there rejoined the fleet.

There was an arrangement—of which, however, Ralegh may not have been fully apprised—that, of the three generals, Essex should devote his attention to Fayal, Howard to Graciosa, and Ralegh to a third island; this was not adhered to. Ralegh, while watering, was suddenly ordered to proceed to Fayal, there to join Essex for an attack upon the place. He sailed at once; but at Fayal there were no signs of the commander-in-chief.

Seeing that the inhabitants were carrying off their effects, and that the works were being rapidly strengthened, Ralegh would have attacked immediately, but was persuaded to wait for four days ere taking action, and then to land only in case the earl should not in the meantime have arrived and assumed the command. Essex did not arrive within the stipulated period, and, at the expiration of it, Ralegh, being denied permission to send his casks ashore for water, landed about four miles from the port, drove the Spaniards before him, filled his casks, and seized the town.

Next day Essex entered the harbour. His friends, more than he himself at first, appear to have resented Ralegh's independent action;

and the latter was summoned to explain his conduct before a council of war. He showed the necessity of the measure and, persuaded by Howard, made some kind of apology. Gorges, who was Ralegh's captain, suggests that, in spite of this affair, Essex seemed to be satisfied with Sir Walter; but Monson is of opinion that, but for the fact that Ralegh was extremely popular in England and that Essex feared public opinion, the rear-admiral would have been severely punished by his chief. The probability is that the earl originally paid, and would have continued to pay, little attention to the matter had not Ralegh's numerous enemies steadily worked upon the mind of the commander-in-chief. It is certain, however, that in the result, first coldness, and then active hatred arose between the two flag-officers, to the great prejudice of the service.

After the fall of the town, the Spaniards abandoned the only fort remaining in their hands. In it the English found an Englishman and a Dutchman with their throats cut. A few days later the guns of the defences were embarked, the place was burnt, and the united fleet sailed to Graciosa, which submitted. Essex had intended to make this island his headquarters while awaiting the homecoming of the Spanish treasure ships from America; but his pilot, Grove, represented that the harbour was inconvenient for the purpose. Essex, therefore, went to Saint Michael's with the bulk of the fleet, leaving a small squadron, comprising the *Mary Rose,* under Sir Francis Vere and Sir Nicholas Parker, to cruise between Graciosa and St. George's, and another, including the *Garland* and the *Rainbow*, under the Earl of Southampton and Sir William Monson, to cruise to the westward.

★★★★★★

Monson says that Essex quitted Graciosa in consequence of having received reports of Spanish vessels, supposed to be the treasure ships, being in the neighbourhood, and that he himself warned Essex that the Spaniards would go to Angra.

★★★★★★

This was a most unfortunate arrangement, for no sooner had Essex departed, and the two small squadrons left for their cruising ground, than the treasure squadron of forty sail—seven of which had specie on board—arrived, and was warned off by the inhabitants. It bore away for Terceira and reached that island, with the exception of only three vessels, which, losing sight of their consorts, were ultimately made prizes by Essex.

★★★★★★

A "great ship" belonging to the Governor of Havana, a frigate of the King of Spain, and a frigate belonging to a private person. Essex's account. The largest was of 400 tons' burden, and very rich. Monson says that Southampton, in addition, sank a pinnace by gunshot.

★★★★★★

At Terceira, the Spaniards took refuge in the well-fortified and garrisoned port of Angra.

Vere, Southampton, and Monson, who had followed, endeavoured to enter the harbour in boats by night and to cut the Spanish cables, so that the vessels might drift to seaward; but the enemy was so alert that the project failed. Word was then sent to the commander-in-chief at St. Michael's of what had happened, with an assurance that the Spaniards should not be permitted to put to sea. In due course Essex, with his whole force, reached the scene of action; but, although at first, he was strongly in favour of hazarding an attack, a reconnaisance convinced him and most of the other officers that the idea was impracticable; and presently the English fleet returned to St. Michael's, and anchored before Punta Delgada.

That place was judged too strong to attempt, and Ralegh was left to hold it in check, while Essex proceeded to Villa Franca, about six miles distant. The town was easily taken, a considerable amount of booty was captured, and for several days the people from the fleet refreshed themselves on shore. (The idea had been to march overland and attack Punta Delgada from the rear, but the difficult nature of the country caused the relinquishment of the project.—Monson.)

While Essex was thus engaged, Ralegh, who awaited his return with great impatience, sighted an East India *carrack*, and a merchant-man from Brazil. The commander of the former ran his ship aground under the town, hurriedly removed as much as possible of her cargo, and then burnt her. The Brazil-man was taken, but, being in a leaky condition, was not manned. Her goods were put on board the English vessels, and she was destroyed.

Very little had been done, and none of the main objects of the expedition had been attained; yet it was decided to return to England, and the fleet accordingly quitted St. Michael's on October 9th. Three days afterwards it was dispersed by a violent storm. The same storm dealt even more hardly with the Spanish fleet, which, taking advantage of the presence of the English at the Azores, had put to sea from Ferrol with the object of effecting a landing in Cornwall and seizing some port there. Several of the ships were lost, and one, sorely damaged and very short of provisions, was driven into Dartmouth. The English vessels, on the other hand, all reached port in safety.

Essex and Ralegh were each blamed for the failure by the friends and partisans of the other, and in consequence the quarrel between the two leaders became very bitter. They, however, agreed upon, and both signed, a common account of the fortunes of the expedition. This account ended characteristically as follows:—

> And now we have given an account of all our whole carriage till we bare for England. If our coming home scattering be objected, we must plead the violence of storms, against which no fore-directions nor present industry can avail. We must conclude with this: that, as we would have acknowledged that we had done but our duties if we had defeated the Adelantada, taken the Spanish treasure, and conquered the islands of the Azores, so, we having failed of nothing that God gave us means to do, we hope her majesty will think our painful days, careful nights, evil diet, and many hazards deserve not now to be measured by the event. The like honourable and just construction we promise ourselves at the hands of all my Lords. As for others, who have sate warm at home, and discant upon us, we know they wanted strength to perform more, and believe they wanted courage to adventure so much.

Alluding to the dispersion of the Spanish fleet, Monson says:

> We must ascribe this victory only to God, for certainly the enemy's designs were perilous, and not diverted by our force.

The Spanish design was to seize Falmouth, and to use it as an advanced base for operations against Ireland. England seems to have little realised at the moment the seriousness of the blow which had missed her so narrowly.

A small expedition, which left England in the course of the same year, is of interest, and deserves mention here, on account of its connection with disputes which, in succeeding ages, greatly influenced the relations between Great Britain and France. It was in no sense a naval expedition, but essentially a fishing venture. Nevertheless, like most of the maritime expeditions of the period, it led to some fighting.

Charles Leigh and Abraham van Herwick, merchants of London,

fitted out the *Hopewell*, 120 tons, William Crafton, master, and the *Chancewell*, 70 tons, Stephen Bennet, master, to fish in the waters of Cape Breton and Newfoundland, where the French already fished for cod. Charles Leigh himself and Stephen van Herwick, a brother of his partner, went as managers of the voyage; and the two vessels, with a pinnace of seven or eight tons, quitted Gravesend on April 8th, 1597. On May 18th, they were upon the banks of Newfoundland. On May 20th, the *Hopewell*, without Leigh's knowledge, fought a French vessel. On June 18th, off Ramea Island, other French ships were encountered, and quarrels arising, were fought with. The English fared ill, and were obliged to retire with the loss of their pinnace and an anchor and cable. Worse still befell on June 23rd, when the *Chancewell*, which had become separated from her consort, was wrecked on Cape Breton Island.

GEORGE CLIFFORD, EARL OF CUMBERLAND, K.G.

The French pillaged her people, stripping them to their very shirts; but most of the survivors seemed to have gained the Hopewell, which, ere she returned to England, amply avenged the unfortunates by boarding and capturing a French craft of 200 tons, and spoiling her of her fish and oil. (Hakluyt, iii.)

The year 1598 witnessed the last and most ambitious of the numerous privateering expeditions of that distinguished maritime adventurer, the Earl of Cumberland. The squadron collected on the occasion comprised no fewer than twenty sail of ships, (see list following), none of which belonged to the navy, and it formed a force more formidable than had ever been assembled by a subject.

SHIPS.	COMMANDERS.
Scourge of Malice	The Earl of Cumberland, "Admiral." John Watts. (later) James Langton.
Merchant Royal [1]	Sir John Berkeley, "Lieut.-General and Vice-Admiral"
Ascension [1]	Robert Flicke " Rear-Admiral."
Samson	Henry Clifford (died). Christopher Colthurst.
Alcedo [1]	John Ley. (later) Thomas Cotch.
Consent [1]	Francis Slingsby.
Prosperous	James Langton. (later) John Watts.
Centurion [1]	Henry Palmer. (later) William Palmer.
Constance, gallion [1]	Hercules Foljambe.
Affection	— Fleming.
Guiana	Christopher Colthurst. (later) Gerald Middleton.
Scout	Henry Jolliffe.
Anthony [1]	Robert Careless (died). Andrew Andrews.
Pegasus [1] [2]	Edward Goodwin.
Royal Defence	Henry Bromley.
Margaret and John	John Dixon.
Barkley Bay	(? later) John Ley.
Old frigate [3]	William Harper.

And two barges [1] [4] for landing troops.

[1] Left with Sir John Berkeley at San Juan de Puerto Rico.
[2] Lost, returning, on the Goodwin Sands.
[3] Lost, returning, off Ushant.
[4] One barge was sunk at Puerto Rico, the other was wrecked on the Bermudas.

It sailed from Plymouth on March 6th, 1598. The first intention of the commander-in-chief appears to have been to proceed to the West Indies; but, learning soon after he had put to sea that certain rich Spanish *carracks* were about to cross the Atlantic in company with twenty merchantmen bound for Brazil, he lay in wait for a time for the convoy. The Spaniards, however, apprised of his presence off their coasts, kept their ships in port; and the earl's only captures at the beginning of his voyage were a Hamburger, with a miscellaneous cargo of contraband goods, a Frenchman laden with salt, and two Flamands full of corn.

Convinced that the *carracks* would not venture out while he was in the neighbourhood, Cumberland steered for the Canaries, took and plundered the island of Lanzarote, and then pushed across to Dominica, where he landed on May 23rd, and remained till June 1st, keeping, meanwhile, on good terms with the natives. From Dominica, he sailed to the Virgin Islands, where he landed, mustered all his men, and announced his intention of attacking Puerto Rico. He arrived off San Juan in that island on June 6th, landed a thousand men, and speedily made himself master of the place, with but small loss, though he was at first repulsed. (Here were taken a French and a Spanish vessel, which were added to the squadron.)

His intention was to make the town a base for his future operations, bat it proved so extremely unhealthy to the troops on shore, of whom more than half died, that he decided to quit it. This he did on August 14th, leaving, however, the better part of his squadron, under Sir John Berkeley, his second-in-command, to arrange for the ransom of the island. Before his departure, the earl captured a caravel from the island of Margarita, off the coast of Venezuela, as she came unsuspectingly into harbour, and a ship from Angola. In the first was pearl worth one thousand *ducats*, in the second was a cargo of negroes.

Cumberland, with his division, made the best of his way to the Azores, where he hoped to intercept the Spanish Mexico Fleet, or at least some *carracks*; but he reached Flores only to learn that a few days earlier twenty-nine large Spanish ships had weighed thence. At Flores he was, in course of time, rejoined by Sir John Berkeley, though not until both divisions of the squadron had suffered severely in a storm. The united force sailed again on September 16th, and in the following month reached England without further adventure. The expedition, which must have been a very costly one, does not seem to have materially increased the earl's estate, but it was of undoubted benefit to England, seeing that it greatly annoyed the Spaniards, prevented that year's sailing of their regular *carracks* for the Indies, and caused the postponement of the return of the Elate Fleet from America. It would probably have been more successful had the earl taken greater pains to keep secret his objects and his movements.

Two non-naval events of considerable importance occurred during 1598, and, since they intimately affected naval policy, deserve mention here. One was the conclusion by England of a new and advantageous treaty with the United Provinces of the Netherlands. (*Foedera*, xvi.) The other was the death of Elizabeth's life-long enemy, Philip II. of

Spain, (on September, 13th, the anniversary of the birth of his rival Burghley, who had predeceased him on August 15th.)

Referring to 1599, Sir William Monson says:—

> I cannot write of anything done this year; for though there was never greater expectation of war, there was never less performance. Whether it was a mistrust one nation had of the other, or policy held on both sides to make peace with sword in hand, a treaty being entertained by consent of each prince, I am not to examine: but sure, I am, the preparation was great on both sides, one expecting an invasion from the other. It was, however, generally conceived not to be intended by either.

The Spaniards had collected ships and galleys at Corunna. The object of the concentration was supposed to be a descent upon England or Ireland in 1599; but, as the event proved, the preparations were made against the Netherlands. In Ireland, Essex was supposed. to be hatching schemes of ambition and revenge. Jealous watch, therefore, had to be kept upon at least two quarters; and, to meet the necessities of the moment, a fleet was mobilised with a rapidity previously unexampled. The work of rigging, victualling, and completely fitting out was accomplished in twelve days.

Monson assures us that foreigners declared that "the queen was never more dreaded abroad for anything she ever did." Happily, the fleet was not called upon to act, and, after having lain for three weeks or a month in the Downs, was sent peaceably back to its ports; but, both as a demonstration of the perfection to which the organisation of the English navy had attained, and as an exercise in hurried preparation for war, the experiment was well worth the comparatively small sum of money which it cost.

In more than one respect it resembled the mobilisation of the Particular Service Squadron in January, 1896. Looking, however, to all the circumstances of the two cases, it must be admitted that the results attained in 1599 were much more remarkable than those attained in 1896. The mobilisation of 1599 seems to have really taken officers, men, and dockyards by surprise. The mobilisation of 1896, on the other hand, had been unofficially prepared for several weeks. Yet the interval between the moment when the formal order went forth from London and the moment when the mobilised ships were fully ready to go anywhere and do anything, was actually as short in 1599 as in 1896.

The constitution of this memorable Elizabethan fleet is given below.

SHIP.	Tons.	Men.	Guns.	Commanders.
Elizabeth Jonas . .	900	500	56	Lord Thos. Howard, Admiral.
Ark Royal . . .	800	400	55	Sir Walter Ralegh.
Triumph . . .	1000	500	68	Sir Fulke Greville.
Mere Honour . .	800	400	41	Sir Henry Palmer.
Repulse . . .	700	350	50	Sir Thos. Vavasour.
Garland . . .	700	300	45	Sir Wm. Harvey.
Defiance . . .	500	250	46	Sir Wm. Monson.
Nonpareil . . .	500	250	56	Sir Robt. Crosse.
Lion	500	250	60	Sir Richd. Leveson.
Rainbow . . .	500	250	26	Sir Alex. Clifford.
Hope . . .	600	250	48	Sir John Gilbert.
Foresight . . .	300	160	37	Sir Thos. Shirley.
Mary Rose . .	600	250	39	— Fortescue.
Bonaventure .	600	250	47	— Troughton.
Crane . . .	200	108	24	— Jones.
Swiftsure . .	400	200	41	— Bradgate.
Tremontana . .	140	70	21	— Slingsby.
Advantage . .	200	102	26	— White.[1]
Quittance . .	200	108	25	Carew Reynell.

[1] "White" in the printed 'Tracts'; but "Hore" (? Gore) in MS. in the Cott. MSS.

In 1600, commissioners met at Boulogne to treat for peace between England and Spain. They separated in consequence of disputes concerning precedence, and effected nothing. Elizabeth and her ministers, foreseeing the probability of a lame issue of the sort, and altogether distrustful of Spanish sincerity, meanwhile quietly fitted out the *Repulse*, Sir Richard Leveson, Admiral of the Narrow Seas, *Warspite*, Captain Troughton, and *Vanguard*, Captain Somers, as if intending them to cruise against the Dunquerque *corsairs* on the western coasts. When it was no longer doubtful that the Boulogne negotiations were destined to fail, Sir Richard was suddenly ordered to proceed with his little squadron to the Azores, there to lie in wait for, and endeavour to capture, the homeward-bound Spanish *carracks* and the Mexico fleet.

Spain was equally wary. In view of the failure of negotiations she equipped a squadron of eighteen ships, and sent them also to the islands. The two squadrons heard of, but never sighted, one another; nor did Leveson sight the treasure ships. Having exhausted his supplies, he returned to England. The only good effected by this expedition was the casual relief of some distressed home-coming Dutch East-Indiamen.

The year 1601, which, on February 25th, witnessed the execution of Robert Devereux, Earl of Essex, (and also witnessed Lancaster's voyage to the East Indies), saw an attempted invasion of Ireland by a Spanish fleet of forty-eight sail under Don Diego de Borachero. Upon the news of the intended descent reaching England, Leveson was again placed in command of a small squadron and ordered to hasten to the threatened point. The squadron consisted of the *Warspite* (flag); *Garland*, Sir Amyas Preston; *Defiance*, Captain Gore; *Swiftsure*, Captain Somers; and *Crane*, Captain Mainwaring.

In Ireland, Hugh O'Neill, Earl of Tyrone, was in rebellion at the head of all the tribes of Ulster. In 1598, he had defeated Bagnall at the Yellow Ford, and had roused Munster; and ever since, without risking a general engagement, he had harassed the English power. The arrival of a strong force of allies from Spain seemed to promise triumph to his cause, provided only that he could join hands with the foreigners.

Leveson was not in time to intercept the Spaniards, the main body of whom effected a landing at Kinsale; but he gallantly entered a bay in which a belated Spanish contingent, under Vice-Admiral Siriaco had anchored, and, after a sharp action, destroyed the whole of that division. Siriaco, who escaped, disguised himself, and returned home in a French ship. The remaining Spaniards, under Don Juan d'Aguila, held Kinsale against Lord Mountjoy, who besieged it, until December 24th, when Tyrone, who attempted to succour the place, was defeated; whereupon the invaders surrendered upon condition of being transported to their own country in English ships.

Late in the autumn of the same year an adventurous privateering expedition, under William Parker, of Plymouth, left England to cruise against the Spaniards in the West Indies. It consisted of the *Prudence*, 100 tons, 130 men, William Parker, master and "admiral"; the *Pearl*, 60 tons, 60 men, Robert Rawlins, master and "vice-admiral"; a pinnace of 20 tons and 18 men; and two little shallops. Among the gentlemen embarked for operations on shore were Edward Giles, Philip Ward,—Fugars,—Ashley, and—Loriman.

Sailing in November, the little squadron was at the beginning unfortunate, losing the pinnace and all on board, save three, in a squall. Parker steered for the Cape de Verde Islands, and, upon reaching them, threw a hundred men ashore at St. Vincent, captured the island, and pillaged and burnt the town. Thence he stretched across to the American continent, and attacked La Rancheria, in the small island of Cubagua. Although the Governor of Cumana, with a body of troops, was on the spot and gave the invaders a warm reception, the place was taken. Parker allowed the inhabitants to ransom it for five hundred pounds of pearl. Off Cape de la Vela he fell in with and captured a Portuguese ship of 250 tons, bound from Angola and Congo to Cartagena. Her also he accepted a ransom for.

At Cabecas he transferred a hundred and fifty of his men to the shallops and two small pinnaces, and, proceeding to the Bastimentos, engaged negro guides, with whose assistance he entered the harbour of Puerto Bello on the night of February 7th, 1602. It was moonlight; and the English were hailed by the sentries in the castle of St. Philip, a strong work, mounting thirty-five brass guns. They replied in Spanish, and were ordered to anchor. Parker obeyed, but, an hour later, leaving the pinnaces before the castle, he suddenly landed at Triana with the shallops and thirty men, set the place on fire, and entered Puerto Bello ere the people had fairly recovered from their first confusion.

In front of the Royal Treasury he found a body of troops and two brass field-pieces drawn up to receive him. An obstinate fight resulted; and, if Fugars and Loriman, who had been left in the pinnaces, had not opportunely landed with a hundred and twenty fresh men, Parker's little force would have been annihilated. The timely assistance; soon brought about the fall of the town, in which the victors found 10,000 *ducats* in specie, belonging to the King of Spain, and a considerable amount of other money, plate, and merchandise. This Parker divided among his men. Two small vessels which lay in the harbour were taken possession of and retained.

Parker's behaviour, judged by the standard of those rough times, was unusually generous. Because the town was well built, he abstained from burning it; and because he was pleased at having taken so important a place with so small a force, he dismissed all his prisoners, including the governor, without exacting any ransom. (The governor, Don Pedro Melendez, had fought gallantly, and received eleven wounds.) After remaining for two days he sailed again, and, after an uneventful voyage, reached Plymouth in due course.

Lediard says:

The action of taking a town of so great strength with so few men bred such an idea of the English valour in some of the Spaniards that the Governor of Cartagena, in particular, swore he would give a mule's lading of silver to have a sight of Captain Parker and his company. And had they been sure he would have parted with what he had upon so easy terms as they of

Puerto Bello had done, it is very likely they might have sold him that favour. But his strength being uncertain, as well as his pay, they did not think fit to visit him.

The year 1602, which saw the return of Parker, saw also the setting out of several private voyages which may be briefly mentioned here. Bartholomew Gosnoll, in a small bark, carried a little party of thirty-two persons to Elizabeth's Island, in 41° 10' N., on the American coast, and would probably have established a permanent colony there had not dissensions arisen and compelled the return of the expedition. William Mace, of Weymouth, employed by Ralegh, who was uneasy as to the fate of the colonists left in Virginia in 1587, pretended to make search for them, but wasted his time, and came home prematurely.

Finally, George Weymouth, employed by the Russia Company, sailed with two fly-boats, one of 70 and one of 60 tons, from Ratcliff, hoping to discover a north-west passage. But, meeting with much ice and fog, his men refused to proceed, and he was obliged to return after an absence of little more than four months.

There were also two purely naval expeditions of considerable importance. Both were fitted out with the object of preventing Spain from again attempting to interfere with the course of affairs in Ireland. The first consisted of the following vessels:—

SHIPS.			Tons.	Men.	Guns.	Commanders.
Repulse	.	.	.	700	350	50	Sir Richard Leveson, Admiral.
Garland	.	.	.	700	300	45	Sir William Monson, V.-Admiral.
Defiance	.	.	.	500	250	46	Captain Gore.
Mary Rose	.	.	.	600	250	39	Captain Slingsby.
Warspite	.	.	.	600	300	29	Captain Somers.
Nonpareil	.	.	.	500	250	56	Captain Carew Reynell.
Dreadnought	.	.	.	400	200	41	Captain Mainwaring.
Adventure	.	.	.	250	120	26	Captain Trevor.
A caravel	.	.	.	?	?	?	Captain Sawkell.

The mission of this fleet was the observation of the Spanish coasts, and, generally, the doing of as much damage as possible to the enemy in his own waters. Leveson, with five of the ships, sailed on March 19th, 1602. Monson remained to await the arrival of a Dutch contingent of twelve ships, the co-operation of which had been promised; but news reaching England that the Spanish Plate fleet was at Terceira, his departure was hastened, in spite of the fact that he was still only partially maimed and provisioned; and he followed his chief on March

26th.

Leveson, with his division, met the Plate fleet soon after it had quitted Terceira, and engaged it; but having only five ships, while the enemy had eight-and-thirty, he could effect nothing, and was, indeed, fortunate in being able to escape capture. Had the Dutch and Monson's division been present with the flag, the result must have been very different; and the failure may undoubtedly be regarded as distinctly due to Dutch remissness. A rendezvous off Lisbon had been arranged between the two English admirals. Monson proceeded thither, and then, after waiting in vain for his chief for a fortnight, cruised to the north-west. He presently met with three ships which Leveson had dispatched to look out for him, and at almost the same time spoke some French and Scots vessels which informed him that five galleons lay in San Lucar ready to sail for the Indies, and that two other galleons had sailed three days earlier, (these were fallen in with one night by the *Warspite*, but escaped her), carrying Don Pedro de Valdes, as governor, to Havana.

Taking the three English ships under his orders, Monson steered for the probable course of the San Lucar galleons, and quickly sighted five sail which he at first took to be them. They proved, however, to be English merchantmen coining out of the Straits. Next day he chased a Spanish Indiaman, but although he took her, she led him so far to leeward that during the following night, the galleons passed him in safety. Soon afterwards the two admirals met.

On June 1st, being close to Lisbon, they took two ships from the Levant, bound for the Tagus. While they were examining them, a caravel signalled that she desired to speak. Leveson approached the stranger, and from her learnt of the recent arrival at Cezimbra of a *carrack* of 1600 tons, richly laden from the East Indies. She also reported that sixteen galleys lay in the same harbour, three of them Portuguese, and the rest about to sail for the coast of Flanders, to cruise under Federigo Spinola against the Dutch; and she explained that she had been sent to the admiral by the *Nonpareil* and *Dreadnought*, which were at the moment detached.

Leveson at once ordered Monson to rejoin him, and the ships then in company, *i.e.*, the *Warspite* (flag), (the *Repulse*, being leaky, had been sent home, and Leveson had shifted his flag to the *Warspite*, as her master proved incompetent, he later shifted it to the *Dreadnought*), *Garland, Nonpareil, Dreadnought, Adventure*, and the two captured vessels, proceeded off Cezimbra, and that very night exchanged a few gunshot with the galleys there.

Early in the morning of June 2nd, a council of war was summoned on board the commander-in-chief, and after considerable discussion, it was determined to attack next day.

The place and shipping were most advantageously situated for defensive purposes. The town stands at the head of a bay which affords a good anchorage in northerly winds. Before the town, and close to the waters, was a strong and well-armed fort, and upon a hill behind the town was a fortified convent commanding the whole. Immediately under the fort lay the great *carrack*. Behind a neck of rock on the west side of the bay lay the eleven galleys, so disposed with their sterns foremost, that with their bow guns, of which each had five, they could cover the advancing English, while they were themselves protected by the rock, so long as the enemy remained out of gunshot of the fort and the *carrack*. In addition, the place was full of troops.

On June 3rd, a breeze springing up at about 10 a.m., the admiral weighed, fired a warning gun, and hoisted his flag at the maintop. The vice-admiral hoisted his at the foretop. It had been arranged that Leveson should lead in and anchor as near as possible to the *carrack*, and that the other vessels following should fight under sail, striking as opportunity might offer and occasion suggest; but this plan was not followed out. Leveson led in as stipulated, but Monson, who entered last, instead of fighting under sail, luffed up as close to the shore as he could, dropped his anchor, and hotly engaged town, fort, *carrack* and galleys all at once, fighting both broadsides simultaneously, while Leveson, owing to the mismanagement of his master, drifted altogether out of the roadstead, and his ship was unable to enter it again until next day. Leveson in person, however, missed very little of the action, for he shifted his flag to the *Dreadnought*. In the course of the afternoon he went on board the *Garland*, and publicly embracing Monson, assured him that he had won his chief's heart for ever.

Monson was so placed as to be able to enfilade the galleys, which soon fell into disorder, many of the slaves leaving them and swimming ashore. At 2 p.m. the *Dreadnought* anchored near him, but the fight went on steadily until 5 p.m., at about which time Monson, who perceived that the two prizes, which had been ordered to run on board the *carrack* and burn her, were not doing their duty, went to them and made preparations for himself leading them on that service. Leveson, however, had begun to hope that the *carrack* might be taken, and, following Monson to the prizes, carried him back with him to the *Dreadnought* to concert measures to that end.

In the result, the English ships were directed to cease firing, and one Captain Sewell, an English prisoner who, in the course of the fight, had escaped from the town, was sent to the *carrack* to offer terms, and to represent that, the galleys being beaten and the English in possession of the roadstead, further resistance would merely provoke the victors.

The captain of the *carrack*, Don Diego Lobo, sent representatives on board the *Dreadnought* to treat, but it appearing that the people in the *carrack* were not all disposed to surrender, Monson expedited negotiations by going in his own boat and personally arranging matters with Don Diego, who, after some discussion, surrendered his ship. (Her name was *São Valentino*. She belonged to the vice-royalty of Portugal, and had lately come from the Indies, wintering by the way at Mozambique.) She was worth a million *ducats*. Of the galleys, two were taken and burnt, (the *Trinidade* and *Occasion*), and all the rest would have shared the same fate had the English had at their disposal boats wherewith to board them. The loss on the side of the victors was but six killed and about as many wounded.

On June 4th, the fleet sailed on its return to England. On the way, it fell in with a packet bearing dispatches to the effect that a new English squadron was in readiness to reinforce the one already out, and that the Dutch squadron (it passed the fleet unseen in the course of the following night), was at length on its way south. Upon receipt of this news it was decided that Leveson should continue his voyage, and that Monson should return to the Spanish coast to assume command of the reinforcing fleet upon its arrival on the station.

The *Garland* being in need of a refit, Monson shifted his flag to the *Nonpareil*, which was in better condition than the other ships, and in her he parted company and went south again. Very severe weather, however, overtook him, and after it had continued for ten days, he was prevailed on by his people to put the ship before the wind and run for Plymouth. He reached that port in safety, found that the captured *carrack* had arrived before him, and learnt that the squadron which he had gone back to take charge of had not yet left England.

It should be added here that the nine galleys which had escaped destruction at Cezimbra subsequently left that port under Federigo Spinola to carry out the object of their original commission, and cruise on the coast of Flanders against the Dutch. On September 23rd, while passing through the strait of Dover, they fell in with a squadron which, under Sir Robert Mansell, was there stationed to intercept them. The English attacked with such success that, of the nine galleys, only the one commanded by Spinola himself got away to Dunquerque, all the others being sunk or driven ashore on the Flanders coast. (This is the account of Colliber and others. Camden says that Spinola sailed with six galleys, and lost two sunk and one taken in a conflict with an Anglo-Dutch force in the Channel. With the other three he escaped to Sluis.)

No sooner had Monson reached Plymouth than he was sent for by the queen, and entrusted with the command of another squadron, destined to watch the coast of Spain, and especially the harbours of Corunna and Ferrol. As before, the safety of Ireland was the chief object of the government. If Monson could satisfy himself that the Spaniards were not threatening Ireland, he might join the Dutch squadron at a given rendezvous, and act on the Spanish coast according to his discretion; but his first care was to be for Ireland.

He sailed from Plymouth on August 31st, 1602, with the following force:

SHIPS.			Tons.	Men.	Guns.	Commanders.
Swiftsure	.	.	400	200	41	Sir William Monson, Admiral.
Mary Rose	.	.	600	250	39	Captain Trevor.
Dreadnought	.	.	400	200	41	Captain Cawfield.
Adventure	.	.	250	120	26	Captain Norris.
Answer	.	.	200	108	21	Captain Bradgate.
Quittance	.	.	200	108	25	Captain Browne.
Lion's Whelp [1]	.	.	..	..	..	Captain May.
Paragon [2]	.	.	..	..	..	Captain Jason.
A small caravel	.	.	..	..	..	Captain Hooper.

[1] Bought from the Lord High Admiral, 1601. Pipe Office Accounts, 2239.
[2] A merchantman.

Bad weather attended the squadron, which, however, remained off Corunna until Monson had ascertained that the Spanish ships which had been collected there, and which had been suspected to be intended for Ireland, had gone southward to Lisbon, there to join the force under Don Diego de Borachero. Monson also went south, earning by means of the caravel, which he sent inshore for intelligence, of the presence on the coast of a Spanish fleet of twenty-four sail; and capturing two French merchant vessels, which he liberated upon receiving from them a pledge that they would return home direct instead of proceeding to Lisbon, their port of destination.

In the course of a chase, Monson, in the *Swiftsure*, with the *Dreadnought* in company, was led into Cezimbra, the scene of his exploits earlier in the year. He exchanged shots with the fort, which protected the chase, and while in the roadstead, captured a caravel, which came in unsuspectingly, and which, volunteering information concerning the state of affairs at Lisbon, was allowed to depart again. But he could hear nothing of the Dutch squadron.

Proceeding off Lisbon, which was the appointed rendezvous, he sighted a light on the night of September 26th, and believing it to come from some richly laden vessel bound for the Tagus, chased it. He had with him at the moment, (the other ships had parted company in a storm four nights earlier), besides his flagship, only the *Adventure* and the *Lion's Whelp*. To his astonishment he presently found himself in the midst of the Spanish fleet. The enemy recognised the *Adventure*, and opened fire on her, wounding some of her men; but had darkness lasted a few hours longer, the English would have got away without much fighting. Daylight, however, discovered the *Swiftsure*, *Adventure*, and *Lion's Whelp* only a short distance ahead of the Spanish fleet, and the latter gave chase.

Three of the Spaniards, being better sailers than the rest, soon gained upon the English, and threatened the *Lion's Whelp*; but Monson lay to to await the three, and after a time bad the satisfaction of seeing them recalled by their admiral, who stood in with the shore.

The early autumn was occupied in watching, but in vain, for the home-coming San Domingo convoy. On October 21st, Monson, in the *Swiftsure*, chased a galleon under the castle of Cape St. Vincent, and gallantly attempted to run alongside and carry her by boarding. He was prevented from doing this by the cowardice or ineptitude, of the man at the helm, who bore up at the critical moment; and in the result, he found himself exposed to a very heavy fire which, in his own words, "rent his ship so that a team of oxen might have crept through her under the half-deck, and one shot killed seven men."

During the fight, a Spanish squadron looked on from the westward, and several English men-of-war from the eastward, neither caring to intervene for fear of being hit by friends as well as by foes. Monson, during the night, extricated his ship, and after an ineffectual attempt to reach Terceira, returned to England, dropping anchor in Plymouth Sound on November 24th. The other ships came home independently.

The *Dreadnought* and *Mary Rose*, both very sickly, had returned

before the admiral. The *Adventure* arrived an hour after him, reporting that she had fallen in with the home-coming Brazilian fleet, and
had been badly mauled by it, but had taken nothing. The *Paragon* had
captured a rich prize laden with sugar and spices. As for the *Quittance*,
she had pluckily engaged two Dunquerquers, and had borne herself
very well with them, but had unhappily lost her captain, Browne, in
the action.

This was the last naval expedition of the reign of Elizabeth. That
great queen died on March 24th, 1603.

Charles Howard
Lord Howard of Effingham. Earl of Nottingham. K. G.
Lord High Admiral

The Campaign of the Spanish Armada

★★★★★★

The reproductions from Pine's engravings of the tapestry hangings in the old House of Lords (with which this chapter is illustrated) possess a special historical interest. The tapestries were made, after designs by C. Vroom, for Howard of Effingham himself, probably to some extent under his direction. James I. bought them, and gave them to the House of Lords; and they perished in the fire of 1834.

★★★★★★

The history of the Spanish Armada, regarded from the naval, and not from the political point of view, begins with the year 1583, when the Spanish admiral, Santa Cruz, intoxicated by the success which he had recently gained off Terceira, proposed to Philip to employ his victorious arms against England. (An invasion of England had, indeed, been proposed by Alva as early as 1509.)

★★★★★★

"*La Felicisima Armada*" (the Most Happy Armada), was its official description. The origin of the description, "The Invincible Armada," is a little obscure; but Captain C. F. Duro has adopted it as the title of his book *La Armada Invencible,*

★★★★★★

At considerable length he explained what preparations would be necessary; and he endeavoured, by anticipation, to combat some of his master's possible objections to the scheme. "If," he wrote, "we fall to considering the difficulties of the task, nothing will be done." (Duro).

But, at that early date, nothing was attempted. Santa Cruz did not, however, rest satisfied with making his original proposals. In January,

1586, he again wrote to the king, he began:

> For a long time, your majesty has cherished an idea of under-
> taking something against England. (Duro).

He then stated the arguments in favour of an expedition. Queen
Elizabeth had fitted out vessels to carry war and rapine into Philip's
seas, islands, and Indies. The veteran seaman was frank and honourable
enough to pay his tribute of admiration to the heretical sovereign, he
wrote:

> Looking at the matter, merely from the statesman's standpoint,
> one must admit that she has adopted a courageous policy, and
> one which, while it has won her glory, has enriched and inspir-
> ited her subjects.

Seeing that the Turks and the French were otherwise occupied, the
admiral recommended his sovereign to assume the offensive.

This energetic communication did not fail to produce some effect. At the desire of the king, Santa Cruz sent him, in the following
March, a very detailed list of the vessels, men, ammunition, and stores
which would have to be provided if the necessary fleet and army were
to undertake an eight months' campaign. He also estimated the cost.
His proposed Armada was powerful indeed. It consisted of 556 vessels,
including 150 large ships of war, with a total burthen of 77,250 tons;
and the fleet was to carry no fewer than 94,222 men. (Duro.)

Santa Cruz died in February, 1588, but, ere that, Philip had finally
made up his mind to delay no longer. (Duro.) A fleet was to join Parma for the purpose; and, as its leader, Don Alonso Perez de Guzman,
Duke of Medina Sidonia, was selected. (Ranke suggests that one of
the reasons may have been that the duke had distinguished himself at
the defence of Cadiz.) The choice was an extremely bad one. Medina
Sidonia hesitatingly accepted the command, after having protested his
absolute inexperience at sea and in war. He had only been enough
at sea to discover that he was liable to sea-sickness. But his scruples
were overcome, and Philip wrote thanking him for having accepted
the post.

On March 22nd, the commander-in-chief received his instructions from the king. (Duro, doc. 94. The date, according to the N.S.
then used in Spain, should be April 1st; but as the O.S. was used in
England, all dates in this chapter are given in the English form.) There
was to be no further postponement. The English were not to be al-

lowed to perfect their preparations. Victory being the gift of God, Medina Sidonia was to see to it that crime should not disgrace the Armada, and especially that there should be no blasphemy on board the ships. If committed, blasphemy was to be severely punished, lest all, for suffering so great an iniquity, should incur divine vengeance.

Then the strategical plan was unfolded. The instructions ran:

> When you have received my orders, you will put to sea with the whole Armada, and proceed direct for the English Channel, up which you will sail as far as the point of Margate, there opening communication with the Duke of Parma, and ensuring him a passage across. (Duro. Parma was in the Netherlands).

While still on his voyage, Medina Sidonia was to keep up a correspondence with Parma; and, to facilitate this, the king promised to forward a cryptographic code. In view of the possibility of the ships being dispersed by bad weather, places of rendezvous were appointed. The coasts of France and Flanders, on account of their shallows, were to be carefully avoided. (The old belief in England was that the Spaniards had been instructed to hug the French coast.) On the other hand, the English coast was to be closely followed. An English fleet might create a diversion; but Medina Sidonia was, nevertheless, to continue his voyage, and not to seek an encounter with the enemy afloat.

If, however, Drake should pursue closely, he was to be attacked. (Duro. Philip seems to have specially feared Drake, who in the previous year had "singed the King of Spain's beard.") He was also to be attacked if he were fallen in with near the mouth of the Channel. For Philip was of opinion that only part of the English fleet would be with Drake. In case the Armada should sight the enemy off the point of Margate, "even if Drake's and the Admiral's squadrons were found to be united," the Spaniards would still be in superior force; and, neglecting neither the weather gauge nor any other possible advantage, might attack and hope for victory.

The king issued no special directions as to the order of battle. That was to be formed as circumstances might dictate. He reminded the admiral, however, that the English, on account of their superiority in artillery, would seek to fight at long range. The Spaniards, therefore, should endeavour to get to close quarters. The English, it was also said, mounted their guns so that they could shoot low. (Duro). Philip, moreover, impressed upon his admiral that he must engage the enemy only if it should become apparent that Parma's passage across could not be ensured without an action. For Medina Sidonia was to spare his Spaniards as much as possible, with a view to assisting Parma with six thousand men, in case there should be no battle, or with fewer, in case losses should be incurred. This exhortation to avoid an unnecessary action must have been rather embarrassing to the commander-in-chief, since Philip had elsewhere directed him to fight if Drake pursued, or were fallen in with near the mouth of the Channel.

If Parma landed in England, Medina Sidonia was to station his fleet at the mouth of the Thames, and to guard that river. He would then be able to keep open and safe the communications with Flanders, and to co-operate in the most efficacious manner.

According to the instructions, Medina Sidonia was only to act independently of Parma, in the event of an action having to be fought at sea, which action was nevertheless described as being "after all the chief thing." (Duro). Above all, he was to remain on the English coast until the business should be brought to a satisfactory termination.

These instructions are vague and ambiguous. (Yet Duro comments: "*No cabe nada mas meditado, claro y preciso que esta instruccion.*"—"There is nothing more thoughtful, clear and precise than this instruction.") They leave one in doubt as to what Philip really had in mind. (It is true that Philip had delivered to the two dukes certain plans which have not been preserved. These may possibly have been more precise. Duro.) The orders admit of the following interpretation.

Margate Road was to be the immediate destination of the Armada. There, for the first time, touch was to be gained with Parma, as soon as possible after the arrival of Medina Sidonia. Philip says nothing definite as to Medina Sidonia convoying Parma, but directs him to ensure the latter's passage across. This order is so indeterminate that one may conjecture that after his arrival off Margate, the admiral might act according to circumstances. The king, perhaps, expected that Medina Sidonia would manage to drive the enemy from the Channel as the result of a battle fought off Margate before the fleet anchored in the Road.

In that case, Parma might cross without assistance. But, if the enemy still remained in the neighbourhood, then it would be the duty of Medina Sidonia with part, or the whole, of the Armada, to convoy Parma. This interpretation is the more probable, seeing that Philip, in his instructions, ordered his admiral, after Parma's landing, to guard and keep open the passage between Flanders and the mouth of the Thames.

At first sight, it seems illogical to protect Parma's passage from Flanders from a base at the mouth of the Thames. But it must be remembered that on the coast of Flanders there were no ports suitable for the Armada, whereas at the mouth of the Thames, and in the Downs, there were good anchorages, where storms might be ridden out, and where favourable opportunities might be awaited.

Medina Sidonia's business, then, was to ensure Parma's passage to Margate; to there reinforce his army with, in the most favourable event, six thousand men, (Parma greatly counted upon these men, and called them "*el niervo principal*"—"the main nerve" of his force); and thenceforward to co-operate with him in the mouth of the Thames. The admiral's mission was subsidiary to that of Parma, but might nevertheless be a very important and honourable one, especially in the case of a great action being fought at sea.

It is clear that Philip entirely failed to comprehend the only principles in accordance with which successful invasions of insular States with respectable navies can be carried out. Had he understood them, he must have ordered the projected invasion to wait upon the fighting of a decisive action with the English fleet, instead of exhorting his admiral to avoid a battle. We may, therefore, take it that his characterisation of an action at sea as "after all, the chief thing," was mere consolatory flattery, designed to compensate Medina Sidonia, in some measure, for having been vouchsafed no more than what was intended to be a secondary part in the drama.

The secret instructions, (written March 22nd), confirm the supposition that, after Medina Sidonia's arrival off Margate, Parma was to pass over with his fighting force. But if, they continue, God should fail to permit the hoped-for issue and should prevent Parma from crossing, thus rendering impracticable the desired co-operation, then, still remaining in correspondence with Parma, the admiral should endeavour to make himself master of the Isle of Wight. This would give the Spaniards a secure harbour whence they might pursue the various undertakings rendered possible by their possession of that important position.

With these secret instructions, the king sent a sealed letter which Medina Sidonia was to hand to Parma, either after the latter had landed in England, or after he had abandoned all hope of being able to do so. By this missive, Parma was empowered, in case neither England nor Spain should have gained a decisive victory, to treat for peace. The king prescribed three main conditions, *viz.* (1) Free exercise of the Catholic faith in England, and the repeal of the sentence of exile upon those already expelled from the country on account of holding that faith; (2) Surrender of the places held in the Netherlands by the English, and especially of Flushing; (3) Compensation for the great injuries inflicted on Spanish possessions and subjects. From this it is apparent that some time before the sailing of the Armada, Philip admitted the possibility of the failure, whole or part, of the expedition.

The instructions, secret as well as public, were drawn up on March 22nd. The confusion and ambiguity noted in them may be noted also in the supplementary instructions which were subsequently added to them. The Armada did not leave Corunna until July 12th, so that there was plenty of time for the reconsideration of the plans put forward in March.

On May 18th, Medina Sidonia wrote to the king a letter in which he discussed the project. His views then expressed agree with Philip's instructions, in so far as they indicate that the admiral considered it as settled that he was not to seek the enemy previous to the moment of Parma's junction with him. He does not, however, mention the place of junction. And the letter opens up some entirely new questions. In common with his most experienced officers, Medina Sidonia considered that it would be risky to hand over many of his troops to Parma so long as the enemy's fleet had not been rendered harmless. (In a word, he recognised the gravity of neglecting a "potent" fleet.) His idea was rather to unite with Parma, and then to seek and destroy the English fleet, before attempting a landing. If he should succeed in doing this, he would give Parma as many men as the latter might ask for. The land attack would thereby be rendered the more secure and certain. This pre-supposed, of course, a junction between Medina Sidonia and Parma previous to the discovery and disabling of the enemy.

It is nowhere expressly said that it would be for Parma's transports to wait off the English coast, somewhere near Margate, until the English fleet should be beaten. Yet that seems to have been Medina Sidonia's meaning. At all events, Parma was to have no share worth mentioning in the victory which it was purposed to gain after the junction had been effected. Parma's contingent was not regarded as likely to very considerably strengthen the fighting power of the Armada at sea. The letter further indicates that Philip had proposed that, after the junction had been effected, the English fleet should, if possible, be blockaded in some port, and then harassed simultaneously by land and by sea.

After the departure from Lisbon, Medina Sidonia wrote to Parma that the Armada was on its way, and that the people were in good spirits and burning for a fight, "if the enemy would wait for them." Still, apparently bearing in mind the original instructions, he said that the king had ordered him to proceed directly to Parma's assistance. He laid stress upon the fact that he had only to clear the way, attacking if the enemy annoyed him. But he was not to follow the English fleet far, if it gave way. In this letter, the scheme of junction with Parma was touched upon with the same perplexing vagueness as on previous occasions.

Medina Sidonia begged Parma, immediately upon receiving the dispatch, to set sail in order to meet the Armada, and at the same time to send a messenger to the fleet, to inform the admiral how far Parma's preparations had advanced, and where the junction was to take place. Supposing Margate to have still been the destination of both forces, Medina Sidonia evidently contemplated the possibility of a junction previous to his arrival off that town.

Recalde's opinion of the plan is noteworthy. Recalde was vice-admiral of the entire fleet, (*i.e. almirante*, or second in command. The commander-in-chief was styled Captain-General. Duro); and it would be his duty to exert himself to the utmost in the battle. His remarks are to be found in a letter which, on July 1st, shortly before the final departure of the fleet from Spain, he addressed to the king.

The object of the fleet was, according to the little which Recalde had been able to learn, to fight the enemy at close quarters and disperse him, if he accepted action, as Recalde felt sure he would. (Recalde's expression to this effect indicates how ill-informed even the highest officers were as to the methods to be pursued.) But it has already been shown that Philip preferred that Parma's passage should be managed without a battle. If there should be no fight, continued Recalde, the fleet was to proceed to the Downs, ("*Las Dimas*," but the expression might mean The Dunes, or the banks on the Netherlands' coast), and thence reach out a helping hand to the forces at Dunquerque. The next measure was to be the taking of such precautions as would enable Parma's army to safely reach England, landing at the place which Parma should designate as being the most suitable for the purpose.

If we may trust Recalde's impressions, the orders then in force prescribed neither that the junction should be effected off Margate, nor that Medina Sidonia and Parma, after their junction, should proceed thither. Indeed, he himself offered suggestions as the most suitable place, declaring that it should be one as little as possible removed, either northward or southward, from the mouth of the Thames. Margate would, of course, be such a place; but, if Margate had already been specified to him as the point selected, Recalde would scarcely have written as he did. Parma's passage would, he thought, probably occupy several days, for cavalry was to be sent over; and as all could not cross at once, the transports would have to make at least two trips. After Parma had crossed successfully, it would be necessary, according to Recalde, to seek a port in England for Medina Sidonia's fleet. He suggested several, and expressed the opinion that even if the Spaniards beat the English fleet, the latter would hardly be reduced to so impotent a condition as not to be able to again appear at sea in fighting trim.

As has thus been indicated, the details of the original plan were not adhered to. The plan seems, in fact, to have been modified little by little until not Margate, but the coast of Flanders became the immediate destination of the Armada. For, on July 20th, the day before the first action with the English, Medina Sidonia wanted to remain off the Isle of Wight until Parma's preparations should be so far advanced as to admit of a junction being effected as soon as the Armada should arrive at some place in the neighbourhood of Dunquerque.

It is clear that the admiral then no longer thought of proceeding first of all to Margate Road. Had he contemplated such a step, Margate would have been as convenient a place of waiting as the neighbourhood of the Isle of Wight. (Duro. The duke is therein strictly forbidden to attempt anything against the Isle of Wight before first proceeding to Margate.) The junction was not to be needlessly postponed, the coast of Flanders being a dangerous one, and the Armada having to fear that many of its ships might be driven ashore in case of heavy weather arising. For this reason, Parma was requested to join immediately upon Medina Sidonia's arrival on the coast, and not to cause the fleet a moment's delay. But again, the exact place of junction was not specified.

Valdes, however, wrote (S. P. Dom. ccxv.), that, on July 20th, Dunquerque was the point of destination. On July 21st, after the first battle, Medina Sidonia's idea (expressed in a letter to Parma of July 21st), was to continue his passage without halt, until he should learn from Parma what to do, and where to wait for him. If Margate was still the goal, it is evident that Medina Sidonia understood that the junction was to be effected before his arrival off that place. The coast of Flanders, then, in spite of the dangers of its shoals, may be accepted as the locality for the intended meeting. Moreover, on July 26th, Medina Sidonia, as Valdes had done previously, indicated Dunquerque as the point. Parma was to join the Armada as soon as it came in sight of Dunquerque.

But when the Spanish admiral drew near Calais, he was informed by the pilots that, owing to the currents, it would be risky to proceed farther on his intended course. He therefore altered his plan. The new scheme was that Parma should join off Calais. (And Medina Sidonia to Parma, July 27th, in Froude's Transcripts.) After the junction had been effected, the combined fleet was to seek some secure harbour, in default of which the large ships of the Armada would certainly drive ashore. Nor is it clear that there was any longer an idea of making Margate the common point of destination. On the contrary, Medina Sidonia seems to have again turned his mind to the Isle of Wight, and to have proposed to Parma to seize the requisite secure harbour in that neighbourhood.

In spite of all this vagueness, alteration, and ambiguity, one perceives that the leading idea of the expedition was that if the English fleet should follow Medina Sidonia, it was to be dispersed, so that, the Channel being cleared, Parma could cross it. If the English fleet should not appear, or if it should appear and be decisively defeated, the minor details of subsequent operations would present no difficulties, provided that a secure harbour or anchorage could be found for the Armada, and that Parma should have favourable weather for his passage. The actions fought before the arrival of the Armada off Calais imperilled the carrying out of the leading idea. It is not astonishing that the scheme of minor details, vague as it was even before the first action, became afterwards hopelessly confused.

So much for the general plan of operations. The preparations in Spain may now be returned to. And, first of all, Medina Sidonia's general orders to his fleet demand attention. They laid stress upon the religious aspect of the expedition. The people were to understand that they were participating in a crusade. Their behaviour must be worthy of their holy aims.

All, high and low, must realise, above all things, that the king undertook the expedition mainly for the service of God, and for the leading back to the bosom of the Church of souls subjected to the enemies of the Holy Catholic faith. Lest they should forget these aims, the people, before proceeding on board, were to humbly confess, and to receive the Sacrament. No one in the fleet, on pain of severe punishment, was to "idly make use of the name of our Lord, or of our Lady, or of the Saints." Even less sinful exclamations were to be punished, apparently by stoppage of the offender's ration of wine. As men swear most lightly while at play, certain games were to be forbidden, and others were to be played as little as possible. In no case was play by night to be permitted.

During the entire duration of the expedition, and for a month afterwards, all contentious questions, challenges, and so on, were, upon pain of death, to be referred to Medina Sidonia. This rule applied to all, great as well as small. Loose women were not to be suffered on board the ships. (But there were some women with the Armada. A lady and children were with Oquendo's second in command: and "*la urea de las mujeres*" "women's urea" is mentioned: Duro.) Every morning at sunrise, in accordance with the Spanish custom, the ships' boys were to call out the morning salutation at the foot of the mainmast. On the approach of night, they were to recite the *Ave Maria*, and, on certain days, the *Salve* and *Litany*. As symbolising the Catholic faith and Spanish dominion, banners bearing the figure of Christ, the figure of the Virgin, and the arms of Philip, were to be carried by the fleet.

At last the Armada was in a condition to sail. It put to sea from Lisbon on the morning of May 20th, 1588, and on June 9th, Medina Sidonia, with part of it, entered Corunna. The rest of the fleet was to have entered the same port on the following day, but was scattered, and to some extent damaged, by a violent storm. Medina Sidonia was at once disheartened, and advised Philip, seeing that the ships were separated, many of the people sick, provisions bad and scarce, and officers and men unfit for their work, to make an honourable treaty with the English.

The commander-in-chief of the Armada, in a word, wished to give up his undertaking before he had left Spain or caught sight of the enemy. And, indeed, he had reasons for not feeling entirely satisfied. He mentioned the absence of many of his ships; and that the crews had complained of the victuals. Yet he showed clearly enough, by his attitude on that occasion, how unsuitable he was for the leadership of men.

It is remarkable that Philip, thus informed by Medina Sidonia himself of the character of that officer, did not appoint a stronger man to supersede him. Philip, however, kept his admiral, while he wholly neglected his admiral's advice. He directed Medina Sidonia to await the arrival in port of his heaviest ships, and expressed a hope that they would be ready for sea on July 2nd.

In the course of a short time, almost all the missing vessels safely reached Corunna and other Spanish ports. Some of them had been driven nearly as far as the Scilly Isles. (Where they sighted and chased several English traders about June 13th: S. P. Dom. ccxi.) Haste was made over the repairs of the damaged ships, and in the furnishing of proper victuals. In the meantime, the religious aspect of the expedition was kept prominently in view by the erection on an island in the harbour of tents and altars, where the people once more confessed, and received the Sacrament.

Philip's motives, viewed from our present standpoint, are sufficiently apparent. He was animated by personal pique, for his matrimonial advances had been repulsed by Elizabeth, and he knew that he was detested in England. He had patriotic reasons for his action; for his huge empire oversea had suffered sorely from the depredations of the wild spirits of England, and his subjects in the Low Countries were being abetted in their struggle for freedom by English help and sympathy. And he had the religious incentive; for, himself a zealot of the most extreme type, he could have regarded no mission as more glorious or more worthy of a Christian sovereign than the bringing back of England to the fold of the Roman Church.

Yet, in the eyes of the England of the third quarter of the sixteenth century, Philip, naturally enough, found no justification whatsoever. If he had been repelled by England and her queen, his gloomy and fanatic character had richly merited the rebuff. If he had suffered in his possessions oversea, the attitude of his representatives there had invited, nay, even compelled, hostile English action. If his Netherlands subjects were in arms against him, Spanish tyranny and oppression were merely meeting with their inevitable reward. And, if he stood for the Roman Catholic faith, Elizabeth stood as conspicuously for a faith which, though new, was already much dearer to the majority in England. Even the English Roman Catholics were not, with very rare exceptions, won over by Philip's assumption of the Crusader's cross.

They were not religiously free, it is true, in those days; yet they knew well that, upon the whole, they were little worse off under Elizabeth than they would have been under Philip. In England, liberty had shown its head, and could not but grow and flourish. Already toleration was slowly extending. And the inspirations of a new and lusty youth had seized upon all Englishmen and rendered them proud of their nationality, no matter whether they agreed or disagreed with the Reformation. So, it was that many English Roman Catholics gallantly fought for England in that crisis, with arms as well as with diplomacy; and that few, indeed, cared to range themselves, even passively, against her.

After the Armada had failed, an official English account of the proceedings against it was drawn up, and has been preserved. (Cotton MS. Julius F. x. The credit of showing that this document has an official character, and, moreover, that it represents the views and conclusions of Howard himself, is due to Professor Laughton, R.N.) It will be much quoted from later, since it possesses the signal merit, from the naval point of view, of having been prepared under Howard's direction. But it is also interesting because it contains, in the form of a curious preamble, a statement of what was certainly the generally accepted English case against Spanish ambition and duplicity, it runs:

Whereas the Queen's most excellent Majesty had of late years sundry and most certain intelligences of the great warlike preparation both for sea and land which the King of Spain of late years made from all parts, not only of the mightiest and most puissant ships and vessels that he could prepare, as well from foreign places as in his own dominions, and by arresting of the ships of other countries that came into his dominions, but also of all kind of munition and victuals, and of captains, soldiers and mariners, and of all other provisions for a mighty army by seas, to come out of Spain and Portugal.

For the more strength whereof it was notorious to the world how he had drawn into Spain and Portugal his principal and most experimented captains and old soldiers out of Naples, Sicilia, Lombardy, and other parts of Italy, yea, and from sundry remote places of the Indies; the preparation whereof, with the numbers of ships, men, victuals, ordnance and all kind of munition, was made patent to the world by sundry books printed and published both in Spain, Portugal, and in many other countries of Christendom, carrying the titles of the *Happy Armada of the King of Spain*, and, in some, specially expressed to be against England.

And, in like sort, where(as) Her Majesty had the like knowledge of the mighty and puissant forces of horses and footmen, sufficient to make many armies, prepared in the Low Countries under the conduct of the Duke of Parma, the King's Lieutenant-General, and of multitude of ships, bilanders, boats and other vessels fit for the transporting and landing of the said forces, armies from the coast of Flanders, with a general publication to the, world that all these so mighty forces, both by sea and land, were intended to the invasion of Her Majesty's realms, and, as was pretended, to have made therewith a full conquest.

Yet for that, in this time of their preparation, the King of Spain, by his Lieutenant-General, the Duke of Parma, caused certain offers to be made to Her Majesty for a communication of a peace betwixt their Majesties: howsoever, by the common judgment of the world, the same was done but to abuse Her Majesty and to win time whilst his preparations might be made complete; Her Majesty, nevertheless, like a most godly and Christian prince, did not refuse to give ear to so Christian an offer, for which purpose she sent certain noblemen (The English Commissioners were Henry, Earl of Derby; William, Lord Cobham; Sir James à Crofts; and Doctors Valentine Dale and John Rogers), of her Privy Council into Flanders to treat with certain commissioners, who continued there without any good success by reason of the unreasonable delays of the King's Commissioners; yea, they continued there until the Navy of Spain was overcome and forced to fly.

AN ENGLISH SHIP OF WAR, 1588.

The impression, therefore, in England was to the effect that Philip was bent not so much upon the settlement of grievances, if he had any, as upon the subjugation of the country; and the prevalence of this impression cannot but have had an important influence upon the attitude of an independent and self-reliant people.

While, therefore, Spain prepared for the spring, England made ready to receive the shock without flinching.

Early in the year (February 1st: S. P. Dom. ccviii. From on board the *White Bear*), the Lord High Admiral, Lord Howard of Effingham, had warned Walsyngham that it would be dangerous then to weaken the English fleet. (Howard had been specially commissioned on December 21st, 1587, to command against the Spaniards: S. P. Dom. ccvi.) He was of opinion that Parma, at Dunquerque, was hatching something against Scotland, and complained that English prestige had diminished. He wrote that the enemy was aware that the English were like bears tied to stakes, and that the dogs might worry them with impunity. On the same day Hawkyns appealed to Walsyngham, (from on board the *Bonaventure*), for bold and decisive action he wrote.

> Having of long time seen the malicious practices of the papists combined generally throughout Christendom to alter the government of this realm and to bring it to papistry, and consequently to servitude, I have a good will from time to time to do and set forward something as I could have credit to impeach their purpose. But it. hath prevailed little, for that there was never any substantial ground laid to be followed effectually. . . . If we stand at this point in a mammering and at a stay, we consume, and our Commonwealth doth utterly decay. . . . We have to choose either a dishonourable and uncertain peace, or to put on virtuous and valiant minds, to make a way through with such a settled war as may bring forth and command a quiet peace.

He went on to recommend:

> That there be always six principal good ships of Her Majesty's upon the coast of Spain, victualled for four months, and accompanied with some six small vessels, which shall haunt the coast of Spain and the islands, and he a sufficient company to distress anything that goeth through the seas. And when these must return, there would be other six good ships, likewise accompanied, to keep the place. . . . For these six ships we shall

not break the strength of the navy; for we shall have a sufficient company always at home to front any violence that can he anyway offered unto us. . . . And therefore, I conclude that with God's blessing and a lawful open war, the Lord shall bring us a most honourable and quiet peace, to the glory of His Church, and to the honour of Her Majesty and this realm of England.

On February 29th, Howard learnt that the Armada was about to sail from Spain. He had recovered from his dejection, and, writing to Burghley, (from on board the *Ark*), said:

If I may have the four great ships come to me in time, and 20 good hoys, but with 20 men apiece, which is but a small charge, and each of them but with two iron pieces, I doubt not but to make Her Majesty a good account of anything that shall be done by the Spanish forces, and I will make him wish his galleys at home again. . . . I protest before God, and as my soul shall answer for it, that I think there were never in any place in the world worthier ships than these are, for so many. And as few as we are, if the King of Spain's forces be not hundreds, we will make good sport with them. And I pray you tell her Majesty from me that her money was well given for the *Ark Ralegh*, (bought from Sir W. Ralegh for £5000. The sum was in 1592 deducted from his debt to the Crown), for I think her the odd ship in the world for all conditions: and truly I think there can no great ship make me change and go out of her. We can see no sail, great nor small, but how far soever they be off, we fetch them and speak with them.

And Sir William Wynter, writing on February 28th, to the Principal Officers of the Navy (from on board the *Vanguard* in the Downs), after the winter had tried the fleet, spoke with equal enthusiasm of the vessels.

Our ships do show themselves like gallants here. I assure you it will do a man's heart good to behold them; and would to God the Prince of Parma were upon the seas with all his forces, and we in the view of them. Then I doubt not but that you would hear that we would make his enterprise very unpleasant to him. But with sorrow I speak it, I am afraid that they will keep me from the baths of Bath by their long detraction, where I meant to have been to seek health by the beginning of May next.

Drake was another of those who advised and longed for an energetic offensive. Writing on March 30th to the Council, (from Plymouth), he said:—

If Her Majesty and your Lordship thinks that the King of Spain meaneth any invasion in England, then doubtless his force is and will be great in Spain; and thereon he will make his groundwork or foundation, whereby the Prince of Parma may have the better entrance, which, in mine own judgment, is most to be feared. But if there may be such a stay or stop made by any means of this fleet in Spain, that they may not come through the seas as conquerors—which, I assure myself, they think to do—then shall the Prince of Parma have such a check thereby as were meet.

But he added that the ships had not enough powder on board for more than a day's, or a day and a half's fighting, and that more ought to be sent to them; "for it importeth but the loss of all." Nor did he underrate the importance of increasing the active navy. To the queen, on April 13th, he wrote, (from Plymouth):—

If your Majesty will give present order for our proceeding to the sea, and send to the strengthening of this fleet here four more of your Majesty's good ships, and those 16 sail of ships with their pinnaces which are preparing in London, then shall your Majesty stand assured, with God's assistance, that if the fleet come out of Lisbon, as long as we have victual to live withal upon that coast, they shall be fought with. . . . God increase your most excellent Majesty's forces both by sea and land daily; for this I surely think, there was never any force so strong as there is now ready or making ready against your Majesty.

Drake continued to press his opinion that the Spaniards should be met and fought off their own shores. On April 28th, he again wrote to the queen:

These great preparations of the Spaniard may be speedily prevented as much as in your Majesty lieth, by sending your forces to encounter them somewhat far off, and more near their own coasts.

But the Channel was to be the scene of England's defence. This, however, was not the desire of the naval commanders. Writing to

Burghley, (from Plymouth), on May 23rd, the Lord High Admiral related what had so far been done.

> Upon Tuesday last, being the 21st of this instant, the wind serving exceedingly well, I cut sail at the Downs, assigning unto my Lord Henry Seymour those ships appointed to stay with him on the Narrow Seas; and so parting companies the same morning athwart of Dover, and with a pleasant gale all the way long, came and arrived this day, being the 23rd, about eight of the clock in the morning, at this port of Plymouth, whence Sir Francis Drake came forth with sixty sail very well appointed to meet with me; and so, casting about, he put with me into the haven again, where I mean to stay there two days to water our fleet, and afterwards, God willing, to take the opportunity of the first wind serving for the coast of Spain, with intention to lie on and off betwixt England and that coast to watch the coming of the Spanish forces.

When, on May 28th, Howard again wrote to Burghley the fleet was, contrary to the commander-in-chief's expectations, still at Plymouth.

> I have received a letter from my man Burnell, (Francis Burnell, of Acton Burnell, then captain of the *Mary Rose*, and later joined the *Ark*. From one branch of his family are descended the Italian Actons, and Lord Acton; from another, Captain John Coke Burnell; 1883, R.N.), whom I left to come after us with the ten ships with victuals. I perceive by his letter that the ships, and also the victuals, be nothing in that readiness that I looked they should be in, nor as Mr. Quarles, (James Quarles was Baeshe's successor in the Victualling Department), did promise me; for he did ensure me that within seven or eight days at the farthest they should be dispatched after my departure from the Court, which was the 14th of this month. Burnell's letter unto me beareth date of the 20th, and signifieth unto me that Mr. Quarles and Mr. Peter told him that it would not be ready to depart in 12 or 14 days after; and besides that the ships were in no readiness that should bring it, and that there would be no mariners gotten for them. . . . We have here now but 18 days' victual, and there is none to be gotten in all this country: and what that is to go withal to sea, your Lordship may judge.

He had already learnt that the Armada was to have sailed with the first fair wind; and, realising the danger of delay, expressed his intention of sailing, short of stores though he was, "for go we will, though we starve"; seeing that he did not know whether the Spaniards were bound for England, Ireland, or Scotland, he added:

> I believe surely, if the wind hold here but six days, they will knock at our door. It they do so, the fault is not ours; for I hope we have lost not one hour nor minute of time, nor will suffer any after to be lost."

And in a second letter of the same day he said:

> There is here the gallantest company of captains, soldiers, and mariners that I think ever was seen in England. It were pity they should lack meat, when they are so desirous to spend their lives in her Majesty's service.

Walsyngham on June 9th, at the queen's direction, wrote to Howard, desiring him not to cruise, as he had intended, so far to the southward as Bayona, since the Spaniards, by taking a westerly course, might circumvent him and "shoot over to this realm" during his absence. ("The isles of Bayona." Bayona is near the south point of Galicia, and numerous islands lie off the coast to the northward of it.) Howard received this command on June 14th, and was much embarrassed by it, Drake, Hawkyns, Frobiser, and, in fact, all the most experienced captains, being in favour of endeavouring to meet the Spaniards as near as possible to their own coasts, where, it was then the admiral's conviction, they intended to remain while the English wore themselves out and expended their supplies. (From on board the *Ark* in Plymouth Sound. S. P. Dom. ccxi. 26., June 15th, also from the *Ark* in Plymouth Sound). Howard remonstrated vigorously, he said:

> If we had been on their coast, they durst not have put off, to have left us on their backs; and when they shall come with the south-westerly wind, which must serve them if they go for Ireland or Scotland, though we be as high as Cape Clear, yet shall we not be able to go to them as long as the wind shall be westerly. And if we lie so high, then, may the Spanish fleet bear with the coast of France, to come for the Isle of Wight; which for my part, I think, if they come to England, they will attempt. Then are we clean out of the way of any service against them. But I must and will obey; and am glad there be such there as are

able to judge what is fitter for us to do than we here.

On June 19th, Howard was still waiting at Plymouth for supplies. (Howard to Walsyngham). Nor had they reached him by June 22nd, when he wrote, (to the Council):—

> If they come not, our extremity will be very great, for our victuals ended the 15th of this month; and if that Mr. Darell had not very carefully provided, us of 14 days' victuals, and again with four or five days more, which now he hath provided, we had been in some great extremity. . . . Men have fallen sick, and by thousands fain to be discharged, and others pressed in their stead. (Marmaduke Darell, victualling agent for the navy. He was knighted in 1603.)

At about that time the Lord High Admiral naturally became exceedingly anxious, and on June 22nd, being still at Plymouth, he wrote to Walsyngham:

> I am very sorry that Her Majesty will not thoroughly awake in this perilous and most dangerous time. . . . I put out on Wednesday to the sea in hopes to have met with some of our victuallers, but on Friday we were put in again with a southerly wind. I hope now shortly we shall hear of our victuals, for the wind doth now serve them. I pray God all be well with them, for if any chance should come to them we should be in most miserable case. For the love of God let the Narrow Seas be well strengthened, and the ships victualled for some good time.

He was, no doubt, the more anxious in consequence of having heard, although he could hardly credit, that a squadron of nine great ships had been sighted on June 13th between Ushant and the Scilly Isles by an English trading bark, and that other vessels had been chased, and even fired at, by the enemy. (These were some of the vessels which had been dispersed by the storm of June 9th.)

But at length a month's victuals arrived. Writing to the queen (from on board the *Ark*, at Plymouth), on Sunday, June 23rd, Howard said:

> On Saturday, late at night, they came to us. They were no sooner come, although it were night, but we went all to work to get in our victuals, which I hope shall be done in 24 hours, for no man shall sleep nor eat till it be dispatched; so that, God willing, we will be under sail tomorrow morning, being Monday, and the 24th of this present.

On the same day, he wrote to Walsyngham, at 12 p.m., "God willing, I will set sail within this three hours," and expressed his belief that the Armada was bound to the coast of France to pick up an army under the Duke of Guise.

The fact that English traders had been sighted, chased, and fired at by Spanish ships at the mouth of the Channel on June 13th, and two or three following days, was, as has been seen, scarcely credited at first by Howard. But the report undoubtedly created in time a very general impression, among himself and his subordinates, that the whole Armada was then close to England.

We know now that the report was correct, but that the Spanish vessels were merely a few which, by the tempest of June 9th, had been driven from off Corunna, and that most of them returned thither before the final sailing of the Armada on July 12th. For some time after June 13th there was no further definite news of the whereabouts of the enemy; and it was therefore generally concluded that the Spaniards had, for some unknown reason, put back. Upon that assumption, Brake and Thomas Fenner strongly counselled that the English fleet should proceed in a body to the coast of Spain.

The advice, however, did not find favour. The dispositions which were actually made are set forth in a letter, addressed by Howard to Walsyngham, on July 6th. The commander-in-chief had put to sea, probably on June 24th, for a cruise in the Channel, and had been subsequently informed by a dispatch from Walsyngham that there was no danger of France assisting the Spaniards. After describing how he had looked for Spanish ships off the Scillies, and failed to find them, he wrote:

> I have divided myself here into three parts, and yet we lie within sight one of another, so as, if any of us do discover the Spanish fleet, we give notice thereof presently the one to the other, and thereupon repair and assemble together. I myself do lie in the middle of the Channel, with the greatest force. Sir Francis Drake (vice-admiral), hath 20 ships and four or five pinnaces, which lie towards Ushant; and Mr. Hawkyns, (rear-admiral, for many generations afterwards it was customary to write of otherwise untitled flag-officers in this way), with as many more, lieth towards Scilly.

If the Armada were destined for England, he did not doubt of falling in with it; if it were aimed at Scotland, he would follow it through the Narrow Seas. He did not believe that it was bound for Ireland. At the same period Lord Henry Seymour, with his flag in the *Rainbow*, commanded a detached force in the Downs, to watch Flushing, Dunquerque, and the Straits of Dover; and two Netherlands fleets were under orders to co-operate.

✶✶✶✶✶✶

A Netherlands contingent, of about 30 vessels, was under the supreme command of Justinus van Nassau, Lieutenant-Admiral of Zeeland, a natural son of Prince William I. The other flag-officers of this squadron were Jan van Wassenaer, Lord of Warmond, Pieter van der Does, and Joos de Moor. This force watched the ports, and especially Dunquerque. Another Netherlands squadron, under Jan Gerbrandtszoon, cruised off the northern coasts of the United Provinces. A squadron under Captain Cornelius Lonck van Roozendaal seems to have been intended to join Howard's fleet; but did not do so.—Jonge: *Het Nederlandsche Zeewezen*, i. Justinus van Nassau, with 40 sail, visited Dover in the middle of August. Seymour wrote to Walsyngham, on August 17th: "I find the man very wise, subtle, and cunning, and therefore do trust him. S. P. Dom. ccxv. 24.

✶✶✶✶✶✶

On July 12th, the very day when the Armada quitted Corunna, Seymour wrote to Walsyngham, and, after recounting how the summer weather on his station had been unusually bad, and admitting that the gales were often favourable for the Spaniards, should they choose to come into the Channel, added:

Yet shall they be as greatly damaged by the raging seas as by their enemies. And to heap on braveries for conquering little England, that hath always been renowned, and now most famous by the great discovered strength, as well by sea as by land, the same also united with thousands (of) resolute civil minds—how can the same enter into my conceit they should any ways prevail?

Thus, there was an admirable spirit in his division. On July 13th, Howard wrote to Walsyngham that he had four pinnaces looking out on the Spanish coast, and then, echoing Seymour, continued:

I know not what weather you have had there, but there was never any such summer seen here on the sea. God of His mercy keep us from sickness, for we fear that more than any hurt the

Spaniards will do.

In the meantime, Howard, having found no Spaniards in the Channel, had cruised farther to the southward from July 8th to July 10th, and then, fearing lest the enemy might pass him unsighted, had put about, and returned to Plymouth on July 12th, to re-water and refresh his ships. He seems to have been a little puzzled, for he wrote thence to Walsyngham, on July 17th:

> I make all the haste I can possible out. . . . Seeing the advertisements (*i.e.* reports concerning the enemy), be no surer, I mean to keep the three great ships with me yet awhile, to see what will come of it. Some four or five ships have discharged their men; for the sickness in some is very great, so that we are fain to discharge some ships to have their men to furnish the others.

But, though perplexed and worried, he was in good spirits, and full of confidence. And, indeed, all in the fleet were in like mood. Thomas Fenner, for example, wrote to Walsyngham (from on board the *Nonpareil*), on July 17th:

> There never happened the like opportunity to beat down the Spanish pride, if it he effectually followed.

The movements and fortunes of the Spaniards must now, for a time, be followed.

The weather at Corunna had for some days been stormy, when, on the evening of July 11th, it began to improve. Medina Sidonia thereupon ordered his captains to lie at single anchor only; and at midnight, the firing of a gun from the flagship served as a signal to the fleet to weigh. At daylight, a second gunshot from the San Martin directed the ships to make all sail. The light southwest breeze was not sufficient to fill the canvas, and between daybreak and 2 p.m. on July 12th, the Armada did not make three miles' progress, and, at the latter hour, had not rounded Cape Priorino. It then fell quite calm; but after a short time, the wind got up again a little, and the coast was slowly left behind.

All went well until July 17th, when the Armada encountered a violent storm. The Spanish seamen declared that, at a corresponding time of year, they had never witnessed such a heavy sea as was soon aroused. The 18th was clear and sunny, with light winds. Forty ships were found to be missing; and Medina Sidonia sent forward a dispatch-vessel in the direction of the Lizard, in order to look for them.

The gale, however, had done little damage to the vessels which were still in company. A detailed list of the entire Armada, as of the fleet opposed to it, will be found in an appendix at the close of this chapter.

At Lisbon, (on April 29th), the Spanish fleet had consisted of 130 sail, made up of 65 galleons, (in addition to twenty small *caravels* and *feluccas*); 25 *urcas* or hulks, of from 300 to 700 tons; 19 *pataches* or dispatch-vessels, of from 70 to 100 tons; 13 *zabras*; 4 *galleasses*; (very large galleys), and 4 galleys; with 2431 guns, and an aggregate burthen of 57,868 tons, and carrying officers, seamen, and troops to the number of 30, 656, (this, the paper strength, no doubt exceeded the real force: Duro, doc. 113.

The estimated strength at Corunna was only 22,500 all told), besides volunteers, servants, priests, and other civilians. The supplies for this huge expedition included 110,000 *quintals*, (1 *quintal* is 101.4 lbs), of biscuit, 11,117 *mayors*, (1 *mayor* is 56.2 gals), of wine, 6000 *quintals* of pork, 3000 *quintals* of cheese, 6000 *quintals* of fish, 4000 *quintals* of rice, 6000 *fanegas*, (1 *fanega* is 1.5 bushels), of beans and peas, 10,000 *arrobas*, (1 *arroba* is 3.5 gals), of oil, 21,000 *arrobas* of vinegar, and 11,000 pipes of water. There were stores of sheet lead and leather for the repair of shot-holes; 21 fieldpieces, with 40 mules to draw them, and 3500 shot for them; and, as extra ordnance supplies, 7000 arquebusses, 1000 muskets, 10,000 pikes, 1000 spears, 6000 half-pikes, with spades, axes, shovels, baskets, etc., etc., for work ashore. (Duro).

Nine days after the departure from Corunna, that is, on July 20th, the Armada was but nine craft short of its Lisbon strength; and of the missing vessels, two had never got as far as Corunna; so that the dispersion occasioned by the gale of the 17th may have been quickly repaired, although the Armada, since leaving Lisbon, had possibly been reinforced, and, probably, had not been rejoined by all the ships separated from it outside Corunna on the night of June 9th. Of 62 ships "of the first class," 59, averaging 726 tons and 26 guns, were still with the fleet.

Captain Duro, and Professor Laughton following him, seem to be of opinion that, upon the whole, the Spanish vessels were much more lightly armed than their enemies. Dr. W. F. Tilton is somewhat opposed to this conclusion. Of the guns, Professor Laughton says:

> As a rule they were small—four, six, or nine pounders: they were comparatively few, and they were very badly worked.

Dr. Tilton imagines that he can trace the origin of this assertion to the fact that, on July 26th, the day after the fight off the Isle of Wight, Medina Sidonia sent to Parma a request for shot of four, six, and ten pounds. A list, dated May 4th, shows that the Spanish fleet had 1497 bronze guns (nearly all the larger guns of the time were bronze or brass), of all calibres, including many "cannon," *i.e.*, ships' guns of the largest size then employed. Besides them there were 934 iron pieces of all sorts. Dr. Tilton says:

> For these 2431 weapons, there were only 123,790 shot sup-
> plied—an average of about 50 shot per gun. It is almost certain
> that for the lighter pieces the supply was larger than for the
> greater; but, supposing that the allowance was the same for all,
> the quicker running short of the small shot becomes only the
> more natural.

And Medina Sidonia's request ought not to be tortured into an implication that he had very few guns bigger than nine or ten-pounders. Dr. Tilton, moreover, points out that Professor Laughton bases at least part of his conclusions upon a statement of force drawn up on July 9th (N.S.), 1587, and that he appears to ignore that, as late as March 4th, 1588, Philip ordered the armament of the Armada to be strengthened.

It is, however, probable that the thirty-four ships of the English Royal Navy, which were engaged, had a slight superiority of armament over any thirty-four vessels belonging to the Armada; and it is quite certain, not only that the Spanish gunnery was very inferior, but also that the Spanish practice of making portholes so small as barely to admit the muzzles of the guns mounted behind them, prevented many guns, which might otherwise have rendered excellent service, from being effectively employed.

On the other hand, there is plenty of testimony that, besides their thirty-four best ships, the Spaniards possessed many vessels which must be regarded as having serious fighting importance; while the testimony is equally strong that, beyond the thirty-four vessels belonging to the queen, Howard commanded very few that could serve a much better purpose than, as Wynter put it, "to make a show." (Wynter to Walsyngham, August 1st, 1588, from the *Vanguard*) The superior handiness of the English ships, and the superior seamanship of the English officers and men, are undoubted.

The largest Spanish ships were but little bigger than the largest English; and their relatively greater height above the water, although it gave their crews an advantage when boarding or repelling boarding was attempted, was a source of weakness which ought not to be lost sight of. Their excessively lofty poops and forecastles rendered them very leewardly, and caused them to present magnificent targets to the English gunners.

On July 19th, the Armada, with a favourable wind from the westward, pursued its course. On that day the dispatch-vessel, which had been sent in the direction of the Lizard to search for the missing vessels, rejoined the fleet with the intelligence that they were ahead, under Don Pedro de Valdes, and that he was keeping them together and awaiting the main body.

By the English this detached portion of the Spanish fleet was sighted off the Lizard. The discoverer of them was Captain Thomas Flemyng, of the *Golden Hind*, a vessel which had been apparently placed on scouting duty by Howard himself. Flemyng was not, as has often been asserted, a pirate, but an honest man, and a connection of the Hawkyns family. He reported, or at least conveyed the impression, that he had seen as many as fifty ships in company, and he reached Plymouth on the 19th.

On the afternoon of that day almost the whole of the Armada was once more with the flag, the four galleys and one other vessel only being missing; and the invaders, as a whole, had their first sight of the English coast. Upon an announcement to this effect being made to him, Medina Sidonia hoisted at the fore a flag bearing a crucifix and the figures of Our Lady and St. Mary Magdalene; and fired three guns as a signal for general prayer and thanksgiving.

On the morning of the 20th, the coast was seen to be studded with signal fires. (The arrangement of the beacons in Kent is shown in the map. There was a similar arrangement in each of the other southern counties.) That day a council of war was held, and it was decided to make for the entrance of Plymouth Sound, and, if circumstances favoured, to endeavour to attack the English fleet at its anchorage. (It is difficult to understand how the instructions justified any such scheme.) But the English were not to be caught napping.

As soon as Flemyng had reported, although the wind was very scant, Howard (to Walsyngham, July 21st), warped out of harbour, (with fifty-four sail. Cott. MS. Julius, V. About forty sail did not get out until later); but on Saturday, July 20th, he found himself impeded by a south-west breeze.

He writes:

About three of the dock in the afternoon, (we) descried the Spanish fleet, and did what we could to work for the wind, which by this morning (July 21st) we had recovered, descrying their fleet to consist of 120 sail, (John Popham, writing to Walsyngham from Wellington on July 22nd, says one hundred and sixty-two sail), whereof there are four *galleasses*, and many ships of great burthen. At nine of the clock we gave them fight, which continued until one. In this fight, we made some of them to bear room, (bear away), to stop their leaks; notwithstanding we durst not adventure to put in among them, their fleet being so strong. (The English fleet was, of course, on this and several following days, without Lord Henry Seymour's division.) . . . The captains in Her Majesty's ships have behaved themselves most bravely and like men. . . . For the love of God and our country let us have with some speed some great shot sent us of all bigness(es): for this service will continue long: and some powder with it.

Drake, by Howard's orders, at once wrote to Seymour and Wynter, who were detached to the eastward, to apprise them of what had occurred, and to warn them to be in readiness for the enemy when he should reach their neighbourhood. Writing on the 22nd, apparently

A SHIP OF THE ARMADA, 1588.

to the Earl of Sussex, Howard urgently asked for reinforcements, and added in a postscript:

> The ships you send shall find me east-north-east, following the Spanish fleet. Since the making up of my letter there is a *galleass* (that of Don Pedro de Valdes, the *N. S. del Rosario*, elsewhere called a *galleon* and a *gallega*), of the enemy's taken with 450 men in her; and yesterday I spoiled one of their greatest ships, (the *San Salvador*, of the squadron of Guipúzcoa), that they were fain to forsake her.

An account of this first action of July 21st, is thus given in *A Relation of Proceedings*, the document already mentioned as having been drawn up under Howard's direction:—

> The next morning, being Sunday, the 21st of July, 1588, all the English ships that were then come out of Plymouth had recovered the wind of the Spaniards two leagues to the westward of Eddystone; and about 9 of the clock in the morning the Lord Admiral sent his pinnace, named the *Disdain*, to give the Duke of Medina defiance, (Carleton, in his *Thankful Remembrance*, says: "To denounce the battell by shooting off some peeces"; but wrongly gives the name of the pinnace as *Defiance),* and afterwards in the *Ark* bare up with the admiral of the Spaniards wherein the duke was supposed to be, and fought with her until she was rescued by divers ships of the Spanish Army.
> In the meantime, Sir Francis Drake, Sir John Hawkyns, and Sir Martin Frobiser fought with the galleon of Portugal, wherein John Martinez de Recalde, vice-admiral, was supposed to be. The fight was so well maintained for the time that the enemy was constrained to give way and to bear up room to the east-

ward, in which bearing up, a great galleon, (*N. S. del Rosario*), wherein Don Pedro de Valdes was captain, became foul of another ship, which spoiled and bare overboard his foremast and bowsprit, whereby he could not keep company with their fleet, but being with great dishonour left behind by the duke, fell into our hands. (On July 22nd.) There was also, at that instant, a great Biscayan, of 800 tons or thereabouts, (*San Salvador*, of Guipúzcoa, really of 958 tons), that, by firing of a barrel of gunpowder, had her decks blown up, her stern blown out, and her steerage spoiled. This ship was for this night carried amongst the fleet by the *galleasses*.

This fight continued not above two hours; for the lord admiral, considering there were forty sail of his fleet as yet to come from Plymouth, thought good to stay their coming before he would hazard the rest too far, and therefore set out a flag of council, where his lordship's considerate advice was much liked of, and order delivered unto each captain how to pursue the fleet of Spain; and so, dismissing each man to go aboard his own ship, his lordship appointed Sir Francis Drake to set the watch that night.

That night the Spanish fleet bare alongst by the Start, and the next day, in the morning, they were as far to leeward as the Berry. (That day Howard wrote urgently for more ships, even if they were victualled only for two days.) Our own fleet, being disappointed of their light, by reason that Sir Francis Drake left the watch to pursue certain hulks which were descried very late in the evening, lingered behind, not knowing whom to follow; only his lordship, with the *Bear* and the *Mary Rose* in his company, somewhat in his stern, pursued the enemy all night within culverin shot; his own fleet being as far behind as, the next morning, the nearest might scarce be seen half-mast high, and very many out of sight, which with a good sail recovered not his lordship the next day before it was very late in the evening.

This day Sir Francis Drake, with the *Revenge*, the *Roebuck*, and a small *bark* or two in his company, (the *Margaret and John* of London, John Fisher, master, played an important part in the capture, having engaged Valdes's ship long before Drake fell in with her), took Don Pedro de Valdes, which (Valdes's ship was the *N. S. del Rosario*), was spoiled of his mast the day before;

and having taken out Don Pedro (Don Pedro de Valdes made the rest of the campaign in the Channel as Drake's guest), and certain other gentlemen, sent away the same ship and company to Dartmouth, under the conduction of the Roebuck, and himself bare with the lord admiral, and recovered his lordship that night, being Monday. (Howard's immediate object was not so much to decisively defeat the Spaniards as to prevent them from landing. Cott. MSS. He was still without Lord Henry Seymour.)

This Monday, being the 22nd of July, 1588, the Spaniards abandoned the ship (*San Salvador*), that the day before was spoiled by fire, to the which his lordship sent the Lord Thomas Howard and Sir John Hawkyns, Knight, who together, in a small skiff of the *Victory's*, went aboard her, where they saw a very pitiful sight—the deck of the ship fallen down, the steerage broken, the stern blown out, and about fifty poor creatures burnt with powder in most miserable sort.

The stink in the ship was so unsavoury and the sight within hoard so ugly, that the Lord Thomas Howard and Sir John Hawkyns shortly departed and came unto the Lord High Admiral to inform, his lordship in what case she was found; whereupon his lordship took present order that a small *bark* named the *Bark Flemyng*, (the *Golden Hind*, here named after her owner), wherein was Captain Thomas Flemyng, should conduct her to some port in England which he could best recover, which was performed, and the said ship brought into Weymouth the next day.

The Spanish accounts of what happened after the two fleets had for the first time sighted one another, throw but little further light upon the events of the 21st and 22nd.

On the night of July 20th, the Armada lay to, while Medina Sidonia sent Don Juan Gil, who knew English, to reconnoitre the land, and to ascertain how things went there. At about the same time, an English craft from seaward approached the Armada to reconnoitre it, and was chased off in the direction of the land by Captain Ojeda, who, however, had to retire before he could come up with the Englishman. Towards 1 a.m. on the same night, Don Juan Gil returned, bringing with him four English fishermen whom he had seized in their boat. They were taken on board the flagship, but communicated nothing of importance. At 2 a.m. (P. C. Calderon's account), the moon appeared, and by its light the Spaniards perceived that the English were working to windward of them.

At daybreak on the 21st the wind blew from W.N.W., (Duro; Calderon says W.), and the Armada was a little to the westward of Plymouth. To the westward of them the Spaniards saw the English, to the number of about sixty sail, (some of the documents given by Duro say 80), besides eleven more, including three large ones, which were under the land. These last had not then the advantage of the wind, and bore about N.E. from the Armada; but they presently gained the wind and joined the main body of the English fleet. (They seem to have worked round to seaward of the Spaniards, as shown in Adams's chart.) While this manoeuvre was being performed, the manoeuvring division exchanged shots with the nearest Spanish vessel.

Perceiving the English fleet to be united to windward, the Spaniards prepared for action, and Medina Sidonia hoisted the royal standard at the fore, the pre-arranged signal for battle. The Armada was organised in three squadrons. The van was under Don Alonso de Leyva, the main body under Medina Sidonia himself, and the rear under Juan Martinez de Recalde; but it would appear that, in his course up Channel, Medina Sidonia had Leyva's squadron on his left, and Recalde's squadron on his right; and that the terms van and rear applied rather to the relative ranks of the commanders of the squadrons than to the positions of the squadrons in the fleet. The Armada, there is little doubt, went at this time before the wind in the form of a huge crescent, of which the main body constituted the centre and foremost portion, and the van and rear the wings.

The English (Calderon says that they were in very fine order), contented themselves with a long-range fire upon the Spanish port (Leyva's) squadron, and, pressing across the rear of the crescent, hotly engaged Recalde, (ships which engaged Recalde were chiefly those of Drake), who, continues Medina Sidonia in the report sent home by the hands of Don Baltasar de Zuñiga,—

> . . . stood fast and abode the assault of the enemy, although he saw that he was being left unsupported, (most of) the (other) ships of his rear-guard taking refuge (both Calderon and Vanegas admit that some captains behaved disgracefully), in the main body of the Armada. The enemy assailed with heavy gunfire, but did not close, and his vessel suffered much in her rigging,

her forestay being cut, and her foremast having two large shot in it. (Calderon says that other Spanish ships were damaged also.)

In the rear (of the squadron), supporting Recalde, were the *Gran-Grin*, with Don Diego Pimentel, and Don Diego Enriquez, of Peru. The commander-in-chief's flagship struck her foretopsail and let fly the sheets; and, coming to the wind, waited for the rear squadron in order to convoy it into the main body of the fleet. (Duro, (account of Captain Alonso Vanegas, says that three English ships attacked the commander-in-chief. Vanegas praises the manner in which the English guns were served.)

Seeing this, the enemy drew off, and the duke collected his force; but was unable to do more, because the enemy always had the wind, and the enemy's ships were so fast and handy that there was nothing which could not be done with them. That day, in the evening, Don Pedro de Valdes ran foul of the ship *Santa Catalina*, of his division, losing his bowsprit and foresails, and withdrew into the main body of the fleet to repair damages. The Armada manoeuvred until 4 p.m., to recover the wind of the enemy.

At that hour, on board (the flagship) of the vice-admiral of Oquendo's division, some powder-barrels took fire, and her two decks and poop were blown up. In her was the paymaster-general of the Armada, (Juan de Huerta or Juan de Juerta), with part of the king's treasure. The duke, seeing the vessel remaining behind, headed the flagship for her, and fired a gun as a signal that the fleet should do the same. He also ordered boats to be sent to her assistance. The fire was put out, and the enemy's fleet, which had been standing towards the ship, ("at about 2 p.m.": Duro and Calderon, but it must have been later), stayed its course when it saw that the commander-in-chief approached her. The vessel, therefore, was protected, and carried into the main body of the Armada.

In the course of this casting about, the foremast of Don Pedro's ship (the *N. S. del Rosario* which collided with two other vessels), broke off near the deck, and fell upon the mainyard. The duke turned to help her and to give her a hawser; but, in spite of all efforts, wind and sea rendered this impossible, and she was left unmanageable. This was in consequence of Diego Flores

182

(Medina Sidonia's official adviser as to seamanship), having told the admiral that, as it was night, if he shortened sail, the Armada, being far ahead, would not see him; that by morning more than half the fleet would inevitably be missing; and that, looking to the proximity of the foe, the Armada must not be imperilled,—for it was certain that, if sail were shortened, the expedition would be brought to nothing.

On the strength of this opinion, the duke directed Captain Ojeda to remain with four pinnaces near Don Pedro's flagship. He also ordered the second flagship (*San Francisco*), of Don Pedro's squadron, the flagship (*San Cristóbal*), of Diego Flores, and a *galleass*, to be ready to tow her and take off her people; but nothing of the sort was found practicable, owing to the heavy sea, the darkness, and the state of the weather. (Valdes, writing to the king, said nothing of any efforts to aid him. Calderon and Vanegas say that when a boat was sent to him, he refused to quit his ship. Valdes does not even mention this.) As for the duke, proceeding on his course, he rejoined the fleet, and took pains to draw it together for whatsoever might happen on the day following.

On Monday, July 22nd, the duke ordered Don Alonso de Leyva to carry over his van to the rear, and so make one squadron of van and rear; and directed the combined divisions, with three *galleasses*, (the fourth was in the van), and the galleons *San Mateo, San Luis, Florencia* and *Santiago*—being in all forty-three of the best vessels of the Armada—to turn upon the enemy, so as to avoid all hindrance of the junction with the Duke of Parma. As the duke, with the rest of the Armada, formed the van, the whole fleet was now divided into but two squadrons, Don Alonso de Leyva having command of the rear, and the duke himself taking charge of the van.

The latter summoned all the sergeants-major, and ordered them to go in a pinnace and pass through the fleet in a prescribed order; and directed each of them in writing to put every ship in his assigned station, and, without delay, to hang (this was no mere threat), the captain of any ship which should leave her station and not keep order. . . . . At eleven this same day the captain of the *Almiranta* (*i.e.* flagship of the second in command of Oquendo's division. She was the *San Salvador*, and if her scuttling was ever attempted, it was unsuccessful), this was no mere threat), of Oquendo advised the duke that his ship was in a sinking condition; and the duke ordered the king's treasure and her people to be removed, and the vessel scuttled. On the same day, in the evening, the duke dispatched the ensign-bearer, Juan Gil, in a pinnace, to the Duke of Parma, to advise him of the position of the Armada.

Such was the first battle of the campaign. (It was visible from Plymouth. S. P. Dom.) Howard gained a success, but not an important one. He had, however, made important discoveries. He had found by experience that his ships were faster and handier, and that his gunnery was much better, than the Spaniards'; and he had seen some of the Spanish captains disgrace themselves by their abandonment of Recalde. The day was, upon the whole, a very encouraging one for England, and it was correspondingly discouraging for Spain, although neither in his report, nor in his letter to Parma, does Medina Sidonia hint at anything of the kind. Others did not conceal the truth. Vanegas wrote:

The desertion of the ship which had blown up, and the loss of Don Pedro de Valdes, shook the spirits of the people. From that time forward there was no real heart in them.

Another Spaniard wrote:

These misfortunes presaged our failure. The evil omen depressed the whole Armada.

The Spaniards continued on their course up Channel. *A Relation of Proceedings* says:

The night of Monday, July 22nd, fell very calm, and the four *galleasses* singled themselves out from their fleet, whereupon some doubt was had lest in the night they might have distressed some of our small ships which were short of our fleet, but their courage failed them, (Vanegas also says this, others attribute the failure to the wind), for they attempted nothing.

The next morning, being Tuesday, the 23rd of July, 1588, the wind sprang up at north-east, and then the Spaniards had the wind of the English Army, which stood in to the north-westward, towards the shore. So, did the Spaniards also. But that course was not good for the English Army to recover the wind of the Spaniards, (probably because of the nearness of the shore), and therefore they cast about to the eastwards, whereupon the Spaniards bare room, offering (to) board our ships. Upon which coming room there grew a great fight. (This action was fought off Portland.) The English ships stood fast and abode their coming, and the enemy seeing us to abide them, and divers of our ships to stay for them, as the *Ark*, the *Nonpareil*, the *Elizabeth Jonas*, the *Victory*, etc., and divers other ships, they were content to fall astern of the *Nonpareil*, which was the sternmost ship.

In the meantime, the *Triumph*, with five ships, *viz.*, the *Merchant Royal*, (merchantman under Drake's command), the *Centurion*, the *Margaret and John*, (both ships equipped by the City of London), the *Mary Rose*, (Francis Burnett's victualler, not H. M.S. of the name), and the *Golden Lion*, (equipped by the City of London); were so far to leeward and separated from our fleet, that the *galleasses* took courage and bare room with them, and assaulted them sharply. But they were very well resisted by those ships for the space of an hour and a half.

At length, certain of her majesty's ships bare with them, and then the *galleasses* forsook them. The wind then shifted to the south-eastward, and so to S.S.W., at what time a troop of her majesty's ships and sundry merchants assailed the Spanish fleet so sharply to the westward that they were all forced to give way and to bear room; which his lordship perceiving, together with the distress that the *Triumph* and the five merchant ships in her company were in, called unto certain of her majesty's ships then near at hand and charged them straitly to follow him, and to set freshly upon the Spaniards, and to go within musket-shot of the enemy before they should discharge any one piece of ordnance, thereby to succour the *Triumph*; which was very well performed by the *Ark*, the *Elizabeth Jonas*, the *Galleon of Leicester*, (with the exception of this vessel, which was a merchantman of Drake's squadron, all the relieving ships belonged to the Royal Navy), the *Golden Lion*, the *Victory*, the *Mary Rose*, the *Dreadnought*, and the *Swallow*; for so they went in order into the fight.

Which the Duke of Medina perceiving, came out with sixteen of his best galleons to impeach his lordship and to stop him of assisting of the *Triumph*. At which assault, after wonderful sharp conflict, the Spaniards were forced to give way, and to flock together like sheep. In this conflict one William Coxe, captain, of a small pinnace of Sir William Wynter's, named the *Delight*, showed himself most valiant in the face of his enemies at the hottest of the encounter, (who) afterwards lost his life with a great shot. Towards the evening some four or five ships of the Spanish fleet edged out of the south-westwards, where some other of our ships met them, amongst which (the) *Mayflower, of London*, discharged some pieces at them very valiantly, which ship and company at sundry other times behaved themselves stoutly.

This fight was very nobly continued from morning until evening, (Vanegas, Calderon and Manrique agree in saying that Medina Sidonia's ship fired one hundred and fifty rounds. She had several shot-holes in her hull below water), the lord admiral being always (in) the hottest of the encounter; and it may well be said that for the time there was never seen a more terrible value of great shot, nor more hot fight than this was; for although the musketeers and harquebusiers of crock (some of the arquebusses of the time were fired from a rest called a crock or crook), were then infinite, yet could they not be discerned nor heard, for that the great ordnance came so thick that a man would have judged it to have been a hot skirmish of small shot, being all the fight long within half musket-shot of the enemy.

This great fight being ended, the next day, being Wednesday, the 24th of July, 1588, there was little done, for that in the fights on Sunday and Tuesday much of our munition had been spent; and therefore the lord admiral sent direct *barks* and pinnaces unto the shore for a new supply of such provisions.

This day the lord admiral divided his fleet (Miranda that day counted one hundred and twenty English sail), into four squadrons, whereof he appointed the first to attend himself; the second his lordship committed to the charge of Sir Francis Drake; the third to Sir John Hawkyns, and the fourth to Sir Martin Frobiser. This afternoon his lordship gave order that, in the night, six merchant ships out of every squadron should set upon the Spanish fleet in sundry places, at one instant in the night time, to keep the enemy waking; but all that night fell out to be so calm that nothing could be done.

Medina Sidonia's relation of events of the two days is as follows:—

On Tuesday, July 23rd, the day broke fine, and the enemy's fleet, being to leeward, was standing in towards the land, endeavour-

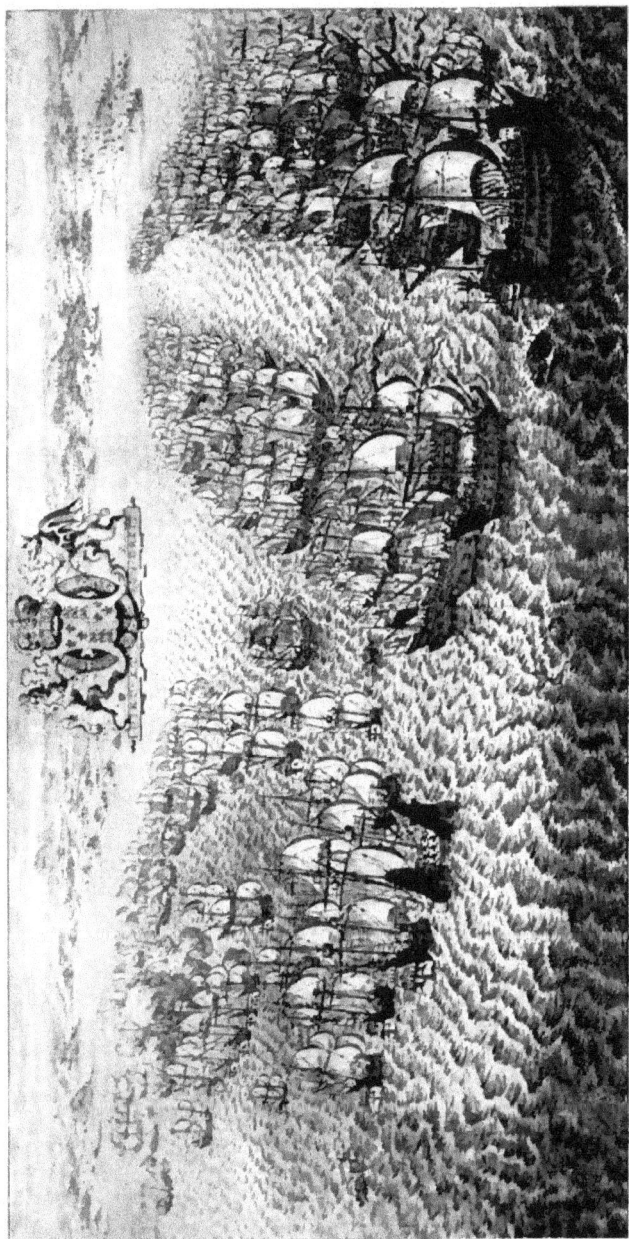

JULY 2nd, 1588. THE ARMADA RE-ENGAGED: AND THE CHASE CONTINUED.

ing to the best of its ability to recover the wind. The duke also tacked towards the land in order to keep the wind, the *galleasses* going with him in the van, and the rest of the fleet following. The enemy seeing our admiral standing towards the land, and that he could not in this manner regain the wind, cast about to seaward; whereupon those of our ships that had the wind of the enemy bore away for him and attacked him. Captain Bertendona (of the *Regazona*, flagship of the Levant contingent), very gallantly engaged the English admiral's ship, and would have boarded her, but as he neared her she bore away and stood to seaward.

In this action there also participated the *San Marcos, San Luis, San Mateo, Rata,* Oquendo's flagship, the *Santa Ana, San Felipe, San Juan de Sicilia,* in which was Don Diego Tellez Enriquez, who had been in action with the foe since the morning, the galleons *Florencia, Santiago, San Joan* of Diego Flores's squadron, in which was Don Diego Enriquez, son of the Viceroy of Peru, and the *Valencera, (Trinidad Valencera),* of the Levant squadron, in which was the camp-master Don Alonso de Luzon. The *galleasses* of the vanguard being carried by the current almost within culverin shot, the duke sent them directions that by oar and sail they should endeavour to close with the enemy, to which end he also headed his flagship towards him.

The *galleasses* threatened the ships of their rear, which were engaged with some of our vessels that had closed with and were seeking to board them. These were the galleons *Florencia,* in which was Gaspar de Sosa, (commanding a body of three thousand Portuguese troops); the flagship of Oquendo; the *Begoña,* (N. S. de Begoña, of the squadron of Diego Flores), in which was Garibay; the *Valencera,* in which was Don Alonso de Luzon; and the galleon *Juan Bautista,* in which were Don Juan Maldonado and Don Luis de Maeda; but all to little purpose, for the enemy, seeing that we endeavoured to come to arm's length, bore away, avoiding our attack, thanks to the lightness of his vessels; and afterwards the English returned with tide and wind in their favour, and engaged Juan Martinez de Recalde, who was in the rear.

Don Alonso de Leyva went to his aid, the admiral's flagship (*San Martin*), being still in the hottest of the fight, occupied in supporting those vessels which were in action, at a distance from both fleets, with the English rear. Captain Marolin de Juan (one of the duke's staff in the *San Martin*), was ordered away in a boat to direct those ships which were nearest to him to afford assistance to Juan Martinez de Recalde, which they did; upon which the enemy relinquished Juan Martinez, and made for the flagship, which was on her way to reinforce the ships above spoken of; and the commander-in-chief, seeing the enemy's flagship in the van, turned towards her and lowered topsails.

And the enemy's flagship and all the fleet passed him, firing at him ship by ship, while he, on his side, fired his guns very well and quickly, so that half the enemy's fleet did not draw near, but fired at him from a distance. When the fury of the action had worn itself out, there came to the support of the commander-in-chief Juan Martinez de Recalde, Don Alonso de Leyva, the Marquis of Peñafiel, who was in the *San Marcos*, and Oquendo; whereupon the foe bore away and stood out to sea, their admiral shortening sail, having, as it seemed to us, sustained some damage, and re-assembling those of his vessels which had been engaged with our van. In this action, which endured for more than three hours, the galleon *Florencia* was one of the foremost vessels, and was in close fight with the enemy.

On Wednesday, July 24th, Juan Martinez de Recalde once more took command of the rear, (Laughton thinks that at about this time he shifted from his original flagship, the *Santa Ana*, which as early as the 21st had been badly damaged, to the *San Juan*), Don Alonso de Leyva remaining with him, and they dividing between them the forty or more ships belonging to it. The enemy approached our rear and attacked the admiral. (Apparently Recalde.) The *galleasses* fired their stern guns, as also did Juan Martinez and Don Alonso de Leyva and the other ships of the squadron, without quitting station. Thus, the enemy drew off without any success, the *galleasses* having damaged their admiral's rigging, and brought down his main-yard. (Manrique to Philip. But there seems to be no English mention of this, or of the loss of the main-yard.)

The fight off Portland was even more indecisive than the fight off Plymouth. Neither side lost a ship, neither side gained any tactical or strategical advantage. But Medina Sidonia had been betrayed into contravening his instructions by seeking an action.

A Relation of Proceedings continues:

The next morning being the 25th of July, 1588, there was a great galleon of the Spaniards short of her company to the southwards.

★★★★★★

Recalde's flagship, the *Santa Ana*. She had been severely mauled on the 21st and 23rd. Recalde probably shifted his flag from her on the 24th. After the rough handling which she received on the 25th, she parted company from the Armada during the night, and drifted to La Hogue, whence she went to Le Hâvre, where at length she became a complete wreck.

★★★★★★

They of Sir John Hawkyns his squadron, being next, towed and recovered so near that the boats were beaten off with musket shot; whereupon three of the *galleasses* and an *armado* (*i.e.* a galleon or large ship belonging to an armada, of which *armado* is an English corruption), issued out of the Spanish fleet, with whom the lord admiral, in the *Ark*, and the Lord Thomas Howard, in the *Golden Lion*, fought a long time, and much damaged them, that one of them was fain to be carried away upon the careen, (*i.e.* heeled over, probably in order to raise her shot holes above the water); and another, by a shot from the *Ark*, lost her lantern, which came swimming by; and the third his nose. There was many good shots made by the *Ark* and *Lion* at the *galleasses* in the sight of both armies, which looked on and could not approach, it being calm, for the *Ark* and the *Lion* did tow to the *galleasses* with their long boats. At length, it began to blow a little gale, and the Spanish fleet edged up to succour their *galleasses*, and so rescued them and the galleon, after which time the *galleasses* were never seen in fight any more, so bad was their entertainment in this encounter. (Yet Medina Sidonia considered that the *galleasses* that day did very well.) Then the fleets, drawing near one to another, began some fight, but it continued not long, saving that the *Nonpareil* and the *Mary Rose* struck their topsails, and lay awhile by the whole fleet of Spain very bravely, during which time the *Triumph*, to the northward of the Spanish fleet, was so far to leeward (the wind, nowhere expressly given, must have been S. or S.S. W.), as, doubting that some of the Spanish Army might weather her,

190

she towed off with the help of sundry boats, and so recovered the wind. (Vanegas says that the way in which the *Triumph* was handled was much admired by the Spaniards.) The *Bear* and the *Elizabeth Jonas*, perceiving her distress, bare with her for her rescue, and put themselves, through their hardiness, into like perils, but made their parties good notwithstanding, until they had recovered the wind; and so that day's fight ended, which was a very sharp fight for the time. (It took place off the Isle of Wight, and, according to Miranda, lasted for about four hours.) Now, forasmuch as our powder and shot was well wasted, the lord admiral thought it was not good in policy to assail them any more until their coming near unto Dover, where he should find the army (*i.e.* armament), which he had left under the conduction of the Lord Henry Seymour, and Sir William Wynter, knight, ready to join with his lordship, whereby our fleet should he much strengthened; and, in the meantime, better store of ammunition might he provided from the shore.

On Friday, being the 26th of July, 1588, his lordship, as well in reward of their good services in these former fights, as also for the encouragement of the rest, called the Lord Thomas Howard, the Lord Sheffield, Sir Roger Townshend, Sir Martin Frobiser, and Sir John Hawkyns, and gave them all the order of knighthood aboard the *Ark*. (Sir George Beeston was also knighted that day. Drake was already a knight.) All this day, and Saturday, being the 27th of July, the Spaniards went always before the English Army like sheep, during which time the justices of peace near the sea-coast, the Earl of Sussex, Sir George Carey, and the captains of the forts and castles along the coast, sent us men, powder, shot, victuals and ships to aid and assist us.

The Spanish version of the same events, as given in Medina Sidonia's relation, runs:—

On Thursday (July 25th), the Feast of St. Dominic, the *Santa Ana* and a Portuguese galleon were somewhat astern, (Calderon also mentions a second vessel, though the English accounts say nothing about her), and the enemy attacked them with great fury. The *galleasses*, the vessel of Don Alonso de Leyva, and other ships went to their assistance; and the *galleasses* did so well that they succeeded in rescuing them, although surrounded by many of the enemy. While this fight was in progress in the rear,

JULY 25th, 1588. ENGAGEMENT WITH THE ARMADA OFF THE ISLE OF WIGHT.

the enemy's admiral, with other large ships, attacked our flag-ship, approaching nearer than on the first day, and firing their large lower-deck guns. (It may be that the weather had previously prevented them from using these, the lower-deck ports of those days being but little raised above the water.) They severed the flagship's mainstay and killed some soldiers.

To the help of the flagship came the *San Luis* (in which was the camp-master Don Augustin Mexia, who checked the enemy), Juan Martinez de Recalde, and the *San Juan* of Diego Flores's squadron, in which was Don Diego Enriquez, together with Oquenda. These ranged themselves for the protection of the flagship, though they were prevented by the currents from keeping together; and other ships did the same. Thereupon the enemy retired. His admiral, being much damaged, drove a little to leeward of our fleet. (Clearly not the *Ark*, flagship of Howard, but the *Triumph*, flagship of Sir Martin Frobiser, commanding the fourth squadron.)

Our flagship cast a, boat towards her, as did Juan Martinez de Recalde, the *San Juan de Sicilia*, the flagship of the galleons of Castille, the *Gran Grin*, and all the other ships of our Armada; while the enemy's ships recovered the wind, and guarded their flagship, which was so mauled in the action that she struck her standard and fired guns as signals of distress, and was at length towed by eleven of the enemy's long boats. Our flagship, and the second in command, and the rest of the ships gained on her so much that the enemy drew close about her to support her, it appearing certain that we would that day succeed in boarding her, that being the only way to victory.

But at that moment the wind freshened in favour of the enemy's admiral, and she began to slip away from us, (Calderon says that she sailed so fast that two ships of the Armada in pursuit of her, seemed to him to be, comparatively speaking, anchored), and to leave the boats which had been towing her; and thereupon the enemy's fleet, which had previously fallen a little to leeward, recovered the wind. The duke, seeing that in the intended attack the advantage would no longer he with us, and that we were near the Isle of Wight, fired a gun and proceeded on his course, the rest of the Armada following in very good order, and the enemy remaining far astern.

The same day the duke dispatched Captain Pedro de Leon to

Dunquerque, to the Duke of Parma, to advise him not only of the place where the duke was, but also of his success, as also that it was desirable that lie should come out and join the fleet with as little delay as possible. The duke gave the charge of the squadron of Don Pedro de Valdes to Don Diego Enriquez, son of the viceroy, since he had noted him to be able and careful in matters belonging to the sea.

Friday, the 26th, broke calm, with the fleets in sight of one another. (Several Spanish ships which drifted from the main body of the Armada had to be towed back to it by means of their boats.) The duke dispatched a pinnace to the Duke of Parma, with Domingo Ochoa as pilot, to obtain from him 4-lb., 6-lb., and 10-lb. shot, because much of his munition had been expended in the successive fights; and begging him also to send as soon as possible forty fly-boats to join the Armada, so that with them we might close with the enemy, our ships being very heavy in comparison with those of the enemy, and it being impossible, in consequence, to get at close quarters with them. The pilot was also to inform the duke that it would be well for him to be ready to come out and join the Armada on the day when it should arrive in sight of Dunquerque. Thither the Duke of Medina Sidonia was proceeding cautiously, fearing lest Parma might not be there, seeing that Don Rodrigo Tello had not returned, nor had any other messenger come thence. At sunset the wind got up, and the Armada, pursued a course toward Calais.

On Saturday, the 27th, at daybreak, the two fleets were very near one another, but did not fire. The Armada had a fair wind, and the rear was close up and in excellent order. At ten o'clock we sighted that part of the coast of France near to Boulogne; and proceeding towards Calais, we arrived off that place at four o'clock in the afternoon.

For the third time, the fight was indecisive; but, as before, the balance of advantage turned in favour of the English. The Santa Ana was obliged to leave the Armada, which she never again rejoined; and, by the admission of a Spanish eye-witness, (Duro), the English inflicted more damage than they received.

Plymouth, Portland, and the Isle of Wight had previously been considered in England as likely places for an attempted landing by

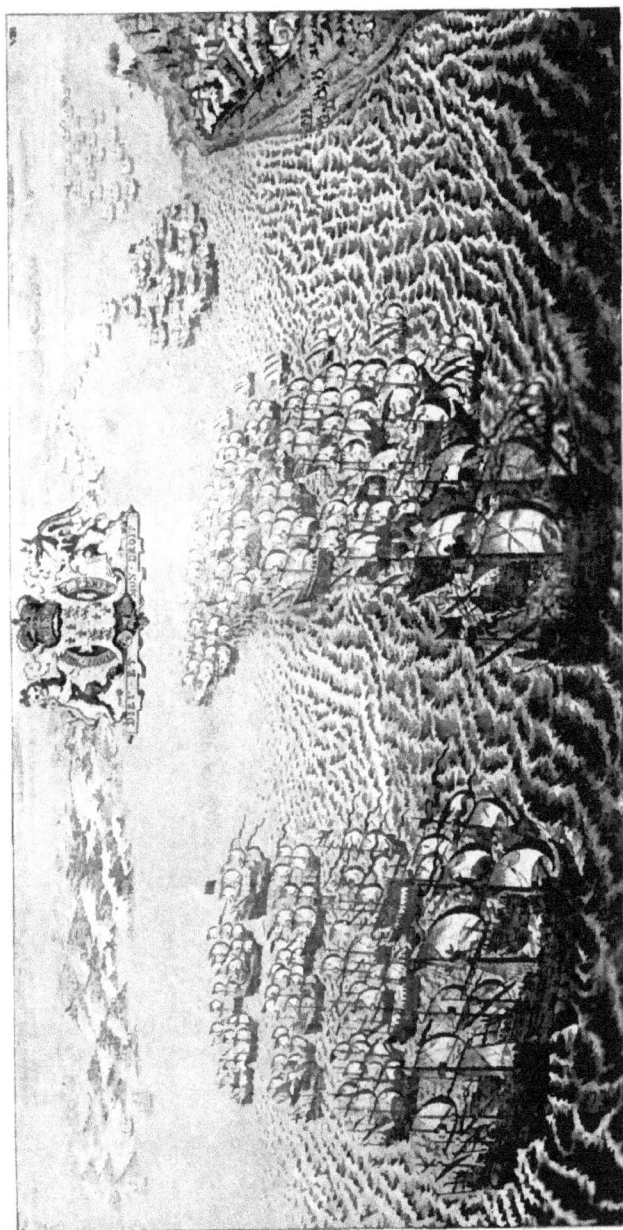

JULY 27th. 1588.   THE ARMADA CHASED TOWARDS CALAIS

the Spaniards. It is curious that the first three battles of the campaign took place off those spots; but the fact seems to be a mere chain of coincidences, and nothing more. Medina Sidonia certainly had no thought of landing, and made no attempt to land, at either Plymouth or Portland; and although he had thought at one time of seizing the Isle of Wight, and, at another, of remaining near it until Parma should be ready to join him, he had before July 25th, surrendered both those ideas. That the fight of July 25th ever became heavy, and to some extent general, is far more probably due to the fact that it was St. Dominic's Day, and that Medina Sidonia had specially devoted himself to that saint, in whose honour the Armada had from early morning been dressed with flags.

The official English story in *A Relation of Proceedings* is continued as follows:—

> On Saturday (July 27th), in the evening, (Lord Henry Seymour and Sir William Wynter joined the commander-in-chief that evening off Calais at about 8 p.m.) the Spanish fleet came near unto Calais on the coast of Picardy, and there suddenly came to an anchor over against, betwixt Calais and Calais Cliffs; and our English fleet anchored short of them, within culverin shot of the enemy.
>
> The Spaniards sent notice of their arrival presently unto the Duke of Parma, but, because there should be no time detracted to permit their forces to join, the lord admiral, the 28th of July, 1588, about midnight, caused eight ships to be fired and let drive amongst the Spanish fleet, (while Howard was discussing this scheme with Wynter, the *Ark* narrowly escaped being run down by the *Bear* and three other ships. Carleton says that the fireships were commanded by Yonge and Prowse): whereupon they were forced to slip or cut cables at half and to set sail.
>
> By reason of which fire the chief *galleass* (the *San Lorenzo*, she became a complete wreck), came foul of another ship's cable and brake her rudder, by means whereof he was forced the next day to row ashore near the haven's mouth and town of Calais; whereupon the lord admiral pent his long boat, under the charge of Amyas Preston, (wounded on this service; commanded an expedition to the Spanish Main in 1595; was captain of the *Ark* in the expedition to Cadiz, in 1596, when he was knighted), gentleman, his lieutenant, and with him Mr. Thomas

Gerard, (probably created Baron Gerard in 1603, if so, eldest son of Sir Gilbert Gerard, Master of the Rolls), and Mr. William Harvey, (knighted at Cadiz, in 1596; captain of the *Bonaventure* in 1597), together with other gentlemen, his lordship's followers and servants, who took her (Captain William Coxe, of the *Delight*, was the first to board her. He seems to have been killed in the fight off Gravelines), and had the spoil of her. There entered into her above one hundred Englishmen. And for that she was aground and sewed two foot, (*i.e.*, aground in water two feet too shallow to float her), and could not be gotten off, they left her to Monsr. Gourdan, Captain of Calais, where she lieth sunk. (Don Hugo de Moncada, commanding the *galleasses*, was killed in this fight. Gourdan drove the English away.)

Now that the Lord Henry Seymour and Sir William Wynter were joined with us, our fleet was near about one hundred and forty sail, ("There were but fifteen of these which bore the burden of the battle." Carleton: *Thankful Remembrance*.) of ships, *barks* and pinnaces, etc. During the time that this *galleass* was in taking by the lord admiral, (Howard committed an error in wasting time over the stranded *galleass*; for Medina Sidonia and Parma were so close to one another, that it had become imperative to concentrate all efforts for a decisive victory over the Armada.)

Sir Francis Drake, in the *Revenge*, accompanied with Mr. Thomas Fenner in the *Nonpareil*, and the rest of his squadron, set upon the fleet of Spain and gave them a sharp fight. And within short time Sir John Hawkyns, in the *Victory*, accompanied with Mr. Edward Fenton, in the *Mary Rose*, Sir George Beeston, in the *Dreadnought*, Mr. Richard Hawkyns, in the *Swallow*, and the rest of the ships appointed to his squadron, bare with the midst of the Spanish Army; and there continued a hot assault all that forenoon.

★★★★★★

July 29th, off Gravelines. The Spaniards were in half-moon formation, with the admiral and large ships in the centre, and the *galleasses*, Portuguese galleons, etc., to the number of about sixteen, on each wing. But the exigencies of the fight seem to have quickly destroyed all formation.

★★★★★★

Sir George Beeston behaved himself valiantly. This fight continued hotly; and then came the lord admiral, the Lord Thomas Howard, the Lord Sheffield, near the place where the Victory had been before, where these noblemen did very valiantly. Astern of these was a great galleon (probably the *Gran Grin*), assailed by the Earl of Cumberland and Mr. George Raymond, (lost captain of the *Penelope*, 1591), in the *Bonaventure*, most worthily; and, being also beaten with the Lord Henry Seymour, in the *Rainbow*, and Sir William Wynter, in the *Vanguard*, yet she recovered into the fleet. (Wynter was wounded in the hip, by the overturning of a demi-cannon.) Notwithstanding, that night she departed from the army and was sunk.

After this, Mr. Edward Fenton, in the *Mary Rose*, and a galleon encountered each other, the one standing to the eastward and the other to the westward, so close as they could conveniently one pass by another, wherein the captain and company did very well. Sir Robert Southwell that day did worthily behave himself, as he had done many times before; so, did Mr. Robert Crosse, (knighted at Cadiz, 1596), in the *Hope*, and most of the rest of the captains and gentlemen.

This day did the Lord Henry Seymour and Sir William Wynter so batter two of the greatest *armados* (*San Felipe* and *San Mateo*), that they were constrained to seek the coast of Flanders, and were afterwards, being distressed and spoiled, taken by the Zeelanders and carried into Flushing. In this fight, it is known that there came to their end sundry of the Spanish ships besides many others unknown to us.

The Spanish story (Duro), of the occurrences off Calais and Gravelines, as set forth in the relation of Medina Sidonia, is as follows:—

"There were divers opinions as to whether we should anchor there (off Calais), or should proceed further; but the duke, learning from the pilots who were with him that if he went further the currents would force him out of the English Channel and into the North Sea, decided to anchor off Calais, seven leagues from Dunquerque, whence the Duke of Parma might join him. At five o'clock, therefore, in the afternoon, (of July 27th), order was given for the whole fleet to anchor; and the duke sent Captain Heredia (Pedro de Heredia, attached to the duke's staff in the *San Martin*), to visit Monsieur de Gourdan, Governor of Calais, not only to advise him of the cause of our presence

JULY 28th, 1588. THE ARMADA, OFF CALAIS, DISLODGED BY FIRESHIPS.

there, but also to assure him of our friendship and good intentions. This evening thirty-six ships joined the enemy, whereof five were large galleons. This was supposed to be the squadron which Juan Acles ("Acles" was the Spanish name for Hawkyns. The supposition about the squadron was, as we know, incorrect.) had had under his charge before Dunquerque. They all anchored about a league from our Armada. That night Captain Heredia returned from Calais, and said that the governor made great offers of service on the part of his majesty, and showed his goodwill by offering the same on his own part. That night also the duke sent the secretary Arceo to the Duke of Parma, to apprise him of the place where he then was, and of the fact that he could not wait there without imperilling the entire Armada. On Sunday, July 28th, at dawn, Captain Don Rodrigo Tello arrived, coming from Dunquerque. The duke (of Medina Sidonia) had sent him away on the 19th of the month. He reported that the duke (of Parma) was at Bruges, whither he had proceeded to him; and that, although he had shown great satisfaction at the news of the arrival of the Armada, yet, on the evening of the 27th, when Tello had quitted Dunquerque, the duke had not appeared there, and that neither men nor stores were being embarked.

That day, in the morning, the Governor of Calais sent his nephew, with a present of refreshments, to visit the duke, and to inform him that the neighbourhood where he had anchored was very dangerous to remain in, because the currents and countersets of that channel were extremely strong. The duke, seeing the goodwill of the Governor of Calais, sent the purveyor-general, Bernabe de Pedroso, to buy victuals. With him went the comptroller. That night likewise the duke sent Don Jorge Manrique to the Duke of Parma to urge him to come out speedily. On the Sunday night, the secretary Arceo sent a man from Dunquerque to report that the Duke of Parma had not arrived there, that the stores were not embarked, and that in his view it was impossible that things could all be got ready in less than a fortnight.

On Sunday, at sunset, nine ships joined the enemy, and at their coming a squadron of twenty-six ships moved nearer to the land. (The English accounts have no mention of these movements.) This caused us to suspect that they had arrived with

JULY 29th, 1588. THE *SAN LORENZO* AGROUND OFF CALAIS. THE ARMADA IN FLIGHT TO THE NORTHWARD.

some intention of employing fire; wherefore the duke ordered Captain Serrano to go away in a pinnace, taking with him an anchor and cable, so that, if any fireship should be directed at us, he might tow her ashore. The duke also sent to warn all the ships to be on their guard, and, for that purpose, to have both men and boats ready. At midnight two fires were seen bunting in the English fleet. These increased to eight; (of the fireships, which cost £5100, five were: the *Thomas* (*Drake*), 200 tons; *Bark Talbot*, 200 tons; *Bark Bond*, 150 tons; *Hope* (*Hawkyns*), 180 tons: and *Bear Yonge*, 140 tons.

The rest, among which was the *Elizabeth*, of Lowestoft, were probably smaller), and suddenly eight ships with sails set, and wind and tide behind them, came direct towards our flagship and the rest of our fleet. All were burning fiercely. The duke seeing that, as they drew near, our men did not arrest them, and fearing lest they might be explosion vessels, weighed, and ordered the rest of the Armada to do the same, (many of the ships undoubtedly cut or slipped their cables, and so were un-prepared to re-anchor later), designing, when the fire should have passed by, to return and take up the same station.

The commander of the *galleasses*, (*i.e.* his ship, the *San. Lorenzo*) while keeping clear of the ship, drifted on board the *San Juan de Sicilia*, and so damaged herself that she bad to remain close to the shore. The current was so strong, and drove our Armada in such a manner, that although the flagship and several of the vessels near her anchored again and tired a gun, the rest did not see them, and were carried as far as off Dunquerque.

On Monday, the 29th, at daybreak, the duke, perceiving that his fleet was very far off, and that the enemy was coming up under a press of sail, weighed to collect his ships, and, with them, to recover station. The wind was N.W., (Wynter says S.S.W., and later W.N.W.), and strong, blowing nearly straight on to the coast, and the enemy's fleet of one hundred and thirty-six ships came on so fast with both wind and tide in its favour, that the duke, who was in the rear, chose rather to save his Armada by awaiting the enemy's attack, than to bear away; for bearing away would be destruction, seeing that, as the pilots assured him, the Armada was already very near the shoals of Dunquerque.

He therefore cast about to meet the enemy, and fired guns and dispatched pinnaces to order all the ships to keep a close luff, unless they would drive amid the shoals of Dunquerque. The enemy's admiral, with the greater part of his fleet, attacked our flagship with a heavy fire delivered within musket, and even within arquebuss, shot; and this went on without cessation from daybreak; nor did the flagship bear away until our fleet was clear of the shoals. During the whole time, the galleon *San Marcos*, in which was the Marquis de Peñafiel, remained by the admiral.

The commander of the *galleasses*, (in the *San Lorenzo*), not being able to follow our fleet, made for Calais, and ran himself ashore near the entrance of the port, whither several of the enemy followed him. It is reported that the French in the fortress of Calais covered the *galleass* with the fire of their guns, and that her people reached the land.

Don Alonso de Leyva and Juan Martinez de Recalde, the flagship of Oquendo, all the ships of the camp-masters, Castillian as well as Portuguese, the flagship of Diego Flores, that of Bertendona, the galleon *San Juan*, of the squadron of Diego Flores, in which was Don Diego Enriquez, (son of the Viceroy of Peru), and the *San Juan de Sicilia*, in which was Don Diego Tellez Enriquez, (son of the *commendator*), sustained the enemy's onset as stoutly as was possible; and in consequence all their vessels were very much mauled, and almost reduced to silence, the greater part of them being without shot for their guns.

In the rear, (*i.e.* on the Spanish right wing), Don Francisco de Toledo (in the *San Felipe*), awaited the attack and endeavoured to grapple with the enemy, whose vessels engaged him, and, by their gunfire, brought him to great extremity. Don Diego Pimentel (in the *San Mateo*), went to his assistance, and both were hard pressed; upon which Juan Martinez de Recalde, with Don Augustin Mexia, went to their help and rescued them from their difficulties. In spite of their experience, these vessels returned, and again attacked the enemy, as did Don Alonso de Luzon, (in the *Trinidad Valencera*), and the *Santa Maria de Begoña*, (in the list, *N. S. de Begoña),* in which was Garibay, and the *San Juan de Sicilia*, in which was Don Diego Tellez Enriquez.

These drew near to the enemy's ships to board them, but failed to grapple with them, they using their great guns at very short range, and our men returning the fire with arquebuss and musket. (Shot and powder for their heavy guns were probably exhausted. This was at 3 p.m.)

When the duke heard the arquebuss and musketry fire in the rear, (*i.e.* the Spanish right wing), but could not, owing to the smoke, see from the top what was the occasion of it, except that two ships of ours were surrounded by the enemy, and that the whole English fleet, having quitted our flagship, was engaging them, he ordered the flagship to cast about for their assistance, although she was badly mauled by great shot between wind and water, it not being possible to stop her leak, and although her rigging was much damaged. Yet when the enemy saw our flagship approaching, he left the ships which he was engaging, namely, the ships of Don Alonso de Luzon, of Garibay, of Don Francisco de Toledo, of Don Diego Pimentel, and of Don Diego Tellez Enriquez.

The last three (*San Felipe, San Mateo*, and *San Juan de Sicilia*), of these had been most closely and warmly occupied with the enemy, had all suffered great damage, and were unfit for service, all their people being killed or wounded, (*i.e.* probably nearly all); and only the ship of Don Diego Tellez Enriquez, (*San Juan de Sicilia*), in spite of her injuries, made shift to follow us. The duke collected his fleet, and the enemy did the same.

The duke ordered boats to go to bring away the people from the *San Felipe* and *San Mateo*; and by this means all the people were taken out of the *San Mateo*, but Don Diego Pimentel declined to leave the ship, and sent Don Rodrigo de Vivero and Don Luis Vanegas to the duke to beg him to send someone to see if it were not possible to save her; whereupon the duke sent a pilot and a diver from this galleon, (flagship *San Martin*), though there was much risk in sparing the latter; yet in consequence of the lateness of the hour and of the sea being very heavy, they could not reach the *San Mateo*, and only saw her at a distance, drifting towards Zeeland.

★★★★★★

She made a point between Sluis and Ostend, and on July 31st she as attacked there by three men-of-war, and, after a two hours' fight, surrendered. Holland, Borlas to Walsyngham. She and the *San Felipe* appear to have been taken by ships of North Holland, under Count Justinus of Nassau, assisted by a few English small craft. Kyllygrew to Walsyngham.

★★★★★★

The galleon *San Felipe* got alongside the hulk *Doncella*, ("*La urca Doncella*"), into which all her people had made their way, when Don Francisco, who was on board of her, heard a cry that the hulk was sinking. Upon this, Captain Juan Poza de Santiso leapt back into the *San Felipe*, as did also Don Francisco de Toledo, (preferring, if he must die, to perish with his own ship), which was a great mishap, for the hulk was not indeed sinking; and Don Francisco was carried in the *San Felipe* towards Zeeland, (the *San Felipe* drove ashore on July 31st, between Ostend and Nieuport, whither the officers escaped. Both the *San Felipe* and the *San Mateo* were taken into Flushing), while the duke understood that he and all his people were safe on board the hulk *Doncella*. The sea was so high that nothing more could be done; nor could the damage done to the flagship by great shot be repaired, so that she ran risk of being lost. (Vanegas says that she was struck one hundred times, but only mentions twelve soldiers as killed and twenty as wounded.)

That day the duke had desired to turn on the enemy with the whole of the Armada, rather than leave the Channel, but the pilots told him that this was impossible, because with sea and wind setting upon the coast direct from the north-west, it was absolutely necessary either to go into the North Sea or to let the entire Armada drive on to the shoals. Thus, leaving the Channel was inevitable. Moreover, nearly all the best ships were unfit, and unable to resist longer, firstly on account of the damage which they had received, and secondly because they had no shot for their guns.

★★★★★★

The losses in men are put by Vanegas at six hundred killed and eight hundred wounded. Duro; Rich. Tomson, writing on July 30th, says: "Of the one hundred and twenty four sail that they were in Calais Road, we cannot now find by any account above eighty-six ships and pinnaces." S. P. Dom. ccxiii.; The English losses in men, apart from losses by sickness, do not appear to have exceeded sixty in the whole campaign. Fenner to Walsyngham, S. P. Dom. ccxiv.

★★★★★★

The battle off Gravelines was really the decisive action of the campaign. The direction of the wind, which put the Spaniards on a lee shore, was most favourable for the tactics which Howard had pursued from the beginning. His policy was to concentrate ships upon stragglers lying to leeward of him, and to cripple or cut them off. Howard, however, did not at once grasp the nature of his success. He wrote to Walsyngham, (July 29th):

> Their force is wonderfully great and strong; and yet we pluck their feathers by little and little.

But that it should be more or less decisive was entirely in accordance with Howard's plans; for he had deliberately determined, if possible, to postpone a general engagement until after the junction with him of Seymour and Wynter. Drake was a little more clear-sighted, he wrote to Walsyngham, (July 29th):

> God hath given us so good a day in forcing the enemy so far to leeward, as I hope in God the Prince of Parma and the Duke of Sidonia shall not shake hands this few days; and whensoever they shall meet, I believe neither of them will greatly rejoice of this day's service.

Neither Drake nor Howard can have known that many ships of the Armada had no cannon shot left, (Wynter, however, suspected the truth); and both, no doubt, overrated the amount of fight still left in the Spaniards. That Gravelines had destroyed the morale of the enemy did not become apparent until several days afterwards, when, making no attempt to return for Parma, and so abandoning its main object, the Armada was fairly on its hazardous course of *sauve qui peut* round Scotland.

On Tuesday, July 30th, Howard ordered Lord Henry Seymour (to the great disgust of Seymour, as expressed in his letters), and Sir William Wynter to return to the Narrow Seas to guard the coasts there against any raids which might be attempted by Parma or others; and with the main body of the fleet he followed the Spaniards, determining to pursue them "until they should come so far northward as the Frith in Scotland, if they should bend themselves that way." The squadrons parted company between seven and eight o'clock on the evening of Wednesday, being then apparently on the line between Lowestoft and the Brielle; but the formal resolution to chase as far northward as the latitude of the Frith of Forth was not come to until Thursday, August 1st, when a council of war agreed to the project. Seymour's squadron thenceforward consisted of the *Vanguard, Rainbow, Antelope, Bull, Tiger, Tremontana, Scout, Achates, Merlin, Sun, Cygnet, George,* and Captain William Borough's galley, besides merchant vessels.

The decision to pursue as far as the Frith of Forth was not carried out, it becoming clear to Howard that the Spaniards had no designs on Scotland, and were only endeavouring to make the best of their way home round Scotland and Ireland.

A Relation of Proceeding says:

> When we were come into 55 degrees and 13 minutes to the northward, 30 leagues east of Newcastle, the lord admiral determined to fight with them again on the Friday, being the 2nd of August; but by some advice and counsel his lordship stayed that determination, partly because we saw their course and meaning was only to get away that way to the northward to save themselves, and partly also for that many of our fleet were unprovided of victuals; for our supply, which her majesty had most carefully provided and caused to be in readiness, knew not where to seek us.

> It was therefore concluded that we should leave the Spanish fleet, and direct our course for the Frith in Scotland, as well for the refreshing of our victuals as also for the performing of some other business which the lord admiral thought convenient to be done; but the wind coming contrary—*viz.*, westerly—the next day the lord admiral altered his course, and returned back again for England with his whole army, (except "certain pinnaces" ordered "to dog the fleet until they should be past the isles of Scotland", whereof some recovered the Downs, some Harwich, and some Yarmouth, about the 7th of August, 1588. (The following reached Harwich on August 8th: *White Bear, Victory, Nonpareil, Hope, Swiftsure, Foresight, Moon, White Lion,* and *Disdain*, with twenty-six ships of London.)

The Spanish account of what befell the Armada after Gravelines is here continued from the relation of Medina Sidonia:—

> On Tuesday, July 30th, the eve of San Lorenzo, at two o'clock in the morning, the wind freshened, so that our command, though it had remained in hope of returning to the Channel, was driven towards the coast of Zeeland, in spite of the fact that it kept as close a luff as possible. At break of day the N.W. wind was not so strong. The enemy's fleet of one hundred and nine sail was visible astern, little more than half a league distant. Our flagship remained in the rear with Juan Martinez de Recalde and Don Alonso de Leyva, and the *galleasses*, and the galleons

San Marcos and *San Juan*, of the squadron of Diego Flores, the rest of our fleet being far to leeward. The enemy's ships stood towards our flagship, which lay to; the *galleasses* also awaited them, as did too the other ships in the rear; whereupon the enemy brought to. The duke fired two guns to collect his Armada, and sent a pinnace with a pilot to order his ships to keep a close luff, seeing that they were very near the banks of Zeeland.

For the same cause, the enemy remained aloof, understanding that the Armada must be lost; for the pilots on board the flagship, men of experience on that coast, told the duke at the time that it would not be possible to save a single ship of the Armada, and that with the wind at N W., as it was, everyone must needs go on the banks of Zeeland, God alone being able to prevent it. The fleet being in this danger, with no kind of way of escape, and in six and a-half fathoms of water, God was pleased to change the wind to W.S.W.; and with it the fleet stood to the northward, without damage to any vessel, the duke having sent orders to every ship to follow the motions of the flagship, at peril of driving on the banks of Zeeland.

That evening the duke summoned on board the generals and Don Alonso de Leyva, to consider what was best to be done; and having explained the state of the Armada and the lack of shot—for which all the largest ships had made demands—he desired them to say whether it would be best to turn back to the English Channel, or, seeing that the Duke of Parma had not sent word that he would soon be able to come but, to return to Spain by the North Sea. The council was unanimously of opinion that the Armada should return to the Channel, if the wind permitted; but that, if not, it should, under the stress of weather, return by the North Sea to Spain, there being great lack of provisions in the fleet, and the vessels that had previously withstood the enemy being damaged and unfit for service. The wind, coming from S.S.W., continued to increase, and the duke stood to seaward, the enemy's fleet following him."

★★★★★★

The 30th, one of the enemy's great ships was espied to be in great distress by the captain (Robert Crosse) of her majesty's ship called the *Hope*; who, being in speech of yielding unto the said captain, before they could agree on certain conditions, sank presently before their eyes."S. P. Dom. ccxiv.

★★★★★★

As to the fighting, and the turning to relieve and assist his ships, and the awaiting the attack of the enemy, the duke took counsel with the camp-master, Don Francisco de Bobadilla, whom, on account of his many years' experience of war by land and sea, he had ordered at Corunna to go on board the flagship, and to quit the *San Marcos* of the same squadron. The Marquis de Peñafiel, who also was in the *San Marcos*, had remained there, not desiring, by removing to the flagship, to leave the gentlemen who were with him. On the question, however, of the conduct of the fleet, and of matters relating to the sea, the duke had the advice of the general Diego Flores, whom also he had caused to remove into the flagship, he being one of the oldest and most experienced officers in sea affairs.

On Wednesday, July 31st, the Armada pursued its course with a strong wind from the S.W. and a high sea, the enemy's fleet continuing to follow it. In the evening the wind decreased, and the enemy, under all sail, closed with our rear; whereupon the duke, there being few ships in the rear with Juan Martinez de Recalde, struck his topsails and lay to to wait for the rear, firing three guns for the main body also to lie to and wait for the rear and the flagship. Don Baltasar de Zuniga will report what our Armada did in consequence. But when the enemy perceived that our flagship had brought to, and that the *galleasses* of the rear and as many as twelve of our best ships had done likewise, their vessels also brought to and shortened sail, without firing at us. That night Juan Acles (it was not Hawkyns, but Seymour, who then returned), turned back with his squadron.

On Thursday, August 1st, we pursued our voyage with the same strong wind, the enemy's fleet keeping a long way off. In the evening, under all sail, it approached our Armada, and we counted the ships of Juan Acles (the ships, really, of Seymour), to be missing. Again, the *galleasses* and our flagship lay to and waited for the enemy; whereupon he also brought to, and did not come within gunshot.

On Friday, August 2nd, at dawn, the enemy's fleet was close up with ours. Seeing that we were in good order, and that our rear had been strengthened, it desisted, and turned back towards England, until we lost sight of it. After that time, we had always the same wind, until we were out of the channel of the Sea of Norway, without having found it possible to return to the English Channel; although we desired to return until today, the 10th of August, when, having passed the isles at the north of Scotland, we are sailing for Spain, with the wind at north-east.

The Armada passed between the Orkney Islands and the Shetlands, and, turning gradually southwards, skirted the Outer Hebrides, and the west coast of Ireland. The story of its misfortunes, after Howard had given up the chase, scarcely belongs to English Naval History, and may be very briefly summarised.

On August 11th, Medina Sidonia sent to Philip a dispatch in which he admitted that the undertaking had failed, he wrote:

God has seen good to direct matters otherwise than we expected.

He went on to lay down the reasons which had prompted the decision to give up the expedition. His fleet was almost destroyed; the best vessels had no ammunition; the survivors had no confidence or spirit remaining. The queen's fleet, owing to its peculiar methods of fighting, had proved its superiority to his. The English strength lay in gunnery and in seamanship. The Spanish strength, on the contrary, lay, unfortunately, in small-arms and in fight at close quarters; and as the Spaniards had been unable to get to close quarters, this advantage had not availed them. Looking to all the circumstances, Medina Sidonia deemed that he would best serve Philip by endeavouring to save the fleet by taking the admittedly perilous course home round Scotland. Indeed, the wind, which had steadily blown from the southward, left him no option. Besides his many wounded, he had three thousand sick among his people.

But the Armada had still the worst of its mishaps before it. In the course of the voyage round Scotland and Ireland, it lost by storm and shipwreck at least nineteen vessels, (Duro's estimate. Irish accounts give seventeen as lost in Ireland alone), and probably several more; for the exact fate of no fewer than thirty-five missing vessels of the great Spanish fleet remains to this day unknown. In addition to almost continuous bad weather, two exceptionally heavy storms were encountered.

The *galleass Girona* went to pieces near Giant's Causeway, on a rock still called Spaniards' Rock, and carried down with her Don Alonso de Leyva, the Count of Paredes, and all her crew. The *urea* or hulk, *El Gran Grifon*, which belonged to Bostock, was lost on Fair Island, where Juan Gomes de Medina, admiral of the hulks, remained with his men during the whole winter. The *Rata Coronada*, or, to give her her full name, *La Rata Santa Maria Encoronada*, went ashore and became a wreck on the coast of Erris. Don Alonso de Leyva, who later went on board the *Girona*, narrowly escaped losing his life in her. The *Duquesa Santa Ana*, into which he first removed, was lost in Glennagiveny Bay, near Inishowen Head, and again De Leyva barely escaped with his life, only to lose it a little later in the *Girona*. *The N. S. de la Rosa* went to pieces among the Blaskets.

The *San Marcos*, the *San Juan*, (with Don Diego Enriquez), of the squadron of Diego Flores, the *Trinidad Valencera*, and the *Falcon Blanco Mediano*, also left their bones in Ireland. And the *San Pedro Mayor*, (this wreck was on October 28th, 1588), after having escaped the perils of Scotland and Ireland, lost her way in the mouth of the Channel, and met her end in Bigbury Bay, Devonshire. These are about all that can be identified, but they are by no means all that perished. Writing on October 1st, to Walsyngham, Sir Richard Bingham, Governor of Connaught, said:—

> After the Spanish fleet had doubled Scotland and were in their course homewards, they were by contrary weather driven upon the several parts of this province and wrecked, as it were, by even portions, 3 ships in every of the 4 several counties bordering upon the sea coasts, *viz.*, in Sligo, Mayo, Galway, and Thomond. So that 12 ships perished, that all we know of, on the rocks and sands by the shore side, and some 3 or 4 besides to seaboard of the out isles, which presently sank, both men and ships, in the night time. And so, can I say, by good estimation, that 6 or 7000 men have been cast away on these coasts, save some 1000 of them which escaped to land in several places where their ships fell, which sithence were all put to the sword. (A few, however, escaped, in spite of Bingham and his people.)

The cruelties practised on the shipwrecked Spaniards, whose miserable situation should have given them a claim to protection, were as bad as any practised by Alva in the Low Countries. There were other wrecks, both in Munster and in Ulster. The ships must have been in terrible straits for lack of provisions, and especially of water. The *San Juan*, flagship of Juan Martinez de Recalde, seems to have landed a party at Dingle and to have obtained water by force. A prisoner, taken in a skirmish there, said, when examined, that in the *San Juan* three or four men a day had died of hunger or thirst, although she was one of the best furnished ships in the Armada; and that men had been dying daily of sickness. Another prisoner averred that two hundred persons in the *San Juan* had died.

Of the one hundred and twenty-eight or one hundred and thirty sail, of which the Armada originally consisted, no fewer than sixty-three are believed by Duro to have been lost. These he thus classifies: abandoned to the enemy, two, (*N. S. del Rosario* and *San Salvador*); lost in France, three, (*Santa Ana, San Lorenzo,* and *Diana);* lost in Holland, two, (*San Felipe* and *San Mateo*); a sunk in the action (off Gravelines), two, (probably *Gran Grin* and *San Juan de Sicilia);* wrecked off Scotland and Ireland, nineteen; fate unknown, thirty-five. Of the lost vessels, twenty-six were galleons and ships, thirteen were *ureas*, or hulks, twenty were *patasses*, three were *galleasses*, and one was a galley.

Appendix

SHIPS ENGAGED IN THE ARMADA CAMPAIGN.

ENGLISH SHIPS.

HER MAJESTY'S SHIPS	Built	Tons	MEN Mariners	Gunners	Soldiers	Total	GUNS Cannon	Demi-Cannon	Culverin	Demi-Culverin	Saker	Minion	Small Pieces	Total	Remarks
1. *Ark*	1587	800	270	34	126	430	4	4	12	12	6	—	17	55	Rebuilt 1608.
2. *Elizabeth Bonaventure*	[1581]	600	150	24	76	250	—	2	11	14	4	2	12	47	Broken up etc. 1610.
3. *Rainbow*	1586	500	150	24	76	250	—	2	10	14	2	—	20	54	Rebuilt 1602.
4. *Golden Lion*	[1582]	500	150	24	76	250	—	4	8	10	9	—	8	38	Broken up 1599.
5. *White Bear*	1563	1000	300	40	150	490	2	—	7	14	—	—	9	40	Rebuilt 1599.
6. *Vanguard*	1586	500	150	24	76	250	—	1	10	12	2	4	20	54	Rebuilt 1599 and 1615.
7. *Revenge*	1577	500	150	24	76	250	—	8	2	8	6	1	11	43	Taken by Spain 1591.
8. *Elizabeth Jonas*	1559	900	300	40	150	490	4	6	8	12	9	—	20	56	Rebuilt 1598.
9. *Victory*	[1586]	800	270	33	126	430	2	—	12	8	9	—	8	42	Rebuilt 1610.
10. *Antelope*	[1581]	400	120	30	30	170	—	—	4	11	8	—	4	30	Rebuilt 1618.
11. *Triumph*	1561	1100	300	40	160	500	2	3	17	10	6	—	5	42	Rebuilt 1596.
12. *Dreadnought*	1573	400	130	20	40	190	2	—	4	8	9	—	7	32	Rebuilt 1592 and 1613.
13. *Mary Rose*	1556	600	150	24	76	250	2	4	11	11	4	—	6	36	Rebuilt 1589.
14. *Nonpareil*	[1584]	500	150	24	76	250	—	3	7	—	2	—	18	38	Rebuilt 1603.
15. *Hope*	1584	600	160	25	85	270	—	4	9	11	4	—	—	48	Rebuilt 1602.
16. *Bonavolia*, galley															Sold 1599.
17. *Swiftsure*	[1573]	400	120	20	40	180	—	—	5	12	8	2	15	42	Rebuilt 1592 and 1607.
18. *Swallow*	[1573]	360	110	20	30	160	—	—	—	4	—	3	6	28	Condemned 1604.
19. *Foresight*	1570	300	110	20	20	150	—	—	4	8	8	4	12	37	Condemned 1599.
20. *Aid*	1562	250	90	16	14	120	—	—	—	—	—	—	4	18	Condemned 1599.
21. *Bull*	[1570]	200	80	12	8	100	—	—	2	—	8	—	10	—	Condemned 1593.
22. *Tiger*	[1570]	200	80	12	8	100	—	—	—	6	2	1	2	30	Condemned 1605.
23. *Tremontana*	1586	150	55	8	7	70	—	—	—	5	—	—	9	21	Broken up 1618.
24. *Scout*	1577	120	45	6	7	70	—	—	—	—	8	2	5	10	Condemned 1604.
25. *Achates*	1573	100	45	6	7	60	—	—	—	—	2	1	5	13	Condemned 1604.
26. *Charles*	1586	70	32	5	8	45	—	—	—	—	4	—	13	16	Sold 1616.
27. *Moon*	1586	60	30	5	5	40	—	—	—	—	—	4	8	9	
28. *Advice*	1586	50	30	5	5	40	—	—	—	—	8	1	4	9	
29. *Merlin*	1579	50	26	5	4	35	—	—	—	—	4	—	3	7	
30. *Spy*	1586	50	30	5	5	40	—	—	—	—	4	3	6	5	
31. *Sun*	1586	40	24	4	2	30	—	—	—	—	—	—	7	5	
32. *Cygnet*	1585	30	—	—	—	20	—	—	—	—	—	1	4	8	
33. *Brigandine*	1583	90	—	—	—	35	—	—	—	—	—	—	2	—	
34. *George*, hoy	1601	100	—	—	—	24	—	—	—	—	—	—	—	—	Rebuilt 1601.
34 ships		**6720**				**8289**									

N.B.—The dates in the "Built" column, when enclosed in square brackets, indicate "Rebuilt."

213

1. Lord Howard of Effingham, Lord High Admiral.
   Sir Edward Hoby, Secretary.
   Thomas Gray, Master.
   Amyas Preston, Lieutenant.
   — Morgan, Captain of soldiers.
   Samuel Clerke, Master Gunner.
   John Wright, Boatswain.
   Richard Leveson, Volunteer.
   Thomas Gerard,   "
   William Harvey,   "
   John Chidley,   "
   Thomas Vavasour,   "
   Francis Burnell, "Admiral's man."
   — Newton,   "   "

2. Earl of Cumberland.[1]
   George Raymond, Captain.
   James Sewell, Master.
   Tristram Searche, Boatswain.
   Robert Carey, Volunteer.

3. Lord Henry Seymour.
   Richard Laine, Boatswain.
   Sir Charles Blount, Volunteer.
   Francis Carey,   "
   Brute Brown,   "

4. Lord Thomas Howard.

5. Lord Sheffield.
   (?) Richard Poulter, Master.
   H. Sheffield, Lieutenant.
   Robert Baxter, Boatswain.

6. Sir William Wynter.
   John Wynter, Lieutenant.

7. Sir Francis Drake, Vice-Admiral.
   John Gray, Master.
   Jonas Bodenham, Lieutenant.
   (?) Martin Jeffrey, Purser.
   Richard Derrick, Boatswain.
   Nicholas Oseley, Volunteer.

8. Sir Robert Southwell.
   (?) John Austyne, Master.
   John Woodroffe, Boatswain.

9. Sir John Hawkyns, Rear-Admiral.
   (?) — Barker, Master.
   John Edmonds, Boatswain.

10. Sir Henry Palmer.

11. Sir Martin Frobiser.
    (?) — Eliot, Lieutenant.
    Simon Fernandez, Boatswain.

12. Sir George Beeston.
    (?) — Harvey, Boatswain.

13. Edward Fenton.
    Lawrence Cleer, Boatswain.
    Henry Whyte, Volunteer.

14. Thomas Fenner.
    I— C——, Boatswain.

15. Robert Crosse.
    (?) John Sampson, Master.
    John Vayle, Boatswain.

16. William Borough.

17. Edward Fenner.
    William Mychell, Boatswain.

18. Richard Hawkyns.[2]
    John Borman, Boatswain.

19. Christopher Baker.
    James Andrews, Boatswain.

20. William Fenner.
    (?) Richard Blucke, Purser.
    John Russell, Boatswain.

21. Jeremy Turner.
    Myhyll Pyrkyne, Boatswain.

22. John Bostocke.

23. Luke Ward.
    John Pratte, Boatswain.

24. Henry Ashley.

25. Gregory Riggs.

26. John Roberts.
    William Monson, Volunteer.[3]

27. Alexander Clifford.[4]

28. John Harris.
    Tristram George, Boatswain.

29. Walter Gower.

30. Ambrose Ward.

31. Richard Buckley, Master.

32. John Sheriff, Master.
    George Wilkynson, Boatswain.

33. Thomas Scott.

34. Richard Hodges, Master.

[1] Cumberland's real position seems to have been only that of a volunteer. He received no pay.
[2] Son of Sir John Hawkyns; died 1622.
[3] Monson describes himself as having been lieutenant of the *Charles*, but she was allowed no lieutenant.
[4] Knighted 1596.

214

	Tons.	Men.	Captains and Officers.	Remarks.
35. *Galleon Leicester*	400	160	George Fenner.	Cavendish made his last voyage in her, 1591.
36. *Merchant Royal*	400	160	Robert Flicke.	Belonged to the Levant Company.
37. *Edward Bonaventure*	300	120	James Lancaster.	Belonged to the Levant Company. Made the first English successful voyage to India and back, 1591–93.
38. *Roebuck*, of Dartmouth	300	120	Jacob Whiddon.	Belonged to Sir Walter Ralegh.
39. *Golden Noble*	250	110	Adam Seager.	
40. *Griffin*	200	100	William Hawkyns. Saml. Norfolk, Master.	
41. *Minion*	200	80	William Wynter. Nicholas Maunder, Master.	
42. *Bark Talbot*	200	90	Henry Whyte. John Hampton, Master.	Burnt as a fireship before Calais.
43. *Thomas Drake*	200	80	Henry Spindelow. John Tranton, Master.	Belonged to Sir Francis Drake. Burnt as a fireship before Calais.
44. *Spark*	200	90	William Spark. Richard Loarie, Master.	
45. *Hopewell*	200	100	John Marchant.	
46. *Galleon Dudley*, of Barnstaple	250	96	James Erisey.	
47. *Virgin God Save Her*, of Barnstaple	200	70	John Greynvile.	Belonged to Sir Richard Greynvile.
48. *Hope Hawkyns*, of Plymouth	200	80	John Rivers. Roger Haley, Master.	Belonged to William Hart. Burnt as a fireship before Calais.
49. *Bark Bond*	150	70	William Poole. John Rock, Master.	Belonged to Sir John Hawkyns. Burnt as a fireship before Calais.
50. *Bark Bonner*	150	70	Charles Cæsar. William Loggin, Master.	
51. *Bark Hawkyns*	150	70	—— Prideaux. William Snell, Master.	
52. *Unity*	80	40	Humphrey Sydenham. William Cornish, Master.	

4030

215

	Tons.	Men.	Captains and Officers.	Remarks.
53. *Elizabeth Drake,* of Lyme . .	60	30	Thomas Cely. Thomas Clerke, Master.	
54. *Bark Buggins* .	80	50	John Langford.	
55. *Elizabeth Founes*	80	50	Roger Grant.	
56. *Bark St. Leger* .	160	80	John St. Leger.	
57. *Bark Manington*	160	80	Ambrose Manington.	
58. *Heartsease* . .	?	24	Hannibal Sharpham.	
59. *Golden Hind* .	50	30	Thomas Flemyng.	Brought in the first news of the Armada. Was not Drake's *Golden Hind.*
60. *Makeshift* . .	60	40	Piers Lemon.	
61. *Diamond,* of Dartmouth .	60	40	Robert Holland.	
62. *Speedwell* . .	60	14	Hugh Hardinge, Master.	
63. *Bear Yonge,* of Lyme . . .	140	70	John Yonge.	Belonged to John Yonge. Burnt as a fireship before Calais.
64. *Chance* . . .	60	40	James Founes. Hugh Cornish, Master.	
65. *Delight* . . .	50	40	William Coxe.	Belonged to Sir William Wynter.
66. *Nightingale* . .	40	30	John Grisling. Habbakuk Percy, Master.	
67. Small Caravel .	30	20	?	
68. Fly-boat *Yonge* .	50	50	Nicholas Webb.	
34 ships	1140	2394		

216

	Tons.	Men.	Captains and Officers.	Remarks.
69. *Hercules* . . .	300	120	George Barne.	
70. *Toby* . . .	250	100	Robert Barrett.	
71. *Mayflower* . .	200	90	Edward Bancks.	
72. *Minion* . . .	200	90	John Dale.	
73. *Royal Defence* .	160	80	John Chester.	
74. *Ascension* . .	200	100	John Bacon.	
75. *Gift of God* . .	180	80	Thomas Luntlowe.	
76. *Primrose* . .	200	90	Robert Bringborne.	
77. *Margaret and John* . . .	200	90	John Fisher. John Nash, Master. Richard Tomson, Lieut. John Watts, Volunteer.	Belonged to John Watts. In 1590, present at a severe action off Cadiz between English merchantmen and Spanish galleys. Watts was knighted, 1603; and was Lord Mayor in 1606.
78. *Golden Lion* .	140	70	Robert Wilcox.	
79. *Diana* . . .	80	40	Edward Cock.	
80. *Bark Burr* . .	160	70	John Serocold.	
81. *Tiger* . . .	200	90	William Cæsar.	
82. *Brave* . . .	160	70	William Furthow.	
83. *Red Lion* . .	200	90	Jervis Wilde.	
84. *Centurion* . .	250	100	Samuel Foxcraft.	
85. *Passport* . . .	80	40	Christopher Colthurst.	
86. *Moonshine* . .	60	30	John Brough.	
87. *Thomas Bonaventure* . .	140	70	William Aldridge.	Belonged to the Levant Company
88. *Release* . . .	60	30	John King.	
89. *George Noble* .	120	80	Henry Bellingham. Richard Harper, Master.	Carried 14 calivers and 10 muskets.
90. *Anthony* . . .	100	60	George Harper. Richard Dove, Master.	Carried 12 calivers and 8 muskets.
91. *Toby* . . .	120	70	Christopher Pigot. Robert Cuttle, Master.	Carried 14 calivers and 10 muskets.
92. *Salamander*, of Leigh . .	110	60	— Damford. William Goodlad, Master.	Carried 14 calivers and 8 muskets.
93. *Rose Lion*, of Leigh . .	100	50	Bartholomew Acton. Robert Duke, Master.	Carried 12 calivers and 8 muskets.
94. *Antelope* . . .	120	60	— Denison. Abraham Bonner, Master.	Carried 14 calivers and 10 muskets.
95. *Jewel*, of Leigh .	110	60	— Rowell. Henry Rawlyn, Master.	Carried 14 calivers and 8 muskets.
96. *Pansy* . . .	100	70	William Butler, Master.	Carried 12 calivers and 8 muskets.
97. *Prudence*, of Leigh . .	120	60	Richard Chester, Master.	Carried 14 calivers and 10 muskets.
98. *Dolphin*, of Leigh	110	70	William Hare, Master.	Carried 14 calivers and 8 muskets.
30 ships	4530	2180		

(The above, in addition to the light armaments specially noted, carried sakers, minions, falcons, and fowlers.)

MERCHANT SHIPS SERVING UNDER THE LORD HIGH ADMIRAL, AND PAID
BY THE QUEEN.

(The following served for about eight weeks.)

—	Tons.	Men.	Captains and Officers.	Remarks.
99. *Susan Parnell* .	220	80	Nicholas Gorges.	{ Belonged to the Levant Company.
100. *Violet* . . .	220	60	Martin Hawkes.	
101. *Solomon* . .	170	80	Edmund Musgrave.	
102. *Anne Frances* .	180	70	Charles Lister.	
103. *George Bona-venture* . . }	200	90	Eleazar Hickman.	{ Belonged to the Levant Company.
104. *Jane Bonaven-ture* . . . }	100	50	Thomas Hallwood.	
105. *Vineyard* . .	160	60	Benjamin Cooke.	
106. *Samuel*. . .	140	50	John Vassall.	
8 ships	1340	530		

(The following served the whole time.)

—	Tons.	Men.	Captains and Officers.	Remarks.
107. *White Lion* .	140	50	Charles Howard.	
108. *Disdain* . .	80	45	Jonas Bradbury.	{ "The Lord High Admiral's pinnace," possibly belonged to the R.N. Built 1585.
109. *Lark* . . .	50	20	Thomas Chichester.	
110. *Edward,* of Maldon . . }	186	30	William Pierce.	{ Belonged to Edward Peek.
111. *Marigold* . .	30	12	William Newton, Master.	
112. *Black Dog* . .	20	10	John Davis, Master.	
113. *Katherine* . .	20	10	?	
114. *Fancy* . . .	50	20	John Paul, Master.	
115. *Pippin*. . .	20	8	?	
116. *Nightingale* .	160	16	John Doate, Master.	
10 ships	756	221		

—	Tons.	Men.	Captains and Officers.	Remarks.
117. *Mary Rose* . .	?	70	{Francis Burnell. {William Parker, Master.	
118. *Elizabeth Bona-* *venture* . .	?	60	Richard Start.	
119. *Pelican* . . .	?	50	John Clarke.	
120. *Hope* . . .	?	40	John Skinner.	
121. *Unity* . . .	?	40	John Moore.	
122. *Pearl* . . .	?	50	Lawrence Moore.	
123. *Elizabeth*, of Leigh . .	?	60	William Bower.	
124. *John*, of London	?	70	Richard Rose.	
125. *Bearsabe* (?) .	?	60	Edward Bryan.	
126. *Marigold* . .	?	50	Robert Bowers.	
127. *White Hind* .	?	40	Richard Browne.	
128. *Gift of God* .	?	40	Robert Harrison.	
129. *Jonas* . . .	?	50	Edward Bell.	
130. *Solomon*, of Aldborough .	?	60	George Street.	
131. *Richard Duffield*	?	70	William Adams.	Belonged to—Duffield. William Adams, ten years later went, as chief pilot of some Rotterdam ships, to the Far East, and then entered the service of the Shogun of Japan. He died in 1620.
15 ships		810		

	Tons.	Men.	Captains and Officers.	Remarks.
132. *Bark Webb* .	80	50	?	
133. *John Trelawney*	150	30	Thomas Meek.	
134. *Hart*, of Dart- mouth . .	60	70	{James Houghton (or { Houston).	{Thomas Anthony, { Master.
135. *Bark Potts*. .	180	80	Anthony Potts.	
136. *Little John* . .	40	20	Laurence Clayton.	
137. *Bartholomew*, of Apsam . .	130	70	Nicholas Wright.	{Apsam is now Top- { sham.
138. *Rose*, of Apsam	110	50	Thomas Sandye.	
139. *Gift*, of Apsam	25	20	?	
140. *Jacob*, of Lyme	90	50	?	
141. *Revenge*, of Lyme . .	60	30	Richard Bedford.	
142. Bark of Bridg- water . .	70	30	John Smyth.	
143. *Crescent*, of Dartmouth .	140	75	John Wilson.	{Christopher Wey- { mouth, Master.
144. Galleon of Weymouth .	100	50	Richard Miller.	
145. *John*, of Chichester .	70	50	John Young.	
146. *Katherine*, of Weymouth .	66	30	?	
147. *Hearty Anne* .	60	30	John Wynnall.	
148. *Minion*, of Bristol . .	230	110	John Sachfield.	}
149. *Unicorn*, of Bristol . .	130	66	James Langton.	Belonged to John Sachfield, or Sack- vile.
150. *Handmaid*, of Bristol . .	80	56	Christopher Pitt.	
151. *Aid*, of Bristol .	60	26	William Megar.	}
20 ships	1431	993		

COASTERS UNDER LORD HENRY SEYMOUR, SOME PAID BY THE QUEEN, BUT MOST BY THE PORT TOWNS.

———	Tons.	Men.	Captains and Officers.	Remarks.
152. *Daniel* . . .	160	70	Robert Johnson.	
153. *Galleon Hutchins*	150	60	Thomas Tucker.	
154. *Bark Lamb* .	150	60	Leonard Harbell.	
155. *Fancy* . . .	60	30	Richard Fearne.	
156. *Griffin* . . .	70	35	John Dobson.	
157. *Little Hare* .	50	25	Matthew Railstone.	
158. *Handmaid* . .	75	35	John Gattenbury.	
159. *Marigold*, of Hull. . .	150	70	Francis Johnson.	
160. *Matthew* . .	35	16	Richard Mitchell.	
161. *Susan* . . .	40	20	John Musgrave.	
162. *William*, of Ipswich . .	140	50	Barnaby Lowe.	
163. *Katherine*, of Ipswich . .	125	50	Thomas Grymble.	
164. *Primrose*, of Harwich .	120	40	John Cardinal.	
165. *Anne Bona-venture* . .	60	50	John Conny.	
166. *William*, of Rye	80	60	William Coxon.	
167. *Grace of God*, of Dover .	50	30	William Fordred.	
168. *Elizabeth*, of Dover . .	120	70	John Lidgen.	
169. *Robin*, of Sand-wich. . .	110	65	William Cripps.	
170. *Hazard*, of Feversham .	38	34	Nicholas Turner.	
171. *Grace*, of Yar-mouth . .	150	70	William Musgrave.	{Carried 6 minions and 20 muskets.
172. *Mayflower*, of King's Lynn	150	70	Alexander Musgrave.	
173. *William*, of Col-chester . .	100	50	Thomas Lambert.	
174. *John Young* .	60	30	Reynold Vesey.	
23 ships	2143	1090		

VOLUNTARY SHIPS WHICH JOINED WHEN THE ARMADA WAS ON THE COAST, AND WERE PAID BY THE QUEEN DURING SERVICE.

	Tons.	Men.	Captains and Officers.	Remarks.
175. *Sampson* . .	300	108	John Wingfield.	{ Belonged to the Earl of Cumberland.
176. *Frances*, of Fowey . .	140	60	John Rashley.	Belonged to John Rashley. His pinnace, the *Christopher*, 15 tons, seems to have been also in the fleet.
177. *Heathen*, of Weymouth .	60	30	?	
178. *Golden Rial*, of Weymouth .	120	50	?	{ Belonged to Thomas Middleton.
179. *Bark Sutton*, of Weymouth .	70	40	Hugh Pearson.	
180. *Carouse* . .	50	25	?	
181. *Samaritan*, of Dartmouth .	250	100	?	
182. *William*, of Plymouth .	120	60	?	
183. *Gallego*, of Plymouth . .	30	20	?	
184. *Bark Halse* .	60	40	Grenfield Halse.	
185. *Unicorn*, of Dartmouth .	76	30	Ralph Hawes.	
186. *Grace*, of Apsam . . .	100	50	Walter Edney.	
187. *Thomas Bonaventure*, of Lyme . .	60	30	John Pentire.	
188. *Rat*, of Wight .	80	60	Gilbert Lee.	
189. *Margaret* . .	60	46	William Hubbard.	
190. *Elizabeth* . .	40	30	?	
191. *Raphael* . .	40	40	?	
192. Fly-boat . .	60	40	?	
193. *John*, of Barnstaple . .	?	65	?	{ Belonged to Sir Richard Greynvile.
194. *Greyhound*, of Aldborough.	?	40	Michael Pullison.	
195. *Elizabeth*, of Lowestoft .	90	30	?	{ Belonged to Thomas Meldrum. Burnt as a fireship before Calais.
196. *Jonas*, of Aldborough. .	?	25	?	
197. *Fortune*, of Aldborough. .	?	25	?	
23 ships	1806	1044		

222

ARMADA OF PORTUGAL, UNDER THE DUKE OF MEDINA SIDONIA.

	Tons.	Guns.	MEN.		
			Soldiers.	Mariners.	Total.
1. *San Martin*, Capitana General[1] .	1000	48	300	177	477
2. *San Juan*, Almiranta General[2] .	1050	50	321	179	500
3. *San Marcos*[3]	790	33	292	117	409
4. *San Felipe*[4].	800	40	415	117	532
5. *San Luis*	830	38	376	116	492
6. *San Mateo*[4].	750	34	277	120	397
7. *Santiago*	520	24	300	93	393
8. *Florencia*	961	52	400	86	486
9. *San Cristóbal*	352	20	300	78	378
10. *San Bernardo*	352	21	250	81	331
11. Zabra *Augusta*	166	13	55	57	112
12. Zabra *Julia*	166	14	44	72	116
12 ships					4623

[1] Returned to Santander with 180 dead, and nearly all the rest sick.
[2] Probably J. M. de Recalde's flagship till July 21st, and again from July 24th. Returned to Corunna. Burnt there 1589.
[3] Lost on the coast of Ireland.   [4] Grounded at the mouth of the Scheldt.

ARMADA OF BISCAY, UNDER JUAN MARTINEZ DE RECALDE.

	Tons.	Guns.	MEN.		
			Soldiers.	Mariners.	Total.
13. *Santa Ana*, Capitana[1] . . .	768	30	256	73	329
14. *El Gran Grin*, Almiranta . .	1160	28	256	73	329
15. *Santiago*	666	25	214	102	316
16. *La Concepcion de Zubelzu* . .	486	16	90	70	160
17. *La Concepcion de Juanes del Cano*	418	18	164	61	225
18. *La Magdalena*	530	18	193	67	260
19. *San Juan*	350	21	114	80	194
20. *La Maria Juan*	665	24	172	100	272
21. *La Manuela*	520	12	125	54	179
22. *Santa Maria de Monte-Mayor* .	707	18	206	45	251
23. Patax *La Maria de Aguirre* . .	70	6	20	23	43
24. Patax *La Isabela*	71	10	20	22	42
25. Patax de Miguel Suso . . .	36	6	20	26	46
26. Patax *San Estéban*	96	6	20	26	46
14 ships					2692

[1] Probably J. M. de Recalde's flagship from July 21st to July 23rd. Was wrecked near Le Hâvre.

	Tons.	Guns.	MEN.		
			Soldiers.	Mariners.	Total.
27. *San Cristóbal*	700	36	205	120	325
28. *San Juan Bautista*	750	24	207	136	343
29. *San Pedro*	530	24	141	131	272
30. *San Juan* [1]	530	24	163	113	276
31. *Santiago el Mayor*	530	24	210	132	342
32. *San Felipe y Santiago* . . .	530	24	151	116	267
33. *La Asuncion*	530	24	199	114	313
34. *Nuestra Señora del Barrio* . .	530	24	155	108	263
35. *San Medel y Celedon*	530	24	160	101	261
36. *Santa Ana*	250	24	91	80	171
37. *Nuestra Señora de Begoña* . .	750	24	174	123	297
38. *La Trinidad*	872	24	180	122	302
39. *Santa Catalina*	882	24	190	159	349
40. *San Juan Bautista*	650	24	192	93	285
41. Patax *N. S. del Socorro* . . .	75	24	20	25	45
42. Patax *S. Antonio de Padua* . .	75	12	20	46	66
16 ships					4177

[1] The ship in which was Diego Enriquez. Apparently lost on the coast of Ireland.

	Tons.	Guns.	MEN.		
			Soldiers.	Mariners.	Total.
43. *N. S. Del Rosario*, Capitana [1] . .	1150	46	304	118	422
44. *San Francisco*, Almiranta . . .	915	21	222	56	278
45. *San Juan*	810	31	245	89	334
46. *San Juan de Gargarin* . . .	569	16	165	56	221
47. *La Concepcion*	862	20	185	71	256
48. *Duquesa Santa Ana* [2]	900	23	280	77	357
49. *Santa Catalina*	730	23	231	77	308
50. *La Trinidad*	650	13	192	74	266
51. *Santa Maria del Juncal* . . .	730	20	228	80	308
52. *San Bartolomé*	976	27	240	72	312
53. Patax *Espíritu Santo*	?	. .	33	10	43
11 ships					3105

[1] Taken, and broken up at Chatham. Don Pedro de Valdes, after about three years paid a ransom of £3000.

[2] Lost in Glennagiveny Bay.

	Tons.	Guns.	MEN.		
			Soldiers.	Mariners.	Total.
54. *Santa Ana*, Capitana[1]	1200	47	303	82	385
55. *N. S. De la Rosa*, Almiranta[2] . .	945	26	233	64	297
56. *San Salvador*[3]	958	25	321	75	396
57. *San Estéban*	736	26	196	68	264
58. *Santa Marta*	548	20	173	63	236
59. *Santa Bárbara*	525	12	154	45	199
60. *San Buenaventura*	379	21	168	53	221
61. *La Maria San Juan*	291	12	110	30	140
62. *Santa Cruz*	680	16	156	32	188
63. Urca *Doncella*	500	16	156	32	188
64. Patax *La Asuncion*	60	9	20	23	43
65. Patax *San Bernabe*	69	9	20	23	43
12 ships					2600

[1] Returned to Spain, but accidentally blew up.

[2] Lost among the Blaskets.

[3] Seems to have been "Almiranta" when partially blown up on July 21st. Was taken to Weymouth, and lost at Studland.

ARMADA OF LEVANT SHIPS, UNDER MARTIN DE BERTENDONA.

	Tons.	Guns.	MEN.		
			Soldiers.	Mariners.	Total.
66. *La Regazona*, Capitana[1] . . .	1249	30	344	80	424
67. *La Lavia*, Almiranta	728	25	203	71	274
68. *La Rata Coronada*[2]	820	35	335	84	419
69. *San Juan de Sicilia*[3]	800	26	279	63	342
70. *La Trinidad Valencera*[4] . . .	1100	42	281	79	360
71. *La Anunciada*	703	24	196	79	275
72. *San Nicolas Prodaneli*	834	26	374	81	455
73. *La Juliana*	860	32	325	70	395
74. *Santa Maria de Vison*	666	18	236	71	307
75. *La Trinidad de Scala*	900	22	307	79	386
10 ships					3637

[1] Flag of Bertendona, who is said by Duro to have been the captor of the *Revenge* in 1591. Burnt at Corunna, 1589.

[2] Wrecked off Erris.

[3] In her was Diego Tellez Enriquez. Seems to have foundered while negotiating surrender to Captain Crosse.

[4] Lost on the Irish Coast.

	Tons.	Guns.	MEN.		
			Soldiers.	Mariners.	Total.
76. *El Gran Grifon*, Capitana [1] . .	650	38	243	43	286
77. *San Salvador*, Almiranta . . .	650	24	218	43	261
78. *Perro Marina*	200	7	70	24	94
79. *Falcon Blanco Mayor* [2] . . .	500	16	161	36	197
80. *Castillo Negro*	750	27	239	34	273
81. *Barca de Amburg*	600	23	239	25	264
82. *Casa de Paz Grande*	650	26	198	27	225
83. *San Pedro Mayor* [3]	581	29	213	28	241
84. *El Sanson*	500	18	200	31	231
85. *San Pedro Menor*	500	18	157	23	180
86. *Barca de Anzique*	450	26	200	25	225
87. *Falcon Blanco Mediano* [4] . . .	300	16	76	27	103
88. *Santo Andres*	400	14	150	28	178
89. *Casa de Paz Chica*	350	15	162	24	186
90. *Ciervo Volante*	400	18	200	22	222
91. *Paloma Blanca*	250	12	56	20	76
92. *La Ventura*	160	4	58	14	72
93. *Santa Bárbara*	370	10	70	22	92
94. *Santiago*	600	19	56	30	86
95. *David*	450	7	50	24	74
96. *El Gato*	400	9	40	22	62
97. *Esayas*	260	4	30	16	46
98. *San Gabriel*	280	4	35	20	55
23 ships					3729

[1] A ship of Rostock. Lost on Fair Island.

[2] A Hamburg ship. Captured and taken to Plymouth while returning from Lisbon to Hamburg, January 22nd, 1589.

[3] Wrecked in Bigbury Bay, Devonshire.　　　　[4] Lost on the Irish Coast.

PATACHES AND ZABRAS, UNDER DON ANTONIO HURTADO DE MENDOZA.

	Tons.	Guns.	MEN.		
			Soldiers.	Mariners.	Total.
99. *N. S. del Pilar de Zaragoza,* Capitana	300	11	109	51	160
100. *La Caridad* (Inglesa)	180	12	70	36	106
101. *San Andres* (Escoces)	150	12	40	29	69
102. *El Crucifijo.*	150	8	40	29	69
103. *N. S. del Puerto*	55	8	30	33	63
104. *La Concepcion de Carasa* . . .	70	5	30	42	72
105. *N. S. de Begoña*	64	..	20	26	46
106. *La Concepcion de Capetillo* . .	60	10	20	26	46
107. *San Jeronimo*	50	4	20	37	57
108. *N. S. de Gracia*	57	5	20	34	54
109. *La Concepcion de Francisco de Latero*	75	6	20	29	49
110. *N. S. de Guadalupe*	70	..	20	42	62
111. *San Francisco*	70	..	20	37	57
112. *Espíritu Santo*	75	..	20	47	67
113. *Trinidad*	?	2	..	23	23
114. *N. S. de Castro*	?	2	..	26	26
115. *Santo Andres*	?	2	..	15	15
116. *La Concepcion de Valmaseda* . .	?	2	..	27	27
117. *La Concepcion de Somanila* . .	?	..	..	31	31
118. *Santa Catalina*	?	..	..	23	23
119. *San Juan de Carasa*	?	..	..	23	23
120. *Asuncion*	?	..	..	23	23
22 ships					1168

GALLEASSES OF NAPLES, UNDER DON HUGO DE MONCADA.

	Tons.	Guns.	MEN.		
			Soldiers.	Mariners.	Total.
121. *San Lorenzo*, Capitana [1] . . .	?	50	262	124	386
122. *Patrona Zuñiga*	?	50	178	112	290
123. *Girona* [2]	?	50	169	120	289
124. *Napolitana*	?	50	264	112	376
4 ships					1341 [3]

[1] Driven ashore and became a wreck at Calais.
[2] Wrecked near the Giant's Causeway, probably with Don Alonso de Leyva, the Count of Paredes, and all hands.
[3] With 1200 rowers.

GALLEYS OF PORTUGAL, UNDER DON DIEGO MEDRANO.

	Tons.	Guns.	MEN.		
			Soldiers.	Mariners.	Total.
125. *Capitana*	?	5	..	106	106
126. *Princesa*	?	5	..	90	90
127. *Diana* [1]	?	5	..	94	94
128. *Bazana*	?	5	..	72	72
4 ships					·362 [2]

[1] Wrecked at Bayonne.   [2] With 888 rowers.

SUMMARIES OF THE TWO FLEETS.

ENGLISH.

Divisions.	Ships.	Men.
Her Majesty's ships	34	6289
Merchant ships under Sir Francis Drake . . .	34	2394
Ships paid by the City of London	30	2180
Merchant ships under the Lord High Admiral :—		
For about eight weeks	8	530
For the whole campaign	10	221
Victuallers	15	810
Coasters under the Lord High Admiral	20	993
Coasters under Lord Henry Seymour	23	1090
Voluntary ships	23	1044
Total	197	15,551

SPANISH.

Divisions.	Ships.	Men.
Armada of Portugal	12	4623
Armada of Biscay	14	2692
Armada of the Galleons of Castille	16	4177
Armada of Andalusia	11	3105
Armada of Guipúzcoa	12	2600
Armada of Levant ships	10	3637
Armada of Hulks	23	3729
Pataches and Zabras	22	1168
Galleasses of Naples (1200 rowers)	4	2541
Galleys of Portugal (888 rowers)	4	1250
Total	128	29,522

Tonnage: English 33546; Spanish 57868

Voyages and Discoveries, 1485–1603

The work at sea, which is now done by three services, the mercantile marine, the royal navy, and the much-neglected expeditions of discovery, was, in the whole earlier period of our maritime history, combined; our merchant ships going forth to trade peaceably, if this way was permitted, if not to fight, and always to explore and to discover. All distant lands, if unvisited and unexplored by Englishmen, were practically discoveries, so far as England was concerned, and the daring seamen who readied then were explorers and discoverers as well as traders.

In the study of our maritime history we are checked at the outset by the want of records. It is certain that in early times many voyages were made to distant countries of which no accounts are preserved, and that there was a spirit of enterprise abroad among our merchants, and great activity in our seaports. The foundations of our naval supremacy were laid in silence, so far as posterity is concerned; and it seems important that this should be borne in mind. Continuous efforts were made, and splendid work was done at sea of which we know little or nothing.

Through casual sentences in some of the old chroniclers—of Botoner, of Fabyan, or of Stow—we get a few glimpses of what was going on. Richard Eden gives us a little light; but even Hakluyt, with all his devoted energy and perseverance, was able to preserve only portions of the early part of the glorious history of our maritime enterprises. He could not find a single scrap of the writings of John Cabot. Yet during a long life he "waded on still further and further in the sweet studie of the historie of cosmographie," and strove "to incorporate into one bodie the torn and scattered limnes of our ancient and later navigations by sea." To no writer does England owe so deep a debt of gratitude as to Richard Hakluyt.

In the fifteenth century William Botoner, better known as William of Worcester—the accomplished secretary of that doughty old warrior, Sir John Fastolf, of Caistor—gives us some insight into the activity and enterprise of one of our great seaports. He tells us of William Canyng, the merchant prince of Bristol, who, for many years, employed eight hundred seamen and one hundred artificers, and possessed ten ships which, as mentioned in an earlier chapter, traded to the Mediterranean, to the Baltic, and even to Iceland, where one of his vessels of 160 tons was lost. We hear also how Robert Sturmy, Mayor of Bristol, sent a ship to the Mediterranean in 1457, which was "spoilt by the Genoese," for which wrong the Genoese in London were arrested and imprisoned until they made good the loss.

A book of sailing directions for the coasts from Scotland to Gibraltar was written in the fifteenth century, and has been preserved. At the time when the Portuguese vessels, under the auspices of Prince Henry, were slowly and cautiously creeping along the coast of Africa, dreading to be out of sight of land, English sailors had no such fears, but habitually faced the storms of the North Atlantic and made voyages to Iceland. They may have gone farther. A map of the coasts from the British Isles nearly to Cape Verde in Africa, was drawn in London in 1448, including the Azores and other islands in the Atlantic.

It has recently been brought to the notice of geographers by Mr. Yule Oldham. Its author was a Venetian galley captain named Andrea Biancho, who is also well known as an accomplished cosmographer. In the margin of his map the outline of a coast is added, with the inscription—"An authentic island distant to the west 1500 miles" ("*Ixola otinticha x longa a ponente 1500 mia*"). As the map was drawn in London, this new information was probably received there. The distance might mean 1500 miles to the westward of the English coast, on about the parallel of London, where Biancho drew the map. The information would come from some expedition in the days of William Canyng. (Mr. Yule Oldham, however, suggests a Portuguese source for the information which induced Biancho to draw the outline on the margin of his map.)

About twenty years later, voyages of discovery began to be dispatched from Bristol, to discover or re-discover an island called Brazil, reported to be in the ocean to the westward of Ireland. William Botoner knew something about one of these voyages, because his brother-in-law, John Jay, took part in it. He says that the commander's name was Thylde, and that he was the most scientific seaman in all England.

Sailing from the port of Bristol, on the 15th of July, 1480, he preceded Columbus by upwards of twelve years. His task, however, was far more difficult and perilous than that of the Genoese. Columbus merely ran down the trades in lovely weather.

But Thylde and his gallant Englishmen, in a little vessel of 80 tons, had to battle against the gales of the North Atlantic in the roaring forties. They failed to discover land, but they deserved success. The time occupied by the voyages of Columbus and Thylde respectively was about the same, one sixty-nine and the other sixty-four days; but while the Spaniards enjoyed the pleasant weather of the trade wind, the English adventurers fought a brave fight against the mighty seas and adverse gales of the boisterous North Atlantic. Thylde returned to Bristol on the 18th of September; and we owe it to the accident that one of his crew was related to one out of the very few chroniclers of that time, that any record was preserved of the existence of the most scientific seaman in all England, or of his voyage of discovery.

Other similar voyages followed; but the English sailors, in their more stormy latitudes, had no trade wind to carry them easily across the ocean: while Thylde, as a scientific observer, for a long time had no English successor. The unknown facts which led to the insertion of the coast-line on the margin of Andrea Biancho's map, possibly account for the subsequent efforts of Thylde and others to rediscover that land which they called Brazil. It seems certain, from what we are told by William Botoner, that such efforts were actually made.

The minds of English mariners were thus quite prepared for another attempt, when the news of the discoveries of Columbus reached them. To those among them who were accustomed to sail from Bristol, a voyage of discovery to the westward was no new idea. When, therefore, a scientific Genoese seaman, with Venetian citizenship, named John Cabot, and his three sons, obtained letters patent for this discovery to the westward from Henry VII. in 1496, the voyage was made in a Bristol ship called the *Matthew*, with a crew of eighteen men, chiefly English seamen. The surgeon was a Genoese, and one of the men was a Burgundian.

It is possible to gather a few particulars respecting this voyage from State papers, and from the letters of two Italian news' writers who were in London at the time. The *Matthew* sailed from Bristol in May, 1497, first steering northwards, after passing Ireland, and then westward for a month, during which time the vessel must have been set to the south. For, passing Newfoundland on the starboard hand, the first sight of land (the "*Prima Vista*") was obtained on St. John's Day, the 24th of June, 1497. The "*Prima Vista*" is shown on a map drawn in 1544 by John Cabot's son Sebastian, to be the northern end of Cape Breton. The explorers can only have remained a very short time on the newly discovered coast, for the *Matthew* had returned to Bristol by the end of July or first days of August. On the 10th of August, Henry VII. granted Cabot the munificent sum of £10. (Mr. Harrisse disbelieves in the legend on the Sebastian Cabot map of 1544—which is the authority for the "*Prima Vista*"—both as regards the date and the place. He places the landfall of Cabot on the coast of Labrador in 51° 15' N.)

The aspirations of Thylde and the other English explorers of the fifteenth century were thus at length realised. There was every encouragement to repeat the voyage, and on February 3rd, 1498, Henry VII. granted his second letters patent to John Cabot. Nothing whatsoever is known of the important second voyage of Cabot from any English source, except the facts that the expedition consisted of five vessels, and that it sailed from Bristol before the 25th of July, 1498. English seamen named Lancelot Thirkill and Thomas Bradley each received a loan of £30 from the king towards fitting out two of the ships. There was also a gratuity of £40 5s. to John Carter "going to the newe ile." Nothing more is recorded. We know nothing more of John Cabot, nor of the expedition, except that Captain Thirkill returned home—for he is again mentioned in a document dated June 6th, 1501.

But when the Spanish pilot, Juan de la Cosa, produced his famous map in 1500, he painted flags with the Red Cross of St. George to show the discoveries made by the English along the coasts of the New World, which extend from Cape Breton to a point which is probably Cape Hatteras. He calls these discoveries "Sea discovered by the English terminating to the north with the Cape of England." This grand achievement was the work of the expedition of 1498. The results, in the shape of a map, must have been obtained by the Spanish ambassador in London, forwarded to his government, and handed over to Juan de la Cosa as material for his great map. So, it came to pass that the only record of the discoveries of the English Expedition of 1498 is preserved on the bullock's hide which now hangs in the navy office at Madrid. (At time of first publication).

This is a very striking example of the absence of materials for the history of English maritime adventure during its earlier development. The Cabot voyages are generally considered to mark an epoch; and to form the commencement of British maritime discovery. They did nothing of the kind. It has been seen that voyages of discovery preceded them; and they also followed them in quick succession. The importance of the Cabot voyages lies in their success, not in their forming a starting point. English maritime enterprise had been fully aroused half a century before letters patent were granted to Cabot, and its development steadily continued without any break.

Three years after John Cabot disappeared from the scene, letters patent were granted for the discovery and settlement of what was called the "New Island" to Richard Ward, Thomas Ashehurst, and John Thomas of Bristol, in conjunction with three natives of the Azores. In 1502, letters patent, for a fourth time, were granted to Hugh Eliot and Thomas Ashehurst; and Dr. Thorne tells us that his father, with another merchant of Bristol named Hugh Eliot, were the discoverers of Newfoundland. Cabot, according to the legend on his son's map of 1544, had left it to the north, and discovered Cape Breton. The State Papers furnish incidental evidence that these and other voyages were actually made across the Atlantic. In 1503, we read of "one who brought hawks from Newfoundland," and in 1504, of "a Preste going to the New Islande." Another expedition returned in September, 1505.

Maritime discovery was a plant of slow but steady growth in England, established in a rich and fertile soil and destined to spread over the whole earth, to the benefit not only or chiefly of England, but of all mankind. Progress was continuous. In 1505, the famous Company of Merchant Adventurers received their Charter and enlarged their commercial relations with the Low Countries and Germany; while the number of English ships trading to ports in the Mediterranean increased year by year. The voyage to the Levant occupied twelve months, and was beset by all kinds of perils, which were faced and overcome by the fighting seamen of London and Bristol.

Voyages to the westward were also continuous from the days of Canyng and Thylde; and some record of at least two—which were made during the reign of Henry VIII.—has been preserved. In 1527 the king sent out two ships, the *Sampson* and *Mary of Guildford*, well manned and victualled, under the command of John Rut of Ratcliff, yeoman of the Crown, and having on board a canon of St. Paul's and "divers cunning men to seek strange regions." They sailed on the 10th of June; but the *Sampson* was cast away on the coast of Labrador, and the other vessel returned in the following October. The letter from

John Rut to Henry VIII., dated at St. John's, Newfoundland, on August 3rd, 1527, is given by Purchas. In the same year, Master Grube, with two ships, reached Cape Race. Nine years after, in 1536, a voyage was undertaken by a number of gentlemen of the Inns of Court, led by Master Hore of London, a man of goodly stature, great courage, and learned in the science of cosmography.

The expedition consisted of thirty gentlemen volunteers, including a son of Sir William Butts of Norfolk, and a hundred seamen, in two vessels, the *Trinity*, of 140 tons, and the *Minion*, commanded by Captain Wade. Sailing from Gravesend they reached Cape Breton, after a voyage of two months, and proceeded thence to an island which, in those days, was frequented by thousands of great auks. The men drove numbers of these helpless birds into their boats and took their eggs, finding them to be "very good and nourishing meat." Many Basque, Breton, and English vessels came every season, and the wholesale destruction of the birds brought about their extinction in less than two centuries.

The exploring vessels were then on the coast of Newfoundland, and "great want of victuals" was brought about by inexperience and mismanagement. The young barristers began to eat each other, which induced Captain Wade to preach a sermon on the impropriety of such conduct. Eventually a French vessel came in sight and was seized by the adventurers, who appropriated provisions sufficient to enable them to return to England. Hakluyt rode two hundred miles to obtain the particulars of this voyage from young Mr. Butts; and to his indefatigable perseverance we owe the preservation of records of this and other voyages, which would otherwise have been lost. They may be taken as enterprises typical of many long since forgotten.

The maritime enterprises of the days of Henry VIII. were not confined to these northern voyages. Hakluyt tells us how old Mr. William Hawkyns of Plymouth, who was much esteemed for his wisdom, valour, and skill in sea canoes, would not be contented with short voyages along the known coasts of Europe. He fitted out a tall and goodly ship of 250 tons, called the *Pole*, of Plymouth, and made three long and once famous voyages to Brazil, which, in those days, was an enterprise of very rare occurrence. His first voyage was in 1530, when he reached the Rio Cestos on the Grain Coast of Guinea, and took in elephants' teeth and other commodities.

Thence he continued his voyage to the coast of Brazil, where he behaved with such prudence and judgment that he not only formed friendships with the natives, but even induced one of the chiefs to come to England. These three voyages of William Hawkyns were memorable, and others followed in his footsteps. Several wealthy merchants of Southampton sent ships to Brazil in 1540; and trade was carried on with the ports of Barbary from London. But one of the first voyages to Guinea was disastrous, owing to the inexperience, and perhaps to the misconduct, of the commander. The *Primrose* and *Lion* left Portsmouth in August, 1553, and returned with the loss of the captain and of a hundred men, out of one hundred and forty men forming the crews of the two ships.

These Guinea voyages were indeed very perilous in those days. Their commanders needed to be men of high qualifications—to be endowed with courage, patience, perseverance, zeal, and sympathy for their men. Long voyages, the ravages of scurvy, and bad provisions had certainly to be faced, besides the usual perils of the sea, and a probable encounter with a superior force of Portuguese. This was the training of most of the great naval officers of the Elizabethan age; and such a man appears to have been Captain John Lock, who commanded a fleet of three ships for the Guinea voyage, fitted out by merchants of London, in 1554. He exchanged his outward cargo with the commodities of the country at a place four leagues to the east of Lamina.

His journal describes the people and the climate, and contains notes on the variation of the compass and on the native products, such as gold, elephants' teeth, dragons' blood, and cinnabar. He suggested instructions for those who would make a voyage to Guinea. They should make a chart with the correct latitudes of places; learn what commodities belong to each port; what help may be depended upon from the natives; ascertain particulars respecting water-supply; and explore the country both along the coast and inland. The voyage of John Lock was followed, from 1555 to 1557, by three voyages sent to Guinea by a merchant of London, named William Towerson, his ships fighting the Portuguese successfully, and bringing back gold and ivory.

The meagre history which Hakluyt has thus preserved, proves that there was an increasing spirit of enterprise among the merchants and seamen of our principal seaports for at least a century before the formation of the great companies gave an additional and abiding impulse to maritime discovery. Nor was this spirit of adventure confined to those whose regular business it was to make trading ventures and to navigate distant seas. Young gentlemen from inland counties, barristers from the Inns of Court, and even a canon of St. Paul's, came forward as volunteers; while the policy of the Government was generally to give reasonable encouragement to these undertakings, by sharing in the ventures, by occasionally even fitting out expeditions, and eventually by granting charters.

Young Edward VI. appears to have taken a personal interest in the advancement of the maritime prosperity of his country, and in the science which is a necessary part of a seaman's education. During his reign Sebastian, the son of John Cabot, returned to England, after having served the Spanish Government for many years, been initiated into all the secrets of the hydrographic office at Seville, and been entrusted with the high position of Chief Pilot. He in fact deserted; and application was made for his surrender by the Emperor Charles V., which was refused because it was thought that his services would be useful to England. Sebastian was very young at the time of the voyages of John Cabot, and it is doubtful whether he accompanied his father.

When he returned from Spain he was an old man, and he was welcomed as a learned cosmographer, possessed of the secrets of the Spanish Government. In reality, he was a treacherous intriguer, disloyal to all his employers, alike to England as to Spain. But this was never known until the Venetian archives revealed it, centuries after his death. King Edward's government received him as a valuable acquisition, and granted him a pension.

When the monopoly of the foreign merchants of the Steelyard was withdrawn, the Company of Merchant Adventurers resolved to seek for new outlets for English manufactured goods, and, after much consideration, it was resolved that the vessels should be fitted out, to undertake a voyage to Cathay by the north-east. One of the leading promoters was Lord Howard of Effingham, father of the great admiral; and Sebastian Cabot was chosen as the first governor of the company.

The choice of the commander for this expedition fell upon Sir Hugh Willoughby, a younger son of an ancient Nottinghamshire family. His portraits at Wollaton and in the painted hall at Greenwich, show us a tall, handsome man, with a small head and amiable expression of countenance. He had the title of captain-general, with his flag on board the *Bona Speranza*, of 120 tons. His second in command, on board the *Edward Bonaventure*, of 160 tons, was Richard Chancellor, an experienced seaman, who had already seen service in the Mediterranean. Stephen Borough was with Chancellor as master, and John Buckland as mate. The third vessel was the *Bona Confidentia*, of 90 tons. Rather elaborate ordinances and instructions were drawn up for

Willoughby's expedition, borrowed from similar documents in the office of the Chief Pilot of Spain. One, as Mr. Harrisse has pointed out, is copied from the instructions which the Council of the Indies prescribed, in 1523, to Cabot himself, for the expedition to the River Plate. In these instructions, the captains were enjoined to enter daily in their journals the navigations of every day and night. The journals of the different ships were to be compared periodically, and, after debate and consultation, to be entered in a common ledger.

On the 20th of May, 1553, the three ships forming Sir Hugh Willoughby's expedition were towed down the Thames by boats, with the crews dressed in sky-blue cloth. The ships saluted as they passed the royal palace of Greenwich, the roofs and towers of which were crowded with spectators. But the poor young king was too ill even to come to a window. The evidence points to his having been poisoned, probably not through criminal intent, but owing to ignorance and neglect. Five years of terror and misgovernment were to follow his death, during which period the sister he had loved so well was in deadly peril, expecting to be offered a sacrifice to bigotry and jealousy, "*tanquam ovis*," as she plaintively said. But then all the clouds cleared away, the sun appeared in its splendour, and the spirit of maritime enterprise was fostered for nearly half a century by the great queen.

As Willoughby's ships were towed down the river, great crowds lined the banks, salutes were fired, and cheers resounded from the crews of all vessels at anchor. The fate of Willoughby's ship is well known. Sir Hugh came in sight of what is now called the "Goose Coast" of Novaya Zemlya, and afterwards took refuge in the Bay of Arzin ain Lapland. Here he and all his crew perished during the following spring, after making some efforts to find habitations of the natives and to seek their aid.

Chancellor was more fortunate. He succeeded in reaching the Russian settlement of Kholmogori on the White Sea, proceeded to Moscow, and returned safely to England in the autumn of 1554. Commercial relations were thus commenced with this distant and previously unknown country, which were kept open by vessels periodically dispatched to the White Sea by the Muscovy Company, the title by which it was henceforth known. For in February, 1555, it was granted a charter of incorporation by Philip and Mary, for the discovery of unknown lands.

In June, 1555, the company sent out two ships, the *Edward Bonaventure* and *Philip and Mary*, commanded by Richard Chancellor

SIR HUGH WILLOUGHBY, KT.

(Taken, by kind permission of Lord Middleton, from the picture, by an unknown artist, at Wollaton Hall, Notts.)

[Owing to the condition of this very interesting portrait, it has been found impossible to obtain a better reproduction of it than the one above given. The historical value of the print will excuse its imperfections.]

and John Howlet, with George Killingworth on board as the company's agent. The former ship proceeded to the White Sea, probably hearing of the sad fate of Sir Hugh Willoughby and his people at Vardö. On her return, the *Edward Bonaventure*, then in command of John Buckland, visited Arzina and took on board the body of Willoughby, and the papers and merchandise remaining in his ships. The *Edward Bonaventure* and *Philip and Mary* returned to the Thames in November. Mr. Harrisse has pointed out that Milton (*Brief History of Muscovia*) was mistaken in supposing that the vessel with Willoughby's body on board was lost at sea. The same two ships were sent to the White Sea again, in 1556, and a third vessel was added, the *Searchthrift*, under Stephen Borough, with his brother William and a crew of eight men.

Stephen Borough appears to have been in chief command; and he left Gravesend on the 25th of April, 1556. Parting company with the two other ships off the entrance to the White Sea, the *Searchthrift* continued the explorations eastward, and Borough reached the mouth of the Pechora. On August 1st, 1556, he landed on the south-west coast of Novaya Zemlya, and explored the strait between that coast and Waigatsch island. He then proceeded to the White Sea, and wintered at Kholmogori, returning home in 1557.

Meanwhile, Chancellor had again been to Moscow, and returning with a Russian ambassador, embarked at Kholmogori on board the *Edward Bonaventure* in July, 1556. It was not until November that she arrived off Pitsligo, near Aberdeen, where she was driven upon the rocks during a heavy gale. Chancellor, the experienced pilot and gallant seaman, perished in an attempt to reach the shore in a boat.

Then, from 1557 to 1572, followed the voyages of Anthony Jenkinson, an able negotiator and intrepid traveller. Jenkinson was the first Englishman to navigate the Caspian Sea. He penetrated as far as Kazvin and Bokhara, and obtained a new charter from the *Tsar*, for the Russia Company, in 1567.

There are reasons for paying special attention to the careers of Stephen and William Borough. They are the first in the long roll of illustrious seamen who commenced life in the merchant service, became distinguished as explorers, and ended as valuable officers of the Royal Navy. They began the establishment of the proof, which the experience of three centuries since their day has now completely demonstrated, that voyages of discovery are the best training-grounds for naval officers. They were the first to perceive that the only point in which English seamen were then inferior to Spaniards or Portuguese was in scientific knowledge; and the elder Borough was the first to seek a remedy.

Stephen and William Borough were born at Borough in the parish of Northam, near Bideford. After Stephen returned from the White Sea in 1557, he induced Richard Eden to translate the *Arte de Navegar*, of Martin Cortes, the navigation text-book of the Spaniards, into English. He thus secured the means whereby our seamen could obtain instruction. In 1563, he received the appointment of Chief Pilot in the Medway, and assumed the duty of instructing and examining seamen in the art of navigation. This meritorious officer died in July, 1584, in his sixtieth year, and was buried at Chatham. His brother William's services were of the same character. He was ten years younger than Stephen, and he continued to serve the Russia Company in voyages to the White Sea.

In 1570, he commanded a fleet bound for Narva in the Baltic. The brothers had been attentive in observing the variation of the compass during the voyage of 1556, and in 1581 William Borough published his *Discourse of Variation of the Compass*. In 1583, he became Comptroller of the Navy, and two years afterwards he commanded the fleet which conveyed the Earl of Leicester from Harwich to Flushing. He constructed charts and prepared sailing directions, besides serving with Drake at Cadiz, and under Lord Howard against the Spanish Armada. Such were the services of these two brothers, who received their training in expeditions of discovery.

But they were only the two first among that galaxy of explorers and discoverers who created the English navy and saved England. They were the first, but their compeers Drake and Hawkyns were perhaps the greatest as commanders in war and as administrators in time of peace. John, the son of that famous old William Hawkyns of the Brazil voyages, was born in 1532, and in his youth made divers voyages to the Canary Islands, where he obtained much information respecting the trade of the West Indies. He heard, among other things, that there was a great demand for negroes at St. Domingo and in the Spanish Main, and that they could easily be obtained in Guinea. His plan was approved by several London capitalists, as well as by Mr. Benjamin Gonson, the Treasurer of the Navy, who became the father-in-law of the young adventurer, probably before he sailed.

John Hawkyns was thirty years of age in 1562, when he received command of three ships, the *Solomon*, of 120 tons, the *Swallow*, of 100 tons, and the small *barque Jonas*. The orders he gave to his sailors were:—

Serve God daily; love one another; preserve your victuals; beware of fire; and keep good company.

Proceeding to Sierra Leone, he got on board, partly by force and partly by other means, as many as three hundred negroes, besides other merchandise. Crossing the Atlantic, he visited the ports of Isabela, Puerto de Plata, and Monte Christi, on the north coast of the island of Santo Domingo. He disposed of all his negroes, and received in exchange so valuable a cargo that he returned home in September, 1563, with much profit, both to himself and to the merchant adventurers who fitted out the expedition. But Hakluyt was only able to get but a brief account of the first West Indian voyage of John Hawkyns.

The story of the second voyage of John Hawkyns is well told by John Sparke the younger, who was on board one of the ships as a volunteer. On the 18th of October, 1564, four vessels, named the *Jesus of*

Lübeck, of 700 tons, the *Solomon*, of 140 tons, and the *Tiger* and *Swallow* of 50 and 30 tons respectively, sailed from Plymouth under the command of Hawkyns, who proceeded, as on the previous voyage, to the Coast of Africa, and in January, 1565, made sail from Sierra Leone for the West Indies with a cargo of slaves. After touching at Dominica and other islands, Hawkyns anchored off Burburata on the coast of Venezuela. Here he was told that the Spaniards were forbidden to trade with any other nation; but the authorities agreed to supply him with provisions and water; and in the end Hawkyns also received payment for a number of his negroes. At Rio de la Hacha, by a display of force, Hawkyns again obliged the Spaniards to trade with him, and thus disposed of more negroes.

On the 31st of May, 1565, the English adventurers departed from the South American coast, sighted Jamaica and Cuba, and arrived at the river in Florida where the French, under Laudonier, had built a fort. Hawkyns found these settlers in want of provisions, and presented them with supplies of meal and beans, and also with one of his *barques*, to help them on their return. Taking leave of the Frenchmen, Hawkyns began his homeward voyage on the 28th of July, and arrived at Padstow on the 20th of September, 1565. This second voyage of Hawkyns was also profitable, and encouraged the adventurers to

SIR JOHN HAWKYNS, KT.

tempt fortune a third time.

Hawkyns sailed from Plymouth on the 2nd of October, 1567, with a fleet consisting of the *Jesus of Lübeck*, lent by the queen, the *Minion*, the *Judith*, of 50 tons, and two small *barques*; and in command of the *Judith* was his renowned cousin, Francis Drake. The needy vicar of Upchurch on the Medway, driven by persecution from his native Devonshire, found it hard to bring up several sons, and Francis was apprenticed to the master of a small vessel which traded along the coast, and across the Channel to Zeeland and France.

As a boy of twelve or thirteen, he might have seen, and probably did see, the fleet of Sir Hugh Willoughby go down the river, and he probably joined in the cheering. He was such a good and honest lad that the old sailor who owned the coasting vessel bequeathed it to his apprentice on his death. This was the small beginning of Drake's fortune. He continued in the same business for several years, but in 1565 he made a voyage with Captain John Lovell to the West Indies, which was disastrous, and caused ruinous loss to young Drake. He was, therefore, glad to receive command of the little *Judith* in the fleet of his relative.

Pursuing his former course of procedure, Hawkyns went first to the coast of Africa, took between four hundred and five hundred negroes on board, and sailed with them for the West Indies, arriving at Dominica on the 27th of March, 1568. He seems to have found no difficulty in inducing the Spaniards on the coast of Venezuela to trade with him, except at Rio de la Hacha and Cartagena. At the former place Hawkyns found it necessary to land his men and take the town by storm before its citizens could be induced to enter into commercial relations, but after that decisive step, they came by night and purchased two hundred negroes from the English.

Leaving Cartagena on the 24th of July, and commencing the homeward-bound voyage, the adventurers encountered a hurricane off the west end of Cuba, which lasted four days, and the Jesus sprung a leak. This was followed by another gale, and Hawkyns was obliged to seek a refuge for his battered ships in the bay of Vera Cruz on the coast of Mexico, on the 16th of September.

Hawkyns made a request to the Audience of Mexico, which was in charge of the government until the new viceroy should arrive, that, having been driven to the anchorage of San Juan de Ulloa by stress of weather, he might be supplied with provisions and allowed to depart peaceably. Meanwhile, the Spanish fleet arrived, having on board the new viceroy of Mexico, Don Martin Henriquez. The viceroy made an agreement with the English commander that his ships should be provisioned; the fleets saluted each other, and amity was apparently established. But the Spaniards intended treachery, and at a given signal a general attack was suddenly made on the English ships. The *Minion* slipped her cables, hauled away on a sternfast, and thus escaped from the first assault. The *Jesus* was next attacked, but she also hauled out, and both the English ships got to a distance of two ships' lengths from their Spanish assailants.

Then a heavy fire was opened on the Jesus from a battery on shore, and her masts and yards were so cut about that all hope was abandoned of getting her out to sea. She was left to her fate, while the *Minion*, hastily taking Hawkyns on board, made sail, followed by some of the survivors of the crew of the *Jesus* in a boat. The rest were slaughtered. The *Minion* and *Judith* put to sea, but parted company next day. The *Minion* was thus crowded with men, while the provisions had run short, and there was no possibility of feeding so many. After sailing about for several days in the Gulf of Mexico, she was anchored off the coast, near Tampico.

The unfortunate people, pressed by hunger, demanded to be put on shore. There was no alternative. A hundred men were landed, and Hawkyns commenced the voyage home with about a hundred survivors, who died in great numbers from scurvy and famine. Some relief was obtained from English ships in Vigo Bay, and on the 25th of January, 1569, the battered *Minion*, with her suffering crew, was anchored in Mount's Bay.

The men who were put on shore on the coast of Mexico were made prisoners, and were at first treated with humanity, but the Inquisition was established at Mexico in 1570, and the most horrible atrocities were committed on the English captives. Only two, named David Ingram and Miles Philips, ever returned home, and their accounts of the cruelties of the Inquisition, and of the terrible sufferings of themselves and their comrades, sent a thrill of horror through the land. Both Hawkyns and Drake vowed vengeance, and they were men who kept their word.

John Hawkyns had thus received his training in the conduct of difficult and perilous adventures by sea. The rest of his life was devoted to the naval service of his country. This great sea captain acquired his rare qualifications during his long service in exploring voyages to the Canaries, to the coast of Africa, and to the West Indies.

The captain of the *Judith* was ten years younger than his cousin Hawkyns, and was resolved to see more of the West Indies. The treatment of his comrades who had been forced to land at Tampico made Francis Drake an implacable enemy of the Spaniards. Whether there was peace or war between England and Spain, there was henceforth to be unceasing war between Drake and the countrymen of the Spanish Inquisitors. In 1570, Drake made a voyage to the West Indies with two small vessels, called the *Dragon* and *Swan*, and in 1571 he went out in the *Swan* alone. He was collecting information and maturing his plans for a hostile expedition on a more considerable scale.

When he returned to Plymouth, he began to make a very careful selection of young able-bodied seamen to form the crews of two vessels, forty-seven men and boys for one, and twenty-six for the other. A year's provisions were taken on board, and three pinnaces were specially constructed, to be taken out in pieces. The *Pasha*, of 70 tons, was commanded by Drake himself, and the *Swan*, of 25 tons, by his brother John. They sailed from Plymouth on the 24th of May, 1572, and Drake shaped a course for the Spanish Main, until he sighted the high land about Santa Marta. He seems to have known of a small unfrequented bay, which he called "Port Pheasant," and here his ships were anchored, and the pinnaces were put together. He was joined by a barque belonging to Cowes, with a crew of thirty men, under the command of a seaman named James Reuse.

Drake's scheme was desperate, but it was very carefully planned. He intended to attack Nombre de Dios in the pinnaces, the point on the isthmus to which all the wealth of Peru converged for shipment to Europe. The three pinnaces came silently before the town in the dead of night. At three in the morning of the 22nd of July, the English, landing, captured a battery of six brass guns, and spiked them. Unluckily a gunner escaped and alarmed the town. When Drake entered the market-place at the head of his men, the Spaniards opened fire, but were put to flight. John Oxenham, Drake's trusty lieutenant, found an immense heap of silver bars in the treasure-house.

The gallant commander of the expedition had, however, been severely wounded. He fainted from loss of blood, was carried down to his pinnace, and taken to an island where he might be cured of his wound. Here the ships joined them, and Reuse parted company to return home with his share of the spoils. Drake continued to harass the Spaniards. His brother John was killed in boarding an enemy's ship, and another brother Joseph died of fever with twenty-eight of the men, but several prizes were captured in the autumn of 1572.

During these closing months of the year, the active brain of the illustrious leader was elaborating a plan for crossing the isthmus of Darien, and intercepting the train of treasure mules. He made his preparations with great care. He had succeeded in opening friendly relations with a chief of the Cimarrones or runaway slaves named Pedro, and he selected the best of his own men. His expedition finally consisted of eighteen picked English seamen and thirty Cimarrones, and he started for the journey across the isthmus on the 3rd of February, 1573. The way led through dense tropical forests, up steep declivities, and along rocky watercourses.

On the 11th, they reached the top of a hill on which, the narrative tells us, there was "a goodlie and great high tree." Francis Drake climbed into the branches by means of notches cut in the trunk, and, for the first time, beheld the South Sea stretching away to the western horizon. His mind was filled with enthusiasm, and when he reached the ground he knelt down and besought God "to give him life and leave once to sail an English ship on that sea."

The little party had reached the water-parting of the isthmus. They now began to force their way through the almost impervious tangle of forest vegetation until at length they came in sight of the city of Panama. Drake had intelligence that eight mules laden with gold were about to make their way from Panama to Nombre de Dios. He secreted his men near the roadside, and after about an hour the tinkling of the leading mule's bell was heard. One of the seamen, unable longer to restrain his excitement, dashed forward. This prevented the plan of a surprise, but Drake was not to be beaten. He got his little force in order, and boldly attacked the escort. The Spaniards were seized with panic and fled, leaving their precious charge in the hands of the victors. Drake then re-crossed the isthmus and, near Nombre de Dios, captured another train of 109 mules, each carrying 300 pounds of silver. The quantity was so great that only a portion could be taken away.

When Drake came down to the appointed place of embarkation he found that, instead of his pinnaces, there were seven armed Spanish boats at anchor in the bay. It is on such occasions that the value of a training in exploring expeditions is brought out. Men have to decide on the instant, when one false step would be fatal. The habit of alertness and presence of mind is acquired; and the necessary training cannot be secured by study and exercise, but only by long service in the midst of perils and difficulties and of sudden emergencies. Taking every precaution that his people should be neither seen nor heard, Drake led them quietly down to a part of the bay which was concealed from the Spaniards by a jutting point. Here they built a raft and embarked to search for their comrades with a bread-bag for a sail, and the branch of a young tree for a rudder. They were up to their middles in water, but the ships were found, and Drake prepared for the homeward voyage after dismissing the faithful Cimarrones loaded with presents.

Drake returned to Plymouth on the 9th of August, 1593, and found himself a rich man. He served for some years in Ireland, and on his return, he was, through the good offices of Sir Christopher Hatton, presented to the great queen.

John Oxenham was not so patient. He was devoted to the service of Drake, whom he had accompanied through all the stirring incidents of his marvellous voyage to the isthmus, but, while waiting for his old master, he must needs scrape together money from among his Devonshire friends, fit out a small vessel of 140 tons at Plymouth, and start on an expedition of his own in 1575. Proceeding to the same place on the isthmus he heard from the Cimarrones that, since Drake's incursion, the mule trains were guarded by much larger escorts. So, he conceived the project of embarking on the South Sea and intercepting the treasure ships before they reached Panama. Oxenham concealed his ship in a creek and buried his guns. He then made his way across the isthmus with all his crew and a large body of Cimarrones.

On reaching a river flowing into the Pacific, trees were felled, timbers wen; shaped, and a pinnace was built, with forty-five feet length of keel. On board this little craft Oxenham and his intrepid followers sailed down the river and across the bay to one of the Pearl Islands, thus being the first Englishmen to navigate the Pacific Ocean. They captured two vessels from Callao and Guayaquil laden with treasure, but Oxenham committed the fatal mistake of allowing the crews to depart and give the alarm. The English returned to the isthmus and went up the river where the pinnace had been built, on their way to their own ship on the other side.

Meanwhile, an expedition in pursuit, consisting of a hundred soldiers under Don Juan de Ortega, was sent from Panama to surprise them. Ortega reached the delta of the river, but he was at a loss which mouth to enter, for it discharged its waters into the sea by three channels. Presently a quantity of feathers of plucked fowls came floating down one of them. Ortega at once went up that channel, and on the fourth day came to the pinnace with only six men in her. Soon the Spaniards discovered where the booty was concealed, and were returning to their boats, when they were overtaken by Oxenham and the main body. The fearless Englishman led on a desperate attack, and his men fought with impetuous valour.

But they were overpowered by numbers. Eleven were killed, and twelve, including the gallant leader, were captured and sent to Lima. All were put to death except two boys. It was a sad ending for an exploit almost without an equal in the annals of maritime daring. Its reckless audacity has been condemned, though it is a quality which should be fostered and encouraged, for it has made England the mistress of the sea. It must be remembered too that Oxenham and his men showed that, although they knew no fear and counted no odds, they, and especially their leader, had the minds to plan out an undertaking of extreme difficulty, and to execute it with skill and foresight.

Above all we should be proud that the cause of their disaster was their generous humanity. If they had done to their prisoners what the Spaniards did to theirs, they would have returned home safely with their little ship laden with treasure. The training of an explorer alone could have enabled Oxenham to achieve what he did. The noble attribute of mercy to the vanquished caused his failure and death.

While Drake, fired by the sight of the South Sea from the tall tree on Darien, was dreaming of a great voyage round the world, the attention of some of his brother adventurers was turned to the discovery of a way to the Indies by the north-west. Michael Lok was a leading spirit in advocating an attempt; and the bold Yorkshireman who commanded the expedition was fortunate in having a man on board who was so well able to give an interesting account of his voyages. Mr. George Best knew what he was writing about, for he had "applied himself wholly to the study of cosmographie and the secrets of navigation." He tells us that Captain Martin Frobiser fitted out two very small vessels—the *Gabriel* of 25, and the *Michael* of 20, tons—and sailed on the 1st of July, 1570, to attempt a passage which has baffled all the skill, energy, and devotion of later times.

After a stormy voyage Frobiser sighted high and rugged land, with great store of ice along the coast, which he judged to be the Friesland described by the Venetian brothers Zeni at the end of the fourteenth century. In reality, it was the east coast of Greenland, near Cape Farewell. Here the pinnace was lost with four men. The *Michael* deserted her consort and went home; but Frobiser, in the little *Gabriel*, continued his westward course. He crossed what was afterwards called Davis' Strait, and sighted "Queen Elizabeth's Forlande" on the 20th of July. On this voyage Frobiser discovered the deep bay, long called a strait, which bears his name. He returned in August, 1590, bringing home a shining piece of stone, from which the gold-finders "promised great matters." This was fortunate, for it led to the dispatch of two more expeditions under Frobiser. It often happens that such searches for "El Dorado," Prester John, or even for ores existing only in the imaginations of assayers, lead to important geographical discoveries, or, at all events, to voyages being undertaken which form an admirable nursery for seamen; "which things," says Mr. George Best most truly, "are of so great importance as, being well wayed, may seem to countervail the adventurers' charges."

Frobisher's second expedition consisted of three vessels—the *Aid* of 200 tons, with the commander of the expedition himself on board; lieutenant, George Best; master, Christopher Hall; and mate, Charles Jackman. The *Gabriel* was commanded by Captain Edward Fenton, and the *Michael* by Gilbert Yorke. Sailing on the 26th of May, 1577, they anchored in Kirkwall Bay to send home letters, and sighted the coast supposed to be Friesland on the 4th of July. Proceeding onward to the land discovered in the previous year, a more careful survey was made of Frobiser's (Strait) Bay: the names of Yorke and Jackman were given to sounds, and that of the master, Christopher Hall, to an island. During this second voyage only one man was lost.

On Frobiser's return it was found that the assayers and goldsmiths had become more excited than ever over the worthless, though glittering, bits of mica, and adventurers were ready to equip a large fleet to seek for more. The queen named the country discovered by Frobiser "Meta Incognita," and, in the spring of 1578, that valorous commander found himself at the head of an expedition consisting of no less than fifteen vessels. As his companions we again find Fenton, Yorke, and Best, besides others not unknown to naval fame, Carew, Courtenay, Newton, Kendal, Kinnersley. Edward Sellman was the historian of the third voyage.

Much experience in ice navigation was acquired during this third voyage. Frobiser himself landed on the coast of Greenland, which he still called Friesland, and obtained some dogs from the natives—the first communication with Greenland Eskimos since the days of the Norsemen. He called some high land near Cape Farewell "Charing Cross." Jackman, who was chief pilot of the fleet, succeeded in guiding the ships through all the perils of floes and icebergs in the strait, though Captain Fenton was beset for twenty days and in great danger.

The "*Meta Incognita*" was further explored in several directions; and a small house was built on an island named after the Countess of Warwick. The American explorer Hall discovered its remains in July, 1861. The ships returned home, and by that time it had been ascertained that the glittering stones were rubbish. The most distinguished of the ice navigators, Frobiser and Fenton, did good service ten years afterwards at the repulse of the Spanish Armada.

Charles Jackman, who had served as a pilot in two of Frobiser's voyages, continued his Arctic work. It was resolved once more to attempt the north-east passage, and two little vessels set out in the spring of 1580, named the *George* and the *William*, under the command of Arthur Pet and Charles Jackman. Mr. Hugh Smith wrote the account of their gallant but ill-fated enterprise. Doubling the North Cape on the 22nd of June, they parted company off Kegor to rendezvous at Waigatsch. They attempted to enter the Kara Sea, but were stopped by the ice, and in returning westward they again parted company. The *George* returned to the Thames in November. The *William* wintered on the coast of Norway and, sailing for England in February, 1581, was never again heard of.

This was nearly the last attempt by the north-east, but an interest was maintained in the north-west passage by such eloquent appeals as the *Discourse* of Sir Humphrey Gilbert, and the *Hydrographical Description* of John Davis.

Uniting the qualities of a daring seaman and a skilful pilot to those of a scientific scholar, Davis was, in some respects, one of the most notable of Queen Elizabeth's marine worthies. He was a native of Dartmouth, and the neighbour and friend of the Gilberts and of Ralegh, so that an ardent zeal for northern discovery was early implanted in his breast. Through the munificence of Mr. William Sanderson, a wealthy London merchant of the Fishmongers' Company, Davis was enabled to equip two vessels for a northern expedition of discovery—the *Sunshine* of 50, and the *Moonshine* of 35 tons. Sailing from Dartmouth in June, 1585, Davis touched on the coast of Greenland and acquired experience in ice navigation. Returning in September, he started on a second voyage in May, 1586, returning in August. Undaunted by failure he induced his employers to fit out a third expedition, this time consisting of three vessels—the *Elizabeth, Sunshine*, and a small pinnace of 20 tons called the *Ellen*.

The third was the most important of the three Arctic voyages of John Davis. Being very anxious to make it remunerative to his generous and enterprising employers, he sent the two larger vessels to fish, while he prosecuted his discoveries along the coast of Greenland on board the little twenty-ton pinnace. He sailed northwards, in an open sea, until he reached 72° 12" N., where he named a lofty, and now well-known, headland, "Sanderson, his hope of a north-west passage." He reached this point on the 30th June, 1587, hoping to proceed on a prosperous voyage. But soon afterwards he was beset in the ice for several days, which diverted him from his course, and he sailed across the strait that bears his name, returning safely to Dartmouth in September, 1587.

Davis did a great work in the course of these three voyages. He discovered Davis' Strait; he lighted the way to others who were destined to penetrate farther north and further west; he set a bright example of scientific skill, consummate seamanship and dauntless gallantry which was followed by numerous successors; and he firmly believed in the possibility of making the voyage; under more favourable circumstances, as he stated in an interesting letter, which has been preserved, to his old friend Francis Drake.

Ten years before Davis commenced his Arctic voyages, Francis Drake had returned from his Irish service resolved to put his plans into execution. For his dreams of navigating English ships in the South Sea had become solid and carefully thought out plans. His age in 1577 was thirty-seven. He had been at sea nearly all his life. He had received the training of an explorer, and was a thorough seaman and a scientific pilot. He was a wise and prudent commander. He carefully collected all available information, and weighed every argument before deciding upon a line of action.

He carried his designs into execution with dauntless courage, but he always remained cool, and his presence of mind never deserted him. He respected the personal property of an enemy. His men felt absolute confidence in his judgment and sense of justice. They knew that he sympathised with them and understood their feelings. They loved him, and would follow him anywhere. Technically the Spaniards were entitled to apply the term "*Corsario*" to the renowned "*Francisco Drague*," whom they feared and hated: at least until 1585. But to call him a pirate in the ordinary acceptation of the term conveys an entirely false impression.

The proposal of Francis Drake to navigate the South Sea, in spite of the Spaniards, received the support of several great men at court, especially of Sir Christopher Hatton, who was the renowned sailor's most active friend. Funds were therefore raised for the equipment of five vessels. Drake himself sailed in the *Pelican*, of 100 tons, as general. He was surrounded with some state, keeping a good table, with music playing during dinner, and having several gentlemen volunteers as his messmates. Among them was his youngest brother and heir, Thomas Drake. He had already lost two other brothers, John and Joseph, in the West Indies. The second ship of 80 tons was the *Elizabeth*, commanded by John Wynter, with William Markham, a younger son of Markham of Sedgebrook in Lincolnshire, and surnamed the "Otter Hunter," as master. The *Marygold*, commanded by John Thomas, was a vessel of 30 tons; the *Swan*, under John Chester, was a fly-boat of 50 tons; and there was a little pinnace of 15 tons called the *Christopher*. Drake's famous expedition sailed from Plymouth on the 13th of December, 1577.

The fleet shaped a course for the Cape Verde Islands, and, after leaving them, Drake steered southward into a region quite unknown to Englishmen. For fifty-five days, they were out of sight of land, and during three weeks in the equatorial calms there was great heat, the line being crossed on the 7th of February, 1578. Drake attended personally to the health of the men, making regular inspections and seeing that they were suitably clothed and fed. He also took the precaution of bleeding them before encountering the great heat of the equator. In all these respects, he showed the qualities of a great commander, and in some points, he was in advance of his age.

The fearful ravages of scurvy in those days were of course mainly due to ignorance, partly also to overcrowding; and this seems to have been suspected; for commanders sometimes thought that they would escape sickness by having their vessels under-manned. Still, much saving of life might doubtless have been effected by close personal attention on the part of the commander to the comforts of the men; and in this respect Drake was distinguished above all the seamen of his time.

At length, the terraced shores of Patagonia came in sight, and the little fleet anchored in Port St. Julian. Fifty-seven years before, Magellan had suppressed a mutiny at this very place with violence, treachery, and bloodshed. Knowing that the captain of one of his ships was disaffected, he sent an officer to him with a letter and with orders to stab him while he was reading it. This was done; and he ordered another captain to be strangled. The two bodies were quartered, while a third captain and a priest were turned adrift on the shore to die of starvation.

Francis Drake, unfortunately, had to deal with a similar matter, but he did so in a different spirit. One of the gentlemen volunteers, named Thomas Doughty, was accused of insubordination and mutiny. He was an accomplished gentleman and a scholar, but he was also a "sea lawyer," striving to stir up discontent; and the success of his machinations would, at the very least, have led to the failure of the enterprise. He received a fair trial, and was found guilty of mutiny by a jury. He was executed with all proper formality, after receiving the sacrament with Drake from Mr. Fletcher, the chaplain. Drake's own feeling towards Doughty was friendly, but, in the isolated and somewhat hazardous position of the fleet, he came to the conclusion, undoubtedly with reluctance, that the execution of a just sentence was necessary for the safety of the people entrusted to his charge, and for the success of the enterprise.

He afterwards spoke kindly, and even in praise, of the deceased. Doughty's young brother, who was in the general's own ship, continued to mess at Drake's table and to be treated in all respects as the other gentlemen volunteers. It was a melancholy business, but the emergency was met by Drake with coolness, firmness, and moderation. It was unfortunate, also, that a skirmish with the natives resulted in the death of Robert Wynter, a brother of the captain of the *Elizabeth*, and of the master gunner.

The fleet left Port St. Julian and, steering south along the Patagonian coast, came in sight of the land at the northern side of Magellan's Strait, which that commander had named the Cape of the Eleven Thousand Virgins, having come in sight of it on the 21st of October, 1520, St. Ursula's day. On entering the strait, being the third navigator to do so since Magellan, on the 20th of August, 1578, Drake changed the name of his ship from the *Pelican* to the *Golden Hind*, in honour of his patron Sir Christopher Hatton, whose crest was a hind *statant Or*.

Drake took his fleet through the strait in sixteen days, Magellan having taken thirty-one days in the same navigation. The English sailors obtained plenty of fresh provisions. In one day three thousand penguins were killed on an island which Drake named after the queen. There was also some friendly intercourse with the natives. Emerging into the South Sea on the 6th of September, the fleet encountered a terrific storm. The little *Marygold* was never heard of again. The *Golden Hind* was driven far to the south, and when the gale moderated,

Drake landed on an island at the extreme south of Tierra del Fuego. Although the Dutch were the first to sail round Cape Horn in 1615, Francis Drake undoubtedly discovered that famous island. He named it, and the adjacent islets, the Elizabethides.

The *Elizabeth* ran back into the strait and, after some hesitation, Captain Wynter resolved to return home, despairing of being able to join his consorts again. This decision was made we are told "full sore again the mariners' minds." Wynter remained three weeks in the strait to recruit the strength of his men, and during his sojourn he collected some aromatic bark from an evergreen tree since named by Foster *Drimys Winteri*. He used it on the voyage home as a remedy for scurvy, and the remedy, still known as a useful tonic, has ever since been called "Winter's bark." The *Elizabeth* arrived safely at Ilfracombe.

The small pinnace *Christopher*, with a crew of only eight men, was also driven out of sight of the other ships by the force of the storm. The crew got back into the strait, killed and salted many penguins, and eventually brought the little *Christopher* into the River Plate. Here she was dashed to pieces on some rocks. Six of the crew were killed by the natives. The two survivors, named Peter Curden and William Pitcher, lived on crabs and wild berries for two months, at the end of which time Pitcher died, and his comrade buried him in the sand. After nine months, Peter Curden almost miraculously found his way back to his native land, and related his marvellous adventures.

The *Golden Hind* was now left alone to complete the wonderful voyage of circumnavigation. Drake proceeded along the west coast of America, with the intention of waging a war of retribution on the Spanish settlements and shipping. This resolution would have been still more firmly fixed in his mind if he had known of the cruel fate of his gallant lieutenant John Oxenham and his men. But the news had not yet arrived when Drake sailed from Plymouth.

Having obtained supplies at the island of Mocha, off the coast of Chile, and at Valparaiso, the *Golden Hind* appeared off Callao, the seaport of Lima, the capital of Peru, and residence of the viceroy. Drake there found seventeen loaded Spanish vessels, and, having obtained tidings of the recent departure for Panama of a richly freighted ship called the *Cacafuego*, he proceeded in chase.

His unexpected appearance at Callao caused the utmost consternation. The viceroy, Don Franciso de Toledo, a younger son of the Count of Oropesa, was astonished. No one had ever passed through the strait since the days of Magellan and Loaysa, and that English ships should have the audacity to make such a voyage had never been conceived possible. (Garcia de Loaysa and Sebastian del Cano passed through the strait in 1526. Simon de Alcazava entered it in 1535, but he was murdered by his men, and his ships never got through.) All the fancied security of the west coast of America was gone, and a new and quite unexpected state of affairs had to be faced.

The viceroy Toledo was a cruel and heartless politician. He was red-handed with the blood of young Tupac Amaru, the last of the Incas, and with the blood of John Oxenham and his gallant comrades. At the same time, he was a statesman of considerable ability. His first step was to fit out two armed vessels, and to send them to Panama in pursuit of the *Golden Hind*. But it was too late. He then resolved to have Magellan's Strait properly surveyed, with a view to its fortification, and to preventing the passage of any more English ships into the South Sea.

For this service, he selected the ablest officer in Peru. Don Pedro Sarmiento had served under Mendana in the discovery of the Solomon Islands. He had accompanied the viceroy in his great tour of inspection through all the provinces of his government, had constructed maps of Peru, and had written a history of the Incas. Toledo prepared elaborate, but judicious, instructions, and entrusted Sarmiento with the command of the expedition. No better man could have been found. He was a scientific seaman, devoted to his duties, and true as steel.

He made a careful survey of the channels leading from the Gulf of Trinidad, and of the Strait of Magellan; and he then proceeded to Spain and strongly recommended that the narrow channel near the eastern entrance should be fortified, and that a colony should be established to raise provisions, in connection with the garrisons. His plan was approved by King Philip II., a large fleet was fitted out, and colonists were put on board. But the business was shamefully mismanaged, owing to the command being given to an incapable and jealous officer, while Sarmiento was to be kept without power until he actually landed on the shore of the strait.

At length, however, Sarmiento was put on shore, with the survivors of the colonists and with a small remnant of the supplies intended for them. Two towns were founded; but food ran short, and Sarmiento returned to Brazil for help. His subsequent efforts were all thwarted, until at length he was taken prisoner by a ship belonging to Sir Walter Ralegh, and brought to England. No succour was sent to the colonists, who perished of starvation and misery. These events were the direct consequences of Drake's appearance in the South Sea.

While the viceroy Toledo was elaborating these defensive schemes, which were destined to terminate so tragically, Drake was pursuing his successful career. He crossed the line on the 28th of February, 1579, sighted the chase off Cape San Francisco, on the coast of the province of Quito, and soon came to close quarters. A defence was attempted by the *Cacafuego*; but one of her masts was shot away, and she was captured by boarding. The prize yielded eighty pounds' weight of gold, thirteen chests of coined silver, and a quantity of bar silver and precious stones, the whole value being £90,000.

A few days afterwards another Spanish ship laden with linen, silks, and china dishes, was overhauled. Drake made prize of the cargo, but not of the private property of the owner, Don Francisco de Zarate, who was himself on board. He did not, as is asserted in Barrow's *Life of Drake*, rob from the owner's person a golden ornament in the shape of a falcon, with a large emerald set in its breast. A most interesting letter has quite recently been found at Seville, from this very Don Francisco de Zarate to the Viceroy of Mexico, giving an account of the capture of the ship. Here we learn the truth, which was, that Drake did nothing of the kind alleged. Zarate wrote that Drake exchanged a sword with a costly hilt, and a silver chafing-dish, for certain toys of his, and he added: "I promise you I did not lose by the bargain."

The whole passage, in Zarate's letter, relating to Drake and his ship is extremely interesting. He wrote:

The English general is about thirty-five years of age, short of stature, with a red beard, and one of the best sailors that sail the seas, both in respect to boldness and to capacity for command. His ship is of near 400 tuns burden, with a hundred men on board, all young and of an age for battle, and all drilled as well as the oldest veterans of our army of Italy. Each one is bound to keep his arquebus clean. Drake treats them all with affection, and they him with respect. He also has with him nine or ten gentlemen, the younger sons of great people in England. Some of them are in his counsels, but he has no favourite. These sit at his table, and he is served in silver plate with a coat of arms engraved on the dishes; and music is played at his dinner and supper. The ship carries about thirty pieces of artillery, and plenty of ammunition and warlike stores.

This is the testimony of a stranger and an enemy, and is particularly valuable because it gives us a glimpse of the internal economy of the *Golden Hind*. We get some idea of the general's personal appearance, of the sort of state that was observed at his meals, of the discipline he maintained, of his relations with his men, and of the ship's armament. The *Golden Hind* was evidently kept like a man-of-war, with all the order and discipline of a queen's ship, and as efficient as she could be made by an able commander, working with a zealous and willing crew.

After the capture of the two valuable prizes, Drake shaped a course for the west coast of Mexico, and anchored in the port of Guatulco, where he took in water and fresh provisions. He then steered northwards, intending to try whether it were possible to find a passage home along the northern shores of America. He had punished the Spaniards for their treachery at Vera Cruz, and for their cruelty to the shipwrecked English sailors who fell into their hands. He had enriched himself and his friends. His voyage now became one of geographical discovery northwards, beyond the farthest limit known to the Spaniards.

In 1542, Juan Rodriguez Cabrillo had been as far as Cape Mendocino, in 40° N. on the Californian coast. Drake, sailing onward, succeeded in reaching the 48th parallel, having thus discovered 480 miles of a new region, to which he gave the name of New Albion. Want of provisions obliged him to give up the project of exploring farther in that direction, and to shape a course for the Ladrone Islands. He therefore resolved to circumnavigate the globe. During a voyage of sixty-eight days, without seeing land, Drake crossed the Pacific. At length, he reached one of the Pelew Islands, and on the 4th of November, 1579, he arrived at Ternate. He refitted at an island near Celebes, and in the course of some intricate navigation the ship grounded on a shoal, but was got off after an anxious day. On January 9th, 1580, the *Golden Hind* passed the Cape, was at Sierra Leone on the 22nd of July, and arrived in Plymouth Sound on the 26th of September.

She was taken round to Deptford, and, on the 4th of April, 1581, the queen dined on board, conferring the honour of knighthood on the great circumnavigator. The *Golden Hind* was placed in dock, with orders that she should be preserved as long as she would hold together, and the cabin was converted into a banqueting-room. In 1587, Sir Francis Drake purchased Buckland Abbey, near his old home in Devonshire. This was inherited by his younger brother Thomas; whose descendants continue to possess it.

Drake was the first commander of an expedition who circumnavigated the globe. Magellan was slain in a brawl with the natives of the Philippine Islands, and one of his ships was brought home by a junior pilot. The English explorer, on the other hand, completed the voyage himself, maintaining discipline and order, giving constant attention to the health and comfort of his men, and avoiding disputes with the natives as far as possible. But he did much more; he discovered Cape Horn, and he discovered 480 miles of new coast to the northward of California. His voyage was the greatest maritime achievement of that century.

The rest of the life of Sir Francis Drake was devoted to the naval service of his country. Like nearly all the other great naval commanders of that age, he owed his training to voyages of exploration and discovery. The habits thus acquired—of coolness and presence of mind, of forming a decision at the moment, of bringing the resources of a mind stored with knowledge and experience to bear quickly and effectively, and his magnetic influence over men—were all now devoted to the service of his queen and country in their great need. First among explorers and discoverers, Sir Francis Drake was, for that very reason, one of the greatest naval commanders of his age. For it cannot be too often repeated that voyages of discovery form the best nursery for a navy.

The next expedition which shaped a course in the direction of Magellan's Strait was not a success, as it never got beyond the coast of Brazil. It was equipped under the auspices of the Earl of Leicester, and the queen contributed two of her ships. But the instructions were ambiguous. The North-West Passage was to be discovered if it was to be found south of 40° N., but the ships were not to be taken north of that parallel; they were not to pass through Magellan's Strait; yet they were to visit the Moluccas. The command was given to Captain Edward Fenton, the companion of Frobiser in his Arctic voyages. He was on board the galleon *Leicester*, of 400 tons, with young William Hawkyns, a nephew of Sir John, and Mr. Maddox, the chaplain and historian of the voyage.

The other vessels were the *Bonaventure*, of 300 tons, commanded by Luke Ward, and the *Francis*, of 40 tons, under Captain John Drake, with William Markham, who had been in the *Elizabeth* with Captain Wynter, as master. There was also a pinnace. The expedition sailed in May, 1582, and went to the coast of Guinea, anchoring at Sierra Leone on the 10th of August. It would appear, from the journal of young

Hawkyns, that Fenton wanted from a very early period to give up the voyage, and that he was only induced to proceed owing to the protests of his officers. On the 1st of November, the ships crossed the line; and Fenton seems to have gone as far as 33° S. But he then turned back, and anchored in the Bay of St. Vincent, on the coast of Brazil.

At this time Don Pedro Sarmiento, with indomitable patience and perseverance, was striving to induce the incompetent commander of the Spanish fleet to proceed to Magellan's Strait, and land his colonists. Once this incapable officer, whose name was Valdez, sailed to the entrance of the strait; but, on the excuse of bad weather, he returned with the ships to ports on the coast of Brazil. Fenton was in the Bay of St. Vincent when, on the 23rd of December, 1582, three of these Spanish ships arrived and opened fire at about ten o'clock at night. The action continued until noon next day.

The English succeeded in sinking one of the Spanish ships, and then put to sea, with a loss of six killed and twenty wounded. After being nearly a month off the coast, Fenton anchored in the mouth of the River Espiritu Santo, and obtained a small cargo of sugar, with which he sailed home, arriving at Kinsale on the 14th of June, 1583. This was a mismanaged business, although Fenton afterwards did good service in the defeat of the Spanish Armada. He died at Deptford in 1603.

The Francis parted company in a gale before Fenton put into the Bay of St. Vincent; and reached the River Plate. Here she was wrecked, but officers and crew succeeded in reaching the shore. They were kept among the Indians for fifteen months, when the officers appear to have been given up to the Spaniards. Drake and Markham were sent to Lima, but their fate is unknown.

War was declared between Queen Elizabeth and Philip II. in 1585, and from that time there could be no further talk about piracy. A gentleman named Thomas Cavendish, of Trimley in Suffolk, had been for some time desirous of emulating the deeds of Sir Francis Drake, and in 1586 he equipped an expedition consisting of three vessels, the *Desire* of 120 tons, the *Content* of 60 tons, and the *Hugh Gallant* of 40 tons. Mr. Francis Pretty, another Suffolk man, accompanied Cavendish and was the historian of the voyage.

The fleet touched at Sierra Leone, at San Sebastian in Brazil, and at Port Desire on the coast of Patagonia. Cavendish then entered Magellan's Strait, and, after passing the two narrows, he anchored the ships and proceeded to explore in his boat along the shore. Presently he saw two men waving to him from a rock. He pulled in and took one

Animum fortuna
fequatur

THOMAS CAVENDISH.

of them into his boat. The man turned out to be one of the survivors
of Sarmiento's colony, and he told a harrowing tale. Nearly all had
died of starvation. For months they had lived on shell-fish picked off
the rocks. Fifteen were still alive about a mile distant, including two
women. The man's name was Tomas Hernandez.

Cavendish promised to take them all on board, but a fair wind
springing up he made sail and left them to their fate. Hernandez was
the only one who escaped to tell the tale. Cavendish visited the deserted town called Felipe which the colonists had built. They had
abandoned it when their provisions came to an end, and had hoped
to maintain life by scattering themselves along the shore and living
on shell-fish until the long-deferred succour arrived; and so, they
perished slowly, the weakest first. The English commander called the
place Port Famine.

Hernandez was frequently consulted by Cavendish, especially on
the occasion of an encounter with the natives near Cape Froward, the
most southern point of America—so named on this occasion. After
entering the South Sea, Cavendish sailed northwards along the west
coast of South America, and anchored at Quintero, a little bay near
Valparaiso, for wood and water. Hernandez landed with the; water-

ing party, as a guide, several horsemen having been seen on the hills. Through his treachery the party was surprised, and a dozen English sailors were taken prisoners and hanged at Santiago, Hernandez escaping behind one of the horsemen.

Sir Richard Hawkyns tells us that retribution overtook the treachery of Hernandez. In the fight with the *Dainty*, he served on board one of the Spanish ships and was severely wounded. Three years afterwards Sir Richard saw him begging on crutches, and in such a miserable state that he had been better dead than alive. He lived afterwards at Lima, and. in the days of the Viceroy Prince of Esquilache (1620), he made a deposition giving a full account of the sufferings of the colonists in the Strait of Magellan, of his rescue by Cavendish, and of his treachery at Quintero.

Touching at Arica, Cavendish, with his little squadron of three vessels, made his way to the island of Puna in the Gulf of Guayaquil. Here he sank a Spanish ship of 250 tons, and landed a party which was repulsed by the Spaniards with a loss of twenty men. Cavendish then went on shore at the head of a stronger force, routed the victors, and burnt their town. On leaving Puna the *Hugh Gallant* was sunk, as it had been found that she impeded the progress of the other two ships. A course was next shaped across the line to the west coast of Mexico, and on the 27th of July Cavendish arrived in the Bay of Guatulco and burnt the town. He then proceeded to a port, which appears to have been San Bias, in order to refit and take in water and provisions. The ships were there several months. Hitherto Cavendish had done some injury to the Spaniards by burning towns and sinking ships, but he had not secured any rich prizes.

Sailing from San Bias the *Desire* and *Content* cruised off Cape San Lucas, the southern point of California, a lofty and barren headland, with outlying rocks which reminded the English explorers of the Needles off the Isle of Wight. On the 4th of November, a tall ship hove in sight, and was captured after a brief resistance. Cavendish had at last secured a rich prize. The *Santa Ana*, a ship of 700 tons, had on board 122,000 *pesos de oro*. The Spanish crew was landed at Aguada Segura, a little port, with supplies of fresh water, almost under the shadow of Cape San Lucas.

The two English ships then steered for the Eastern Archipelago, but a few days afterwards the *Content* parted company and was never heard of more. The *Desire* touched at the Ladrones and Philippines, and passed along the south coast of Java on her way round the Cape of Good Hope. She reached home in the autumn to 1588.

Thus, was the world circumnavigated for a second time by English sailors. Cavendish, though fortunate on this occasion, was more remarkable for energy and violence of methods than for seamanlike skill, fitness for command, and humanity. The desertion of starving men and women, the burning of towns, and hanging of a Spanish pilot without sufficient cause, make us feel that we have not here a true disciple of Drake and Ralegh.

The enthusiasm for these voyages continued to prevail, and the year after the return of Cavendish, in 1589, a country gentleman of Devonshire, named Chudleigh, fitted out a vessel, called the *Wild Man*, for the South Sea. She was joined by the *Delight* of Bristol, under the command of Captain Merick. We have no details of Chudleigh's voyage. The young leader appears to have visited Trinidad. He died in the Strait of Magellan, and his ship returned. But the *Delight* had on board Mr. Magroth, who wrote the story of her passage out and home. She reached the Strait of Magellan, where sickness, want of resources, and other misfortunes led to a resolution to return without succeeding in the objects of the voyage. The sole survivor of the miserable colonists who had been abandoned to their fate by Cavendish was found at Port Famine and taken on board the *Delight*, but he died on the passage to Europe. The ship was wrecked on the coast of France, and only a few survivors found their way home again, including Mr. Magroth, the historian of the voyage.

Cavendish also fitted out a second expedition, which he mismanaged and which was a total failure. He himself reached the Strait of Magellan, shaped a course homeward, and died on the passage. Another ship deserted and returned.

The interest of this expedition lies in the fact that John Davis, the great Arctic navigator, commanded one of the ships, with the idea of attempting to make the voyage intended by Drake, from the coast of New Albion, round North America, to the Atlantic. Davis, on board the *Desire*, sailed from England in August, 1591. The ship was ill-found, both as regards stores and provisions, and when Davis reached Port Desire, on the coast of Patagonia, he strove to make good some of the defects. His crew fished for smelts with crooked pins, and caught many seals, which enabled him to salt down twenty hogsheads of seal flesh. He again put to sea with the intention of passing through Magellan's Strait, and on the 14th of August. 1592, he discovered the group now called the Falkland Islands.

He then passed through the Strait, but on entering the South Sea he was driven back by gale after gale of wind. In one furious squall, the cable of the *Desire* parted and an anchor was lost. Davis now only had one anchor with one of the flukes gone, and a cable spliced in two places. Still the dauntless seaman resolved to make another attempt. But again, he was met, on passing Cape Pilar, by a furious storm, with hail and snow, and with such a sea running that the people expected every moment to be their last.

At length, worn out with fatigue and the desperate struggle against the elements, even Davis began to despond. The sails were nearly worn out. The foot-rope of the foresail had parted, so that nothing held it but the cringles or eyelet-holes in the clews. The seas constantly broke over the poop and dashed with great force against the lower sails.

After nine days of an unequal contest the gallant commander of a resolute crew reluctantly bore up for the Strait. The provisions were spent and the *Desire* was quite unfit to continue the voyage. It would be necessary to lay in provisions for the return voyage while anchored in the Strait, of which Davis had already made a careful survey. He made salt by evaporation from the sea water, and stored in the hold fourteen thousand salted penguins. The allowance on the passage home was five ounces of meal per week for each man, three spoonfuls of oil a day, five penguins between four men, and six quarts of water for four men. In the hot weather the penguins, having been insufficiently salted, went bad. Scurvy broke out and all the crew died but sixteen, of whom only five were able to move.

The whole work of the ship was done by Davis himself, the master, two men and a boy. The captain and master at first went aloft to the topsails, but latterly they were too weak, and finally topsails and spritsail were blown away. Davis sailed homewards under courses, he and the master taking turns at the helm. Thus, did the great navigator, in spite of almost insuperable difficulties, bring his ship into Berehaven, on the Irish coast, on the 11th of June, 1593.

Such was the type of seamen created by a training in the Arctic regions. Davis was not found wanting when the trial came. He had learnt courage of the highest order, perseverance, readiness of resource, patience, and sympathy for his men, in the best school. No man, without these qualities, would have struggled against adverse circumstances as he did, nor would any less gifted seaman have ever brought the *Desire* home. The life of Davis was still preserved for useful service to his country as a scholar and as a pilot.

The last Elizabethan voyage to the South Sea, with its memorable fight against hopeless odds, belongs rather to the militant than to the exploring department of our naval service. Yet its leader inherited the traditions of an explorer, and was himself a born lover of everything that appertained to the work of maritime discovery.

Richard Hawkyns was the only son of Sir John Hawkyns, and was brought up to a sea life from a boy. Born about 1562, and losing his mother at an early age, he became his father's constant companion, and his boyhood was passed in dockyards and on board ships. At the age of twenty he made his first long voyage to the West Indies, with his Uncle William, and displayed both boldness and sagacity. One of the ships had been reported to be unseaworthy, and it had been arranged that the stores should be taken out of her and that she should be sunk. But young Richard volunteered, with as many men as would stand by him, to take her home. From his return in 1583 to 1588 he was constantly employed, and he commanded the *Swallow* in the fleet which defeated the Spanish Armada.

At the end of the same year, with the consent and help of his father, he prepared for a voyage to India by way of the Strait of Magellan and the South Sea, with the intention of discovering and exploring unknown lands, and reporting upon their inhabitants, governments, and the commodities they yielded. With this object, he caused a ship to be built in the Thames, "pleasing to the eye, profitable for stowage, good for sayle, and well-conditioned." His stepmother asked to be allowed to christen the ship, and named her the *Repentance* , saying it was the safest ship we could sail in to purchase the haven of heaven.

But when Queen Elizabeth passed on her way to Greenwich Palace she ordered her bargemen to row round her, and said that she misliked nothing but the name. Her majesty christened her anew, and ordered that henceforth she should be called the *Dainty*. She was a ship of about 350 Ions. Other duties delayed the voyage, and meanwhile the *Dainty* was employed in the queen's service; but in April, 1593, Richard Hawkins sailed on his daring enterprise. He was then in his thirtieth year, with several years' experience as a sea-captain, observant and eager to adopt every improvement, and paying close attention to each detail of his work. The most important event in his voyage across the Atlantic was the sighting of land on the 2nd of February, 1594, in 50° S., and about fifty leagues from the Strait of Magellan. He called it "Hawkyns's Maiden Land," not being aware that it had already been discovered by John Davis in 1592.

On the 10th of February, Richard Hawkyns entered the Strait of Magellan. He described the appearance of the land, the different birds met with, and those available for fresh food, and prepared useful sailing directions throughout. His was the mind of an observant explorer. He also enriched his narrative with valuable suggestions respecting the sheathing of ships' bottoms and the repairing of anchors. He took the opportunity offered by his detention in the Strait to caulk the ship throughout, and employed the men in collecting Winter's bark, and in various sports, to keep them cheerful and healthy.

Having made a prosperous voyage through the Strait into the South Sea, the *Dainty* anchored off the island of Mocha, on the coast of Chile, which was occupied by independent Indians, of whom he wrote an interesting account. They supplied him plentifully with fresh provisions, and he then steered northwards with the intention of passing Callao out of sight of land, so that his presence on the coast might not be known to the Spaniards. But his plan was overruled by the officers and crew, who urged him to attack some of the ships in the enemy's ports. He very reluctantly consented, and bore up for Valparaiso, where he ransacked four ships and the warehouses on shore, but found nothing worth taking away, except fresh provisions. When leaving the port, however, a ship was taken with some gold on board, and with important passengers who paid ransoms.

Hawkyns touched at Coquimbo and Arica, and off Quilca he caused the empty prize to be burnt. But meanwhile news of the arrival of an English ship on the coast had been sent to Lima. The Marquis of Cañete, a most distinguished soldier both in the wars in Europe, and in those against the Araucanian Indians when he was Captain-General of Chile, was the Viceroy of Peru. With all possible diligence, he sent six ships in search of the *Dainty* under the command of his brother-in-law, Don Beltran de Castro y de la Cueva. She was sighted off Cañete, and the Spanish ships, being much more windwardly, rapidly came up with their chase. Then a fresh breeze began to blow, the Spanish admiral sprung his mainmast, the vice-admiral split his mainsail, and for that time the *Dainty* escaped. The Spanish ships returned to Callao, while Hawkyns steered for the Bay of Atacames, in the province of Quito, intending to take in wood and water, and then leave the coast.

The *Dainty* anchored in Atacames Bay on the 10th of June, 1594. In five days, all the empty water-casks were filled, wood was cut and taken on board, and the pinnace was put to rights. On the 15th, sail was made to the Bay of San Mateo, and a few days afterwards Hawkyns weighed with the intention of finally leaving the coast of South America. But it was not to be. The Spanish squadron hove in sight, and the admiral bore down on the little *Dainty*. Richard Hawkyns and his splendid crew, hopelessly outnumbered, prepared to make a desperate fight for the honour of their country. First with noise of trumpets and then with artillery did the *Dainties* defy their enemies, but the Spaniards answered two to one; for they had twice the number of guns, and ten times the complement of men.

Hawkyns had but 75 men and boys, while the Spaniards numbered 1300. All day the action continued, and in the evening the Spanish vice-admiral came alongside the *Dainty* with the intention of boarding. But he met with such a reception from the English sailors that his decks were completely cleared. He forged ahead with a loss of thirty men. The English also suffered severely, Hawkyns himself having received six wounds. The Spanish ships then remained at a more respectful distance, keeping up, however, a continual fire, and at intervals calling upon the *Dainty* to surrender "*a buena guerra*." Hawkyns had been carried below, and at last his captain, named Ellis, came down to his wounded chief and suggested the impossibility of further resistance.

But Richard Hawkyns declared that he had not come into the South Sea to hang out flags of truce. Like Richard Greynvile he cried, "Fight on! fight on!" His captain and men took fresh heart, fought on all that night, and sustained the unequal struggle for the next day and night, and the third day after, being battered constantly with great and small shot by six ships. On the second day, a master's mate named William Blanch, by a capital shot, carried away the mainmast of the Spanish vice-admiral close to the deck. But the *Dainty* could not free herself from the other ships, and, when nearly all were dead or wounded, Captain Ellis surrendered "*a buena guerra*" on a solemn promise from Don Beltran de Castro that all should have their lives and liberties with a passage to their own country.

Richard Hawkyns was received by the noble Spaniard with great courtesy, and accommodated in his own cabin. The *Dainty* was taken to Panama and re-christened the *Visitation*. Hawkyns and his fellow-prisoners were brought to Lima, and the Marquis of Cañete treated them with kindness and consideration. But before long, Hawkyns was claimed by the Inquisition. The honour of the viceroy's brother-in-law was, however, at stake. The Marquis of Cañete defied the Inquisitors, and sent his prisoners to Spain after a detention of three years at Lima. On reaching Spain, Hawkyns was thrown into prison at Seville, in defiance of the terms of surrender. Don Beltran de Castro was indignant at this breach of faith, which compromised his honour, but many years passed away.

At length a more powerful man, the Count of Miranda, took up the case. He declared that all future agreement would be impossible if faith in Spanish honour were destroyed. After eight long years of imprisonment Richard Hawkyns was released. He was knighted by James I. and made Vice-Admiral of Devon; and he died in 1622, when about to sail as vice-admiral of a fleet for the punishment of Algerine pirates.

The *Observations of Sir Richard Hawkyns* were published in 1622, and reprinted by the Hakluyt Society in 1847 and 1878. They are a perfect storehouse of valuable naval information of all kinds, every incident of the voyage leading the writer into reminiscences of former experiences, or into dissertations on subjects having reference to navigation, seamanship, gunnery, or naval discipline. Richard Hawkyns was the ideal of an ardent explorer and of a brave and thoroughly efficient naval officer. If fortune had favoured, he would have made a great name. He has only left us a most charming book; and Englishmen read it with feelings of pride that the author was their countryman, and with warm regret and sympathy for his misfortunes.

The three Elizabethan voyages into the South Sea did not lead directly to commercial intercourse, because the Spanish monopoly was uncompromising, and the undertaking was too difficult and perilous. But in other directions the first voyages of discovery were the forerunners of an active and prosperous trade to the Mediterranean, to the coast of Guinea, to Russia, and to Newfoundland, while the fearless English seamen continued to frequent the West Indies. In 1581 a charter was granted to the Turkey Company, and consuls were appointed in the Levant; and in 1588 the first Guinea Company received its charter, with the privilege of exclusive trade to the Senegal and the Gambia.

But the oldest and most continuous traffic was that connected with the fishery on the banks of Newfoundland. According to Mr. Anthony Parkhurst, who reported on "the true state and commodities of Newfoundland" in 1578, there were from thirty to fifty sail frequenting the banks from the west of England, one hundred from Spain for cod, and thirty Basque vessels for whales, fifty Portuguese, and one hundred and fifty Breton vessels of about 40 tons.

On the 11th of June, 1578, Sir Humphrey Gilbert received letters patent to found a colony in Newfoundland, and for the discovery of Norumbega. His training had been rather in the war against Spaniards in the Low Countries than at sea; but he was a man of far-seeing views, a patriotic and high-minded gentleman. He made one disastrous voyage with his half-brother, Walter Ralegh, in 1579, and in 1583 he equipped a more important expedition.

Five vessels left Cawsand Bay on the 11th of June; but the largest, named the *Ralegh*, put back owing to the outbreak of a mortal sickness. The others were the *Delight*, of 120 tons, the *Swallow* and *Golden Hind*, each of 40 tons, and the little *Squirrel*, of 10 tons. On the 30th of July, they had crossed the Atlantic and sighted land, visiting the island where the Bretons were accustomed to salt down quantities of great auks in casks. At St. John's, Newfoundland, Sir Humphrey Gilbert found thirty-six sail of vessels of all nations, and, in accordance with his orders, he took possession in the name of the queen.

On the 4th of August he landed, and was entertained by the English merchants. Leaving St. John's on the 20th of August, the ships were steered in the direction of the Isle of Sables, and on the 20th the *Delight* ran on shore and became a total wreck. Among those who perished were Stephanus Parmenius of Buda, who was to have been the historian of the expedition, the captain, and many others. The master, Richard Clarke, got away in a small boat, which was dangerously overcrowded. One of the party, named Hedley, proposed that they should draw lots for four to be thrown overboard.

But Clarke said, "No! We will live or die together!" After having been four days without food they succeeded in landing, and relieved their hunger by eating berries. Finally, they were taken on board a vessel belonging to St. Jean de Luz, and were landed at Pasajes in Spain, whence they found their way home.

These disasters induced Sir Humphrey Gilbert to resolve upon returning to England, with the intention of continuing the enterprise in the ensuing spring. He was urged to go on board the *Hind*; but as the *Squirrel*, owing to her small size, would be exposed to the greatest danger in crossing the Atlantic, he chose to go in her, and his resolution could not be shaken. On the evening of the 9th of September, he was seen sitting with a book in his hand, and he cried out to those on board the *Hind*, when within hailing distance, "We are as near to heaven by sea as by land." On the same night, being ahead of the *Hind*, the *Squirrel's* lights were noticed to have disappeared. The vessel had gone down with all hands. The *Hind* arrived at Falmouth on the 22nd of September.

Hakluyt has preserved the journals of four Bristol ships which made successful sealing voyages to Newfoundland and Cape Breton in 1593 and 1594.

The mantle of Sir Humphrey Gilbert fell upon his half-brother, Walter Ralegh. This illustrious Englishman was the embodiment of all that was best in the chivalry, the culture, and the enterprise of the Elizabethan age. Born at Hayes, near Sidmouth, in 1552, Ralegh was educated at Oxford, and passed six years of his life in Huguenot camps in France, probably serving in the Battles of Jarnac and Moncontour. He then saw service in Ireland; and in 1582, at the age of thirty, he was received into high favour by the queen. His greatness then began, and in 1584 he leased Durham House in the Strand. He was knighted in 1585, and became Captain of the Queen's Guard and Lord Warden of the Stannaries in the following year.

On the 25th of March, 1584, Sir Walter Ralegh received letters patent for the discovery and settlement of the region then vaguely known as Norumbega, the coasts of which had been discovered by the English in 1498, as shown by the map of Juan de la Cosa. Ralegh first sent two vessels, under Philip Amadas and Arthur Barlowe, to proceed to their destination by way of the West Indies, and thus avoid the storms of the North Atlantic. They sailed on the 27th of April, 1584, touched at the Canaries and at one of the West India islands, and, on the 18th of July, landed on a low and sandy beach, and took possession. The country received the name of Virginia, in honour of the great queen, but the spot where they landed is in North Carolina. They found a broad, wooded island, with great abundance of wild grapes. Seven leagues farther on was the village of Roanoak, consisting of a hundred houses of cedar. A banquet was given them by the king, and they returned to England with two natives.

Ralegh's second expedition was on a larger scale. It was commanded by the renowned Sir Richard Greynvile, and consisted of five vessels—the *Tiger*, of 140 tons, the *Lion*, of 100 tons, the *Elizabeth*, of 50 tons, the *Dorothy*, a small *barque*, and the fly-boat *Roebuck*. Among the volunteers were Ralph Lane, the Governor of Kerry, Cavendish, the future circumnavigator, Arundel, Raymond, Stukeley, and Vincent. Sailing on the 5th of April, 1585, Greynvile touched at Puerto Rico and at Isabela, on the north coast of St. Domingo. Passing along the mainland of Florida, he anchored at Wocoken (now called Ocracoke Inlet) on the 26th of June; but one of his ships went on shore and was lost.

In exploring the country, Greynvile crossed the south part of Pamlico Sound, and visited three towns called Pomeick, Aguascogoc, and Lecoto, where he was well received. The plan was, that a small colony should remain under the command of Ralph Lane, and that Sir Richard Greynvile should return home with the ships. He reached Plymouth on the 18th of October, having during the voyage captured a richly laden Spanish ship of 300 tons. He boarded her in a boat made of the boards of chests, and the fragile craft went to pieces as he and his men sprang up the ship's side.

The colony under Ralph Lane was to remain and explore the mainland. There were with him Captain Philip Amadas, the learned Thomas Heriot, Courtenay, Stafford, Acton, Marmaduke Constable— all historic names—and a hundred men. They made the best use of their time, and Heriot studied the resources of the country, especially the vegetable products, and wrote an important work on the subject, which was of great use to future colonists. In June, 1586, Sir Francis Drake arrived with a fleet, and offered to supply the settlers with provisions; but they decided to return home. Meanwhile, Ralegh had sent out supplies to the colony in a vessel of 100 tons. Not finding the settlers, she returned to England. Sir Richard Greynvile also came out with three well-appointed vessels, and, failing to find the settlers, he also returned. He, however, left fifteen men at Roanoak, with provisions for two years.

In 1587, Ralegh obtained a charter for the "Governor and Assistants of the city of Ralegh in Virginia." He fitted out a ship of 120 tons, a fly-boat, and a pinnace, and sent out a colony of one hundred and fifty souls, under the leadership of John White, with Simon Fernando as pilot. They reached Hatorash on the 22nd of July, but found no signs of the fourteen men left by Sir Richard Greynvile. A colony was landed, consisting of ninety-one men, seventeen women, and nine boys; and John White went back to England for supplies.

But it was not until the 20th of March, 1590, that he was able to return with three vessels. He landed at Hatorash on the 15th of August, and went to the place where the colony had been left in 1587. All was desolation. At length, he found the word "Cruatoan" carved on a post. It was the name of the place whither the settlers had gone or had been taken. No effort was made to communicate with them, and the ships returned to England. Ralegh had now spent £40,000 on the work of colonising Virginia. In 1602, he again sent a vessel to succour the lost colony, under Captain William Mace, but she returned without reaching Roanoak. The colonists intermixed with the natives, and were finally massacred by order of King Powhatan, instigated by his priests. Four men, two boys, and one young maid were spared, and from them the Hatteras Indians were descended.

Although the first colony was unfortunate, the patriotic efforts of Ralegh were, without doubt, the incentives to future colonisation. He aroused the spirit of colonial enterprise, and thus planted a sturdy tree, which bore fruit even in his own lifetime. The people of the United States must look to Sir Walter Ralegh as the original founder of their nation, and they could not have a nobler nor a purer origin. For Sir Walter's connection with Virginia is a monument of patriotic self-sacrifice; and that his great merits are not forgotten was shown when a window to his memory was placed by Americans in St. Margaret's Church, Westminster.

Sir Walter Ralegh turned his attention to the discovery of Guiana in 1594. In that year, he sent Captain Jacob Whiddon on a preliminary voyage of discovery, but Whiddon was thwarted by the Spanish Governor of Trinidad, and returned. Meanwhile, Ralegh himself made an exhaustive study of the subject. He derived his knowledge of Peru and the Incas from Gomara; he had studied Andrew Thevet and Diego de Ordas, and he knew the particulars of the voyages down the Amazon by Orellana and Aguirre. He had heard of the discovery of gold in the Orinoco basin, of El Dorado, and of the fabulous city of Manoa.

He obtained the services of such experienced seamen as Captains Whiddon, Keymis, Canfield, Gifford, and Dowglas; and he was accompanied by a number of gallant young gentlemen volunteers, some of them being his own relations. John Gilbert was his nephew, Greyn vile and Gorges were cousins. Leaving England on the 9th of February, 1595, with five ships, with the object of exploring the Orinoco, the expedition arrived at the island of Trinidad on the 22nd of March, anchoring at Parico within the Gulf of Paria.

The Spaniards had a settlement called San Jose on the island of Trinidad, and at that time the governor was an officer of some distinction. Don Antonio Berreo had married a daughter of Gonzalo Jimenes de Quesada, the famous conqueror of Nueva Granada. Berreo had made a very remarkable journey from Bogota, by descending the rivers Meta and Orinoco; and he was only waiting for the arrival of his son from Bogota to undertake the establishment of a settlement on the Orinoco River.

Ralegh's first step was the capture of the Spanish town of San Jose. This was done by break of day, and Berreo was taken prisoner. His captor treated the governor with all possible respect as an honoured guest, and received from him as much information respecting Guiana as he possessed; but Berreo vainly attempted to dissuade Ralegh from attempting to ascend the Orinoco.

The ships were to be left at Trinidad, and the ascent of the river was to be undertaken by a hundred men with provisions for a month. The little flotilla consisted of an old galley, a barge, two wherries, and the long-boat of the *Lion's Whelp*. Ralegh himself, with most of the volunteers and fifty men, were in the galley; Captain Gifford and ten more, in one wherry; Captain Canfield, with young Gorges and eight men, in the other; and the rest, in the two ships' boats.

Reaching the Orinoco delta, Captains Whiddon and Dowglas sounded the Capari mouth, while Captain Canfield examined that of Manamo. The boats then entered the Orinoco, good supplies of cassava bread being obtained from the natives, with whom Ralegh kept on very friendly terms. He was thus able to collect a large amount of valuable information respecting the tribes and the resources of the country. The stories he was told respecting the yield of gold were chiefly from Spanish sources, and were grossly exaggerated; but Ralegh was quite correct in his opinion that Guiana was a gold-yielding country.

The expedition was on the whole successful. The explorers suffered considerably from hardships and privations in the ascent of the river, rowing against the stream, but they got as far as the mouth of the Karoni, and forty miles up that river. The Orinoco was rising rapidly, which obliged them to return. Ralegh's principal native friend was an old chief named Tapiawari, with whom he held long conversations. It was arranged that two volunteers, a man named Francis Sparrow and a boy named Hugh Godwin, should remain to learn the language, and that they should take merchandise into the interior, so as to explore and collect information. A son of Tapiawari returned with Ralegh. The boats reached the sea by the Capari mouth, and the explorers found the ships as they had left them, at Curiapan in Trinidad, and returned safely home.

In this ably conducted expedition, Sir Walter Ralegh showed himself to possess all the qualifications of an explorer. He took great pains, before starting, to inform himself, from every available source, of all that was known respecting the region he was about to explore. He equipped his expedition and selected his companions with great care, and with reference to the work that had to be done. He took every precaution in sounding the different mouths of the Orinoco, in navigating the river, and in his intercourse with the natives, that could suggest itself to a thoughtful leader. He was indefatigable in the collection of all useful information. The result was the publication of an interesting narrative which is read with pleasure and instruction down to the present day. The map was not finished when the book was published in 1596, but it is in the British Museum, and has recently been reproduced.

The Guiana voyage of Sir Walter Ralegh led to many others in the direction both of the Orinoco and of the West Indian Islands. In January, 1596, Captain Laurence Keymis left Portland in the *Darling*, of London, and again visited the Orinoco. He found that Sparrow had been captured by the Spaniards and taken to Cumana. In the same year Thomas Masham, in the pinnace *Watte*, went up the Essequibo.

The most romantic biography of all the Elizabethan worthies is that of Sir Robert Dudley, the repudiated heir of the Earl of Leicester. A gallant soldier, a scientific seaman, a gunner, an engineer, he was above all an enthusiastic explorer. He tells us that:

> Having, ever since I could conceive of anything, been delighted with the discoveries of navigation, I fostered in myself that disposition till I was of more years and better ability to undertake such a matter.

Yet he was only twenty-one when he sailed for the West Indies in command of an expedition consisting of the *Bear*, of 200 tons, the *Bear's Whelp*, and two pinnaces, called the *Frisking* and the *Earwig*. He ordered his master, Abraham Kendall, to steer for Trinidad, and, anchoring at Curiapan, he landed with an armed party, and marched through the woods. He was joined by a pinnace from Plymouth, commanded by Captain Popham, and the leaders intended to have extended their explorations to Guiana.

But the crews refused, and young Dudley was obliged to return. Leaving Trinidad in March, 1595, he touched at Puerto Iiico and the Azores, encountering very severe weather. In May he arrived at St. Ives in Cornwall, having sunk and burnt nine Spanish ships and expended all his powder. Owing to unjust treatment after the great queen's death, Sir Robert Dudley abandoned his native country and lived at Florence, where he wrote that superb work, *Del Arcano del Mare*, and where he died in 1630.

In 1595 also Amyas Preston harassed the Spaniards in the West Indies, with two ships, the *Ascension* and the *Gift*. He sacked the towns of Coro and Santiago de Leon, and obliged Cumana to pay a ransom. In 1590 Sir Anthony Shirley followed in Preston's track with nine vessels. He took Santa Marta and Jamaica, visited Puerto Cabello and Truxillo, and returned home by way of Newfoundland; and in the same year William Parker, in the *Prudence*, made good prizes in the Bay of Campeachy. These audacious voyagers were supplied with a good "*Ruttier*," or book of sailing directions for the West Indies, translated from the Spanish.

The value of an explorer's training was shown at the taking of Cadiz. Sir Walter Ralegh commanded a division of the fleet, and among those who had been engaged in exploring adventures with him, or at the same time, in the Orinoco and the West Indies, no fewer than four received the honour of knighthood from the Earl of Essex at Cadiz for their gallantry. These were Sir Robert Dudley, Sir George Gifford, Sir Francis Popham, and Sir Amyas Preston.

In the closing years of the brilliant reign of Queen Elizabeth, the first chapter in the history of British India was commenced. The establishment of factories by the Turkey Company in the Levant led the way. In 1583 Fitch, Leedes, and Newberry found their way to India overland, and their story drew attention in England to the wonders of the East. But no English ship had yet made the voyage to India, although Drake and Cavendish had rounded the Cape, coming from the East.

The first English voyage to India was undertaken by James Lancaster in 1591. Lancaster was a native of Basingstoke, who had been serving in Portugal both as a soldier and a merchant, though he is only known to fame as an adventurous and able sea-captain. The expedition consisted of three tall ships, the *Penelope* as admiral, commanded by George Raymond, the *Merchant Royal*, under Abraham Kendall, who had been master to Sir Robert Dudley in his West Indian voyage, as vice-admiral, and the *Edward Bonaventure* under James Lancaster as rear-admiral. The historians of the voyage were Edmund Barker, Lancaster's lieutenant, and a mate named Henry May.

The expedition sailed from Plymouth on the 10th of April, 1591, and, touching at the Canary Islands, the ships made the best of their way to the Cape of Good Hope. Near the line the English explorers fortunately captured a Portuguese *caravel* laden with wine, oil, and olives. During the long detention by equatorial calms the scurvy broke out, there were many deaths, and the crews were in a very weakly state when the ships reached Table Bay. There oxen and sheep were obtained from the natives, and the sailors began to recover their strength. It was resolved to send the *Merchant Royal* back to England with all the weakly men, and to proceed with two strong crews in two ships. Accordingly, Captains Raymond and Lancaster, in the *Penelope* and *Edward Bonaventure*, proceeded on the voyage. On the 14th of September, they encountered a great storm, during which the *Penelope* parted company, nor was she ever heard of again.

The *Edward Bonaventure*, after losing the master and several men through the treachery of the Comoro Islanders, arrived at Zanzibar on the 7th of November. Lancaster remained there until February, 1592, opening friendly relations with the native merchants, who were disabused of the stories told by the Portuguese to the disadvantage of the strangers. On leaving Zanzibar a course was shaped for Cape Comorin, and then for the Nicobar Islands; but the first port in which the ship was anchored was Penang, on the coast of Malacca, where Lancaster remained until August. He lost his master, one of the merchants, and twenty-six men during his stay at that place; and when he put to sea there were not more than twenty-two men fit for duty.

Having captured some Portuguese ships laden with pepper and rice, and cruised for some months on the coast of Malacca, Lancaster anchored at Point de Galle. There the crew declared they must return to England, and the homeward voyage was commenced on the 8th of December, 1593. After a long rest at St. Helena, Lancaster took the ship in the direction of the Brazilian coast, and thence to the West Indies, at last finding himself off the island of Mona, between St. Domingo and Puerto Rico, whence, after receiving provisions and water, he directed his course to Newfoundland. Baffling winds prolonged the voyage, so that the provisions were exhausted, and it was resolved to return to the West Indies.

Mona was again reached on the 20th of November, 1593, but while the captain and a party of men landed to seek for provisions, the carpenter secretly cut the cable, and the ship drifted away to sea with only five men and a boy on board. Lancaster, with his lieutenant Barker, and the men who had landed, were left on the island. During twenty-nine days, their only food was the stalks of purslane boiled in water, with a few pumpkins. At length, a French ship came to off the island, and took the unfortunate Englishmen on board. Lancaster and Barker were taken home, arriving at Dieppe on the 19th of May, 1594.

It had been arranged by Captain Lancaster that Henry May, one of the mates, should take a passage home in another French ship, to report to the owners the proceedings of the *Edward Bonaventure* and the mutinous condition of her crew. This ship was commanded by M. de la Barbotière, who made sail northwards from the port of Laguna in Santo Domingo. It appears that the pilot was quite out in his reckoning, and on the 17th of December the ship was run on a rock, at about midnight, on the western reef of Bermuda.

About twenty-six men, including Henry May, reached the shore on a raft. Luckily the carpenter's tools were saved, and they began to cut down trees, and succeeded in building a small vessel of eighteen tons. Water was stored in two great chests, well caulked, and secured one on each side of the mainmast, and the provisions consisted of thirteen live turtles. On the 11th of May, 1594, they put to sea and made for the banks of Newfoundland, where a vessel from Falmouth took them on board. Henry May's adventures, of which he wrote an interesting narrative, came to an end when he landed at Falmouth in August, 1594.

This first English voyage to the East Indies was disastrous. Lancaster's next enterprise was of a warlike character, and was elided by some merchants of London, who fitted out several vessels to attack Pernambuco. James Lancaster was appointed to the command, with his old lieutenant, Edmund Barker, and John Audley of Poplar as his captains. The expedition was ably and resolutely conducted, and was a complete success. The port of Pernambuco was surprised, taken and held for thirty days in spite of repeated assaults by the Portuguese. About thirty ships were captured, and rich cargoes of sugar, dye-wood, and cotton were brought home.

But Captain Barker fell in one of the skirmishes, and several other valuable officers lost their lives. Lancaster was engaged on this service from September, 1594, to July, 1595, when he brought his ship back to Blackwall in safety. These two expeditions showed him to be an able, prudent, and courageous officer, well qualified for the high trust that was about to be placed in him.

In 1599 the merchants and adventurers of London projected an expedition, and eventually formed a company, with the object of establishing a trade with the East Indies. A sum of £72,000 was subscribed, and the preparations were steadily pushed forward throughout the autumn. On the 10th of December Captain James Lancaster was appointed "general" of the fleet, with a commission of martial law from the queen. His flag was on board the *Dragon*, a ship, formerly named the *Scourge of Malice*, which had been bought from the Earl of Cumberland for £3700. She was of 600 tons burden, (some accounts make her to have been of 800 tons.—W. L. C.), and had a crew of two hundred and two men. The chief pilot was John Davis, the Arctic navigator, who had just returned from the East Indies as pilot of the first Dutch India fleet. The "vice-admiral" was the *Hector*, of 300 tons, and a crew of one hundred and eight men, commanded by John Middleton. The *Ascension*, of 260 tons, with a crew of eighty-two men, was under William Brand; and John Hayward commanded the *Susan*, of 240 tons, and eighty-eight men. The *Guest* was to accompany the fleet as a victualler.

On the 31st of December, 1599, Queen Elizabeth laid the foundation stone of the British Empire in India. The Charter of Incorporation of the East India Company was granted to George Clifford, Earl of Cumberland, and two hundred and fifteen knights, aldermen, and merchants; Alderman Sir Thomas Smith being chosen the first governor of the company, and James Lancaster and John Middleton being in the list of the first directors. The queen, in council, framed this great instrument with foresight and wisdom, and, it would almost seem, with some prevision of the future. Her majesty had cordially and graciously approved of the voyage before the issue of the Charter, and she sent John Mildenhall as her envoy to the great Emperor Akbar at Agra, by way of Constantinople and Persia.

All through the month of January, 1600, the expedition was being fitted out in the Thames. Each ship was provided with twelve streamers, two flags, and an ensign. Stores and provisions of all kinds were stowed in the holds, as well as merchandise; and merchants were appointed to each ship to superintend the trading operations. The queen prepared letters to the princes of India, including one to the Sultan of Acheen; and suitable presents accompanied them. Mr. Richard Hakluyt compiled much useful information respecting the commodities of the different countries, instructions "touching the preparing of the voyage," and several maps. The officers and others received "bills of adventure" on the gains of the voyage—that is to say, each was to receive a reward on a fixed scale with reference to the yield of the return cargo.

The fleet sailed from Woolwich on the 13th of February, 1600, but it was long delayed in the Downs by calms, and the ships had to put into Dartmouth to complete their stores; so that it was the 2nd of April before they finally sailed for the Canaries. The usual fatal sickness broke out while the fleet was detained by equatorial calms. Captain Lancaster, however, captured a Portuguese ship and got out of her 146 casks of wine, 176 casks of olive oil, and a quantity of meal, which proved a great addition to the supply of provisions. The victualler *Guest* was emptied and turned adrift. The expedition crossed the line on the last day of June.

The ravages of scurvy continued, so that when Table Bay was reached on the 9th of September, Captain Lancaster had first to anchor his own ship, and then to send his boats away, with working parties, to perform the same office for his consorts, whose crews were too weak to bring their ships to. The *Dragon's* working parties also hoisted out the boats for the rest of the fleet.

The reason why the men in Lancaster's ship were so much healthier than the others was that he took the precaution of providing a supply of lemon-juice. He gave three spoonfuls to each man every morning fasting, by which means he cured many of his sailors and kept the rest from scurvy. The sick were landed and put under canvas on shore. Very good arrangements were made for the traffic with natives, cattle and sheep were purchased, and the sick soon began to gain strength on a diet of fresh meat and vegetables. But the terrible disease had carried off one hundred and five men before any effective remedy could be applied.

On the 20th of October, the fleet left Table Bay and, towards the end of December, anchored in the Bay of Antongil, in Madagascar, where excellent fresh provisions were again obtained. But dysentery broke out, and there were several deaths. After encountering numerous dangers in crossing the Indian Ocean, and having touched at the Nicobar Islands, Lancaster anchored his fleet in the road of Acheen, in Sumatra, on the 5th of June, 1601. His reception by the *sultan* was cordial and satisfactory in every respect. In the first audience, the letter from Queen Elizabeth was presented; and on subsequent occasions Lancaster made progress with the negotiations for opening trade. Pepper, cloves, and cinnamon were bought for the return cargo; and in October the *sultan's* answer to the queen's letter was brought on board.

The fleet finally left Acheen on the 9th of November, the *Ascension* proceeding direct to England with the news, and the *Dragon* shaping a course along the coast of Sumatra in search of the *Susan*, which had been previously sent to Priamon for a cargo of pepper. She joined off Priamon, and the ships anchored in the road of Bantam, in Java, on the 16th of December. Here the merchants landed to sell the goods brought from England, in exchange for which further supplies of pepper were shipped.

A factory was established under Mr. William Starkey, to provide lading for the ships which were to be sent out on the Company's second venture. The King of Bantam sent a letter and presents to Queen Elizabeth, and on the 20th of February, 1602, the ships began their homeward course. Captain John Middleton of the *Hector* was taken ill and died at Bantam. His brother Henry, who was in the *Susan*, was destined to command the Company's second voyage.

On the 3rd of May a great storm was encountered between Madagascar and the Cape; and early next morning the *Dragon's* rudder was torn clean away from the stern of the ship. She drifted for some days at the mercy of the waves, once almost down to 40° S. in sleet and snow, the *Hector* always manfully keeping company. At last the mizzen-mast was taken out, and passed over the stern to serve as a temporary rudder, but it was found to shake the ship in such a way as to be dangerous, and it was got in again with all convenient speed. The carpenters then set to work to shape a rudder out of the mizzen-mast; but the irons had also been carried away, and there were only two wherewith to hang the new rudder. The men wanted to abandon the ship and go on board the *Hector* Lancaster said: "Nay, we will yet abide God's leisure, to see what mercy He will show us." The sea became smooth, the rudder was temporarily fixed, and there was no small rejoicing when the Island of St. Helena hove in sight. Here the rudder was properly hung, and plentiful supplies were obtained.

On the 11th of September, the sailors of the East India Company's first venture arrived at the Downs, and completed this memorable voyage. Great credit is due to the master, Sanderbole, of the *Hector*, for the way in which he stuck by his rudderless consort when she was drifting helplessly about in the stormy sea to the south of the Cape. Even when Captain Lancaster gave him written orders to make the best, of his way home, he disobeyed, and continued to keep near the *Dragon*, ready with all the help he could give, until they both got safe to St. Helena:

> For the master was an honest and a good man, and loved the general well, and was lothe to leave him in so great distress.

The gallant commander of the first voyage received the honour of knighthood and became Sir James Lancaster. He afterwards served as a director of the East India Company in London, where his great experience was invaluable in preparing subsequent ventures, and in the general conduct of the Company's affairs. He died in June, 1618, unmarried and childless, leaving large legacies to the grammar-school, and to the charities, of his native town of Basingstoke. Before the Company's second voyage commenced, the great queen had passed away, and the glorious roll of Elizabethan adventure and discovery was completed.

It is indeed a roll of surpassing splendour:—In the far north, the "*Meta Incognita*" and Davis Strait, as far as 72° 12' N.. discovered, and the intercourse with Russia, by the White Sea, strengthened and organised; the Caspian Sea navigated and Bokhara visited; a great fishing trade established on the Newfoundland banks, besides a considerable seal fishery; Virginia discovered, and a sure foundation laid for the future thirteen colonies which should form the United States; the charter granted to the Turkey Company, and British trade placed on a solid footing in the Levant: lucrative trade on the coast of Guinea and the West Indies and Spanish Main kept alive In English cruisers; the Orinoco explored as far as the mouth of the Karoni; the world twice circumnavigated; the Falkland Islands, Cape Horn, and 480 miles of the west coast of North America discovered; the Cape of Good Hope first rounded by an English ship; and a charter of incorporation granted to the East India Company, which opened the first chapter of the history of the British Empire in India.

One of the results of Elizabethan exploration and discovery was the extension of British commerce in all directions, to the remotest parts of the earth. Almost every important voyage of discovery led to the establishment of a lucrative trade, and was, therefore, of lasting benefit to mankind. Another result was, in the highest degree, to stimulate an enthusiastic feeling of patriotism which no difficulties or hardships could daunt and no disaster could quench. But the greatest result of all was the creation of an admirable training-ground for the Royal Navy; so that, when the day of imminent peril came, the great queen's explorers and discoverers saved her throne and her country.

Civil History of the Royal Navy, 1603–1649

Elizabeth had brought the navy to a point of force and efficiency to which it had never before attained. She had made England respected abroad, and she had preserved peace and order in the Narrow Seas. On March 24th, 1603, James VI. of Scotland became also King of England, and received the glorious legacy of the fleet which, under his predecessor, had created for itself a world-wide reputation.

There is no evidence that James took less interest than Elizabeth in the navy; indeed, in some respects, he may be said to have taken more; and, undoubtedly, he spent more money on it. Yet, owing to his weakness of character, his usually unfortunate choice and employment of officials, and perhaps also the growing softness and corruption of the times, the navy, during the greater part of his reign, went steadily downwards; and, but for Buckingham's exertions in 1618, would have become absolutely contemptible ere Charles I. succeeded to the throne in 1625.

Buckingham was a meritorious re-organiser, and Buckingham was,

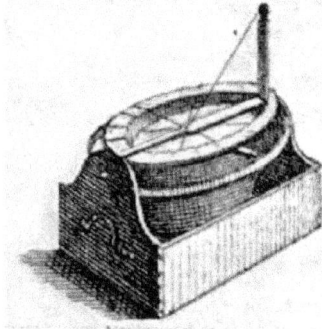

of course, James's selected favourite. Save, however, in the appointment
of Buckingham to share in the management of naval affairs, James,
in spite of his excellent intentions, did considerably more harm than
good to the service. The numerical decrease of the fleet during the
two and twenty years, was not particularly striking, though there was
a decrease. What was significant was that whereas Elizabeth left a navy
fit to go anywhere and do anything,

James left one largely composed of vessels unfit for any duty whatsoever.

The art of the shipbuilder does not seem to have greatly advanced
during the reign. (The Shipwrights' Company, however, was incor-
porated in 1605; and this may be taken as evidence that the subject
was receiving attention). Among the ships built under James, one, the
Royal Prince, was a larger man-of-war than had up to that time been
constructed in England; but there is no evidence that she was a more
seaworthy or less leewardly craft, or that she carried her guns better than the best of her Elizabethan predecessors. Speaking generally,
indeed, the ships of the period gave dissatisfaction to those who had
to handle them and to all who were best qualified to criticise them.

Ralegh, (*Observations on the Navy*), after enumerating the most desirable qualities in a man-of-war, *i.e.*, strong build, speed, stout scant-
ling, ability to fight the guns in all weathers, ability to lie to easily
in a gale, and ability to stay well, declared that in none of these re-
quirements were the King's ships satisfactory. And Captain George
Waymouth, (Add. MSS. 19,889: *The Jewell of Artes*), a professional ex-

A SHIP OF WAR OF THE SEVENTEENTH CENTURY.

Sectional elevation.

pert, and a contemporary authority on the theory of shipbuilding, lamented that he:

> . . . . could never see two ships builded of the like proportion by the best and most skilful shipwrights, though they have many times undertaken the same . . . because they trust rather to their judgment than their art, and to their eye than their scale and compass.

Mr. Oppenheim, (*Admin, of Royal Navy*), cites, as an illustration of the loose methods of calculation in vogue, that when the *Royal Prince* was built, Phineas Pett and William Bright, her constructors, estimated that 775 loads of timber would be required, whereas 1627 loads were actually used, with a consequent increase of £5908 in the cost.

Lead sheathing, which had been employed in the Spanish Navy since 1514, (Duro's *Armada Española*), and which had been applied to English merchant ships since 1553, was still untried in the navy, possibly because it had been found to set up galvanic action with the iron of the rudder pintles, etc. Nor was Hawkyns's sheathing of double planks, with tar and hair between them, as generally adopted as it should have been, though it remained in some favour until late in the seventeenth century. Much more care, in fact, was devoted to making ships look well than to making them really serviceable; and the result

A SHIP OF WAR OF THE SEVENTEENTH CENTURY.
Spars, rigging and sails.

often was that after her completion a vessel was found to be so crank that it was deemed necessary to "fur" or "girdle" her with a partial, or even an entire external planking beyond her original skin.

As the *Royal Prince*, (often called *Prince Royal*, or simply *Prince*), was the greatest constructive effort of the reign of James I., some account must be here given of her. Her keel was laid at Woolwich on October 20th, 1608, her chief constructor being Phineas Pett. Her nominal tonnage was 1200, but, measured according to the rules in force in 1632, it was 1035 nett, and 1330 gross. After the work had been some time in progress, and had met with much adverse criticism from rival shipwrights, a commission, consisting of Captain George Waymouth, Matthew Baker (who had been a principal constructor for more than half a century), William Bright, Edward Stevens, and others, was ordered to report on what was being done. Pett hated Waymouth, and Baker despised the Pett family, while Bright was particularly jealous of Phineas.

But Pett had powerful protectors in the Lord High Admiral and Sir Robert Mansell; and after there had been not only inquiry and further inquiry, but also a special scrutiny by the King and Prince Henry, Phineas Pett emerged triumphant. An attempt to launch the ship was made on September 24th, 1610, but it failed, owing to the dock head being too narrow to allow her to pass. She was, however, successfully launched a little later. (Oppenheim, *Admin. of Royal Navy.*)

Pett, on this occasion, owed more to his protectors than to the merits of his work, for the *Royal Prince,* though a striking object in the water, was both ill-designed and ill-built. As early as 1621, it was reported to Buckingham that although she had cost £20,000, a further £6000 would be needed to make her fit for service, she being built of decaying timber and of green unseasoned stuff. At that time, she had, nevertheless, been tried by no hard work. (She was rebuilt in 1641, and was renamed *Resolution* under the Commonwealth.)

The *Royal Prince* has often been described as the first three-decker of the Royal Navy; but, in the modern sense, she was not a three, but a two-decker. She had, that is to say, two complete covered batteries, and an armed upper deck. Stow says of her:

> This year the king built a most goodly ship for warre, the keel whereof was 114 feet in length, and the crossbeam was 44 feet in length; she will carry 64 pieces of ordnance, (she eventually mounted fifty-five, but had vacant ports to which some of these could be shifted in case of need), and is of the burthen of

285

H.M.S. *ROYAL PRINCE*, 92. BUILT IN 1610

1400 tons. This royal ship is double built, and is most sumptuously adorned, within and without, with all manner of curious carving, painting, and rich gilding.

Writing in 1801, Charnock, (*Mar. Architecture*), says, with some degree of truth:

The vessel in question as most worthy of remark, as it may be considered the parent of the identical class of shipping which, excepting the removal of such defects or trivial absurdities as long use and experience have pointed out, continue in practice even to the present moment. Were the absurd profusion of ornament with which the *Royal Prince* is decorated removed, its contour, or general appearance, would not so materially differ from the modern vessel of the same size as to render it an uncommon sight, or a ship in which mariners would hesitate at proceeding to sea in, on account of any glaring defect in its form, that, in their opinion, might render it unsafe to undertake a common voyage in it.

Stow's expression, "double built," means double planked. All the bulkheads were also double bolted with iron. Both these features were innovations. Yet by far the greatest amount of attention was given to the decorations. The carvings, including fourteen lions' heads for the round ports, cost £441, (*Pipe Off. Accts.* 2249), and to Robert Peake and Paul Isaackson was paid at one time a sum of £868 for painting and gilding.

The *Royal Prince* remained the show ship of the service until 1637, when the *Sovereign of the Seas* was launched. She was the first of the real three-deckers; and it is curious and significant that, although the authorities of Trinity House, as late as 1634, declared that "the art or wit of man cannot build a ship fit for service, with three tier of ordnance," (Oppenheim, *Admin. of Royal Navy*), the very vessel which they stigmatised as impossible was afloat three years later.

In January, 1635, an estimate for a ship of 1500 tons was called for; and in the following March, Phineas Pett was ordered to prepare a model of the projected craft, and was informed that he was fixed upon to superintend the building of her. In April, Pett met, and consulted as to the dimensions, with Sir John Penington, Sir Robert Mansell, and John Wells, storekeeper at Deptford; and it was determined that the tonnage should be 1466 by depth, 1661 by draught, and 1836 by beam. (But it is not apparent how the various computations were made, nor what they mean). The estimated cost was only £13,680; but the sum finally expended on the vessel was, excluding the cost of her guns, no less than £40,833 8s. 1½d. (*Aud. Off. Dec. Accts.* 1703-77, cited by Oppenheim.) In his journal, under the date May 14th, 1635, Pett writes:—

> I took leave of His Majesty at Greenwich, with his command to hasten into the north, and prepare the frame, timber, plank, and tressels for the new ship to be built at Woolwich. . . . I left my sons to see the moulds and other necessaries shipped in a Newcastle ship, hired on purpose to transport our provisions and workmen to Newcastle. Attended the Bishop of Durham with my commissions and instructions, whom I found wonderfully ready to assist us with other knights, gentlemen, and justices of the county, who took care to order present carriage; so that in a short time there was enough of the frame ready to lade a large collier, which was landed at Woolwich: and as fast as provisions could be got ready, they were shipped off from Chapley (Chopwell), Wood, at Newcastle, and that at Barnspeth (Brancepeth), Park, from Sutherland. . . . The 21st of December we laid the ship's keel in the dock. Most part of her frame, coming safe, was landed at Woolwich. . . . The 16th of January, His Majesty with divers lords came to Woolwich to see part of the frame and floor laid, and that time he gave orders to myself and my son to build two small pinnaces out of the great ship's waste. The 28th (month missing; obviously not January, 1636), His Majesty came again to Woolwich with the *Palsgrave* his brother, Duke Robert, and divers other lords, to see the pinnaces launched, which were named the *Greyhound* and *Roebuck*. (Duke Robert better known in English naval history as Prince Rupert. The "*Palsgrave*" was the Elector Friedrich V. of the Palatinate, who married Elizabeth, sister of Charles I.)

The great ship herself was launched in October, 1637.

The dimensions, etc., of the *Royal Prince* of 1610, and of the *Sovereign of the Seas* of 1637 respectively, were, according to statistics which appear to possess official authority, as follows:—

	Length of keel.	Length over all.	Beam.	Depth.	Tons gross.	Guns.	Men.
	Feet.	Ft. in.	Ft. in.	Ft. in.			
Royal Prince	115	. .	43 0	18 0	1187	55	500
Sovereign of the Seas [1]	127	167 9	48 4	19 4	1683	100	600

[1] From a list in the Dept. of the Cont. of the Navy. The number of guns is nominal. She really carried one hundred and two, all brass, which cost £24,753 8s. 8d. S. P. Dom. ccclxxiv. 30, and ccclxxxvii. 87. Pett's original design was for ninety guns only.

H.M.S. ROYAL SOVEREIGN, 100. BUILT IN 1637. CUT DOWN IN 1652.

During the interregnum, the *Sovereign of the Seas* was, on account of her crankness, cut down in 1652 to a 100-gun two-decker. There was a disposition to rename her the *Commonwealth*, but eventually she became known as the *Sovereign* simply. After the Restoration, she became *Royal Sovereign*. She saw much service throughout the Dutch and French wars, and existed until January 27th, 1696, when, being laid up at Chatham in order to be rebuilt, she was accidentally burnt, owing to a candle having been carelessly left alight in the cook's cabin.

Thomas Heywood, who is supposed to have designed the very elaborate decorations of the *Sovereign*, published a, long account of the ship, (*A True Description*), with a picture of her. His facts, so far as they relate to the ornaments, are probably correct enough; but the remaining details, and the picture, seem to be quite untrustworthy. The figure-head, or beakhead, represented King Edgar on horseback, trampling upon seven kings; upon the stern-head was a cupid bestriding a lion; upon the forward bulkhead were six emblematic statues; and the stern was a mass of useless carving and gilding.

In the last year but one of the reign of James I., the Royal Navy consisted of the following effective vessels.

Of Elizabethan ships which existed during part of the reign of James, the *Foresight*, of 1570, had been condemned in 1604; the *St. Andrew* and *St. Matthew*, prizes of 1596, had been given to Sir John Leigh in 1604; the *Mercury*, of 1592, had been sold in 1611; the *Garland*, of 1590, and *Mary Rose*, of 1589, had been used in the construction of a wharf at Chatham; and the *Nuestra Señora del Rosario*, the prize of 1588, after having been placed in support of her ancient antagonists in the dockyard, had been finally broken up in 1622. Most of the remaining ships had been broken up or disposed of, see lists following. (The *Answer* and *Crane*, of 1590, and the *Moon* and *Merlin*, however, survived into the reign of Charles I., though they were then ineffective.)

James also rebuilt two vessels which were disposed of or broken up ere his reign ended. These were the *Lion's Whelp*, purchased in 1601 and rebuilt in 1608, and the *Primrose*, purchased in 1560 and rebuilt in 1612. He also seems to have ordered the purchase in 1622, (order dated August 31st), of the *Mercury* and *Spy*, built by Phineas Pett for his own purposes in 1620, and sent out to Algier, under Captains Phineas Pett and Edward Giles, to Mansell, whom they joined on February 26th, 1621; but there is no evidence that these vessels were ever added to the navy.

	Built, or *Rebuilt.	Tons.	Length of keel.	Beam.		Depth.		Guns.	
			Feet.	Ft.	In.	Ft.	In.		
First rates:—									
1. *Prince* . .	1610	1187	115	43		18		55	
2. *Bear* . . .	*1599	915	110	37		18		40	Sold in 1629.
3. *Merhonour* .	*1611–14	800	104	38		17		44	Sold in 1650.
4. *Anne Royal* .	*1608	800	103	37		16		44	The *Ark Royal*, of 1587, rebuilt and renamed. She was bilged on her anchor in 1636, raised at great cost, and then broken up.
Second rates:—									
5. *Repulse* . .	*1610	700	97	37		15		40	Broken up about 1645.
6. *Warspite* .	1596	648	90	36		16		29	Cut down to a lighter for harbour service, 1635.
7. *Victory* . .	1620	875	108	35	9	17		42	
8. *Assurance*. .	*1603–5	600	95	33		14	6	38	The *Hope*, of 1559, rebuilt and renamed. Broken up about 1645.
9. *Nonsuch* . .	*1603–5	636	88	34		15		38	The *Nonpareil*, of 1584, rebuilt and re-named. Sold under Charles I.
10. *Defiance* . .	*1611–14	700	97	37		15		40	Sold in 1650.
11. *Lion* . . .	*1609	650	91	35	2	16		38	Or *Red Lion*, the *Golden Lion*, of 1582, rebuilt and renamed.
12. *Vanguard* .	*1615	650	102	35		14		40	
13. *Rainbow* . .	*1618	650	102	35		14		40	
14. *Constant Re-formation* .	1619	752	106	35	6	15		42	Named to celebrate Buckingham's accession to office. Carried off, 1648, to the Prince of Wales.
15. *Swiftsure*. .	1621	887	106	36	10	16	8	42	
16. *St. George* .	1622	895	110	37		16	6	42	Renamed *George* under the Commonwealth.
17. *St. Andrew* .	1622	895	110	37		16	6	42	Renamed *Andrew* under the Common-wealth.
18. *Triumph* . .	1623	922	110	37		17		42	
Third rates:—									
19. *Dreadnought* .	*1611–14	450	84	31		13		32	Broken up about 1645.
20. *Antelope* . .	*1618	450	92	32		12	6	34	Carried off to the Prince of Wales, 1648.

* In several cases there is much doubt as to how far the ships were rebuilt. Some of those thus marked may have merely undergone extensive repairs.

	Built, or *Rebuilt.	Tons.	Length of keel.	Beam.	Depth.	Guns.	
			Feet.	Ft. In.	Ft. In.		
21. *Speedwell* . .	*1607	400	..	.. ..	..	..	Lost, Nov. 1624, near Flushing. She was the *Swiftsure*, of 1592, rebuilt and renamed.
22. *Adventure* .	1594	343	88	26	12	26	Broken up about 1645.
23. *Convertine* .	1616	500	..	.. ..	..	34	ex *Destiny*, of Ralegh's last voyage. Carried off to the Prince of Wales, 1648.
24. *Happy Entrance* . . }	1619	582	96	32	6 14	32	Named to celebrate Buckingham's accession to office. Burnt at Chatham, 1658.
25. *Bonaventure* .	1621	675	98	33	15 8	34	Taken by the Dutch, 1652.
26. *Garland* . .	1620	683	93	33	16	34	Taken by the Dutch, 1652.
27. *Mary Rose* .	1623	394	83	27	13	26	Wrecked off Flanders, 1650.

Fourth rates:—

28. *Phœnix* . .	1612	250	70	24	11	20	Sold under Charles I.
29. *Seven Stars* .	1615	140	60	20	9	14	
30. *Charles* . .	..	80	63	16	7	16	
31. *Desire* . . .	1616	80	66	16	6	6	

With four galleys and several hoys.

* In several cases there is much doubt as to how far the ships were rebuilt. Some of those thus marked may have merely undergone extensive repairs.

The additions under Charles I. were as follows:—

—	Built. *Rebuilt. †Prize. ‡Bought.	Tons.	Length of keel.	Beam.	Depth.	Guns.	—
			Ft. In.	Ft. In.	Ft. In.		
1. *St. Claude* . .	†1625	300	..	.. ..	..	..	
2. *St. Denis* . . .	†1625	528	104	32 5	11 9	38	
3. *St. Mary* . . .	†1626	100	..	.. ..	..	..	Given to Sir John Chudleigh, 1629.
4. *St. Anne* . . .	†1626	350	..	.. ..	..	..	
5. *Espérance* . . .	†1626	250	..	.. ..	..	..	
6. *Henrietta* . . .	1626	68	52	15	6 6	6	Sold under the Commonwealth.
7. *Maria*	1626	68	52	15	6 6	6	
8. *Spy*	1626	20	..	.. ..	..	..	

No. & Name	Built † Prize * Rebuilt	Tons	Length of keel (Ft)	(In)	Beam (Ft)	(In)	Depth (Ft)	(In)	Guns	Remarks
9–18. *Lion's Whelps* (10)[1]	1627	185	62		25		9		12	One only survived to the days of the Commonwealth.
19. *Fortune*	†1627	200	..		..		..		..	
20. *St. Esprit*	†1627	800	105		35		..		42	Built in Holland for France. Taken in the Texel.
21. *Vanguard*	*1630	750	112		36	4	13	10	40	Renamed *Liberty* under the Commonwealth. Wrecked off Harwich, 1650.
22. *Charles*	1632	810	105		33	7	16	3	44	
23. *Henrietta Maria*	1632	793	106		35	9	15	8	42	Renamed *Paragon* under the Commonwealth. Accidentally burnt, 1655, in the West Indies.
24. *James*	1633	875	110		37	6	16	2	48	
25. *Unicorn*	1634	823	107		36	4	15	1	46	
26. *Leopard*	1634	515	95		33		12	4	34	Taken by the Dutch.
27. *Swallow*	1634	478	96		32	2	11	7	34	Carried off, 1648, to the Prince of Wales.

[1] Two of the *Whelps* differed slightly in size from the rest. All were square rigged with three masts, and were fitted for using sweeps. The original armament of each was four culverins, four demi-culverins, and two brass sakers; but to these two demi-cannon were added. Two were lost, returning from La Rochelle, while quite new; one blew up in action with a Dunquerquer; No. 6 had disappeared by 1631 and seems to be the one which was given by the King to Buckingham, on August 11th, 1625, for an attempt at the North-West Passage; No. 4 was lost on August 14th, 1636; another was expended for experimental purposes; No. 5 sank off the Dutch coast in 1637. No. 10, the last survivor, remained in commission till 1654. The *Whelps* were built by contract at £3 5s. a ton. S. P. Dom. lviii. 25; ccclxiii. 29, etc.

—	Built *Rebuilt †Prize ‡Bought	Tons	Length of keel (Ft)	(In)	Beam (Ft)	(In)	Depth (Ft)	(In)	Guns	—
28. *Swan*	†1636	..	..		..		..		..	Taken from the Dunquerquers. Lost off Guernsey, Oct. 1638.
29. *Nicodemus*	†1636	105	63		19	9	6		6	Taken from the Dunquerquers. Sold under the Commonwealth.
30. *Roebuck*	1636	90	57		18	1	6	8	10	Carried off, 1648, to the Prince of Wales.
31. *Greyhound*	1636	126	60		20	3	7	8	12	Blown up in action, 1656, by her captain, Geo. Wager.
32. *Expedition*	1637	301	90		26		9	8	30	
33. *Providence*	1637	304	90		26		9	9	30	
34. *Sovereign of the Seas*	1637	1683	127		48	4	19	4	100	
35. *Lion*	*1640	717	108		35	4	15	6	52	

No. Name	Date	Tons						Guns	Notes
36. *Prince*	*1641	1187	115	43		18		64	Renamed *Resolution* under the Commonwealth. Renamed *Prince*, 1660.
37. *Crescent*	‡1642	150	..		..		..	14	Carried off, 1648, to the Prince of Wales.
38. *Lily*	‡1642	80	..		..		..	8	
39. *Satisfaction*	1646	220	..		..		..	26	Carried off, 1648, to the Prince of Wales.
40. *Adventure*	1646	385	94	27		9	11	38	
41. *Nonsuch*	1646	389	98	28	4	14	2	34	
42. *Assurance*	1646	341	89	26	10	11		32	
43. *Constant Warwick*	1646	379	90	28		12		30	Built as a privateer. Bought by Parliament Jan. 20th, 1649.
44. *Phœnix*	1647	414	96	28	6	14	3	38	Taken by the Dutch, Sept. 7th, 1652. Retaken, Nov. 1652.
45. *Dragon*	1647	414	96	30		12		38	
46. *Tiger*	1647	447	99	29	4	12		38	
47. *Elizabeth*	1647	471	101	6 29	8	14	10	38	
48. *Old Warwick*	†1646	..	..		..		..	22	
49. *Falcon*	†	..	..		..		..	..	Merchantman taken from the Cromwellians.
50. *Hart*	†	..	..		..		..	10	Do. do.
51. *Dove*	†	..	..		..		..	6	Do. do.
52. *Truelove*	†	259	..		..		..	20	Do. do.
53. *Concord*	†	..	..		..		..	..	Do. do.
54. *Dolphin*	†	100	..		..		..	..	Do. do.
55. *Fellowship*	†	300	..		..		..	28	Do. do.
56. *Globe*	‡	300	..		..		..	24	Purchased merchantman.
57. *Hector*	‡	300	.		..		..	20	Do. do.

Although the *Sovereign of the Seas* was nominally a 100-gun ship, 102 brass guns were thus classed and distributed in her:—

			Length.	Weight.
			Ft.	Cwt.
Lower deck :				
Broadside guns	20	cannon drakes[1]	9·0	45
Stern chasers	4	demi-cannon drakes	12·5	53
Bow chasers	2	„ „	11·5	48
Luffs	2	„ „	10·0	44
Middle deck :				
Broadside guns	24	culverin drakes	8·5	28
Stern chasers	4	culverins	11·5	48
Bow chasers	2	„	11·5	48
Main deck :				
Broadside guns	24	demi-culverin drakes	8·5	18
Stern chasers	2	demi-culverins	10·0	30
Bow chasers	2	„	10·0	30

Upper deck :				
Forecastle	8 demi-culverin drakes . . .	9·0	20
Half-deck	6 ,, ,, . . .	9·0	20
Quarter-deck . . .	2 ,, ,, . . .	5·5	8
Forecastle, pointing aft	2 culverin drakes	5·5	11

---

[1] The affix "drake" signified that the gun was suited for heavy charges of powder, whereas "perier," after it had ceased to mean a gun throwing a stone shot, meant one suited for low charges.

Throughout the reign of James I. and Charles I., ships were systematically over-gunned, and, in consequence, when at sea, captains often dismounted some of their pieces and stowed them in the ballast in the hold. The price of guns varied from £12 to £15 a ton, and the manufacture of them was practically the monopoly of a few, chief among whom was John Browne, King's Gunfounder, who in 1626 gained a reward of £200 for casting lighter pieces than had been previously made, yet pieces capable, nevertheless, of standing double proof. The place of proof for all guns was Ratcliff Fields. Their export without licence was forbidden; they might be bought and sold only at East Smithfield, and shipped and landed only at Tower Wharf. Yet in spite of these restrictions, many went abroad, and of these not a few had been stolen from royal forts, and probably from ships as well.

Stone shot continued to be carried in certain small proportions until about 1625, after which they seem to have been wholly discontinued. It was not until James I. had been for several years on the throne that the extravagant practice of firing shotted charges as salutes ceased, and up to the time of the Revolution the expenditure of powder in salutes was enormous, although repeated orders were issued in order to check waste. On joyous occasions the number of rounds, as is still the rule, was generally odd; on occasions of death, etc., it was even, but the exact number of rounds was not prescribed, and all sorts of excuses were invented for firing them. In 1628, the fleet at Plymouth "shot away £100 of powder in one day in drinking healths," (Yonge's *Diary*), and Mr. Oppenheim, who cites the above, says elsewhere, (*Admin. of Royal Navy.*)

In one gunner's accounts we find: 'One faucon when the master's wife went ashore . . . One minion the master commanded to be shot off to a ship his father was in.'

The evil was not materially abated until the close of the seventeenth century.

During the reign of James I., the lunar monthly pay of a seaman was 10s. On the occasion of the attack upon Cadiz, in 1625, it was temporarily raised to 14s., and it was raised permanently, in 1626, to 15s., subject to deductions of 6d. for the Chatham Chest, 4d. for the chaplain, and 2d. for the surgeon; and so, the scale remained until the Civil War.

The Caroline Navy was the first to be divided into six rates. The rates of ships were not always determined by the size and importance of the vessels, as was the case in later periods. Indeed, the rating only gradually assumed a systematic plan. But upon the rating of a ship always depended the rate of pay of the officers serving in her. The maximum (first-rate), and minimum (sixth rate) scales, up to the time of the Revolution, per month of twenty-eight days were: captains, £14 to £4 14s. 4d.; lieutenants (allowed only in the first three rates), £3 10s. to £3; masters, £3 13s. 9d. to £2 6s. 8d.; pilots, £2 5s. to £1 10s.; masters' mates, £2 5s. to £1 10s.; boatswains, £2 5s. to £1 3s. 4d.; boatswains' mates, £1 6s. 3d. to £1 0s. 8d.; pursers, £2 to £1 3s. 4d.; surgeons, £1 10s.; surgeons' mates, £1; quartermasters, £1 10s. to £1; quartermasters' mates, £1 5s. to 17s. 6d.; yeomen of sheets, jeers, tacks, or halliards, £1 5s. to £1 1s.; carpenters, £1 17s. 6d. to £1 1s.; carpenters' mates, £1 5s. to 18s. 8d.; corporals, (then newly allowed, they drilled the men in small-arms), £1 10s. 4d. to 18s. 8d.; gunners, £2 to £1 3s. 4d.; gunners' mates, £1 2s. 6d. to 18s. 8d.; cooks, £1 5s. to £1; master trumpeters, £1 8s. to £1 5s.; other trumpeters, £1 3s. 4d.; drummers, (first four rates only) £1; fifers, (first four rates only) £1; armourers, £1 1s.; gunmakers, £1 1s. The pay of gromets was 11s. 3d., and that of boys, 7s. 6d.

The rank of lieutenant had, as has been seen, existed in the navy at the time of the Armada. It had subsequently disappeared, to be revived under Charles I. Mr. Oppenheim, (*Admin of Royal Navy*), cites the Egerton MSS. (2541, f. 13), as declaring that the appointment of lieutenants was—

> . . . .to breed young gentlemen for the sea-service. . . .The reason why there are not now so many able sea-captains as there is use of is because there hath not been formerly allowance for lieutenants, whereby gentlemen of worth and quality might be encouraged to go to sea. And, if peace had held a little longer, the old sea-captains would have been worn out, as that the

State must have relied wholly on mechanick men that have been bred up from swabbers, and . . . . to make many of them would cause sea service in time to be despised by gentlemen of worth, who will refuse to serve at sea under such captains.

The efficiency of the navy, which had steadily deteriorated under James I., continued to decrease during the early years of his son and successor, although Charles took a much more intelligent interest in the fleet than James had ever been capable of taking. In the opinion of Mr. Oppenheim, the Cadiz expedition of 1625 probably indicated the low water mark of English seamanship, he says:

There have been many previous and subsequent occasions when fleets were sent to sea equally ill-found and ill-provided, but never before or since have we such accounts of utter incapacity in the mere everyday work of a sailor's duties. The shameful picture of that confused mass of ships crowded together helplessly, without order or plan, colliding with each other, chasing or deserting at their own will, the officers losing spars and sails from ignorance of the elementary principles of their art, is the indictment against the government of James I., which had allowed the seamanship of Elizabeth to die out in this generation. (*Admin. of Royal Navy*).

The worst feature in the situation—and it was a feature which grew darker as the years of Charles's reign went on—was that the seamen, being ill-fed, ill-clothed, and irregularly paid, were terribly discontented. Wages, as has been seen, were raised, but for many years the increment was practically a paper one only. The men got neither the old scale nor the new, except at uncertain intervals. They mutinied, they rioted, they turned marauders in order to supply their empty stomachs; they even threatened to besiege the Court at Whitehall, and they actually seized the Guildhall at Plymouth. In 1629, Sir Henry Mervyn, commanding in the Narrow Seas, officially set forth the sad state of the men, and prophetically concluded:

His Majesty will lose the honour of his seas, the love and loyalty of his sailors, and his Royal Navy will droop. (S. P. Dom.)

In course of time wages were paid more regularly, but there was no other improvement. The provisions were bad and scanty; the ships were floating pest-houses; the sick were turned ashore starving. And so, it is hardly astonishing that soon after the beginning of the Civil

War large bodies of sailors offered their services to the Parliament, and that when King and Parliament appointed rival commanders in the persons of Penington and Warwick, there was a general adhesion to the latter, in spite of the fact that Penington, the Royalist, was personally popular in the navy.

The opinion among the seamen seems to have been that things were so bad that any change must be a change for the better. If so, it was justified by the event. Wages were raised to 19s. a month, and were regularly paid; the food improved in quality, and the sick were taken care of. The pay of officers was not raised by Parliament until 1647, when it became as follows: Captains, £21 to £1; lieutenants, £4 4s. to £3 10s.; masters, £7 to £3 18s. 8d.; masters' mates, £3 5s. 4d. to £2 2s.; pilots, £3 5s. 4d. to £2 2s.; carpenters, £3 3s. to £1 15s.; boatswains, £3 10s. to £1 17s. 4d., and gunners, £3 3s. to £1 15s.

The prescribed contributions to the Chatham Chest were still invariably deducted, but the fund itself was mismanaged, and often misapplied. Sums, for example, were taken from it to pay wages. A Commission appointed in December, 1635, to inquire into the administration of the Chest, reported in April, 1637, and as a result some reforms were effected.

At the accession of James I., Charles Howard, Earl of Nottingham, was still Lord High Admiral. Before dealing more particularly with the changes and reforms effected in the Administration, it may be convenient here to set down in a succinct form the successive alterations in the high personnel of the Admiralty during the period now under review. These were:—

LORD HIGH ADMIRAL.

July 8, 1585—
Charles Howard, Earl of Nottingham.
Jan. 28, 1619—
George Villiers, Duke of Buckingham.
Sept. 20, 1628—
Richard, Lord Weston.
Robert, Earl of Lindsey.
William, Earl of Pembroke.
Edward, Earl of Dorset.
Dudley, Viscount Dorchester.
Sir John Coke.
Nov. 20, 1632—
Richard, Lord Weston.
Robert, Earl of Lindsey.
Edward, Earl of Dorset.
Sir John Coke.
Francis, Lord Cottington.
Sir Francis Windebank.

Edward Nicholas as Secretary.

May 10, 1618. Sir William Russell.
April 5, 1627. Sir Sackville Crowe.
1629. Sir William Russell.
Jan. 12, 1639. Sir William Russell.
Sir Henry Vane, junior.
1642. Sir William Russell.
Aug. 1642. Sir Henry Vane, junior.

SURVEYOR OF THE NAVY.

Dec. 20, 1598. Sir John Trevor.
1611. Sir Richard Bingley.

CONTROLLER OF THE NAVY.

Dec. 20, 1598. Sir Henry Palmer.
1611. Sir Guildford Slingsby.
[In 1618, the Surveyor and Controller were "sequestered from their posts," and their duties were entrusted to a Board of Navy Commissioners.]

Sir Henry Vane, senior.
March 16, 1636—
William Juxon, Bishop of London.
Francis, Lord Cottington.
Robert, Earl of Lindsey.
Edward, Earl of Dorset.
Sir John Coke.
Sir Francis Windebank.
Sir Henry Vane, senior.
March 18, 1638—
Prince James, Duke of York.
April 13, 1638—
Algernon Percy, Earl of Northumberland (*acting* substitute).

In commission, wit

NAVY COMMISSIONERS.

Feb. 12, 1619.[1] Sir Lionel Cranfield.[2]
Sir Thomas Weston.
Sir John Wolstenholme.
Sir Thomas Smith.
Nicholas Fortescue.
John Osborne.
Francis Gofton.
Richard Sutton.
William Pitt.
John Coke.[3]
Thomas Norreys.
William Burrell.[4]

SURVEYOR OF THE NAVY (re-appointed 1628).

1628. Sir Thomas Aylesbury.
Dec. 19, 1632. Kenrick Edisbury (*alias* Wilkinson).
Sept. 26, 1638. William Batten.

"PRINCIPAL OFFICERS."
TREASURER OF THE NAVY.

Dec. 22, 1598. Fulke Grevill, Lord Brooke.
1604. Sir Robert Mansell.

[1] Date of Letters Patent. These, with few changes, held office until 1628. Pepys ('Diary,' March 14, 1669) calls this the Grand Commission. It was renewed, with alterations, in 1625.

[2] Created a baron in 1621, and later Earl of Middlesex. He was impeached and imprisoned in 1624, and died in 1645.

[3] Knighted 1624.

[4] Burrell had been Master Shipwright to the East India Company, and was one of the chief shipwrights in the reign of James I. He was succeeded as Master Shipwright by Peter Pett in 1629, and died in 1630.

CONTROLLER OF THE NAVY (re-appointed 1628).		
Feb.	1628. Sir Guildford Slingsby.	
	1632. Sir Henry Palmer.	

CLERK OF THE NAVY (later "of the Acts").

1600. Peter (later Sir Peter) Buck.
Denis Fleming.
Feb. 16, 1639. Thomas Barlow.

EXTRA PRINCIPAL OFFICERS.

1629. William Burrell (assist.).
Phineas Pett (assist.).

[1] Darell died in 1622.
[2] Later Apsley became Lieutenant of the Tower. He died in 1630.

Oct. 1630. Sir Kenelm Digby.
Jan. 1631. Phineas Pett.

SURVEYORS OF VICTUALLING.

1595. Marmaduke Darell.
Aug. 16, 1603. Sir Marmaduke Darell.
Sir Thomas Bludder.
Dec. 31, 1612. Sir Marmaduke Darell.[1]
Sir Allen Apsley.[2]
Jan. 8, 1623. Sir Allen Apsley.
Sir Sampson Darell.
1630. Sir Sampson Darell.
Nov. 20, 1635. John Crane.

After the commencement of the Civil War the greater part of the civil staff of the Admiralty went over to the service of the Parliament, which assumed control through the mediumship of committees.

Nottingham was already fifty-two at the time of the defeat of the

Spanish Armada. At the accession of James I., he was sixty-seven. Yet he remained Lord Admiral until he was eighty-two. He was, undoubtedly, an honest man; but in his old age he left far too much to his subordinates, some of whom, especially Sir Robert Mansell, the Treasurer, were not honest, and, in consequence, the administration of the Navy became most corrupt and inefficient.

As early as 1608, the numerous scandals compelled the formation of a commission of inquiry, which consisted of the Earls of Nottingham and Northampton, Lord Zouche, Sir Edward Wotton, Sir Julius Caesar, Sir Robert Cotton, and others; and this sat from May, 1608, to June, 1609. But the only experienced seaman on the commission was the Earl of Nottingham, who never attended the meetings. A report was drawn up, and the king himself lectured the parties who were found to have been guilty of malpractices; but no effective steps were taken for securing reforms.

The evils, in consequence, continued and increased. In 1613, Cotton attempted to obtain another inquiry, but failed. In 1618, however, when, as Gardiner says, "the household was one mass of peculation and extravagance," the efforts of the party of reform met with more success, mainly, perhaps, because Buckingham, who was in the height of his power, desired to have the post of Lord Admiral for himself. Nottingham was superseded and pensioned. Mansell was got rid of; Bingley, the surveyor, and Slingsby, the controller, were "sequestered"; Navy Commissioners inquired, reported, and were given charge of the surveyorship and controllership; and various radical changes were effected.

The report issued by the Commissioners upon their assumption of office was a very long and searching one. It showed, among other things, to quote Mr. Oppenheim, (*Admin. of Royal Navy*) that—

All the frauds of 1608 were still flourishing, with some new ones due to the lapse of time. Places were still sold, and at such high prices that the buyers 'profess openly that they cannot live unless they may steal'; the cost of the navy had of late been some £53,000 a year, 'that could not keep it from decay.' For building a new ship in place of the *Bonaventure* £5700 had been allowed, but, although £1700 had been paid on account of it, no new vessel had been commenced; and, though this same ship 'was broken up above seven years past, yet the king hath paid £63 yearly for keeping her.' Further, 'the *Advantage* was burnt about five years since, and yet keepeth at the charge of £104 9s. 5d.; the *Charles* was disposed of in Scotland two years since, and costeth £60 16s. 10d. for keeping.' For repairing the *Merhonour, Defiance, Vanguard,* and *Dreadnought,* £23,500 had been paid, 'for which eight new ships might have been built as the accounts of the East India Company do prove; yet all this while the king's ships decayed: and if the *Merhonour* were repaired, she was left so imperfect that before her finishing she begins again to decay.' In nine years £108,000 had been charged for cordage: and the commissioners express their intention of reducing the expenditure on this item by two-thirds.

The commissioners made very great reforms in many directions, and, at the close of their first five years of office, delivered a report of the work done by them. They had, they said, found in 1618, twenty-three serviceable and ten unserviceable ships, of together 15,670 tons, with four decayed galleys and four hoys, costing £53,000 a year; and they had, in 1624, thirty-five serviceable ships of 19,339 tons, besides the galleys and hoys, though the expense was little more than £30,000 a year, inclusive of the charges for building ten new vessels. (But the Pipe Office Accounts show the total naval expenditure in 1623—inclusive of that for the fleet sent to Spain for Prince Charles—to have been £62,000)

But even the commissioners themselves were not beyond suspicion. Coke suspected some of his colleagues of bribery in connection with the Algier Expedition, and kept them under espionage. And several gross abuses, such, for example, as the employment as captains of influential landsmen, were not corrected, nor even seriously attacked, until a much later period. (A Special Commission appointed in 1626 to inspire into the state of the navy produced no results.)

And, in course of time, direction by commissioners was found to be slow and cumbersome. Charles I. complained of it to Buckingham in 1627. (*Royal Letters,* Halliwell). After Buckingham's assassination, it was deemed more convenient to put the office of Lord High Admiral into commission, and to allow the principal officers of the navy to resume their full duties. The Treasurer's office had by that time become almost entirely financial. In 1630 his emoluments were increased by the grant of a house at Deptford, and of a poundage of threepence on all payments, including wages, made to him. In 1634, his fixed salary was raised from £270 13s. 4d. to £645 13.s. 4d.

The other principal officers flourished correspondingly, by foul means as well as by fair. Palmer once excused himself for selling government cordage and pocketing the proceeds, by saying that "his predecessors had done the like." Digby, who had no defined duties on the Board, proposed at one time to purchase from Sir Henry Mervyn the latter's command in the Channel; but Mervyn seems to have asked too much, *viz.*, his arrears of pay to the amount of £5000, and the £3000 which he himself had given for his position.

In 1628, the Principal Officers met in St. Martin's Lane; but in 1630 rooms for them were taken in Mincing Lane at a rent of £30 a year. They cost £150 to furnish; twelve months' beer for the officers and their staff cost £13 8s. at a time when beer was but £1 10s. a tun; and, upon the whole, it is clear that so long as comfort and perquisites were obtainable, the efficiency of the service was a secondary consideration.

In 1634, Palmer, Pett, and Fleming, Clerk of the Acts, were suspended for malversation of stores. They were no worse than their inferiors. The dockyard officials robbed wholesale; the captains turned their ships into cargo boats for their own profit, and conspired with the pursers to forge and sell seamen's tickets; carpenters, gunners, boatswains, and pursers, cheated and swindled; imaginary men were borne in nearly all ships, and their wages were shared among the officers; and government storehouses were converted into surreptitious residences for government servants and their families.

There were also sinecurists and pluralists. In 1626, a Rochester man, to sell it again, offered £100 for the pursership of the *Anne Royal*, which he could not himself hold. Another man was simultaneously purser of the *George* and cook of the *Bear*, and filled both offices by deputy. And the pursers made ever increasing profit on the sale of slop-clothes, the issue of which had begun in 1623. ("To avoyde nastie beastlyness by continuall wearinge of one suite of clothes, and therebie boddilie diseases and unwholesome ill smells in every ship."); and derived illegitimate fees from the contractors who delivered them on board. As a result, the seamen bought hardly any slops, and preferred to go ragged.

The Earl of Northumberland, as acting Lord High Admiral, reduced and regulated the pursers' profits on, slop clothes by orders issued in 1641; and, at about the same time, public opinion within the navy apparently began to improve, and, if not actually to condemn, at least to look askance on, peculation, fraud, and the sale of places. But there was no noticeable cessation of the evil practices until the establishment of the Commonwealth; and they flourished again with full vigour for many years after the Restoration.

In the reign of James I., Deptford was still the principal dockyard, but Chatham was beginning to rival it. In the reign of Charles I., Portsmouth drew a little to the front, and Woolwich, temporarily discarded, was leased in 1633 to the East India Company for £100 a year. Under James, the dry dock at Deptford was enlarged, and the yard was surrounded by a paling; and a ropehouse was established at Woolwich. In 1619, the paling at Deptford gave place to a brick wall. Four years later, the dry dock at Portsmouth, the earliest of the kind built in England, was filled up, apparently because that part of the yard was threatened by incursions of the sea.

Chatham obtained two mast docks in 1619 and 1620, and much additional ground, on part of which a dock, a ropehouse, and various brick and lime kilns were erected. Another dock was under construction in 1623. The chief officers of the yard had up to about that time lodged at Winchester House; they appear to have then removed to a house on Chatham Hill, leased from the Dean and Chapter of Rochester. Portsmouth largely owed to Buckingham its growth in importance, and from his time some vessels were always stationed there; but not till 1638 was a master shipwright ordered into permanent residence at the yard; and a new dry dock was not begun there until 1656. As a naval centre, indeed, Portsmouth was still far behind Chatham.

The chain, drawn by Hawkyns across the Medway at Upnor, was repaired in 1606, and, in 1623, gave place to a boom composed of masts, iron, cordage, and the hulls of two ships and two pinnaces. A new boom or a new chain was probably placed in position about 1635.

Naval punishments were, as in previous periods, of a barbarous type, ducking, keel-hauling, tongue-scraping, and tying up with weights about the neck being common. The ancient custom of lashing to the bowsprit a seaman who had four times slept upon his watch, and of letting him drown or starve there, also survived. But some of these punishments were not strictly legal, and in the days of Charles many officers, and especially Penington and Mervyn, leant in the direction of a less ferocious *régime*. Yet the regulations were still strict.

Mr. Oppenheim, (*Admin. of Royal Navy*), says:

Prayer was said twice daily—before dinner, and after the psalm sung at setting the evening watch; and anyone absent was liable to twenty-four hours in irons. Swearing was punished by three knocks on the forehead with a boatswain's whistle, and smoking anywhere but on the upper deck, 'and that sparingly,' by the bilboes. The thief was tied up to the capstan, 'and every man in the ship shall give him five lashes with a three-stringed whip on his bare back.' This is, I think, the first mention of any form of cat.

The habitual thief was, after flogging, dragged ashore astern of a boat and ignominiously dismissed with the loss of his wages. For brawling and fighting the offender was ducked three times from the yardarm, and similarly towed ashore and discharged; while for striking an officer, he was to be tried for his life by twelve men, but whether shipmates or civilians is not said. If a man slept on watch, three buckets of water were to be poured upon his head and into his sleeves; and anyone, except 'gentlemen or officers,' playing cards or dice incurred four hours of manacles. It is suggestive to read that 'no man presume to strike in the ship but such officers as are authorised.'

Neither the public sense nor the law, however, seems to have been outraged when the letter of legality was overstepped by captains, either in the navy or in the merchant service. The master of a Virginia trader hung up an insubordinate boy by the wrists, and tied two hundredweights to his feet. The boy laid a complaint before the Admiralty Court, but the judge. Sir H. Martin, refused redress, on the ground that the maintenance of sea discipline was necessary.

During the whole of this period it was usual, when extra vessels were needed for naval purposes, to hire ships from the merchants, and to arm them. But Penington, like other commanders, had but a low opinion of such craft, considering fifteen of them not a match for two regular men-of-war, their guns being defective, and their ammunition small in quantity. Their discipline also was bad.

In 1625, they had to be forced under fire at Cadiz by threats; in 1628, at Rochelle, they fired vigorously, but well out of any useful or hazardous range. In this year, the captain of one of them killed, injured, and maltreated his men, while he and five gentlemen volunteers consumed sixteen men's allowance of food every day; and in January, 1627, when some of them, lying in Stokes Bay, were ordered westward, they mutinied, and would only sail for the Downs. (*Admin. of Royal Navy.*)

The rate of hire under James I. and his successor was two shillings per month per ton; but this was often not paid for several years. Up to 1624, and again from 1626 onwards, a bounty of five shillings a ton was offered to induce the building of merchant vessels suitable for adaptation to the purposes of war. After 1642, the Parliament, instead of paying so much per ton per month, offered £3 15s. 6d. per man per month, the owner supplying his vessel completely armed, manned, and equipped for sea, and the State being responsible in case of her loss.

The police of the home seas was disgracefully mismanaged under both James I. and Charles I. Dunquerque privateers infested the Channel, and rovers from the Mediterranean hovered about the coasts; while the people of Ireland and the western counties were many of them either pirates themselves or in league with such freebooters. It was sought to cope with the evil by granting warrants to the merchants to cruise against the pirates, and to retain three-fourths of any goods seized from them. In the middle of James's reign, a Sallee rover was taken in the Thames, and a fleet of thirty Mussulman *corsairs* cruised in the Atlantic.

Between 1609 and 1616, no fewer than four hundred and sixty-six British vessels were captured by the Algerines, and their crews enslaved. Mansell's expedition of 1621 checked the evil only for the moment. The Newfoundland Company complained that since 1612 it had received damage from the pirates to the value of £40,000; Swanage was in terror of the Turks, and petitioned for a blockhouse; and Trinity House objected to the Lizard Light on the ground that it would be of assistance to the marauders.

Under Charles I., the nuisance grew even graver. Such men-of-war as cruised to protect trade in home waters were not good enough sailers to come up with the fast Dunquerquers and lateen-rigged Turks. Within only ten days in 1625, according to the Mayor of Plymouth, the pirates took twenty-seven vessels and two hundred men. Nor was this all. On the night of June 30th, 1631, a body of Algerines landed at Baltimore in Munster, sacked the town, and carried off two hundred and thirty-seven British subjects into slavery.

The Government was too much in fear of the adoption of retaliatory measures to be very severe upon such Algerines as were caught from time to time. They were not executed, because there were in

Sallee two thousand English people in peril of their lives. These free-booters had much their own way on the west and south. On the east, the Dunquerquers enforced something almost akin to a blockade; so that at one time, at Ipswich alone, fifty-eight vessels were laid up, and, at another, Lynn was plundered and partially burnt. Tunnage and poundage was supposed to provide for the protection of the coasts; but in 1628, in addition, duties were levied on sea-borne coal from Sunderland and Newcastle to pay for it; yet without any perceptible abatement of the scourge.

Even when the ship-money fleets were at sea, coasters and Dover packets were overhauled and pillaged almost in sight of his Majesty's ships, and the Channel was full of Algerines. (*Admin, of Royal Navy*) Rainborow's expedition to Sallee, like Mansell's to Algier, gave but temporary relief; for in 1640 there were sixty sail of Algerines off the south coast, and the unbelievers executed a successful raid near Penzance.

The comparative impunity with which the Mediterranean *corsairs* carried out their operations was due perhaps almost as much to the disunion of the Christian Powers as to the weakness of Britain. Yet it is strange that while Britain in her own seas was at the mercy of these pirates, she still jealously maintained the right of her flag as against civilised states. Monson enforced it in the Downs in 1604, when a Dutch squadron lay there; Mansell enforced it in 1620 against a French squadron on the coast of Spain; Selden, in 1634, wrote his *Mare Clausum* in defence of it, Charles ordering a copy of the book to be kept for ever as a piece of evidence in the Court of Admiralty. Lindsey was sent to sea in 1635 especially to vindicate the honour claimed by Great Britain, and in 1636 Northumberland received the mark of deference both from the Dutch and from the Spaniards.

★★★★★★

These examples might be largely added to. In July, 1626, for instance, the captain of Deal Castle fired at a Dutchman which came into the roads with her colours flying, and made her master pay ten shillings, the cost of the shot. And in 1632 the captain of a man-of-war, sent to Calais to fetch the body of Sir Isaac Wake, forced the French to lower their flag to him. *Admin. of Royal Navy.*

★★★★★★

The rations of the seamen were nominally, and when they were served out in full, the same as in the age of Elizabeth, *viz.*, one pound of biscuit and one gallon of beer daily, with, on four days of the week, two pounds of salt beef (or alternatively on two of those days one pound of bacon or pork, and one pint of peas), and on the other three days fish, dried or fresh, two ounces of butter, and a quainter of a pound of cheese. The allowance paid to the contractors for these victuals in 1622 was, per head, 7½d. per day in harbour, and 8d. at sea; but in Elizabeth's time the allowance had been but 4½d. and 5d. In 1635 the allowance rose further, the rates being 7½d. and 8½d., but owing to the advance in prices, the contractor, even on those terms, declared that he lost money, and in 1638 he gave notice to terminate the arrangement. At that time beef was about 2¾d. and pork about 1½d. a pound, stockfish about £4 5s. a cwt., biscuit about 15s. a cwt., and beer about £1 16s. a tun.

Previous to the Civil War, the crew of one of H.M. ships received no regular and fixed proportion of the proceeds of their captures, though, under an Order in Council of October, 1626, they were to be given "a competent reward." But in October, 1642, Parliament assigned to the officers and men of a ship, in addition to their pay, one-third of the value of the prizes taken by them. For many years, however, it was the practice to make unjustifiable deductions on various pretexts, and owing to this, and to delays in making payment, there was much naval discontent until the Commonwealth became firmly established.

Soon after the union of England and Scotland in 1603, all British vessels for a time flew the Union Flag of the crosses of St. George and St. Andrew.

★★★★★★

It was carried, under an order of April 13tli, 1606, in the main-top, English and Scotch vessels also carrying their national colours in the lore-top. The first Union Flag is heraldically described as: "Azure a saltire Argent, surmounted of a cross Gules fimbriated of the second." The fimbriation was made one-third of the width of the red cross, and the red cross was made one-fifth of the width of the flag. Contemporary pictures seem to show that ensigns of red, white, or blue, bearing St. George's Cross on a white canton next the staff, were also commonly carried until the time of the Commonwealth.

★★★★★★

But on May 5th, 1634, it was ordered by proclamation, (*Foedera*, xix.), that men-of-war only were to fly it in future, and that merchantmen, according to their nationality, were to wear the St. George's or the St. Andrew's Flag merely. This rule endured until February, 1649, when Parliament directed men-of-war to wear as an ensign the St. George's Cross on a white field.

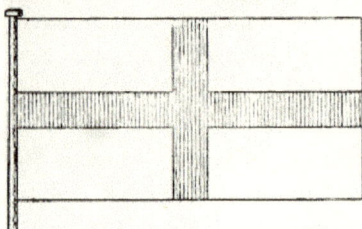

THE ENGLISH FLAG, BEFORE 1603.

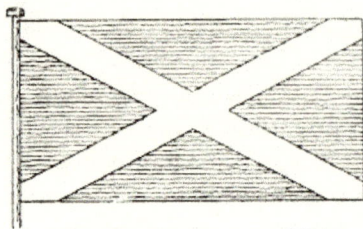

THE SCOTS FLAG, BEFORE 1603.

THE UNION FLAG, AS ORDERED IN 1606.

Little progress was made in the art of signalling at sea. At night two lights from the flagship, to be answered by one light from each private ship, signified "shorten sail"; three lights arranged vertically astern signified "make sail"; waving a light from the poop signified "lie to," etc. Day signalling by means of flags was still in its infancy. In fleets, the van flew the blue at the main, and the Union at the fore; the rear flew the white at the main, and the Union at the mizen; and the centre flew the Union at the main, for distinction of squadrons.

Repeated mention has been made in these pages of the ancient practice of creating fleets by the process of summoning vessels from the port towns and coast counties. Part of the fleet for the Cadiz Expedition of 1625 was collected in the old manner. But in 1634, the position of foreign affairs suggested to Charles I. the advisability of raising a fleet of better fighting value in order to maintain the sovereignty of the seas, prevent the French from taking Dunquerque, assert his right to the North Sea fisheries, and induce the cooperation of Spain in certain projects. Noy, the Attorney-General, suggested that the requisite money for equipment of vessels should be levied from the coast towns, a somewhat similar measure having been occasionally adopted in previous ages, though without parliamentary warrant.

★★★★★★

In 1619, soon after Buckingham's appointment as Lord High Admiral, King James, apprehensive of a rupture with Spain, ordered that six ships of the Royal Navy should be prepared for immediate service. Fourteen other ships were to be equipped by the merchants; and directions were given to the City Companies to pay £40,000 which had been assessed upon them. It was also decided that the old tax of ship-money should be levied at the other ports; and the magistrates were accordingly required to make up the sum of £8550 amongst them. The sums assessed were as follows:—*Bristol*, £2500; *Exeter*, £1000; *Plymouth*, £1000; *Dartmouth*, £1000; *Barnstaple*, £500; *Hull*, £500; *Weymouth*, £450; *Southampton*, £300; *Newcastle*, £300; the *Cinque Ports*, £200; *Yarmouth*, £200; *Ipswich*, £150; *Colchester*, £150; *Poole*, £100; *Chester*, £100; *Lyme*, £100.

★★★★★★

A ship-money writ was accordingly issued in October, 1634, and after some remonstrance was submitted to. In 1635 a second writ required the inland towns and comities to contribute also. There was much opposition, but in December the king obtained from ten judges an opinion that the levy of ship-money upon all was lawful. A third writ was issued in October, 1636, and in spite of a further favourable opinion from the judges, provoked increasing hostility. A fourth writ was issued in the autumn of 1637, a fifth in January, 1639, and a sixth in 1640.

By the writ of 1635, a ship of 450 tons, manned and equipped for six months, or in default a sum of £4500, was demanded from the county of Buckingham. The constitutional struggle arose out of this fact, John Hampden, of Great Hampden, refusing to pay his share, and standing his trial in respect of 20s. claimed from him for lands in the parish of Stoke Mandeville. Judgment was given in June, 1638, seven out of twelve judges deciding for the Crown, three for Hampden on all grounds, and two for him on technical grounds only. Charles I. was at one time willing to allow the judgment to go before the House of

Lords upon a writ of error, and be reversed, but various considerations prevented the carrying out of that plan. When the Long Parliament met, the Commons on December 7th, 1640, and the Lords on January 20th, 1641, agreed to resolutions declaring the levying of ship-money to be illegal, and a bill to the same effect, being brought in by Selden, received the royal assent on August 7th, 1641. (Hampden was mortally wounded at Chalgrove Field on June 18th, 1643.)

The fleets raised by ship-money were ill-found and ill-organised, but of imposing proportions, and Mr. Oppenheim, who nowhere conceals his contempt for the methods of those who raised them, and, indeed, for the Stuarts in general, is forced to admit that but for the forces which the writs enabled King Charles to send to sea:

> The strife with France and Holland might have been precipitated by nearly half a century. That they had some such intimidating influence was shown by the care taken by the French fleets, also cruising, to avoid meeting them, and the efforts of the French Court to evade the question of the dominion of the Narrow Seas. (*Admin. of Royal Navy.*)

Just as the ship-money question had an important bearing upon the internal history of the country, so an episode of 1623 had an important bearing upon the history of the country's foreign relations. This episode was known as the Amboyna affair. Amboyna, one of the Moluccas, had been taken by the Dutch from the Portuguese in 1607. The English, after having been expelled from the place, obtained in 1619 the right to trade there; but the treaty was ill-kept on both sides, and in February, 1623, the Dutch tortured to death several English factors, upon pretence that they had intrigued with the natives. This massacre was one of the main causes of the bad feeling between England and Holland in the middle of the seventeenth century, and although Holland, after the war of 1651–54, submitted to pay £300,000 to the descendants of the victims, the massacre was not forgotten in England, and its memory, for many years afterwards, often provoked ill-blood.

The properties of the geometrical series which constitute the foundation of the doctrine of logarithms seem to have been, known as long ago as the days of Archimedes; they are also touched upon in the writings of sixteenth century German mathematicians. But these properties and their advantageous utilisation were not properly understood until the publication by John, Lord Napier of Merchistoun, in 1614, of his work, *Mirifici Logarithmorum Canonis Descriptio*. The discovery was further improved by Henry Briggs, who at the time of Napier's publication was Professor of Geometry at Gresham College, and who later became Savilian Professor at Oxford. The work of Napier and Briggs, and of their contemporaries Adrian Valcq of Gouda, and Henry Gellibrand of Gresham College, in connection with this subject, had a most valuable influence upon the development of the practice of navigation, as well as of other branches of mathematics, and deserves commemoration here.

While England was drifting towards the great constitutional struggle which more than any other laid the foundations of her freedom, her small transatlantic colonies, though still in their feeblest infancy, were also doing something towards the making of the prosperity and greatness to which, under independent government, they have since attained. A small ship was built at or near Boston, Massachusetts, as early as 1633, and in 1639 laws for the encouragement of the American fisheries were passed. These exempted fishermen during the season, and shipwrights at all seasons, from military duty, and no doubt had much effect in turning the attention of the colonists to the advantages of sea life.

Two years later a ship of 300 tons was constructed at Salem, and in 1646 a vessel of 150 tons was built in Rhode Island. (J. F. Cooper, *History of the Navy of the U.S.A.*) Such were the small beginnings of a mercantile marine which, two hundred years afterwards, seemed about to challenge, at least for a time. Great Britain's supremacy as the ocean carrier of the goods of the world.

LEONAUR

ALSO FROM LEONAUR

AVAILABLE IN SOFTCOVER OR HARDCOVER WITH DUST JACKET

THE FALL OF THE MOGHUL EMPIRE OF HINDUSTAN *by H. G. Keene*—By the beginning of the nineteenth century, as British and Indian armies under Lake and Wellesley dominated the scene, a little over half a century of conflict brought the Moghul Empire to its knees.

LADY SALE'S AFGHANISTAN *by Florentia Sale*—An Indomitable Victorian Lady's Account of the Retreat from Kabul During the First Afghan War.

THE CAMPAIGN OF MAGENTA AND SOLFERINO 1859 *by Harold Carmichael Wylly*—The Decisive Conflict for the Unification of Italy.

FRENCH'S CAVALRY CAMPAIGN *by J. G. Maydon*—A Special Correspondent's View of British Army Mounted Troops During the Boer War.

CAVALRY AT WATERLOO *by Sir Evelyn Wood*—British Mounted Troops During the Campaign of 1815.

THE SUBALTERN *by George Robert Gleig*—The Experiences of an Officer of the 85th Light Infantry During the Peninsular War.

NAPOLEON AT BAY, 1814 *by F. Loraine Petre*—The Campaigns to the Fall of the First Empire.

NAPOLEON AND THE CAMPAIGN OF 1806 *by Colonel Vachée*—The Napoleonic Method of Organisation and Command to the Battles of Jena & Auerstädt.

THE COMPLETE ADVENTURES IN THE CONNAUGHT RANGERS *by William Grattan*—The 88th Regiment during the Napoleonic Wars by a Serving Officer.

BUGLER AND OFFICER OF THE RIFLES *by William Green & Harry Smith*—With the 95th (Rifles) during the Peninsular & Waterloo Campaigns of the Napoleonic Wars.

NAPOLEONIC WAR STORIES *by Sir Arthur Quiller-Couch*—Tales of soldiers, spies, battles & sieges from the Peninsular & Waterloo campaingns.

CAPTAIN OF THE 95TH (RIFLES) *by Jonathan Leach*—An officer of Wellington's sharpshooters during the Peninsular, South of France and Waterloo campaigns of the Napoleonic wars.

RIFLEMAN COSTELLO *by Edward Costello*—The adventures of a soldier of the 95th (Rifles) in the Peninsular & Waterloo Campaigns of the Napoleonic wars.

LEONAUR

ALSO FROM LEONAUR
AVAILABLE IN SOFTCOVER OR HARDCOVER WITH DUST JACKET

THE 9TH—THE KING'S (LIVERPOOL REGIMENT) IN THE GREAT WAR 1914 - 1918 *by Enos H. G. Roberts*—Mersey to mud—war and Liverpool men.

THE GAMBARDIER *by Mark Severn*—The experiences of a battery of Heavy artillery on the Western Front during the First World War.

FROM MESSINES TO THIRD YPRES *by Thomas Floyd*—A personal account of the First World War on the Western front by a 2/5th Lancashire Fusilier.

THE IRISH GUARDS IN THE GREAT WAR - VOLUME 1 *by Rudyard Kipling*—Edited and Compiled from Their Diaries and Papers—The First Battalion.

THE IRISH GUARDS IN THE GREAT WAR - VOLUME 1 *by Rudyard Kipling*—Edited and Compiled from Their Diaries and Papers—The Second Battalion.

ARMOURED CARS IN EDEN *by K. Roosevelt*—An American President's son serving in Rolls Royce armoured cars with the British in Mesopatamia & with the American Artillery in France during the First World War.

CHASSEUR OF 1914 *by Marcel Dupont*—Experiences of the twilight of the French Light Cavalry by a young officer during the early battles of the great war in Europe.

TROOP HORSE & TRENCH *by R.A. Lloyd*—The experiences of a British Lifeguardsman of the household cavalry fighting on the western front during the First World War 1914-18.

THE EAST AFRICAN MOUNTED RIFLES *by C.J. Wilson*—Experiences of the campaign in the East African bush during the First World War.

THE LONG PATROL *by George Berrie*—A Novel of Light Horsemen from Gallipoli to the Palestine campaign of the First World War.

THE FIGHTING CAMELIERS *by Frank Reid*—The exploits of the Imperial Camel Corps in the desert and Palestine campaigns of the First World War.

STEEL CHARIOTS IN THE DESERT *by S. C. Rolls*—The first world war experiences of a Rolls Royce armoured car driver with the Duke of Westminster in Libya and in Arabia with T.E. Lawrence.

WITH THE IMPERIAL CAMEL CORPS IN THE GREAT WAR *by Geoffrey Inchbald*—The story of a serving officer with the British 2nd battalion against the Senussi and during the Palestine campaign.

LEONAUR

ALSO FROM LEONAUR
AVAILABLE IN SOFTCOVER OR HARDCOVER WITH DUST JACKET

ESCAPE FROM THE FRENCH *by Edward Boys*—A Young Royal Navy Midshipman's Adventures During the Napoleonic War.

THE VOYAGE OF H.M.S. PANDORA *by Edward Edwards R. N. & George Hamilton, edited by Basil Thomson*—In Pursuit of the Mutineers of the Bounty in the South Seas—1790-1791.

MEDUSA *by J. B. Henry Savigny and Alexander Correard and Charlotte-Adélaïde Dard* —Narrative of a Voyage to Senegal in 1816 & The Sufferings of the Picard Family After the Shipwreck of the Medusa.

THE SEA WAR OF 1812 VOLUME 1 *by A. T. Mahan*—A History of the Maritime Conflict.

THE SEA WAR OF 1812 VOLUME 2 *by A. T. Mahan*—A History of the Maritime Conflict.

WETHERELL OF H. M. S. HUSSAR *by John Wetherell*—The Recollections of an Ordinary Seaman of the Royal Navy During the Napoleonic Wars.

THE NAVAL BRIGADE IN NATAL *by C. R. N. Burne*—With the Guns of H. M. S. Terrible & H. M. S. Tartar during the Boer War 1899-1900.

THE VOYAGE OF H. M. S. BOUNTY *by William Bligh*—The True Story of an 18th Century Voyage of Exploration and Mutiny.

SHIPWRECK! *by William Gilly*—The Royal Navy's Disasters at Sea 1793-1849.

KING'S CUTTERS AND SMUGGLERS: 1700-1855 *by E. Keble Chatterton*—A unique period of maritime history-from the beginning of the eighteenth to the middle of the nineteenth century when British seamen risked all to smuggle valuable goods from wool to tea and spirits from and to the Continent.

CONFEDERATE BLOCKADE RUNNER *by John Wilkinson*—The Personal Recollections of an Officer of the Confederate Navy.

NAVAL BATTLES OF THE NAPOLEONIC WARS *by W. H. Fitchett*—Cape St. Vincent, the Nile, Cadiz, Copenhagen, Trafalgar & Others.

PRISONERS OF THE RED DESERT *by R. S. Gwatkin-Williams*—The Adventures of the Crew of the Tara During the First World War.

U-BOAT WAR 1914-1918 *by James B. Connolly/Karl von Schenk*—Two Contrasting Accounts from Both Sides of the Conflict at Sea D uring the Great War.